WORKING WOMEN, WORKING MEN

WORKING WOMEN, WORKING MEN

São Paulo and the Rise of Brazil's Industrial Working Class, 1900–1955

JOEL WOLFE

DUKE UNIVERSITY PRESS 1993 Durham and London

For Traci

© 1993 Duke University Press
All rights reserved
Printed in the United States of
America on acid-free paper ∞
Designed by Cherie Holma Westmoreland
Typeset in Weiss by Keystone Typesetting, Inc.
Library of Congress Cataloging-in-
Publication Data appear on the last printed
page of this book.

Contents

CONTENTS

Tables

Acknowledgments

Over the course of researching and writing this book I have been fortunate to receive guidance and encouragement from many friends in the United States and Brazil. This project began as a dissertation at the University of Wisconsin, under the direction of Florencia Mallon and Thomas Skidmore. Tom Skidmore has been a constant source of inspiration and support. From my first days in Madison to the present day, Tom has been a mentor, a friend, and most of all, an example of a historian and teacher for me to try to emulate. Florencia's creativity, passion, and good humor have likewise inspired both me and my work. Her influence on me has been great, and I thank her for it. Steve Stern also provided an intellectually challenging yet supportive environment for me in graduate school. He, along with Tom and Florencia, set an example of a committed scholar for all of us in the Latin American History graduate program. Jeanne Boydston of the Women's History Program also provided invaluable advice and opened new avenues of inquiry. I am grateful for her encouragement and support.

Several other scholars read and commented on the entire manuscript. Even though they are good friends, they didn't pull any punches. I thank Marshall Eakin, Tom Spear, and Barbara Weinstein who read the dissertation and helped me make it a book manuscript, and I thank Tom Holloway and Mike Conniff who helped me make it a book. Their frank and constructive criticism has helped me immeasurably. Larry Malley of Duke University Press has been a wonderful editor and a good friend. Mindy Conner and Jean Brady have contributed careful copy editing and other important assistance.

Many friends contributed to the various stages of this project: I would like to thank Judith Allen, Reid Andrews, Kathy Brown, Paula Consolini, Todd Diacon, Jim Dickmeyer, Dário Euraque, Luis Figueroa, Colin Gordon, Linda Gordon, Michael Greenwald, Michael Hall, Roger Kittleson, Regina Kunzel, Maria Helena P. T. Machado, Jim Mahon, Frank McCann, John Monteiro, Áquilas Nogueira Mendes, Ted Pearson, Sarah Rosenson, Chris Waters, Julius Weinberg, and

Hélio Zylberstajn for their encouragement and friendship over the years.

Librarians and archivists in Brazil and the United States, as well as the interlibrary loan staffs at the University of Wisconsin and Williams College, provided valuable assistance. Carmen Lucia Evangelho Lopes and Carla Donadelli of the Centro de Memória Sindical in São Paulo merit special thanks. Their encouragement and many introductions to unionists and other activists helped me with various stages of the research, especially the interviews. Carlos Battesti (Carlão) of the Federation of Industries also provided timely assistance.

A generous grant from the Department of Education's Fulbright-Hays program funded the research in Brazil in 1986 and 1987. A summer travel grant from the Tinker Foundation allowed me to visit Brazil in 1985 to prepare my dissertation topic. I am grateful for both grants. I should also thank the Department of Education and the University of Wisconsin for fellowships that funded my graduate study. The Williams College History Department has also provided a nurturing environment for me as I completed work on this book, and faculty research support funded a trip to Brazil that allowed me to complete work on this book and to begin my next project. My appreciation is also deeply felt for my fellow activists in the Teaching Assistants' Association, as well as past activists who founded the union in the early 1970s, for helping to include health insurance in TA salaries and fellowships.

My family has supported me intellectually and financially over the years. My parents, Donald and Barbara Wolfe, first piqued my interest in history and politics. My aunt, Florence Greenberg, introduced me to the world outside the Philadelphia area. Her encouragement to study other cultures and her generous support over the years have helped in innumerable ways. My wife Traci has supplied good humor, a healthy dose of cynicism, encouragement and love. I thank her and her family for all of their support.

My final thanks are to the subjects of this book. The workers, union activists, retired workers, and other Brazilians who took the time to tell me their stories provided the most valuable help of all. By taking me into their factories, union halls, and homes they allowed me into their lives. For that I offer my deepest thanks and the hope that I did justice to their history.

Somerville, Massachusetts
November 1992

Acronyms

ANL   Aliança Nacional Libertadora (National Liberation Alliance)

CETEX   Comissão Executiva Têxtil (Executive Textile Commission)

CIFTSP   Centro dos Industriaes de Fiação e Tecelagem de São Paulo (Center for Spinning and Weaving of São Paulo)

CLT   Consolidação das Leis do Trabalho (Consolidated Labor Laws)

COB   Confederação Operária Brasileira (Brazilian Labor Confederation)

CRT   Conselho Regional do Trabalho (Regional Labor Board)

CGTB   Confederação Geral dos Trabalhadores do Brasil (General Workers' Confederation of Brazil)

DIEESE   Departamento Intersindical de Estatísticas e Estudos Sócio-Econômicos (Inter-Union Department of Statistics and Socioeconomic Studies)

DOPS   Departamento de Ordem Política Social (Political Police)

ECLA   Economic Commission for Latin America

FEB   Força Expedicionária Brasileira (Brazilian Expeditionary Force)

FIESP   Federação das Indústrias do Estado de São Paulo (São Paulo State Federation of Industries)

FOSP   Federação Operária de São Paulo (Workers' Federation of São Paulo)

IAPI   Instituto de Aposentadores e Pensões dos Industriários (Industrial Workers' Retirement Pension Institute)

IBOPE   Instituto Brasileiro de Opinião Pública e Estatística (Brazilian Public Opinion and Statistics Institute)

IDORT   Instituto de Organização Racional do Trabalho (Institute for the Rational Organization of Work)

MUT   Movimento Unificador dos Trabalhadores (United Workers' Movement)

PCB   Partido Comunista Brasileiro (Communist Party of Brazil)

PSD   Partido Social Democrático (Social Democratic Party)

PSP   Partido Social Progressista (Social Progressive Party)
PT   Partido dos Trabalhadores (Workers' Party)
PTB   Partido Trabalhista Brasileiro (Brazilian Labor Party)
PUI   Pacto de Unidade Intersindical (Inter-Union Unity Pact)
SENAI   Serviço Nacional de Aprendizagem Industrial (National Industrial Apprenticeship Service)
SESI   Serviço Social de Indústria (Industrial Social Service)
SPSAIC São Paulo Secretaria da Agricultura, Indústria, e Comércio
UDN   União Democrática Nacional (National Democratic Union)
TRT   Tribunal Regional do Trabalho (Regional Labor Tribunal)

WORKING WOMEN, WORKING MEN

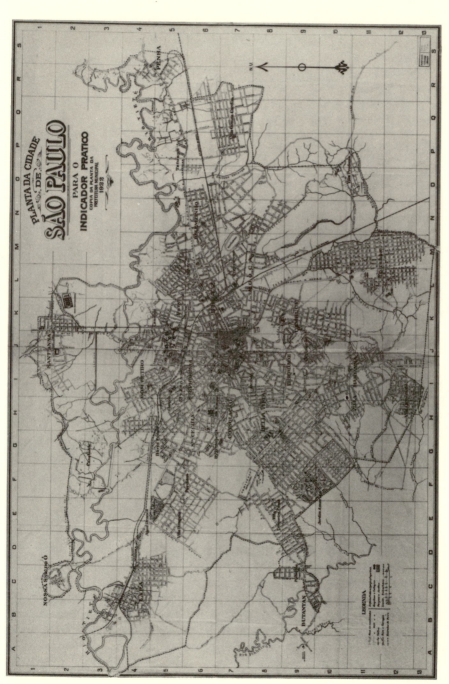

São Paulo, Brazil circa 1922. (*Courtesy Harvard College Library*)

Introduction

Speaker after speaker came forward on the stage to denounce the *pelegos* (government unionists) who controlled the state-sanctioned *sindicatos* in the city. They demanded an end to the onerous *imposto sindical* (union tax), called for the abolition of state intervention in industrial relations, and blasted the cozy relationship between the pelegos and the industrialists. Factory commission activists from metalworking establishments throughout the *município* of São Paulo and its suburbs of Osasco, Garulhos, Santo André, São Bernardo, São Caetano, and Diadema packed the rented hall in the Liberdade section of São Paulo. These insurgents from grass-roots factory commissions staged their rally far from union headquarters to energize rank-and-file metalworkers in São Paulo for the upcoming election of a new union directorate. Speaker after speaker called on those gathered to throw out the entrenched pelegos and bring the open politics of their factory commissions to the closed state-sanctioned unions.

What impressed me most about this May 1987 rally was how much its rhetoric mirrored that of the struggles for union democracy São Paulo's metallurgical and textile workers had waged in the 1930s, 1940s, and 1950s. The 1987 calls for union democracy were near-perfect representations of the language of rank-and-file insurgency expressed in similar meetings held throughout the mid-1940s and early 1950s.[1] Along with the language of union democracy, these workers in 1987 continued to rely on a system of factory commissions as their own form of independent organizing. These factory-based groups of anywhere from five to fifty workers first played a role in grass-roots protests in the 1910s. At times, the commissions were workers' only institutions for negotiating wage increases and changes in work conditions. At other times, the commissions made up the grass roots of the city's unions. In the late 1970s, workers from insurgent factory commissions succeeded in breaking the power of the state-sanctioned sindicatos and created an alternative structure known as the "New Unionism," which workers later institutionalized as the Partido dos Trabalhadores (PT).[2] These calls for a grass-roots insurgency to oust pelegos and to take control of the unions—which have been part of a nationwide PT platform since its founding—reveal the importance of working-class historical memory and the development of a syndicalist tradition among São Paulo's industrial workers that stretches back to the first decades of the twentieth century.

This book is about the rise of Brazil's industrial working class to a position of political prominence in the first half of the twentieth century. It is the story of how workers experienced Brazil's industrialization and how they struggled to gain control over their lives within a highly authoritarian political system. It is also the story of how workers' struggles shaped that political system. By studying those struggles, this book details the historical origins of the New Unionism. But this is not just an exercise in locating origins. Rather, this book places industrial workers firmly within twentieth-century Brazilian history by revealing the important connections among people and ideas from different historical epochs.

This book focuses closely on the experiences of two divergent groups of industrial laborers—textile and metallurgical workers—over a long and formative period in Brazilian history in order to describe the formation and various transformations of São Paulo's industrial working class. Class formation is not an inevitable result of structural circumstances; instead, it is the "making" of a social class by those individuals whose common experiences—in the labor market, neighborhoods, and marketplaces, and in relation to their employers and the state—encourage them to band together to act in their perceived common interests. Further, the process of class formation is an ongoing one, and the composition of the working class, as well as its worldview and goals, changes accordingly.[3] Thus, the story of the formation of São Paulo's industrial working class is not the story of the "masses" lumped together indiscriminately, but of individual workers or groups of workers separated by sex, skill, industry, and ethnicity.[4]

The development of São Paulo's industrial bourgeoisie was closely tied to the rise of the city's working class. The engine of class struggle shaped the formation of both classes, and neither can be understood without reference to the other.[5] This double focus also reveals important aspects of the roots of Brazil's modern bureaucratic-authoritarian state.[6] As both the state and federal governments grappled with the issue of "social control," they created institutions in an effort to manipulate workers and their independent organizations. The bureaucratic-authoritarian state, then, was not the result of a unique post-1945 political conjuncture; rather, it was the product of nearly a century of class struggle between Brazil's working people and their rulers.[7]

This book analyzes how both male and female industrial workers in São Paulo overcame many obstacles to form—during certain key periods—a powerful workers' movement, and by the mid-1950s a representative and vibrant union movement.[8] It examines workers' ongoing struggles within their factories and neighborhoods, and describes how their own informal organizations related to unions, industrialists, and the state. A basic theme is that neither the formation of the working class nor its operation in Brazilian society can be understood without a close analysis of the interaction of four sets of actors: the industrial working class, union and Left organization leaders, industrialists, and state policymakers.

In considering the interaction of these four sets of actors, it is particularly important to make a distinction between the rank and file and leaders of formal Left and labor groups. Compared with some other Latin American countries (e.g., Argentina, Chile, and Mexico), Brazil has not sustained a large-scale, politically active *formal* labor movement. Brazilian labor leaders' and state makers' failures to speak to the rank and file's needs or to deliver real social gains hindered the development of a powerful labor movement in the first half of the twentieth century.[9] Brazilian workers have, however, created and maintained their own local, independent organizations that survive state intervention and violence because of their strong roots among the rank and file, and because their informal levels of organization have made them elusive targets for industrialist and state repression. These very features have also made this type of worker organization and mobilization difficult for historians to locate.[10]

Workers most often organized themselves into factory commissions and avoided participation in formal unions. This fact helps explain two aspects of São Paulo's labor history. First, it reveals the tension workers experienced between their need to maintain their own independent social movement—a working-class movement based in the commissions—and the opportunities and costs associated with tying their commissions to institutions (anarchist and later state-run unions) that they, as the rank and file, had played little or no role in creating.[11] Second, workers' reliance on an informal factory commission structure provided them opportunities and social spaces to articulate and spread their ideas about their bosses, unions, the state, and other issues. By studying workers' factory commissions, this book uncovers workers' "hidden transcripts" of independent rank-and-file activism.[12]

Analyzing these developments over the *longue durée* explains the durability of the working-class movement even when the formal labor movement had been weakened by state intervention. Moreover, the focus on these hidden transcripts challenges the tendency to characterize strikes and other working-class organizing and protest activities as "spontaneous." Instead, this book details how such activities were most often products of an ongoing, informal, popular social movement organized around factory commissions.

Social movements are not abstractions; they are groups of people who organize together to push for common goals. Because this book focuses on Brazil's industrial working people the analysis concentrates on the lives—in their factories, neighborhoods, unions, and other organizations—of two groups of factory workers in the country's leading industrial city, São Paulo.[13] The first group is textile workers. As in most countries, Brazil's first experience with industrialization was with textiles. Textile production took place in large, highly mechanized factories with "semiskilled" labor.[14] Further, women workers tended to dominate this field. The second group of workers studied are those in São Paulo's metallurgical industries. As the city's industrial base expanded, craftsmen opened small machine shops to meet the increasing demand for spare parts and agricultural tools. These shops employed "skilled" workers who retained a large measure of control over the labor process.[15] And the majority of the city's metalworkers were men.

I concentrate on these two groups of workers for several reasons. First, they represent two extremes of factory laborers. Textile workers were considered semiskilled, and metalworkers skilled. Textile factories were large industrial establishments (often employing more than five hundred workers), while metalworking shops tended to be small (generally employing fewer than thirty). These two industries utilized contrasting labor processes with different types of workers. Moreover, these two industries offer the opportunity to compare and contrast the work, living, organizational, and protest experiences of female and male industrial laborers. Finally, the textile and metallurgical sectors employed more factory workers than any other two industrial sectors in Brazil, and they eventually produced two of São Paulo's, and therefore Brazil's, leading industrial unions.[16]

The development of these two leading unions was not a linear or smooth process. Unions, like social classes, are made by workers and individuals who assume leadership roles, and through their relations with industrialists and state policymakers. Moreover, conflicts among various rank-and-file groups—especially between women workers and male unionists—often defined the organization and politics of these unions. Workers' continued reliance on their own factory commissions also contributed to the making of small, unrepresentative formal unions in São Paulo. State intervention in the 1930s and 1940s solidified this process of rank-and-file alienation from the union structure.

Both the factory commissions and the unions that developed out of these processes articulated—often through public pronouncements and always through praxis—highly gendered notions of working-class politics. Because *gender* is defined as a socially constructed set of definitions of appropriate behavior for each sex, it often changes over time. Thus, this book traces not only the role gender ideologies played in shaping working-class organizing and protest activities but also how those activities and the reactions they brought in turn shaped gender ideologies.

The complex issues associated with the concepts of consciousness and hegemony often muddle labor histories. In this book, consciousness is analyzed as the totality of the impressions, thoughts, and feelings that constitute an individual's or group's worldview. And because consciousness is shaped by social experiences, it often changes. Accordingly, I reject the notion that there is one appropriate political class consciousness, especially one that is introduced by intellectuals, a party, or some other non-working-class group.[17] Instead, I argue that people are drawn to ideologies that speak to important aspects of their lives, and they often shape and reformulate those ideologies to address the specifics of their condition. In this way, individuals and groups of both sexes and various ethnicities and classes socially construct ideologies. By uncovering both working-class ideologies and their making, this book reveals the role historical memory has played in helping São Paulo's industrial workers articulate and maintain ideologies of opposition and resistance to both employers and the state. Accordingly, my analysis demonstrates how workers have avoided being duped by so-called hegemonic ideologies.[18] Tracing the development of this working-class historical memory that values local, independent forms of organizing also helps us connect the rhetoric and praxis of São Paulo's New Unionism with the legacy of workers' struggles against their bosses and the state, and for representative and open unions in the first half of the twentieth century.

Industrialization and the Birth of São Paulo's
Working-Class Movement, 1900–1924

Large-scale industry is the factor that most efficiently contributes to social tranquility, for the well-being of the people and for the wealth of the public.

— Antônio Francisco Bandeira Junior
A Indústria no Estado de São Paulo em 1901

Strikes will become more general, more and more frequent, responding to the ever-increasing oppression of capitalism.

— Report of the Second Brazilian Socialist Congress, cited in Dulles, *Anarchists and Communists in Brazil*

The industrialization Antônio Francisco Bandeira Junior praised and the fledgling Socialist party decried had barely begun in the São Paulo of 1900. Neighborhoods such as Brás and Mooca, where large textile factories and small metalworking and other shops would soon dominate, were still swampy lowlands with only a handful of industrial establishments and few inhabitants. Beyond the downtown business triangle, a few elite residential areas, and the immigrant slums of Bexiga, São Paulo still had the look of an agrarian hamlet. Small farms with their fruit trees, cattle, and rustic houses operated in Consolação, Higienópolis, Vila Buarque, Pinheiros, and other neighborhoods of the city. Foreign visitors and local commentators alike praised the beauty of this bucolic town at the turn of the century.[1]

The steady expansion of the state's coffee economy, along with planters' and merchants' desire to diversify their holdings, fostered the development of industry throughout the state of São Paulo, especially in its capital.[2] Industrialization, though, was not the panacea Bandeira Junior and other elites believed it would be;[3] nor was it a linear process that stripped workers of their humanity or agency. Although the growth of industry had a profound impact on the population of São Paulo, that same population, most of whom would become the industrial working class, shaped the process of industrialization. Those same individuals, many of whom were immigrants or first-generation Brazilians, began to form small, independent groups to confront bosses and city leaders about the conditions they faced at work and in their neighborhoods, and they came into contact with the small group of leftist activists who were attempting to build a union movement in São Paulo. The conflicts and compromises among these groups brought changes to São Paulo that neither the proponents nor the critics of the city's early industrialization could have predicted at the turn of the century.

The Development of Industry

New tariffs and the steady demand for the state's coffee exports were circumstances that favored São Paulo's transition from an overgrown agricultural hamlet to the Third World's leading industrial center.[4] The new factories produced light consumer goods, especially textiles, using semiskilled labor. This manufacturing sector at first precluded the rise of a unified industrial bourgeoisie. Some mill owners maintained their primary interest in the coffee trade while others concentrated their investments in industrial production.[5] The expansion of the city's industrial base, along with external economic shocks, led to the creation of a new area of industrial production: São Paulo's capital goods sector. This development in turn increased demand for skilled metalworkers in and around the city. The clothing, shoe, and processed food industries also expanded dramatically (on average, 8 percent per year from 1900 to 1920) in response to the overall growth of the state's economy and population.[6] Ultimately, however, in the early twentieth century São Paulo experienced its first round of industrialization as an ancillary economic activity. The actions of neither mill owners nor their workers were of primary concern to the ruling class of this overwhelmingly agrarian state.

Migrants from São Paulo's coffee *fazendas* filled the city's industrial labor market at this time. The migration of young Italians (especially women) from *colono* (tenant farmer) households to the city meshed with racist ideologies that sought to limit blacks' access to factory labor and created an industrial labor force dominated by women. That is, while men monopolized construction, printing, metalworking, and other trades, women made up the majority of industrial (especially

Table 1.1   Workers by Sex and Age in Thirty-one Textile Mills
in the State of São Paulo, 1912

	Under 12	12–16	17–22	Over 22	Total
Female	244	1,885	2,966	1,706	6,801
Male	127	696	1,825[a]	—	2,648

Source: "Condições do Trabalho na Indústria Têxtil no Estado de São Paulo," BDET 1:1–2 (1st Trimester, 1912), 38.

Note: Of the 31 mills studied, 29 were in the city of São Paulo, 1 was in São Bernardo, and 1 was in Santos.

[a]The categories for male employees end with "older than 16 years."

textile) workers (table 1.1).[7] As we shall see, the prevalence of women in textiles profoundly affected the development of São Paulo's labor movement.

World War I first interrupted, then intensified this process of industrialization. After a brief suspension of coffee and rubber exports, the Brazilian economy quickly recovered. By late 1915, Brazil was again exporting primary products, but its trade axis had shifted from Europe to the United States. The federal government stimulated this rise in exports by devaluing the milréis. Such an exchange rate policy along with shortages of manufactured goods on the international market combined to protect Brazil's nascent industrial sector. Although scholars dispute the exact impact of the war years on São Paulo's industry, all agree that the 1914–18 period witnessed significant increases in industrial output.[8] Expansion of the textile sector grew out of both the increased capacity installed before the war and the intensified use of labor in the factories.

To meet increased demand, industrialists extended work hours, especially the night shifts. Mill owners continued to employ mostly women and children, and foremen did not hesitate to punish them for not meeting production quotas or for falling asleep at their machines. Accordingly, the number of accidents in São Paulo's factories rose steadily during the war.[9] The city's press increasingly reported such accidents. A reporter for O Estado de São Paulo noted in 1917 that many of the children exiting a textile mill appeared to have been not only injured by machinery but also abused by foremen: "Yesterday we watched 60 children entering the factory at Mooca at 7:00 PM. They would leave only at 6:00 AM. That meant that they worked 11 hours straight on the night shift, with only a 20-minute rest break at midnight! Worse is that they complain that they are beaten by the foremen of the spinning rooms. Many of them showed us the black-and-blue marks on their arms and backs. . . . The ears of one are injured from their having been pulled so violently and so often. These are 12-, 13-, and 14-year-old children."[10]

Although exact figures are not available, both foreign observers and Brazilian government officials noted that São Paulo's mill owners reaped substantial profits during the war years.[11] Even the president of the state of São Paulo publicly declared that industrialists were unfairly profiting from workers' labor. He wrote, "It is clear that industrialists and merchants are reaping profits in the current situation, profits never before seen and that demonstrate that the prices of goods that are indispensable for subsistence exceed what is needed to satisfactorily remunerate capital and the activity of workers."[12]

Industrial expansion had a dramatic impact on life in São Paulo. With the city's population and number of buildings more than doubling from 1900 (239,820 people and 22,407 buildings) to 1918 (504,278 and 55,356), residents experienced the many problems and frustrations of living in a metropolis.[13] Along with this expansion São Paulo witnessed the clear demarcation of neighborhoods by social class. The growth of luxury housing and of the city's commercial center forced an increasing number of workers to move into cortiços in the factory districts of Brás, Mooca, Belemzinho, and Cambuci.[14] Before and during the war years, the São Paulo city government carried out an extensive urban planning campaign to manage this growth. Residences and small shops on Avenida São João were demolished to create the sort of boulevard considered appropriate for the downtown. The city also moved to improve transportation and sewage lines.[15] In 1915 and 1916, Mayor Washington Luís Pereira de Sousa encouraged further high-rise construction downtown and attempted to renovate Brás and other working-class neighborhoods. Washington Luís sought not only to spur further growth but also "to purify [the city] morally and physically."[16] Paulistano elites wanted to cleanse the working-class neighborhoods of their "vicious mixture of scum of all nationalities, all ages, all of them dangerous."[17] São Paulo's workers felt the full effects of Washington Luís's reforms. In addition to the changes in the downtown area, the city modified the food distribution system by closing the central market in Anhangabaú and instituted a system of neighborhood

Table 1.2   Index of Wholesale Prices for Foodstuffs
in São Paulo, 1912–1917 (1912 = 100)

	Rice	Beans	Sugar	Mandioca	Chicken
1912	100	100	100	100	100
1913	112	128	85	85	133
1914	106	136	73	67	89
1915	125	92	103	78	75
1916	104	85	125	96	82
1917	98	136	128	96	100

Source: BDET 24 (1917), chart between pp. 580 and 581.

markets known as *feiras livres*. This helped women workers because it freed them from having to travel to the central market for a large selection of food items, but the decentralization of food distribution also created a system in which the goods sold in the working-class feiras were of the lowest quality and highest price in the city.[18]

This system of markets intensified the impact of the wartime inflation for São Paulo's working people in general and women workers in particular. Speculation and increased exports of foodstuffs from the state to Europe forced up the prices for rice, beans, and other working-class staples. Hoarding, speculation, and exports brought wild swings in prices from month to month (table 1.2).[19] During the war workers faced not only higher prices for foodstuffs but extremely unstable supplies as accepted practices and prices for food were discarded.[20] The export of inexpensive foods forced Brazil to increase its imports of Argentine wheat for the bread sold in markets in the city's elite neighborhoods.[21] Then, when Argentina imposed an embargo on wheat exports in early 1917, the São Paulo city government introduced *pão paulista*, bread baked with corn and some wheat flour, for the Italian immigrants in working-class neighborhoods. Bakers were supposed to mark this product clearly and to sell it at half the price of bread made completely from wheat flour, but few retailers obeyed this regulation.[22] All these changes meant that women industrial workers—especially those in the mills—bore the brunt of São Paulo's wartime industrial expansion. Not only did they confront intensified work regimes in the factories, they also faced increasingly difficult conditions in their other jobs as the individuals most responsible for the maintenance of their families' lives.[23]

The Development of the Early Labor Movement

São Paulo's struggling women workers could not hope for much help from the city's anarchist activists, for the ideological, social, ethnic, and gender differences between the leaders of the anarchist movement and São Paulo's working people limited the development of a coherent and effective labor movement.[24] Indeed, Brazil's early anarchist movement owed more to the antistate politics of disaffected Republicans than it did to working-class organizing. Brazilians such as Benjamin Mota, Manuel Curvello de Mendonça, Avelino Foscolo, Fábio Luz, and Lima Barreto rejected the government of the Old Republic as a corrupt and failed experiment. They considered themselves exponents of logic and morality and called for a return to so-called primitive communitarianism.[25] These anarchist activists concentrated their energies on education programs and cultural events such as the Workers' Theater.[26] Further, anarchists attacked, implicitly and explicitly, the Catholic church. While anticlericalism was a fundamental part of anarchist ideology and was expressed often in plays, songs, and study groups, it created a gulf between activists and the majority of São Paulo's working people. When the Italian socialist Enrico Ferri spoke out against the church during a street rally in November 1911, for example, a crowd rioted and attacked the "freethinkers."[27] Whatever their level of religious commitment or attachment to formal or informal churches, most of São Paulo's working people were troubled by the anarchists' anticlericalism.

In 1906 and 1907, São Paulo's anarchists began to focus on organizing the steadily growing number of workers in the city.[28] Even this commitment to working-class politics—as opposed to the previous emphasis on culture and education—failed to produce a large-scale workers' movement. The leaders of the new anarchist movement were primarily artisans from the printing, stonecutting, carpentry, shoemaking, and other trades. As a group, they were better paid and more highly educated than most of the city's industrial workers.[29] The anarchists themselves recognized that they had few ties to most of São Paulo's workers.[30]

The gulf between the rank and file and the anarchist leadership became obvious during the widespread textile strike of May 1907. After the Mariangela mill's workers struck against the brutal treatment they suffered at the hands of foremen who directed them for twelve-hour shifts, six and sometimes seven days a week, textile workers throughout the city organized strike committees to demand improved working conditions. Thinking the workers' discontent could lead to a revolutionary upheaval, the anarchists attempted to take over direction of the strikes from the workers. While the centralized organizing and support for the eight-hour day by the anarchists' Workers' Federation of São Paulo (Federação Operária de São Paulo, FOSP) helped the overall movement, the individual workers' committees rejected a revolutionary platform. Instead they sought reforms designed simply to improve work conditions and pay.[31]

The 1907 strike illustrates why São Paulo's industrial workers had few reasons to embrace the anarchists' revolutionary political platform. These immigrant workers did not place their demands within a framework critical of industry or capitalism as such, and as a group they still identified with their fellow Italians, Portuguese, and Spaniards—including many of their bosses. They had had little or no contact with radical ideologies before arriving in São Paulo, and they did not yet view themselves as part of a subordinate class united against employers; they were in the city to better their social and economic position. Workers were often proud of the achievements of immigrant industrialists like Francisco Matarazzo, the owner of the Mariangela mill, who employed them.[32]

Further, São Paulo's anarchists demonstrated little interest in organizing the city's women workers. Like their elite opponents, the anarchists believed women were weak and required men's protection. Belém Sárrage de Ferrero wrote in 1911, for example, "Let us make of women what they should be: the priestesses of the home, the priestesses of morality."[33] In addition to wanting to expel women from the labor market in order to protect them, anarchist men were often hostile to women's presence in the factories as low-paid workers. A 1914 meeting of Rio de Janeiro's tailors thus concluded that "the woman of our class . . . we are sorry to say, is our most dangerous competition, and this contributes a good deal to her own as well as to our impoverishment."[34] At times, anarchists' frustrations with working women became outright misogyny, as expressed in a 1900 article in the anarchist Il Diritto: "We are not well enough aware of how at present women are a danger, an enemy of the social movement. We could not precisely count the number of militants who have deserted the struggle and abandoned forever the revolutionary ideas they once so avidly espoused so as not to displease their women and to have tranquility on the domestic

12

scene."[35] Some anarchists, though certainly not all, even considered feminism a threat to working-class consciousness and thought all feminists were lesbians (whom they viewed unfavorably).[36]

Anarchist discourse at this time developed a dichotomy between male and female worlds. Men worked outside the home, participated in politics through study and labor groups; women were to work in the home, raising children and caring for their men.[37] Men's opposition to women's factory work was not only based in their belief that women's presence devalued work and so lowered wages for all workers; it also reflected men's desire to protect women. Many men (anarchists, conservatives, etc.) viewed factories as dangerous locations for women and children; not only was the work difficult and at times perilous, but factories were also areas where women were at once independent of their fathers' and husbands' control and potentially threatened by the power of male bosses (foremen). Not surprisingly, anarchist discourse concerning women's work highlighted their need for "protection" and conflated the situations of adult women with those of children. In the final analysis, this discourse not only devalued women's factory work, it also envisioned organizing and protest activities as essentially male.[38]

Such views of women's roles in society certainly limited the success of anarchist organizing among São Paulo's thousands of textile and other female factory workers. In fact, the city's women workers consistently avoided participation in male-dominated unions and chose instead to organize their own formal and informal associations, such as factory commissions comprised solely of women. Women gained employment in the textile mills through family and extended kinship ties—for the Italians often through *paisani*. The work force in a given factory was thus made up of people who had strong bonds among themselves, and those ties were often the bases of informal groups such as those that became factory commissions. In other words, these groups of friends and relatives who worked together in a given section, on a given shift, transformed their social grouping into a loose factory commission structure to bargain with their bosses. Sometimes they chose one of the older women (i.e., someone in her late twenties) or the most articulate as their leader or spokeswoman.[39] Thus, just as the segmenting of the industrial labor market was influenced by immigrants' and Brazilian elites' gender ideologies, those same gender ideologies shaped the organizing and protest activities of twentieth-century São Paulo's labor movement.[40] Anarchist organizers did have some limited success bringing men into their unions, but they could not overcome ethnic rivalries and immigrants' initial disinterest in joining unions and study groups; thus they did not direct a large-scale labor movement during the first two decades of the twentieth century.[41]

Although anarchist leaders and striking workers briefly came together in 1907, the labor movement continued as a small group of craftsmen who had little contact with most of the city's industrial laborers. Anarchist-oriented trade unions representing São Paulo's craftsmen (e.g., printers, hatters, shoemakers, and stonemasons) operated under an umbrella organization, the Brazilian Labor Confederation (Confederação Operária Brasileira, COB), but textile and other industrial workers did not have active unions in São Paulo in 1914. Anarchist activists concentrated on various cultural activities and education through their Modern Schools and so ignored shop-floor organizing of industrial workers. The COB in Rio called on textile workers throughout Brazil to form new unions, but Paulistano anarchists did little actual organizing.[42] In April 1914, the national anarchist newspaper, A Voz do Trabalhador, noted that "the workers' organizations in [São Paulo], once so successful, continue unfortunately in a state of complete paralysis. The labor movement is limited exclusively to the following organizations: the Union of Stonemasons, the Union of Printers, the Syndicate of Workers in Diverse Shops, and the Union of Hatters."[43] The socialist newspaper Avanti! commented, "What most impresses the socialists who arrive here in São Paulo . . . is the lack of working-class organization."[44]

The Left in São Paulo lacked coherence and a strong base in the industrial working class throughout most of the first two decades of the twentieth century because the anarchists and socialists concentrated on national and international politics at the expense of shop-floor union organizing. Then, as already difficult conditions for Paulistano factory workers became worse in 1914, the city's anarchist, socialist, and other leftist political organizations rallied to protest the war in Europe. With São Paulo racked by food shortages, price speculation, and large-scale industrial unemployment, groups such as the Comissão Internacional contra a Guerra, Centro Socialista Internacional, Centro Libertário, Círculo de Estudos Sociais Francisco Ferrer, and Grupo Anarquista "Os Sem Pátria" met in the Largo da Sé (now Praça da Sé) on 2 August 1914 to denounce the European "hemorrhage of blood promoted by capitalism." The gulf between these activists and their audience was so great that workers in the crowd stood up and demanded that the speakers address their problems. They wanted to know what anarchist and social-

Men and women debate labor politics during May Day rally 1915. (*Courtesy Arquivo Edgard Leuenroth, State University of São Paulo, Campinas* [UNICAMP])

ist leaders were willing to do about the shortages of goods in the markets. How did these leaders plan to combat the decreasing number of jobs, increasing work loads in the factories for those still employed, and low wages earned?[45] On May Day 1915, socialist and anarchist study groups and the unions representing stonemasons and hatters formed yet another International Commission Against the War. Its manifesto proclaimed the group's "repulsion and absolute condemnation of the war, with which capitalism, always insatiable for gold and human lives, seeks to deter the growing progress of international socialism."[46]

The tensions exposed by these meetings had existed since the 1907 textile strike. Leftist activists continued to embrace a political agenda that failed to speak to the concerns of the city's workers. The formal labor movement existed only among a minority of skilled workers (e.g., printers, shoemakers, furniture makers, etc.). Neither the anarchists' focus on direct action to spur the revolutionary moment nor the socialists' belief in using the political system to usher in evolutionary change appealed to the city's industrial workers.[47] The war years highlighted this gulf between the rank and file and leftist activists, for the rapid expansion of São Paulo's industrial sector most profoundly affected the city's women workers—the individuals most alienated from the unions and anarchist study groups.

Popular Mobilization for "Reason and Justice"

With anarchists concentrating on antiwar politics, São Paulo's women textile workers—as they had in 1907—had to organize themselves to push for improved conditions and higher wages in the factories. In May 1917, as prices for foodstuffs fluctuated widely and conditions in the mills became ever more dangerous, women weavers at Cotonifício Crespi in the Mooca neighborhood created factory commissions to bargain with their employers.[48] According to the *Diário Popular* and *O Estado de São Paulo*, the commissions submitted a list of demands to management in late May. They sought a 20 percent increase in pay (to meet rapidly increasing food prices), an end to all fines (e.g., those that foremen imposed to deduct several hours of pay for minor irregularities in cloth), and an end to unhealthy and dangerous work conditions. They also demanded that supervisors and foremen treat the women and children workers with "more respect." The women concluded by demanding that "in everything there should be reason and justice."[49] Explicitly they called for respect; implicitly they demanded an end to foremen's abuses, for these women workers were protesting sexual harassment in the factories as well as dangerous machinery.[50]

When management refused to meet their demands, women workers initiated a strike at Crespi that would soon affect industry throughout the city. After two thousand strikers shut down the mill, men and women from Crespi demonstrated in the city's center to expose industrialists' unwillingness to improve conditions in the factories. Women, men, and children marched, and several women spoke at large rallies about inhumane work conditions in the mills. The strikers also declared that their movement was completely independent of São Paulo's anarchists and socialists. City officials responded by calling for negotiating teams to settle the walkout, and women from the factory commissions agreed to meet with employers. Interestingly, however, a group of men with no ties to the factory commissions arrived at police headquarters to negotiate on behalf of the strikers.[51]

Details of the first days of the strike are sketchy, but reports in the *Diário Popular* and *O Estado de São Paulo*, as well as the recollections of male anarchist leaders, seem to indicate that women took the leading role by formulating the first set of demands, initiating the walkout, and spreading the strike through their speeches and other public demonstrations. Edgard Leuenroth, the anarchist activist and editor of *A Plebe*, noted in a memoir about the strike that it began without the knowledge or help of the anarchist movement. "The 1917 General Strike was a spontaneous workers' movement without the interference, direct or indirect, of any known individuals. It was an explosive protest that came out of a long period of tormenting difficulties that burdened the working class."[52] Leuenroth went on to explain that the shortage and high cost of food were central among the causes of the strike. The anarchist Everardo Dias similarly noted in his memoir: "You couldn't say the General Strike of 1917 was a planned strike or a strike organized in the traditional way by the leaders of unions tied to the [anarchist] Workers' Federation. It was a strike that burst out of São Paulo's workers' rage at their starvation wages and exhausting work."[53] Dias then listed the increases in food prices São Paulo's workers faced in May and June 1917.

Leuenroth's and Dias's belief in the spontaneity of the strike reveals the distance between the rank and file and the anarchist leadership, for no social movement is truly spontaneous. Strikes are planned, and the workers at Crespi created their own factory commissions to formulate demands and then to organize their strike after management refused to negotiate. For the participants, then, there was nothing spontaneous about the strike.[54] Moreover, the workers' demands—for better conditions at both the point of production (the factory) and the point of consumption (their neighborhood markets)—could only have come from women textile workers, for they experienced both the harsh intensification of factory regimes and the wartime inflation and changes in the food distribution system. In June 1917, therefore, women textile workers—because of their unique position within the industrial labor market and the sexual division of labor in working-class households— took over as the de facto leaders of São Paulo's labor movement.

Crespi's women weavers set off a wave of strikes in other mills. First, on 22 June, workers at Tecidos Labor in Mooca struck; those at Estamparia Ipiranga followed. Within days, male and female workers at the medium and smaller textile firms struck. They sought 20 percent increases in base pay and 25 percent increases in the wages of those on the night shifts. The strikers also demanded prompt payment of their earnings, for some factories were three to five weeks late in paying workers. More than a thousand strikers rallied outside the gates of the Estamparia Ipiranga pressing for wage hikes. They then added to their demands a call for the city's authorities to increase the regulation of public markets, for they were often forced to purchase adulterated food at inflated prices; some bakers, for example, were selling pão paulista as regular bread at high prices. After about 1,200 striking Ipiranga workers marched to their factory's gate, the management of that mill offered increases of 15 percent, and 17 percent for night work. The strikers refused to return until all their demands were met. They even rallied to protest the jailing of one of their *companheiros* who had been seized while picketing outside the factory. Their march forced his release from prison. In this first week of July, as a steadily increasing number of workers struck the city's large textile mills, the localized protests of women and men weavers inspired other workers to strike and take direct actions. Workers at São Paulo's largest beverage concern, the Companhia Antártica, struck on 7 July. That same day, a crowd of strikers in Brás sacked a truck carrying wheat from the miller, and two more workers were jailed.[55]

By this time many men workers had entered the growing strike movement. And as the number of strikes increased, the level of violence grew. Roving groups of strikers encountered and fought with mounted police and some military troops in Brás and Mooca. Before these clashes in the second week of July, all the workers' protests had been peaceful. The violence no doubt came out of the increasing frustration of the strikers and the provocation that the stationing of troops represented. It also resulted from the increasing number of men among the thousands of strikers, for the police were more likely to use violence against men than against women. Indeed, the men at Antártica had violent clashes with the police during the first day of their strike.[56]

As the strike spread and violence against workers increased, some textile mills settled with their workers, and the state Department of Labor sought authority to increase its inspections of factories in order to promote safer working conditions. A general settlement seemed possible, but the city's police continued to increase the number of guards around textile mills and troops throughout the industrial *bairros* (neighborhoods). Workers responded by seizing streetcars and closing sections of the city to the troops. In one clash on 9 July the police in Brás shot and killed a young shoemaker, Antônio Ineguez Martinez. Strike leaders and anarchists who had taken an interest in the growing popular movement called for a public protest march from the Martinez house in Brás through the downtown area to the Araça municipal cemetery. About two thousand people, mostly women, gathered outside the Martinez home at 7:00 A.M. on 11 July. They marched through the city, and at the cemetery several women and men gave eulogies that were speeches against the violence ordered by the industrialists. Another rally in the Largo da Sé followed in the afternoon. Soon after this, workers sacked food warehouses and markets. Strikers seized more streetcars and sought to keep troops out of their neighborhoods.[57]

The funeral march and later rally played key roles in transforming the strike. The women deliberately held a public funeral—a ceremony honored by society and thus not likely to engender police repression—and marched through industrial neighborhoods and the central business district to spread the word of their strike to those still working, as well as to other Paulistanos not involved with the factories; that is, the women used the funeral to strengthen their solidarity, increase the total number of strikers, and peacefully advertise their grievances.[58]

The course of the movement changed in the days after the funeral. An increasing number of walkouts in textile factories and metalworking and other shops generalized the strike.[59] In addition to the funeral and rally, Crespi workers spread their movement by calling on other workers to boycott products from the closed mills. Some strikers went to factory gates at the lunch hour and tried to persuade their companheiros to strike. This tactic succeeded at the Matarazzo and other large textile plants that had not yet been struck. Workers at the Fiat Lux match factory as well as at a large screw factory and at small metallurgy shops nearby also followed the strikers' lead. At this point, some ten thousand Paulistano workers were on strike. Without a union structure available to expand the walkout, workers were forced to spread the strike through confrontations outside the factories and through meetings in the markets and their neighborhoods.[60] On 12 July the press reported that at least twenty thousand workers were on strike and that the movement seemed to be growing steadily. Soon the walkout spread to the city's industrial suburbs and into the industrial centers of the interior, such as Campinas and Riberão Preto. By 18 July, workers in Rio de Janeiro had followed the lead of São Paulo's working class.[61] Then, for the first time during the strike, the city's industrialists, under the direction of Elói Chaves, the state secretary of justice and public security, met as a group to respond to the uprising. Members of the São Paulo Center for Commerce and Industry had met several times in June and early July, but they did not discuss collective action to end the strike, even though several firms had settled with their workers. The meeting called by Chaves not only started the process of ending the walkout, it also pointed out to the industrialists that their best hope for success against the workers lay in collective action.[62] This move changed the course of the strike and would have a great impact on industrial relations in São Paulo well into the 1920s and beyond.

The final event that affected the strike was the entrance of the all-male anarchist leadership. As I have said, the anarchists had had little contact with textile and other industrial workers during the war years, and they played no role in initiating this strike movement. São Paulo city authorities blamed the anarchist Workers' League of Mooca (Liga Operária) for most of the strikers' activities and therefore closed it, but the evidence indicates that the walkout began without the assistance of the league.[63] At a meeting at the Salão Germinal on 9 July, anarchists and activists in the Printers' Union, such as Edgard Leuenroth, Francisco Cianci, Antonio Candeias Duarte, Gigi Damiani, Rodolfo Felipe, and Florentino de Carvalho, as well as the socialist Teodoro Monicelli, founded the Proletarian Defense Committee (Comitê de Defesa Proletária) to bargain for the various groups of strikers. The committee's first move, however, was to denounce the closing of the Mooca Workers' League and the anarchists' Modern School; it did not begin negotiations on the workers' behalf for several more days.[64]

The entry of these activists added cohesiveness to the unorganized general strike, but the creation of the committee by men with no ties to the striking textile workers changed the course of the popular movement. The committee's demands ignored most of the goals of the striking women. The anarchists called for the right to organize unions without government interference, amnesty for all strikers, freedom for all jailed strikers, the abolition of work for minors less than fourteen years old, the abolition of night work for minors less than eighteen years old and women, an eight-hour workday, pay increases of 25 to 35 percent depending on the base wage, prompt pay, and an increase of 50 percent in overtime pay. In an aside, the anarchists said the city should encourage lower rents and inspect the markets in order to make sure wage gains would not be lost to new price increases.[65] These demands, although in the general interest of the Paulistano working class, demonstrate a significant schism between the aspirations of the strikers and those of the anarchists who assumed leadership of the movement. The demands ignored women's calls for improved working conditions and protection from sexual harassment by foremen. Further, the committee's proposed prohibition on night work for women potentially limited the ability of São Paulo's women workers to earn a living. Because of their duties as mothers, many women textile workers in São Paulo could be at the factories only during the late shifts. Moreover, the calls for the right to organize addressed the committee's desire to use this strike to help create the union structure anarchists had previously been unable to build.[66]

Soon after its creation the committee began negotiations with industrialists, represented by the Center for Commerce and Industry, through a group of journalists who had volunteered to serve as intermediaries. Many middle-class groups and some people in the state Department of Labor supported the strikers' demands, for they recognized how the harsh conditions that had intensified during the war most adversely affected the city's working class. *O Estado de São Paulo* editorialized against the increasing misery workers faced. In the midst of the strike, its editors wrote, "The truth is that at present the situation of workers in São Paulo is in general the worst."[67]

The increasing police violence against strikers, as well as the conditions under which the city's working class lived and worked, outraged many in São Paulo. Mounted police roamed the industrial districts and broke up gatherings of workers. The number of casualties grew in the second and third weeks of July, and on 13 July a twelve-year-old girl was shot and killed in Barra Funda. Fearing a backlash, the state military authorities set up machine-gun nests and blockades at the entrances to the areas where the industrialists and coffee barons lived. By 14 July the city looked like a war zone, with some forty thousand strikers and an ever-increasing number of military personnel roaming the industrial areas. A tense calm hung over the city as state and city military troops and police occupied the working-class bairros and operated the streetcars. Special details guarded all food shipments through these areas. At the same time, the committee's journalist allies met with the industrialists, and the anarchist leadership held a well-attended meeting at the headquarters of the Mooca Workers' League.[68]

The few industrial establishments still operating were soon struck by their workers. Some textile mills quickly offered wage increases of 20 percent, but most workers stayed away from the shops in solidarity with those still on strike. The city's leading industrialists (e.g., Rodolfo Crespi, Ermelino Matarazzo—on behalf of Indústrias Reunides Francisco Matarazzo—and Jorge Street) agreed to the terms presented by the journalists. The strength of the workers' movement as well as the lack of cohesiveness among themselves forced the industrialists to settle. Several large textile mills and many of the small metallurgy shops had granted wage increases during the negotiations. Divided, the entrepreneurs had to meet the workers' demands. The final agreement reached between the journalists and the industrialists called for a 20 percent increase in wages, amnesty for all strikers, complete freedom for unions to organize workers, prompt payment of wages, and a general effort to improve the living and working conditions in the city. The Proletarian Defense Committee accepted these terms and publicly stated that it would pressure the government to regulate the work of minors and the quality of food in the markets. The strikers accepted this agreement.[69] By 16 July, peace had returned to the industrial districts, and the city's smokestacks were soon billowing as workers went back to the factories. On 18 July almost all the strikers were back at work, and the city was moving to increase the number of markets in working-class neighborhoods.[70]

The anarchists' acceptance of the terms presented by the industrialists effectively ended the general strike. It took several more days to gain freedom for the strikers who had been jailed, and the anarchists continued to pressure the city authorities to reduce food prices. The state soon began transporting food from the interior in order to lower prices, and some industrialists sold inexpensive foodstuffs in makeshift stores they opened in factories.[71]

The workers' uprising had taken elite groups by surprise and worried them deeply. Even the textile industrialist Jorge Street admitted that the great deterioration of workers' living conditions made their movement a just one. He wrote at the end of the strike: "I judged the workers' movement as just in order to negotiate certain concessions . . . that the current living conditions have made necessary and urgent. I also said that I saw the strike as a legitimate right of the worker, and an effective means to get justice, because the previous requests made had been denied. But I also said, and very clearly, that the peaceful and orderly strike should not get involved with subversive movements."[72] Street was not alone in recognizing the justice in the strikers' demands. The state Department of Labor, which dealt at this time primarily with issues in the rural sector, reported during the World War I years on the horrible conditions the city's workers faced, and middle-class groups had recognized the harsh impact of rapid industrial growth.[73] The 1917 General Strike, then, was a form of class struggle that did not conform

22

to the anarchists' vision of Brazil. The elite was divided, and the state did not fully support the industrialists' position. Moreover, middle-class reformers had a clearer idea of the rank and file's demands than had the anarchist leadership.

Women Workers and the Anarchist Movement

São Paulo's women workers initiated the strikes of 1917 because they were the first to feel the impact of the intensified exploitation that came with expanded production during World War I. Women's work buying and preparing food for their families also forced them to confront directly the many problems created by wartime speculation and changes in the city's marketing system. The views or consciousness that came out of their leadership position moved them to the forefront of the labor movement.[74]

After the strike, anarchists and other leftist activists responded to the issues women in the rank and file had raised and shifted their focus away from such macrolevel political concerns as the war in Europe and national politics. The anarchists maintained their Modern Schools and other cultural endeavors, but through their newspaper, A Plebe, they began to address seriously conditions in the factories and working-class neighborhoods. In mid-August, A Plebe reported on the sexual harassment of women workers at Nami Jafet's Labor mill. The editors of the leftist newspaper O Combate attacked the continued use of child labor in the mills and the failure of owners and state inspectors to improve work conditions. Anarchist and other leftist newspapers protested the poor quality and high prices of foodstuffs sold to the city's workers: one issue of A Plebe reported that flour mills were adding clay to their product. These activists also proposed state intervention on behalf of workers. O Combate called on the state government to regulate markets in working-class neighborhoods and sought state inspection of conditions in the city's factories. Through A Plebe, anarchists continued to rely primarily on direct action, but they also chided the state for its failure to protect São Paulo's working people.[75] The anarchist and labor press had mentioned such issues in the past, but it is important to note that in the wake of the strike, women's concerns became a central component of anarchist discourse.

Perhaps the most significant lesson leftist activists learned (or relearned) from the city's working women was the importance of labor organizations. Although they had participated in unions, some Brazilian anarchists remained skeptical of any institution that divided workers by trade or region. In late 1916 the Italian-language anarchist newspaper in São Paulo, *Guerra Sociale,* asserted: "As things are at present, trade unions represent an element of disunity. All those people who shout 'Workers unite!' render the greatest possible service to the state and the bourgeoisie. They fractionalize the proletariat into categories, divide humanity into classes, and reduce the social question to a problem of hours and pennies."[76] Anarchists *as a group* embraced unionization campaigns for industrial laborers only after women workers' independent factory commissions had demonstrated the latent power of São Paulo's working class. Edgard Leuenroth and other supporters of the opening of workers' leagues used women's independent organizing to justify their program to the doubters within the movement. In late July 1917, *A Plebe* called on the city's workers to organize into unions: "In the shortest possible time, the working class, here as well as in the interior [of the state], has to be organized in trade unions or workers' leagues, and then tied together in a powerful general federation."[77] Over the coming months and years, the anarchists sought to build a union that was based in the commissions the workers themselves had organized.[78] Still, popular mobilization had preceded the large-scale unionization campaign, and São Paulo's women workers—not the handful of anarchist activists—played the leadership role in the creation of the city's labor movement.

These changes in strategy helped both the anarchist leaders and the city's workers. In September 1917, for example, workers and anarchist organizers at the Labor mill pressed the bosses to shorten work hours for weavers. When the mill fired the organizers, the workers struck, and they stayed out until the owner, Nami Jafet, changed the work hours and rehired the organizers. In late October, three hundred women weavers in Francisco Matarazzo's Belemzinho mill struck to force an end to foremen's sexual harassment of workers.[79] Men and women workers in both of these strikes organized on their own and then turned to the recently founded neighborhood workers' leagues and the reorganized FOSP for support. At this time, anarchist leaders such as Leuenroth hoped to use the FOSP and workers' leagues to help metalworkers and others found their own unions.[80]

These changes in the outlook and goals of the anarchist movement in São Paulo resulted from that movement making one of its weaknesses—an aversion to centralized authority and decision making—

into a strength. Anarchists' tolerance of divergent points of view made it possible for the male leadership to accept women's organizing and protest activities.[81] For the rest, the success of the city's women workers in May, June, and July 1917 both revealed the latent power of São Paulo's expanding industrial working class and demonstrated the efficacy of organizing locally (within neighborhoods and factories) around issues central to workers' lives such as food quality and prices and work conditions. In this way, women workers dramatically altered the trajectory of São Paulo's labor movement.

The Evolving Industrial Relations System

The general strike both resulted from the distinctive formation of São Paulo's industrial working class and shaped the continuing development of that class. By meeting outside their factories' gates to discuss shared problems, and by carrying word of their strike throughout the city, São Paulo's workers gained a stronger sense of themselves as members of a potentially powerful social class.[82] At the same time they built tenuous ties between their factory commissions and the city's anarchist movement.

The success of the general strike also affected the consciousness of São Paulo's nascent industrial bourgeoisie. The threat posed by the city's laborers forced factory owners to recognize their common interests as members of a class (or class fraction) and to form their own organization in order to confront the workers in a unified way. Accordingly, the state's largest mill owners founded the Center for Spinning and Weaving of São Paulo (Centro dos Industriaes de Fiação e Tecelagem de São Paulo, CIFTSP) in 1919 to provide a unified front and to lobby the state for assistance in labor confrontations.[83] By establishing the center, the state's divergent industrial elite of immigrants and native Brazilians came together as a unified class. This process of elite class formation continued into the 1920s as immigrant industrialists gained access to São Paulo's most exclusive social clubs and their children married into native elite families.[84]

The CIFTSP, along with the national Industrialists' Center in Rio, initiated a two-track policy of co-optation and repression to maintain social peace. Soon after the 1917 General Strike, industrialists in São Paulo applied existing labor regulations and lobbied politicians to write further protective legislation.[85] In Rio, progressive politicians (e.g.,

Maurício de Lacerda and Nicanor do Nascimento) and conservatives lobbied for laws on work accidents, night work for women and children, workers' compensation, and the eight-hour day.[86] Brazilian elites not only thought that such legislation would obviate strikes, they also hoped it would keep workers away from revolutionary ideologies such as those at work in Russia.[87]

Along with protective legislation, São Paulo's industrialists violently repressed labor activists. In late 1917 the city's mill owners fired factory commission leaders, and the police attacked the headquarters of the workers' leagues and *A Plebe*. Industrialists also provided lists of foreign-born activists to be deported under the provisions of the 1907 Adolfo Gordo Law. From late 1917 to 1920, the federal government deported thirty-nine of Brazil's forty-eight major labor leaders. In addition to decapitating the formal labor movement, the government wanted these deportations to intimidate the largely immigrant industrial working class.[88] Ultimately, Paulista elites did not think that material conditions and workers' desires for "reason and justice" engendered strikes; their workers would not strike, they were sure, without the encouragement of outside agitators. This attitude was well summarized by Washington Luís, who had been São Paulo's mayor in the 1910s, when he said during his 1920 campaign for governor: "Labor agitation is a question more closely related to public order than to social order; it represents the state of spirit of some workers, but not the state of society."[89]

Industrialists employed this two-track policy of co-optation and repression as workers in São Paulo organized and struck to force their bosses to meet the commitments of the 1917 General Strike accord. After attending a large May Day rally in 1919, for example, weavers in Francisco Matarazzo's Mariangela mill in Brás struck for an eight-hour day, equal pay for women and men, a 50 percent wage increase, double pay for overtime, and an end to night work for minors. Textile workers throughout the city and its suburbs soon struck. Metalworkers and others followed their lead, and some ten thousand strikers closed down São Paulo by the end of the first week of May. Within days, fifty thousand textile, metallurgical, and other workers were out on strike.[90] The city's industrialists responded with a mixture of violence and conciliation. On 5 May, mounted police charged groups of strikers congregated on the Avenida Celso Garcia and on the Rua Belo Horizonte in Brás, attacked other workers in the Mooca and Ipiranga neighborhoods, and killed a worker in São Bernardo. Congressman Nicanor do Nascimento commented, "When I arrived in São Paulo, the general feeling among the workers was of terror; they feared to go to meetings or rallies because they said that the police would [violently] break them up." At the same time, Jorge Street and other industrialists accepted the idea of an eight-hour day, and Governor Altino Arantes called on the Congress in Rio to adopt national labor legislation along the lines suggested by the Paris peace treaty in order to protect workers. These strikes were settled throughout May. Workers won the eight-hour day and wage increases of between 20 and 30 percent.[91]

Beyond these gains for workers, the May strikes revealed São Paulo's evolving system of industrial relations. In the wake of the 1917 General Strike, both workers and employers created institutions to push for their own interests. Workers ran the local strike negotiations through their factory commissions. These local organizations maintained ties to the neighborhood workers' leagues and the newly organized Textile Workers' Union (União dos Operários em Fábricas de Tecidos) and Metalworkers' Union (União dos Metalúrgicos). The unions often met in the headquarters of the FOSP and coordinated their activities through the General Workers' Council (Conselho Geral dos Operários). The industrialists met several times in the headquarters of the Commercial Association of São Paulo and coordinated their negotiations with the various factory commissions through the new CIFTSP.[92]

The city's anarchists, however, did not completely understand the nature of the evolving working-class structure. In October 1919, leaders of the FOSP attempted to help striking trolley workers by declaring a citywide general strike. Textile and metallurgical workers closed a few establishments for a day or two, but the strike call had little impact.[93] The anarchists had once again miscalculated the views of São Paulo's rank and file. They did not consider that workers who had just won an eight-hour day would be uneasy waging sympathy strikes, and they also failed to recognize that a downturn in the economy was already threatening many of the workers' jobs in São Paulo.[94] The anarchists' failure in October 1919 was not the death knell of the labor movement. It simply demonstrated that few among the city's rank and file embraced the anarchist ideal of the general strike as a political act.

Class Struggle in an Industrial City

World War I changed São Paulo and brought a new style of labor relations to Brazil's leading industrial center. The city's expansion and the changes it foisted upon the working class, as well as the expansion of the industrial sector of the economy, laid the groundwork for workers' continuing battles for higher wages and better living and working conditions. The war years also determined how that class struggle would be waged. Labor activists learned they had to build ties to the growing industrial working class if they were going to create a representative and powerful workers' movement. At the same time, the wartime economic expansion and workers' activism—especially the 1917 General Strike—forced industrialists to organize their own class association to coordinate activities among themselves and between them and the state. These changes in São Paulo's economic and social structures brought on a period of intense class struggle in the early 1920s.[95]

Life in an Expanding Metropolis

When Rudyard Kipling first saw São Paulo in the 1920s, he remarked, "One understands without being told that here is a metropolis."[96] Indeed, the city's population had grown from 239,820 inhabitants in 1900 to 579,033 in 1920, and would expand to 1,033,202 people in 1934.[97] In the 1920s, São Paulo shed the remnants of its agrarian past and began its existence as an industrial center. The state government observed this expansion by taking censuses of all things urban. In 1924, the state Department of Labor researched the number of automobiles (8,000), trucks (1,000), trolleys (650), and telephones (21,050).[98] Intellectuals in São Paulo also took note of their city's rapid urbanization. Writers such as Mário de Andrade and António de Alcântara Machado celebrated, and at the same time questioned, the impact of the growth of the city on its residents. Painters, writers, composers, and other artists from throughout Brazil came together in São Paulo in February 1922 for the Week of Modern Art. They congregated in São Paulo, not Rio (Brazil's traditional arts center), because the growing industrial city represented all they considered modern.[99]

São Paulo's workers, in their everyday lives, took note of these changes in the city. The continued expansion of high-rises in the city's commercial center and the expanding luxury neighborhoods, along with growth in the factory districts, forced up rents and pushed an increasing number of workers into unhealthy housing.[100] The situation deteriorated to the point that the governor, who in general was not sympathetic to the plight of São Paulo's workers, told the state legislature that "the shortage of healthy housing for the poor in the capital is constantly growing; as a result, they dwell in basements with unhealthy conditions, or in tenements which have the worst sanitary conditions."[101]

São Paulo's urban expansion also brought new dangers to its inhabitants. Local and foreign commentators noted that as the city expanded in size, life on its streets became increasingly menacing. In addition to the almost daily fatalities caused by cars and trolleys, São Paulo's workers suffered the impact of their poor living conditions as scarlet fever, typhoid fever, diphtheria, and other dangerous diseases spread through the close quarters of the city's tenements and basements.[102] Given the existing sexual division of labor in working-class households, these conditions particularly affected the lives of São Paulo's women workers. In addition to their duties in the factories, women struggled to find unadulterated foods and safe living conditions for their families. Street ballads sung in working-class neighborhoods in the 1920s capture the tone of women workers' struggles:

>Sleep little one
>Enough fighting
>Mommy is going to the movies
>To see the craziness of love
>
>Sleep little one
>That the animal looks for
>Papa left
>He was tired of hoping
>
>Sleep little one
>Let Mama leave
>Mama works too much
>And she needs escape
>
>Sleep little mother
>Mama will be angry
>Sleep quickly
>If you don't want to be hit
>
>Look here, little one
>I'm tired of asking
>You can cry as you wish
>I'll leave, so I won't hear.[103]

In addition to recounting the struggles faced by women workers with children, this ballad reveals the complex working-class culture that developed in São Paulo in the 1910s and 1920s. Workers'—both men's and women's—lives revolved around their streets. Along with everyday activities such as singing ballads, playing music, and debating politics, São Paulo's working people held their own Carnavals in their neighborhoods in the 1920s. Before the municipal government began regulating Carnaval, the celebration in Brás was known among workers as the most enjoyable in the city.[104] At the same time, new forms of entertainment such as movies became central to working-class leisure. North American movies dominated in the city's theaters. According to a U.S. consular official, westerns and "social dramas with luxurious settings are the most popular [films], and beautiful women are especially demanded."[105] By 1923, the city's movie houses, including Brás's famous Olimpia Theater, were admitting between fifteen thousand and twenty thousand people daily.[106] The movies were an escape for workers. Armando Sufrendi and other young metalworkers went to adventure series such as *The Star of Gold* and *The Masked Man*. Assumpta Bianchi and her friends from the textile mill, like the women in the ballad, escaped the reality of life in São Paulo through love stories.[107]

These leisure activities helped shape Paulistano working-class culture. Between community activities such as Carnaval and listening to street music, and the escapist entertainment of the movies, the city's workers developed an expanded set of shared experiences that made up their individual and group consciousness. Indeed, it was at this time that Brás, Mooca, Ipiranga, Cambuci, and other neighborhoods flourished as centers of working-class life and culture.[108] This culture then became part of the glue holding the city's workers together, especially in the face of government attempts to "purify" and regulate working-class life in the 1920s.[109]

Industrial Relations in an Expanding Metropolis

The failed general strike of October 1919 did not slow grass-roots organizing among São Paulo's industrial workers. In addition to the neighborhood workers' leagues, the city's textile workers continued to expand the shop-floor activities of their factory commissions in the early 1920s. This local level of organizing was extremely important for textile workers, who remained sharply divided by sex. Although women made up 58 percent of the textile work force in the state as a whole, they earned only 60 percent of men's wages in the same industry.[110] In the aftermath of the 1917 and 1919 strikes, industrialists did little to correct this imbalance. Further, foremen continued to threaten and harass women workers. Ambrosina Pioli, who worked in the Companhia de Indústrias Têxtis, was repeatedly threatened with firing to make room for the foreman's lover. When she complained, she was severely beaten by her foreman, Paschoal Botti.[111] In the face of such discrimination, women textile workers chose to maintain separate factory commissions that would then affiliate with the workers' leagues.

These divisions did not affect organizing in the new metallurgy sector, for men made up over 95 percent of the state's metalworkers. Spread out in small shops (often employing fewer than thirty), São Paulo's metalworkers relied on contacts outside the shops to organize their Metalworkers' Union in 1919.[112] Ernesto Mendes Dantas, José Albertino, and others recalled the important role anarchists played helping metalworkers organize their union but noted that it was the dangerous conditions in this new, expanding industry more than a revolutionary ideology that drove workers to join. In fact, the rank and file struggled to force shop-floor issues to the fore because the anarchists often concentrated on political questions related to the working class as a whole.[113]

The shop-floor level of orientation in the Metalworkers' Union masked its steadily growing cohesiveness and power throughout the city's factory districts in the early 1920s. Metalworkers in the Lidgerwood do Brasil shop, for example, struck against the long hours they had to work without the customary "time and a half" overtime pay. Metalworkers at the Companhia Martin e Barros, Viuva Craig shop, Associação Paulista das Indústrias Mecânicas e Metais, and other firms initiated strikes a few days later to force bosses to accept rules on hours and pay. And after shops throughout the city accepted work rules, metalworkers as a united group struck to enforce them. These important struggles were more or less ignored by the anarchist leadership in the city, because in April and May the FOSP was busy attempting— unsuccessfully—to initiate a general strike to strengthen textile, railroad, and other workers' strikes.[114]

Industrialists and the state and federal governments again responded with repression. A British diplomat noted in 1920 that "strike meetings are surrounded by troops, and the leaders and orators arrested. If they happen to be foreigners, they are at once deported—if they are Brazilians they are imprisoned for a time, or else they are sent up to the north and disappear altogether."[115] The city's mill owners also recognized the power of the factory commissions. In addition to attacking union headquarters and meetings, they initiated a system of identifying and blacklisting workers who played active roles in the commissions. After the strike in the Scarpa mill in São Bernardo, the Textile Industrialists' Center circulated a special register of workers along with other circulars giving the names and descriptions of rank-and-file workers who had participated. These Paulistas also contacted the national industrialists' association in Rio offering to coordinate the dissemination of such blacklists.[116]

Even in the face of repression, workers' factory commissions negotiated throughout 1921 for improved work conditions and higher pay. In early January 1921, workers at Companhia de Aniagem Paulista struck for payment of their Christmas bonuses. Commissions at Matarazzo's Mariangela mill also demanded bonuses.[117] The factory commissions continued to attract workers with calls for improved work conditions. A handbill circulated in one mill asked: "Do you want to improve your conditions? Do you want to end the abuses in the factories? Do you want to be [treated like] human beings?" It then called on workers to participate in factory organizing and also, if they could, to attend meetings of the Textile Workers' Union.[118] This call to attend union meetings demonstrates that factory commission leaders were not necessarily hostile to the anarchist organization. In the end, however, they saw the commissions as their primary line of defense for dealing with employers.[119] In addition to handling negotiations with bosses, the commissions coordinated acts of sabotage, such as work slowdowns and the theft of materials and equipment.[120]

Factory commissions were much more effective in organizing women workers than was the Textile Workers' Union. After all, the union was dominated by men, conducted its meetings while many women were on the night shift, and often faced police repression. And the male unionists continued to speak of protecting women rather than sharing power with them in the union structure. In May 1921, twenty-two women (eighteen Italians, one Portuguese, and three Brazilians) were expelled—along with one Italian man—from the Luzitania mill for organizing commissions to press for higher wages. The women's commissions did not back down in the face of threats and were broken up only when the mill owners called in the police. A few weeks later, women textile workers in the Companhia Fabril Paulistana struck against fines that were being subtracted from their wages. Twelve women (ten Italians and two Brazilians) led this protest and were arrested and blacklisted for doing so. The city's mill owners maintained extensive blacklists to guarantee they would have "only the real workers" in their factories. What they failed to understand was that the women running factory commissions *were* the real workers.[121]

Women textile workers also used less direct forms of resistance to fight low wages and poor work conditions. The easiest and most common strategy was changing jobs. Women textile workers, through their factory commissions and informal neighborhood social networks, collected information on wages available in the city's factories and discussed which factories had foremen known for harassing women. Women workers also frequently returned to the rural sector to avoid harsh work conditions, earn higher wages during the harvest, or help their families who still lived as colonos.[122] This mobility became such a problem for mill owners that bosses attempted to standardize wages throughout the city and state.[123]

São Paulo's industrial workers continued to use such survival and resistance strategies throughout 1922. The city's Metalworkers' Union again faced police repression, but *metalúrgicos* managed to negotiate directly with their bosses through their factory commissions. Some of these commissions, composed of one worker from each small shop in a given neighborhood, managed to negotiate work rules and wages.[124] The Textile Workers' Union also suffered from police repression and so held few formal meetings in 1922. Although the formal labor institutions had been silenced by violent interventions, arrests, and deportations of leaders, rank-and-file workers in São Paulo continued to organize in their factories and often, in the case of metalworkers, in their neighborhoods.[125] These rank-and-file groups continued to launch strikes, and in textiles, immigrant women remained in the forefront of the protest movements.[126]

Labor and other leftist leaders in São Paulo recognized the independent nature of this working-class organizing. In May 1922, the Italian-language newspaper *Fanfulla* ran a long letter calling on São Paulo's textile workers to join (i.e., become dues-paying members of) the Textile Workers' Union. The letter, which was no doubt written by labor activists, admitted that the union had made many mistakes that alienated the rank and file from the leadership. It promised to "make a new union from the lessons learned from past errors, and the new union will be founded using new methods. . . . All the aspects of power will be eliminated from our environment."[127]

São Paulo's industrial workers had left or failed to join the city's unions because they did not feel those unions adequately represented their interests. Further, by relying on their own local forms of organization they protected themselves from the shifting political alliances and repression that characterized the Left in São Paulo at this time. In February 1922, a group of militants broke from the anarchist movement and, with other leftists, formed the Brazilian Communist party (PCB). The shift from anarchism, with its loose organization that tolerated grass-roots movements (e.g., factory commissions), to Leninism, which featured strict party discipline and hierarchies, further alienated São Paulo's industrial working class from some activists. Few workers in São Paulo joined the Communist party in the 1920s.[128]

The founding of the PCB, along with increasing state repression, strengthened the workers' resolve to maintain their own local organizations.[129] This independence shielded rank-and-file activists from the increasingly effective state repression of formal labor institutions. Moreover, laws authorizing arrest and imprisonment for acts aimed at "destroying the existing social order" and regulations for the closing of unions did not affect factory commissions, for those organizations were concerned primarily with industrial relations issues (wages, hours, conditions on the shop floor, etc.) rather than with overtly political questions (e.g., the destruction of the capitalist system).[130]

These local grass-roots forms of organizing worried the city's industrialists, who in the early and mid-1920s began to "rationalize" production. In the metalworking sector, which was expanding now that the economic climate encouraged reinvestment of local capital in such industries, employers maximized production by changing work rules on the shop floor. In many shops, for the first time workers were forced to stay at their work stations for set periods, and their breaks (including, at the Santa Rosa screw factory, those in the bathroom) were timed. Francisco Matarazzo's Metal Graphica Aliberti shop initiated a 12.5 percent increase in hours but gave only a 5 percent raise.[131] Mill owners felt too that they needed an apolitical, submissive labor force if they were to succeed in the modernization of textile production. In late 1923, Octávio Pupo Nogueira of the São Paulo Textile Industrialists' Center proposed a national identification system so that factory owners could find workers who had no history of participation in "political strikes." Interestingly, Pupo Nogueira felt strikes for increased wages were just, but any work stoppage for changes in work conditions was "political" and thus unjust.[132] Industrialists made this distinction because they were altering work regimes as they installed new equipment. As a part of the rationalization process, employers unilaterally rescinded the eight-hour day. To facilitate these changes, in 1923 mill owners in São Paulo had the police carry out preemptive arrests to clear their factories of leaders of commissions.[133]

Throughout 1923, workers' commissions organized strikes to regain the eight-hour day and end onerous new work rules. In February and March, leaders of various commissions coordinated their activities through the Textile Workers' and Metalworkers' unions, but the strikes remained local by factory.[134] Still, this association with the anarchist unions hurt the strike movement. Workers' demands lost legitimacy in the eyes of industrialists who respected "peaceful" strikes (i.e., those for wages) but repressed "political" strikes (those related to work rules or any movement tied to a revolutionary ideology). Accordingly, employers broke up the walkouts by jailing as many commission leaders as they could identify.[135]

In September 1923, workers responded to this repression by using their commissions to launch strikes that had no *overt* ties to the unions. Women textile workers even phrased their demands to appeal to their bosses. They complained about foremen who lacked the necessary technical abilities to keep the new machines operating efficiently and said that they could not earn a high enough piece rate to meet increasing prices. Workers also threatened to take their skills in using the new machines to other factories. These arguments convinced mill owners to grant wage increases of 10 percent. The strikes succeeded because industrialists did not construe them as political, and because the skills of the women workers (most of them weavers) were highly valued by industrialists in the midst of an expansion program.[136]

As prices for foodstuffs once again increased dramatically, the city's industrial workers renewed their push for higher wages and better work conditions through their factory commissions. In January 1924, women workers from the Crespi, Mariangela, Gamba, Penteado, Tecidos de Juta, and other mills struck against inflation and harsh work regimes; they sought wage hikes, an eight-hour day, and payment of their wages fortnightly instead of monthly. Industrialists recognized the demands as generally just and noted that the strikes were being instigated and run by factory commissions. Factory owners did, however, use the strikes as an excuse to arrest anarchist leaders and move against union headquarters.[137]

The jailing of anarchist leaders did not affect this strike movement, for the walkout had been initiated and was being propagated by workers (especially women) in factory commissions. Throughout February, an increasing number of industrial workers joined the walkout. Although the police continued to attempt to break up the strike, the decentralized nature of the movement protected it. Leaders of the workers' commissions frustrated both the industrialists and São Paulo's anarchist leaders: industrialists could not settle the strike through violence, and the anarchists could not influence its direction.[138] Although the movement did not have the participation of the city's unions, the factory commissions managed to keep it well organized and peaceful, even when the number of strikers reached thirty thousand in February and early March and the police stepped up their attacks against them.[139]

A downturn in demand for textiles allowed mill owners to wait out the strike. Because they valued their skilled work force, however, they offered wage increases of 10 percent and some reductions in hours. Textile and other industrialists wanted to rehire the strikers, but they blacklisted the leaders of the factory commissions. Once again, the vast majority of the blacklisted workers were immigrant women, mostly from Italy. Activist women workers likewise faced arrest after the strikes, for the city's industrialists wanted to cleanse their factories of rank-and-file leaders during this period of reequipping.[140]

The January–March 1924 strike rekindled anarchists' hopes of building an effective and representative union structure in São Paulo. José Righetti, a weaver who had ties to the anarchist movement as well as to the factory commissions, was one of the leaders in this effort. He and other activists founded the new Textile Workers' Union on 14 April 1924, hoping it would bridge the gap between them and the grass-roots workers' movement. They also moved to reopen unions in other industries, and throughout May and June 1924 the anarchist press reported record numbers of new union members. Whether or not these unions appealed to the majority of the rank and file, they did make a conscious effort to address workers' primary concerns (e.g., food prices, rents, and working conditions) along with their usual set of political issues.[141]

Perhaps the contrast with the PCB, with its concentration on political issues, bolstered the image of São Paulo's anarchists in the early 1920s. Further, the anarchists' belief in decentralized authority again allowed them to build loose ties to the factory commissions. This process, however, was abruptly interrupted in early July 1924 when the *tenentes*, a group of young officers, seized the city of São Paulo as part of a rebellion against the regime in Rio. Anarchist weavers such as Righetti, João Castellani, and Paulo Menkitz sought promises from the tenentes of a minimum wage that would meet the cost of living, price controls, an eight-hour day, the right to free association, and an open press. After taking the city, the military men made some foodstuffs available to workers at reduced prices, but they did little more to gain working-class support.[142]

While the rebels held the city (5–28 July 1924), São Paulo's workers ignored political platforms and took direct action. During the second week of July, workers sacked food warehouses in Brás, Mooca, and other neighborhoods in riots carefully targeted against the holdings of industrialists, especially Francisco Matarazzo and Pinotti Gamba. According to the U.S. consul, the attacks were "largely an expression of dislike for large industrialists who were accused of being responsible for the high prices of foodstuffs."[143] Workers stole and destroyed machinery in some factories and burned down certain flour mills they blamed for the highest prices.[144] These attacks set the rebels against São Paulo's workers, for the tenentes feared the "mobs"; the rebels threatened to shoot anyone involved in any form of looting.[145]

The rebellion brought increased misery to São Paulo's workers. The conflict cut off supplies of food to the city, sending prices for available goods out of the reach of most workers. They also endured artillery and aerial bombardment from federal troops, for the rebels had made Brás and Mooca their strongholds. The bombing destroyed workers' homes and places of employment, including sections of the massive Crespi mill, and killed several hundred workers. Roughly 1,000 Paulistanos died, 4,000 were wounded by the bombing and shelling, and an estimated 300,000 fled the city for the interior.[146]

In addition to this physical suffering, São Paulo's workers faced increased repression. After the federal government expelled the rebels from the city, the state government created a special political police, the Departamento de Ordem Política Social (DOPS), and worked with industrialists to close all formal labor institutions in the city. The British consul reported that industrialists were using the 1924 revolt as an excuse to completely repress the city's labor movement. Indeed, the Textile Industrialists' Center bragged: "We have the honor to report, confidentially, that the police, taking advantage of the unusual times we have just experienced, destroyed everything inside the headquarters of workers' associations. . . . This solution, in our view, will keep us safe from future strikes." The government initiated a state of siege, during which it closed *A Plebe* and other labor newspapers. At the same time, political prisoners from São Paulo, including many anarchist and other labor activists, were sent to the Clevelândia penal colony in the jungle on the French Guiana frontier.[147]

Industrialists relied on such repression against labor and the Left in São Paulo in the aftermath of the tenente rebellion. When textile workers in the Companhia Fabril Paulistano, Companhia Anglo-Brasileira de Juta, and other mills struck for higher wages in September and October 1924, owners granted modest 10 percent wage increases and made some discounted foodstuffs available to workers, but they also violently repressed the strike commissions. In addition to blacklisting activists, they requested that the police jail the strike leaders. With the union structure destroyed, industrialists believed they could continue their policies of co-optation and repression to facilitate the rationalization of production in their factories.[148]

The tenente rebellion helped usher in new authoritarian institutions the state and industrialists could use to repress São Paulo's rising working-class movement. Ironically, the very weakness of the developing labor movement—the divisions in strategy and goals between the rank and file (especially women workers who dominated industries such as textiles) and anarchist activists—served to protect it from the growing authoritarian power the state was willing to exercise on behalf of the industrialists. At the same time, both the rank and file and the city's labor and leftist activists began to narrow the gulf that separated them. Women's organizing and protest activities raised important issues that anarchist activists eventually embraced. Through increased contact with these labor radicals—most often during strikes rather than through regular participation in unions or anarchist study groups—Paulistano factory workers began to develop a more coherent critique of politics. This mixing of ideology and praxis by the city's workers and leftist activists led to the development of a unique Paulistano anarcho-syndicalism that valued both local, independent grass-roots organizing (e.g., through the factory commissions) and the organizational and bargaining role played during strikes by labor and Left activists.

The process of class formation that had forced women into industrial labor in large factories continued, however, to shape São Paulo's nascent workers' movement. Not only were women still excluded from higher-paying skilled jobs, they remained separated from power in the city's unions. But women proved to themselves, as well as to their male companheiros, labor and leftist leaders, industrialists, and state policy-makers, that they could and should play a leadership role in organizing and protest activities. Through their actions, these working women had redefined their roles: they would not accept the status of "priestesses of the home." Moreover, by being in the forefront of the evolving workers' movement, these women could no longer be seen as enemies of the social movement. But given the repressive atmosphere of the mid-1920s, their distance from the formal union movement served to protect their own organizations, the factory commissions.

"Order and Progress" and Revolution in Industrial São Paulo, 1925–1935

The history of industrialism has always been a continuing struggle . . . against the element of "animality" in man. It has been an uninterrupted, often painful and bloody process of subjugating natural (i.e., animal and primitive) instincts to new, more complex and rigid norms and habits of order, exactitude and precision which can make possible the increasingly complex forms of collective life which are the necessary consequence of industrial development.

—Antonio Gramsci,
"Americanism and Fordism," in *Selections from the Prison Notebooks*

The basic sociology of today's economic well-being is solidarity. The principle of free competition has been replaced by cooperation. This increasing solidarity leads to the creation of ever more powerful collective groups, under the control of and working with the State. We have entered the phase of the construction of the union movement.

—Getúlio Vargas,
A Nova Política do Brasil

In the wake of the 1924 tenente rebellion, São Paulo's industrialists began the process of consolidating their recent gains. They continued to work with the state government to repress the formal labor movement, and they again employed repression and co-optation to foster social peace among the rank and file. Mill owners, metalworking shop owners, and other entrepreneurs continued to invest their profits in expanding capacity. They also tended to act in state and national politics as a unified industrial bourgeoisie. Through the Textile Industrialists' Center and other trade associations, they pushed for policies that would further help them control their workers, and in turn increase productivity.[1] Ultimately, industrialists used the state of siege to consolidate the rise of industrial capitalism in São Paulo.

The city's workers were not passive victims of these developments. They continued to use their factory commissions to protest and resist many of the industrialists' initiatives. The intervention of national political elites during the 1930s profoundly affected this process. As government attempts to promote and regulate the industrial expansion of Brazil brought new actors into São Paulo's labor relations system, industrialists and workers began to look to the state for assistance in their struggles. Indeed, after the Revolution of 1930, workers, union and leftist activists, industrialists, and state policymakers struggled to implement their version of the "order and progress" promised by Brazilian citizenship. For the first time, labor relations, especially those centered in São Paulo—Brazil's leading industrial center—became national political issues.

Consolidating Industrial Capitalism in São Paulo

In May 1925, the Rio de Janeiro daily, O Jornal, commented on the impressive industrialization of São Paulo and its impact on the "modernization" of Brazil: "We are no longer the classic tropical country with its laziness and dreams, [because] today we work in São Paulo with the fever of the Yankees."[2] São Paulo's industrialists liked such comparisons, for they greatly envied the progress made by North Americans. At the opening of the new Center of Industries of the State of São Paulo, Roberto Simonsen called for his fellow industrialists to emulate the ideology of mass production and consumption associated with "Fordism." This, he told his colleagues, was the future of Brazil: "It is obvious that there is an absolute correlation between the ends that industrialists have in view and the true interests of the nation. The increase in the nation's capacity to consume will represent the opening of a formidable market for Brazilian industrialists; consumption and production, rising in harmony, will increase wealth, will bring greatness to the country, well being and tranquility to the population."[3]

Owners of small industrial establishments, such as the city's metalworking shops, also caught this "fever of the Yankees" in the 1920s and early 1930s. At this time, the founders of the Paulistano metalworking sector sent their sons to study the technical aspects of their industry at the São Paulo Polytechnical School. These students came away from their training with both a knowledge of engineering and the fervent belief that industrial expansion would be the cornerstone of national progress.[4] The intellectuals and military men who established the Republic in 1889 had had similar ideas about the modernization of Brazil: They believed that "order and progress" would come to Brazil if it abandoned its agrarian past and industrialized.[5] By the 1920s and early 1930s, São Paulo's industrialists not only shared this ideology, they implemented it.

Economic Expansion and the Rationalization of Work

São Paulo experienced four distinct economic cycles during the 1920s. In the first years of the decade, the economy continued the expansion begun by World War I. Drought and the reentry of foreign goods brought low growth or stagnation from 1924 to 1926.[6] Tariff adjustments in 1926 engendered rapid growth in 1927 and 1928. Finally, the crash of 1929 brought a downturn.[7] These trends, however, obscure the actual condition of the textile and metalworking industries. The re-equipping of older mills and the establishment of new ones—with imported machinery as well as parts made in the city's expanding metalworking sector—affected the pace and direction of growth in textiles and metallurgy. The textile industry introduced, for the first time in Brazil, automated spinning and weaving equipment. Mills expanded their capacity without having to increase their work forces.[8] Using the profits earned during the war, machine shops in São Paulo began making replacement parts and other equipment for the mills. Although the 1920s have traditionally been seen as a period of renewed interest in old trading patterns (i.e., Brazilian exports of coffee for British and U.S. finished goods) and a decline for industry, the reality was increased industrial capacity (table 2.1).[9]

This expansion had deep and lasting effects on São Paulo's industrial workers.[10] The acquisition of new textile machinery brought with it attempts to rationalize industrial production. For the first time since they had established the textile industry, mill owners sought the latest, most efficient spinning and weaving equipment.[11] The replacement of equipment was quite uneven, however. Those sections of the Crespi mill that had been destroyed during the 1924 bombing were completely rebuilt, but other sections of the industrial complex in Brás continued to use machines built in the 1890s. The Companhia Nacional de Tecidos de Juta utilized some of the newest machinery available in the mid-1920s alongside old equipment from the turn of the century.[12]

Mill owners also wanted these new machines because they required less skill to operate. The older equipment required skilled operators, and its fragility actually empowered workers. That is, weavers and

Table 2.1   Index of Brazilian Industrial Output, 1918–1930 (1928 = 100)

Year	Textiles[a]	Metallurgy	Total industry
1918	85	—	52
1919	89	—	58
1920	92	27	62
1921	88	34	60
1922	108	34	75
1923	107	49	75
1924	100	48	81
1925	93	64	83
1926	93	130	84
1927	102	121	94
1928	100	100	100
1929	83	120	98
1930	82	106	91

Source: Flávio Rabelo Versiani, A Década de 20 na Industrialização Brasileira (Rio de Janeiro: IPEA/INPES, 1987), 39.
[a]This is for cotton textiles.

spinners acquired a vast knowledge of how to keep their often broken machines running throughout their shifts. Their piece rate wages made such knowledge standard fare for textile workers and gave them leverage against their bosses' attempts to fire anyone with ties to the factory commissions.[13] Mill owners convinced the State Industrialists' Center to sponsor a series of conferences on the application of "Taylorismo" in São Paulo's factories. Industrialists studied methods of selecting and educating "good workers," creating efficient work areas, regulating work regimes to provide sufficient rest for workers, and ways to motivate labor.[14]

Mill owners were particularly interested in finding and training workers, for they felt they faced a tight labor market. They opposed a 1926 law restricting child labor on the grounds that, unlike the United States and Great Britain, Brazil faced a shortage of factory workers.[15] Industrialists later argued that this tight labor market had forced up wages and so reduced profits available for their purchases of new machinery.[16] Mill owners' gender ideologies shaped this perspective. Even though they recognized the unique abilities required to operate their machinery efficiently, they still considered mill work unskilled,

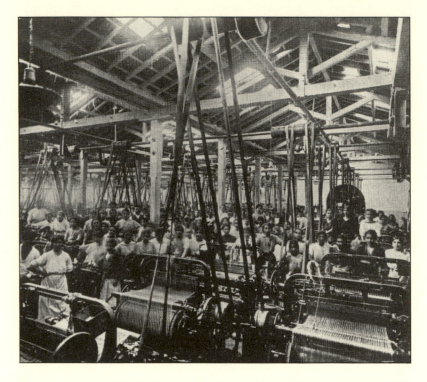

Women weavers of the Fábrica de Tecidos Paulistana. Note the series of belts running from each loom to a central power source. (*Courtesy Arquivo Edgard Leuenroth, State University of São Paulo, Campinas* [UNICAMP])

and thus appropriate for women. In this way they limited their own labor market—mostly to immigrant women.[17]

The metalworking sector likewise expanded its capacity and complexity at this time. Throughout the 1920s and 1930s, the owners of small repair shops used the profits earned during the industrial expansion brought on by World War I to found large machine shops. These new industrial establishments (e.g., Villares, Dedini, Romi, Ribeiro, Andrighetti, and Nardini) increased their capital invested and for the first time attempted to rationalize work regimes.[18] São Paulo's industrialists—owners of metalworking establishments, textile mills, and other factories—looked with great curiosity at the assembly plant the Ford Motor Company built in the city. They noted that the factory had a well-organized division of labor that allowed the workers to use their machines efficiently. O. Pupo Nogueira of the Textile Industrialists' Center believed that "the factory uses Taylorism well and with intelligence." After noting that Ford paid the highest wages in the city, Pupo Nogueira continued, "This factory . . . adapts to local conditions all [of Ford's] experience. It is a school of industrial labor that should be looked at by the owners of some of our industries, whose anachronistic work regimes are inefficient and dreadful in industrial and social terms, not to mention purely human terms."[19]

The one problem new machinery and production techniques could not solve was the volatility of São Paulo's industrial labor market. Throughout the 1920s and early 1930s, São Paulo's workers continued to migrate back and forth to the rural sector depending on employment conditions in the city. In 1926, the high turnover rate in São Paulo's industries, especially in the mills, began to worry industrialists. They complained that these migration patterns forced up the price of labor; mill owners particularly worried about the high cost of training and retraining workers.[20] In order to stabilize the labor market, São Paulo's industrialists adopted one more tenet of Fordism: they instituted a wide range of corporate welfare schemes.

A few textile and metallurgy establishments supplied worker housing, medical care, and food cooperatives as a response to the 1917 strikes, but sponsoring such measures did not become a concerted policy among the city's industrialists until the mid-1920s.[21] Most commonly, industrialists built housing known as *vilas operárias* to rent to their employees. Even though São Paulo grew at a rate of one house per hour in 1925, there was a severe shortage of affordable units available to the city's workers. Indeed, workers often spent more than half their incomes on housing. These high rents were more often than not for tenements, basements, and other forms of substandard housing.[22] To help keep workers in the city, an increasing number of industrialists built vilas operárias in the 1920s. The rents for these small houses were generally one quarter of the market rate for similar dwellings. The houses also increased industrialists' control over their workers, because foremen and other officials decided who would gain access to this valuable benefit. Workers who participated in strikes or other protest activities risked losing their homes.[23]

An increasing number of industrialists offered their workers discounted meals at factory restaurants, foodstuffs below market prices, limited medical care, reading classes, and recreation facilities. These programs had two basic goals: first, industrialists wanted to foster a healthy and capable working class that could efficiently handle the latest machinery in the factories; second, they sought to earn workers' loyalty by building an atmosphere of the "company family." Factories sponsored group picnics and sports leagues (especially for soccer) to this end.[24] Ultimately, industrialists wanted to create a stable, well-trained, and healthy labor force that would not strike or organize other protest activities.[25] Providing social services was also the most efficient way for industrialists to meet workers' needs. The construction of housing, restaurants, and other facilities represented fixed capital investments; wage increases to meet inflation were beyond the control of employers. There was little charity in these social services—they were rational applications of economic resources.[26]

All these measures were aimed at ameliorating workers' conditions outside the factories, and thus providing social peace. On the other hand, such social services represented an implicit bargain that industrialists could alter work regimes (i.e., the rationalization of production) in exchange for improved living conditions. This is an essential component of Fordism. On the other hand, these measures demonstrate the impact of women's organizing on São Paulo's industrialists. Women textile workers were the first to introduce issues related to life outside the factories into the industrial relations system. Industrialists responded with a series of programs aimed at making everyday life in the expanding metropolis a little easier. In addition to helping reproduce their labor force, employers sought to mollify their women workers with these measures.[27]

The federal government also took up the banner of social welfare in 1926 when it instituted regulations limiting women's and minors' (between fourteen and eighteen years old) factory labor to six hours of day work.[28] The government inspectors enforced only the child labor provisions of this law. In doing so, they acted to promote "morality" among the nation's future workers. Government officials were also responding to their perceptions of women's demands that children be protected from the dangerous factory conditions. Whatever the actual impact of this law and industrialists' social welfare policies, it is clear that women workers' protests had not fallen on deaf ears.[29]

Workers Confront Fordism

The changes in production had a much greater effect on São Paulo's industrial workers than did the limited social services made available by

Table 2.2   Daily Wages in São Paulo, 1925–1927 (in milreis)

Position	1925	1926	1927
Metalworker (male)	13$500	16$500	17$500
Factory worker[a]			
Male	9$500	11$500	16$000
Female	5$500	7$000	8$500
Child	1$500	3$000	4$500

Source: São Paulo to Rio, Memo on Daily Wages, 22 June 1927, RG 84, SP Post 850.4, NA.

[a] These figures are averages for workers in textile mills, flour mills, glass factories, breweries, and shoe factories.

their employers. Paulistanos continued to face a steadily increasing cost of living; consumer prices rose 36 percent from 1923 to 1925, for example. And although they enjoyed several significant wage increases after 1925 (table 2.2), workers had to cope with curtailed hours during shortages of electricity for factories. Such shortened shifts forced down real income.[30] In late 1928, the British consul in São Paulo worried that the inability of the city's workers to keep up with the rapidly increasing cost of living was so significant that it was causing a dramatic increase in the number of suicides and murders.[31]

With the formal union structure destroyed by violent state and industrialist action in the aftermath of the 1924 tenente rebellion, São Paulo's industrial workers once again had to rely on their factory commissions to bargain for increased wages and improved work conditions.[32] Accordingly, factory commissions—led by and composed entirely of women—in the Crespi, Belemzinho, and Mariangela mills continued to meet and push for higher wages and improved conditions throughout 1925 and 1926.[33] The strikes these women launched had several key similarities: they were initiated and run solely by the commissions; there was no union role; and the strikers faced immediate, violent state intervention. A British report of one strike in October 1926 noted that "all workers of a jute factory in São Paulo, 200 strong, struck recently on account of the shortening of the working week to four days. . . . In a moment the factory was turned into what looked like an armed camp: it was occupied by hundreds of soldiers equipped with machine guns."[34]

As more and more textile mills in São Paulo installed new weaving and spinning equipment, workers—using their commissions—protested changes in work regimes and decreases in pay.[35] Throughout 1927 the commissions increasingly organized work slowdowns, theft of machinery, and strikes.[36] In January 1928, workers at Matarazzo's Mariangela mill struck when management doubled their work loads from tending eight standard looms to tending sixteen of the semiautomated machines. Matarazzo and other industrialists were surprised by the strike, for the Mariangela mill provided a wide variety of social services to its workers, and Matarazzo had issued a slight wage increase for work with the semiautomated looms.[37] In March, five women (from twenty-one to thirty-eight years old) at the Companhia Fiação São Martinho organized a similar strike. Their boss fired them and added their names to the center's blacklist.[38] In October, nine workers at the Companhia Santista de Tecelagem reacted to the management's refusal to meet their requests for higher wages by destroying equipment in the factory.[39]

These episodes highlight the basic features of industrial relations in late-1920s São Paulo. Workers organized themselves through their independent factory commissions to oppose radical changes in their work regimes and to protect their standard of living in a period of steadily rising prices. These strikes also demonstrate the limited value of Fordism in fostering peaceful industrial relations. No matter what meager social services industrialists offered, São Paulo's workers continued to fight for their rights. In doing so, these workers uncovered the hypocrisy of Fordism, for like Henry Ford himself, São Paulo's industrialists did not hesitate to employ violence to suppress strikes and other organizing and protest activities.[40]

In addition to violent repression of strikes, industrialists increasingly relied on the repressive power of the state. The federal government sent anarchist organizers as well as rank-and-file activists to its penal colony, Clevelândia, located on the Oiapoque River on the border with French Guiana.[41] Indeed, as the president of Brazil (1926–30), São Paulo's former mayor Washington Luís augmented the national government's tools for social control and repression. In August 1927, Congress passed legislation (Decree 5221) providing jail sentences of one to six months and fines of from 200$000 to 500$000 (i.e., from one to two and a half months' wages for a woman textile worker) for instigating a strike. This law also gave the federal government legal grounds for closing unions and prounion newspapers.[42] On the state level, the

DOPS began its own blacklisting system, which included photographs and fingerprints of activist workers.[43]

Ultimately, Washington Luís's administration marked the beginning of the federal government's participation in São Paulo's industrial relations.[44] According to a British diplomat, Washington Luís avoided the "savage repression" practiced by his predecessor, Artur da Silva Bernardes, by using "more subtle and maybe more effective" means of repressing working-class movements.[45] Washington Luís, who as mayor of São Paulo in the 1910s had sought to cleanse working-class neighborhoods of their "vicious mixture of scum," included some limited social legislation to co-opt workers. In 1926 alone the federal government instituted laws regulating work accidents, vacations, and minors' work hours. In 1927 the government promulgated regulations on health insurance. Factory owners successfully avoided implementing these regulations, but their existence demonstrates the national government's interest in using a dual system of co-optation and repression in dealing with workers in the late 1920s.[46]

As the decade ended, São Paulo's industrial workers continued to organize themselves in factory commissions. They did so because violent state intervention, along with policies of co-optation and repression practiced both by industrialists and the state, had severely limited the operation of formal working-class institutions. Further, the city's women workers had little reason to trust the anarchist leadership, and male metalworkers were still groping to establish an effective union structure tied to the weakened anarchist movement (the Communist party remained only a formality in São Paulo at this time).[47] The distance between the city's workers and the unions and Left political parties did not limit the scope or effectiveness of workers' protest activities. Indeed, that distance may have actually legitimized their grievances in the eyes of those elites who had considered most working-class organizing part of a subversive political project.[48]

The Revolution of 1930: A Watershed in Industrial Relations?

The stock market crash of 1929 and subsequent depression in the United States and Europe destroyed the delicate balance between rationalization of production and social peace that São Paulo's industrialists had barely been maintaining in the late 1920s. With demand down for coffee exports and inflows of foreign capital all but stopped, the Brazilian economy quickly felt the impact of the industrialized nations' economic crisis.[49] Factories throughout the city closed in late 1929 and 1930; those mills that remained open operated only two or three days per week. In mid-1930 the state government began transporting factory workers and their families (free of charge) to coffee plantations in the interior.[50]

In addition to the economic downturn, Brazil faced a major political crisis as a result of the 1930 presidential election. After Júlio Prestes, a Paulista, won the March election, the opposition Aliança Liberal, led by the defeated candidate, Getúlio Vargas, conspired over the next few months to topple the administration. At first, the events of October and November 1930 appeared to be just one more political crisis caused by the breakdown of the Republic's "politics of the governors."[51] Soon, however, workers, industrialists, and a wide variety of reformers pushed the new Vargas government to play an active role in the nation's economic affairs. Throughout the early 1930s, Vargas met these pressures with a series of policies geared to expanding industrial output and maintaining social peace in Brazil's factories—especially those in São Paulo and Rio.

Workers and Industrialists Mobilize

On 24 October 1930, in the midst of the national political upheaval, crowds of workers rioted in downtown São Paulo and then sacked and burned the house of the Cambuci prison's warden. The next day they marched to the prison itself, where labor activists—including factory commission members—and others had been tortured and killed, and sacked it. According to the British consul in São Paulo, "The fury of the people knew no bounds, and after depositing all that could be found on to the pavement, a huge bonfire was made, and the building devoured by flames."[52] The prison, which was known as the Bastille of Cambuci, became a symbol of the false promises of working-class life in the São Paulo of the 1920s. The decade had begun with workers hoping that they could improve their working and living conditions through honest bargaining with employers. By the end of the 1920s, however, work conditions and wages had not improved, and strikes were more often than not met by troops, blacklisting, and imprisonment. The Bastille of Cambuci was a fitting target for workers' celebration of the defeat of São Paulo's political leaders in the Revolution of 1930.

The city's factory owners recognized the significance of the attack on the Cambuci prison. On 28 October, both the Textile Industrialists' Center and the State Industrialists' Center advised their members that state authorities still had the means to suppress strikes or any other "worker agitation, for whatever reason."[53] With most factories operating only three days per week (due to the depression) and an estimated 100,000 people out of work in the city, industrialists worried that the breakdown in order would lead to a general insurrection. Strikes, such as those initiated by workers in Lapa's railroad repair shops, were quickly settled by jittery employers.[54]

When Getúlio Vargas entered São Paulo on 29 October on his way to Rio to assume the presidency, the city's workers took advantage of the moment to press for improved wages and conditions. Given the state of industry (the textile sector was operating at only 30 percent of capacity, and metalworking at 40 percent), striking workers had to rely on political appeals to Vargas for him to press their case with the industrialists. After all, Vargas had promised during his presidential campaign to initiate a set of programs promoting social justice for all Brazilians. He specifically promised workers improved conditions, a minimum wage, mandatory vacations, consumer cooperatives, and the regulation of women's and children's labor. The crowds that packed Vargas's route from the train station to the Campos Elíseos palace chanting "We have Getúlio" were offering their support to the Gaúcho in return for his intervention on their behalf.[55] Vargas and his allies quickly met the challenge. João Alberto Lins de Barros, whom Vargas first appointed "delegate" and later "interventor" of São Paulo, ordered the city's factories to provide forty hours per week employment and 5 percent wage increases to all their workers. At the same time, he lowered industrial taxes and other fees to stimulate production.[56]

João Alberto moved to increase industrial employment in order to calm the tense situation in São Paulo. Afrânio de Melo Franco, who became Vargas's first foreign minister (and whose son, Virgílio de Melo Franco, had served with João Alberto), recalled in 1932 that the administration believed that "so long as the great mass of the people was content . . . there was little real danger."[57] To keep São Paulo's working people "content," João Alberto moved to fulfill the labor promises of Vargas's 1930 presidential platform. According to a British diplomat, "In regard to the labor situation, the authorities are combining warnings against agitation on the part of workers with a series of measures, or promises for the restriction of immigration, the institution of some relief to the unemployed, the building of workmen's dwellings, and so on."[58] Soon, however, João Alberto and Getúlio Vargas became captives of their own rhetoric; they had to meet the rising expectations of their new working-class allies. Again according to a British observer, "The ground is ready prepared for the activities of extremist agitators, while the windy promises of universal reform and betterment so lavishly made by the insurgent leaders at the moment of triumph have undoubtedly aroused certain hopes amongst the working class."[59]

In Rio, Vargas moved to meet workers' heightened expectations by creating the federal Ministry of Labor, Industry, and Commerce to regulate industrial relations. One of the ministry's first regulations was the "Law of Two-thirds," which forced all employers to maintain a work force that was at least two-thirds Brazilian. Vargas and his recently appointed minister of labor, Lindolfo Collor, hoped to alleviate unemployment in São Paulo with this and other measures.[60] Then, in March 1931, Vargas and his new Ministry of Labor created a corporatist structure for Brazil's first national industrial relations system.[61] Collor and Vargas put in place a structure through which officially sanctioned unions of employees and employers could negotiate. In 1932, industrialists' unions and workers' unions negotiated through mixed conciliation boards that included representatives of capital, labor, and the Ministry of Labor.[62] In a detailed memorandum to Vargas, Collor explained that this system would help alleviate the situation of "complete and distressing anarchy" through which Brazil's workers were suffering. He explained that the state would have to take a prominent role in managing industrial relations in order for Brazil to maintain social peace and deepen its industrial base. Further, Collor argued that such unions would strengthen capitalist development, for "unionization does not destroy, rather it conforms to the idea of private property."[63]

Collor's ideas were not new. He and others thought that such a government role in guaranteeing social justice for workers had been called for in the Treaty of Versailles. Moreover, Collor and Vargas were accustomed to corporatist organizations and cooperatives, for they had used them in Rio Grande do Sul,[64] and aspects of this structure conformed to the Fordist ideologies São Paulo's entrepreneurs had been embracing. Throughout the 1920s, Paulistano industrialists complained about the volatility of their labor market. Collor's and Vargas's program offered a means of standardizing wages throughout a given industry, and thus stabilizing the labor market. That is, if all Paulistano textile workers belonged to one union, and that union negotiated with the union of the city's textile mill owners, they could establish a single wage rate for all São Paulo textile workers, thus obviating the need to change jobs to bid up wages.

São Paulo's industrialists approved of this unionization program. They believed state control of workers' unions would provide social peace along with a means through which workers could negotiate to improve their conditions. After all, they did not oppose unions per se, they opposed "subversive movements."[65] The city's industrialists did, however, oppose social legislation they felt interfered with the operation of their enterprises.[66] São Paulo's industrialists supported a Fordist program, but they believed *they* had to manage it; in early 1931 they were not yet willing to grant the national government the power to regulate conditions of employment and work regimes in their factories.

Independent Worker Mobilization

In April and May 1931, Paulistano mill owners began laying off workers. They claimed they could not maintain production in the current economic climate, but they really did this to increase their leverage with factory commissions that had been opposing changes in work regimes and decreased wages. With João Alberto forcing employers to negotiate with workers, the mill owners thought their only power lay in stopping production.[67] Factory commissions attempted to negotiate settlements during May and June, but mill owners refused to meet their demands for an eight-hour day, one loom per weaver (this in response to the continuing process of automation), and no decreases in wages or piece rates. Finally, Minister of Labor Collor arrived in São Paulo and opened negotiations with José Righetti and other leaders of the anarchists' Textile Factory Workers' Union (União dos Operários em Fábricas de Tecidos).[68]

Collor's intervention helped the union negotiate settlements with Cotonifício Guilherme Giorgi and Tecelagem de Sedas Joanni D'Arc after strikes that lasted more than two weeks. The strikers apparently received promises of their old wages and future negotiations on their work regimes.[69] At about the same time, the recently reestablished Union of Metalworkers (União dos Operários Metalúrgicos) organized collective protests against the increasing state role in the city's industrial relations system. The anarchist union, which was affiliated with the FOSP, called for workers to reject the government union structure because Vargas would "sacrifice the proletariat to bolster capitalism."

Further, the increased government control of work conditions, these unionists believed, was "soon going to wound the workers' dignity, and weaken them in their struggles against their exploiters."[70]

Whatever their political orientation, workers throughout São Paulo's textile and metalworking industries organized—through their informal commissions—to negotiate for improved conditions (e.g., the eight-hour day) and higher wages.[71] The political opening initiated by the revolution and expanded by Vargas's and João Alberto's rhetoric provided an organizing opportunity for myriad labor groups tied to various ideological positions. Anarchist, communist, Trotskyist, and Catholic labor federations vied for workers' allegiance throughout 1931 and 1932.[72] Although the FOSP played a role in centralizing the separate strike movements in the city (as it had in the early and mid-1920s), São Paulo's workers continued to concentrate their organizing activities on the factory commission level. About thirty men from the idled Fábrica de Tecidos Matarazzo Belemzinho tried to force their way into the closed factory. They sought a resumption of production, eight-hour shifts, their old wages and piece rates, and amnesty for members of their factory commission. These men pleaded with the factory manager for work so that they could provide food and clothing for their families.[73] Women from the Fábrica Brasileira de Sedas also struck. They wanted their old pay scales and piece rates, the firing of an abusive foreman, responsibility for only one loom per worker, and recognition of their factory commission as a legal bargaining unit.[74] This last demand no doubt arose from Vargas's labor legislation. These women did not want to join a union, for they knew of the male-dominated unions that had attempted to represent the textile sector, but they were perfectly willing to participate in an institutionalized industrial relations system as long as they were represented by their own factory commissions.

By 18 July, workers had spread these walkouts throughout the textile and metalworking sectors. Men and women workers called on their employers to create conditions in which they could earn enough money to feed, clothe, and shelter their families. Once again, however, São Paulo's textile workers (especially the women) took the lead in the strike movement. Striking textile workers marched through Brás and other industrial neighborhoods cajoling other workers to join their movement. In the afternoon of 18 July these workers held a large meeting in the Largo de São José in Belem. They rallied for an eight-hour day, the regulation of child labor, and the end of "abuses" by bosses, and then they marched to the city center to spread the news of their strike. By the end of the day, the press and police estimated that some thirty thousand industrial workers throughout the city were on strike.[75]

Within days, the city's conservative press estimated that seventy thousand Paulistano industrial laborers had joined the walkout. Although it neither initiated nor directed the various strike movements, the FOSP played a leading role in the negotiation process. Its demands (eight-hour shifts at all factories—including those closed by the depression—an end to overtime and child labor; wage increases of from 15 to 30 percent; price and rent controls; an end to government control of union organizing, strikes, and other collective activities; paid leaves for pregnant workers; and amnesty for strike leaders) demonstrate the progress São Paulo's union movement had made over the course of the 1920s. The anarchist central did not demand union rights before workers' rights, and for the first time it did not seek to limit women's night work.[76] Indeed, by July 1931 the city's anarchist leadership was willing to let the factory commissions conduct their own strikes; the FOSP would serve only as a central body for coordinating strike activities.

The city's industrialists, who had recently formed their own sindicato and changed the Industrialists' Center to the São Paulo State Federation of Industries (Federação das Indústrias do Estado de São Paulo, FIESP), refused to negotiate with the striking factory commissions or the FOSP. The Federation of Industries went so far as to assert that the work stoppages were not strikes; they were nothing more than "agitations."[77] The industrialists did not trust the federal government to mediate the strike negotiations fairly, so they tried to convince Vargas and Collor that no strikes were taking place.[78] Their fear is understandable. Vargas had entered São Paulo in November 1930 as a hero of the city's workers. He promised them social justice and a government that would speak to their interests. And to implement his program Vargas had installed the progressive João Alberto as the state's interventor.[79] FIESP members had no reason to believe the federal government would be neutral, let alone their ally.

The July 1931 strike movement provided Vargas with the opportunity to demonstrate how his corporatist industrial relations system would actually work. First, Vargas claimed the striking workers had no right to participate in government-sponsored negotiations. This was because neither their strike commissions nor their unions had Ministry of Labor approval.[80] Mill owners followed this lead and refused to negotiate with the Textile Factory Workers' Union because it was not an "official union."[81] Next, Vargas and João Alberto used the government's power to force strikers back to work. In a manifesto to the city's workers, João Alberto said that all the strikers' "just and reasonable demands" would be met through the Ministry of Labor's intervention. This could only take place, he told the workers, if they abandoned their strike.[82] At the same time, the federal government provided the means to violently repress the strikes. Federal authorities directed military and state police to "defend" the factories. These forces escorted strike-breakers into the factories and broke up unauthorized public meetings. The police and the Federation of Industries installed special direct telephone lines that allowed factory owners to call for police assistance twenty-four hours per day. By the end of the strike, FIESP members were so grateful for all the help that they held a banquet to thank the local military commander, Major Lobato Valle.[83]

With strikers conceding defeat and returning to their factories and shops without receiving substantial wage increases or changes in work regimes, some of São Paulo's union activists (especially those tied to the Textile Factory Workers' Union, such as Righetti) petitioned the Ministry of Labor for official recognition.[84] The failure of the July strike movement taught them that they would have to negotiate with employers through the state labor relations system. Vargas had succeeded in his first attempt to bring São Paulo's unionists into an industrial relations system run by the national government.

The experiences of José Righetti and the Textile Factory Workers' Union demonstrate the co-optive nature of this system. Although the union and Righetti were closely identified with the anarchist FOSP, the union head traveled to Rio in August 1931 to press Vargas for help in negotiations with Paulistano mill owners. In the memorial they presented to Vargas, Righetti and Bruno Lopo (a member of the union's executive committee) detailed the increasingly difficult conditions São Paulo's textile workers faced and then called for an increased state role in monitoring wages and factory conditions. This was a natural role for Vargas's government, they said, for he had "promised better days to the people in general and workers in particular."[85] This appeal to Vargas signaled the end of anarchist influence on the Textile Factory Workers' Union and the beginning of the era of state-sponsored corporatist unionism. That is not to say that Righetti and other unionists became agents of the state; rather, they took the only course Vargas made available for the improvement of workers' lives in São Paulo in the early 1930s.

The city's Metalworkers' Union did not follow this path. These workers maintained the anarchist aversion to participating in a state-sponsored industrial relations system.[86] The Metalworkers' Union kept this tradition because many among its rank and file were anarchists from both large and small metalworking shops in the city. The Textile Factory Workers' Union, on the other hand, continued to face problems attracting members. Indeed, Righetti, Lopo, and others on the executive committee hoped to bring in members from the factory commissions—especially women workers—by gaining official recognition for the commissions from Vargas and by working with the Ministry of Labor to improve conditions in the mills.[87] Righetti and Lopo were not alone in recognizing the importance of the women's factory commissions to the rank and file; the Federation of Industries and the police placed their spies not only at union meetings but also in the factories, where they hoped to gather information about the commissions.[88]

In the final analysis, the sexual division of labor in São Paulo's industry fundamentally affected how unionists approached the new government role in labor relations. The leadership in the Metalworkers' Union had a lot in common with its rank and file. Both groups were male, worked primarily in positions defined as skilled, and had had some contact with anarchist ideologies. Unionists in the metalworking sector knew they would gain little by building ties to the new Ministry of Labor. In fact, the anarchist orientation of so many of the city's metalworkers made government affiliation a liability. The textile unionists, on the other hand, had to bridge the gaps between themselves and the largely female rank and file. The developing government role in industrial relations offered them a new tool in this process.

Even though they had come a long way in understanding the important issues for women workers, the male textile unionists still failed to fully comprehend women's concerns. Righetti was willing to grant women workers some autonomy through factory commissions, but he made no move to bring women into leadership positions within the union. Further, the male unionists continued to denigrate women's participation in the labor market. Righetti revealed his view of women's "proper" work when he wrote to Vargas that women's employment in the mills "serves to increase the number of unemployed men, creating . . . a ridiculous spectacle that is shameful and revolting: the woman at work in the factory and the husband at home taking care of the domestic chores and bringing the children to the factory gate to be nursed."[89] This statement reveals quite a bit about gender ideologies and anxieties. Righetti's fears about the reversal of traditional gender roles underscores the fact that São Paulo's textile unionists fundamentally misunderstood the necessity of women's wage labor for the maintenance of their families. More important, however, the letter to Vargas demonstrates that unionists not only believed that men should be the primary economic actors in society, but also that women belonged in the home caring for the children and "taking care of the domestic chores." Such sentiments were probably common among Brazilian men of all social classes in the 1930s.[90] What is significant is that the men who claimed to represent São Paulo's textile workers—most of whom were women—held such views.

1932: A Watershed in Elite Consciousness

Throughout the strike wave of 1931, São Paulo's industrial bourgeoisie remained wary of the federal government's new role in labor relations. FIESP members believed Vargas's system helped to legitimize unionists such as Righetti, Lopo, and others whom they considered subversives.[91] The city's industrialists also worried that the federal government was playing too active a role in their affairs. They not only objected to the Ministry of Labor's interference in regulating conditions in the factories, they also opposed the trend of increased municipal, state, and federal government interference in their business affairs.[92] In fact, Vargas lowered taxes on production, implemented restrictions on textile machinery imports (ostensibly to lower "overproduction"), and fashioned social legislation (e.g., restrictions on child labor) in accordance with industrialists' wishes.[93] During João Alberto's tenure and after, Vargas's labor policy also sought to balance workers' and industrialists' interests.[94] In early 1932, the Ministry of Labor attempted to maintain this balance with a series of regulations—some of which applied only to workers in the state of São Paulo—that granted improved conditions (e.g., an eight-hour day) in exchange for increased government scrutiny of workers' activities (i.e, forcing all workers to carry federal identity cards in order to gain industrial employment).[95] Vargas took these measures as São Paulo's manufacturing sector entered a new period of prosperity after the 1930 downturn (table 2.3).

São Paulo's workers needed Vargas's help. Mill owners were using the economic downturn of the early 1930s to force them into accepting longer shifts in the factories and decreased piece rates. Once again,

Table 2.3   Index of Industrial Output in the State
of São Paulo, 1928–1935 (1935 = 100)

Year	Metallurgy	Textiles	Total manufacturing
1928	69.9	70.5	67.6
1929	71.4	56.7	65.6
1930	53.1	50.2	59.5
1931	42.1	62.7	64.8
1932	50.0	67.6	64.2
1933	59.8	84.2	75.0
1934	96.9	96.2	87.9
1935	100.0	100.0	100.0

Source: A. V. Villela and W. Suzigan, "Government Policy and the Economic Growth of Brazil, 1889–1945," Brazilian Economic Studies 3 (1977): 297.

textile workers' factory commissions responded by fighting to improve conditions. Women from Tecelagem de Sedas Italo-Brasileira struck in March 1932 against a system of speedups that decreased their piece rates and increased their work loads. These women organized their strike independently, but they did welcome the support of some members of the Textile Factory Workers' Union.[96]

The textile workers joined a steadily increasing number of strikers from various industries in the city. From March to May, workers in the railroad repair shops, shoemakers, printers, and others initiated strikes against the continued harsh work regimes. Unionists from the metalworking and textile sectors attempted to help strikers and at the same time bring them into their unions. Accordingly, union and leftist activists supported the strikes and debated Vargas's labor policies during May Day rallies and meetings. This development worried Paulistano industrialists, who interpreted the participation of these activists as a sign that the strikes were the work of outside agitators. FIESP members therefore decided to break the strike movement without addressing their workers' demands.[97] They called upon the police to arrest strike leaders, ban public rallies, and protect strikebreakers.[98]

By 10 May, more than sixty-five thousand workers in the city were on strike. Women from the mills sought an eight-hour day, 20 percent wage increases, recognition of their factory commissions, no more forced overtime, fortnightly pay, bonuses for night work, and equal pay for equal work. Interestingly, the male directorate of the Textile Factory

Workers' Union added several of their own demands: recognition of the union, an end to the identity card system, a code regulating child labor, and a vacation law. Most important, however, was the union's demand that "for each opening in the factories and its sections the male workers [*profissionais ou diaristas do sexo masculino*] who applied would be hired."[99] Once again the gender anxieties of the male unionists determined the direction they felt the strike should take.

Discontent over work conditions, inflation, wages, and the failure of the new government to address their concerns brought a steadily increasing number of workers into the strike. By 12 May, railroad workers, glass workers, shoemakers, hatmakers, cabinetmakers, stone-cutters, and hotel and restaurant workers had joined textile and metal-lurgical workers in a general strike. As they had in 1917, the city's textile workers played the leadership role in this movement. Foreign and local observers agreed that the estimated ninety thousand striking textile workers in and around São Paulo made up the backbone of the general strike.[100] The city's industrialists decided that they would have to break the textile walkout to end the general strike, so they directed police to break in on closed meetings of factory commissions and unionists. The Federation of Industries thought it could end the strike by arresting the leaders and leftist activists and guaranteeing safe passage into and out of the factories for strikebreakers.[101] If the strike had been only the work of outside agitators these measures might have ended it, but because the general strike was a grass-roots movement, the industrialists' actions could not succeed in breaking it.

FIESP members also sought Vargas's help in ending the walkout. Textile, metallurgy, and other industrialists telegrammed the president on 19 May and asked him to help settle the strike. Because Vargas had meddled with the internal affairs of the state and "weaken[ed] the public power just as it is necessary to repress attempts to disturb public order," the industrialists believed he should help them end the strike movement.[102] Even before hearing from the city's industrialists, Vargas and his top aides worried that São Paulo's general strike could, if not handled properly, lead to social revolution. Former minister of labor Collor wrote of the strike, "Tomorrow it could be too late, for the extremists are pushing us to the abyss of social upheaval. The Communists are knocking at the door. . . . It isn't only the present, but the future of Brazil that is in our hands."[103]

Collor's replacement, Joaquim Salgado Filho, moved to settle the general strike by meeting some workers' demands and at the same time bringing them into the state industrial relations structure. He and Vargas extended the eight-hour day to industrial workers and set up conciliation commissions (a tripartite system for negotiating work issues) during the first two weeks of the walkout. And in recognition of women textile workers' leadership role in the general strike, Salgado Filho pushed through legislation guaranteeing equal pay for equal work in industry. To satisfy male unionists, he also promulgated regulations on women's night work. In addition to these new statutes, strikers received wage increases of between 20 and 40 percent.[104] These concessions slowly ended the strike movement. The May strikes demonstrated Vargas's willingness to meet what he believed were workers' legitimate demands, as long as those workers were not associated with "subversive elements." These strikes again demonstrated to the city's industrialists the value of using a combination of co-optation and repression in industrial relations.

In the aftermath of this worker mobilization, São Paulo's elites initiated a civil war against Vargas's government. Above all else, the Revolution of 1930 had brought to power a new national political elite that Paulistas felt threatened their interests. João Alberto's tenure as interventor, as well as national intervention in economic and social policies, convinced Paulista elites to attempt to overthrow the Vargas regime.[105] Whatever the origins and larger political meaning of the 1932 uprising, the war created new opportunities for São Paulo's industrial workers. As they went to war in early July, the state's leaders wondered how they would be able to maintain industrial production in light of the recent general strike. They knew the government in Rio would attempt to blockade shipments of foreign goods (e.g., munitions, uniforms, and transportation equipment) to São Paulo, and that they would have to produce all they needed for the war in their own factories. The city's industrial laborers suddenly became an important factor for victory.[106]

In a revealing move, the rebel leaders first augmented the state militia's firepower by collecting the sizable arms caches of São Paulo's industrial establishments. The Federation of Industries organized the collection of the factories' heavier weapons (particularly thirty-eight- and forty-four-caliber rifles); the FIESP told its members their security forces would have to rely on pistols and hunting rifles during the war.[107] The existence of arms caches in the factories puts industrial relations in

São Paulo into perspective: No matter what role Fordist policies or state mechanisms might play, the city's industrialists were always prepared to rely on violence when dealing with their workers.

In order to keep their factories open to produce war materials, São Paulo's industrialists attempted to bribe workers with a new set of comprehensive fringe benefits. During the war, all the city's workers received full and free medical and dental care. The Federation of Industries hurriedly opened clinics in Brás, Mooca, Lapa, and Belemzinho. By presenting a certificate proving they were employed in a factory, workers could receive any sort of medical care. They had access to specialists who treated eyes, lungs, and ear, nose, and throat problems. The state even opened a special clinic where obstetricians helped women with pregnancies and "other female maladies." After the war, FIESP members noted that thousands of workers had used these services and that the program was quite successful. In addition to the medical services, the city government had also maintained plentiful supplies of affordable foodstuffs in the neighborhood markets.[108]

These measures were a great success. Foreign and local observers noted how enthusiastically the city's industrial laborers worked in the factories, which operated twenty-four hours a day.[109] By the end of the war, factories throughout the state of São Paulo (but primarily those in the capital) had produced sixty thousand steel helmets, 150,000 uniforms, two hundred field kitchens, a number of armored vehicles, mortars, seventy-five-millimeter guns, grenades, and a variety of types of ammunition.[110] Apart from the impressive advances in production, the conflict ushered in a new period of labor relations in São Paulo, for the city's industrialists translated their Fordist programs into a comprehensive system of welfare capitalism. Although they lost the war, São Paulo's industrialists gained a new appreciation of the government's power to guarantee social peace, and therefore high levels of production. That is, they began to accept key components of Vargas's program of state-sponsored corporatist unionism.

The New Era: State-Sponsored Unions versus the Factory Commissions

During the 1931 and 1932 strike waves, Vargas had demonstrated to São Paulo's industrialists that his labor policies were aimed at providing social peace in order to foster expanded production. The Ministry of Labor, like the Federation of Industries, would deal only with so-called

legitimate unionists, not "subversive elements." Paulistano factory owners who doubted the effectiveness of Vargas's version of Fordism saw for
themselves during the civil war how a program of comprehensive social
services kept workers content and thus expanded production. Accordingly, Salgado Filho's Ministry of Labor pushed the program of "class
collaboration" by encouraging workers to join unions that would negotiate through the state structure and distribute social services to their
members.[111] As a British observer noted, Vargas was trying to "on the
one hand . . . keep order, and, on the other to harness the working class
to [his] chariot." Vargas accomplished this not only through benefits
for workers but by offering expanded political rights—and therefore
expanded citizenship—to union members. He placed a loophole in the
regulations for the 1934 elections: illiterates, who could not regularly
vote, would be allowed to do so through ex-officio registration if they
were members of a state-sponsored union.[112]

In late December 1932 and early January 1933, a group of about
thirty men textile workers from the Cotonifício Guilherme Giorgi
responded to Vargas's overtures and decided to form a union. They met
opposition from Righetti and others tied to the existing union, but by
April 1933 their new union had received official recognition from the
Ministry of Labor. The new union presaged the sort of sindicatos that
would come to dominate São Paulo in the 1930s and early 1940s. It had
only about 140 members during 1933 (about .003 percent of the city's
textile workers!), and its directorate maintained close ties both to the
state Department of Labor and the Ministry of Labor in Rio. Further,
the unionists specifically distanced themselves from former labor and
leftist activists as they espoused Vargas's ideology of class collaboration.[113] Likewise, a handful of metalworkers from a few of the city's
larger shops (e.g., Metalúrgicos Matarazzo, Fundição Diez, Cofres
Bernardini, Fundição Pecoraro, and several others) met to found a new
union in late December 1932. Throughout 1933 this union had but 105
members, again about .003 percent of the city's workers from this
industry.[114]

The outlines of how Vargas's industrial relations system would actually work began to take shape in 1933 and 1934. Police in São Paulo
increasingly harassed and imprisoned anarchists, Communists, and
other leftist activists.[115] At the same time, the new group of unionists
came to realize that their fortunes in industrial relations depended
largely on their ties to the state Department of Labor and the Ministry
of Labor in Rio, as well as to Vargas himself.[116] Union officials such as

Mário Rotta of the Textile Workers' Union and Rodolfo Mantorani of the Metalworkers' Union increasingly petitioned Vargas for his assistance in various matters.[117] Interestingly, they did not seem to discuss conditions in the factories, wages, or other "labor" issues in their communications with Vargas. At the same time, industrialists regularly broke agreements on work hours and wages with little fear that the government would interfere. Indeed, Vargas had appeased the state's industrialists in July 1933 by turning over control of the industrial relations system to the state Department of Labor, which worked closely with the Federation of Industries. And in April 1934 Vargas turned over the directorship of the São Paulo state Department of Labor to industrialist Jorge Street.[118] With the federal Ministry of Labor operating only in Rio, the state departments of labor throughout Brazil had the responsibility for implementing Vargas's labor legislation. In the case of São Paulo, that responsibility fell into the hands of a textile industrialist.[119]

This atmosphere of class collaboration shaped the internal politics of São Paulo's new unions. Mário Rotta, who often expressed his sympathies with both the Vargas administration and the quasi-fascist Integralist movement, used his ties to the Ministry of Labor and the state Department of Labor to solidify his leadership of the union. When his opponents challenged him, Rotta called on the DOPS to harass and, at times, arrest them. Rotta avoided dealing with the factory commissions (especially those controlled by women textile workers) and instead brought Melchíades dos Santos and Joaquim Teixeira, neither of them textile workers, into the directorate of the union.[120] Rotta and his cronies succeeded in fashioning a narrow, ineffective union. They called few meetings, and those they had were poorly attended. In 1934, attendance at the four meetings held was 43, 53, 47, and 32 (out of 19,648 textile workers in the city); and in 1935, attendance at six meetings was 34, 131, 48, 70, 28, and 48 (out of 22,156 textile workers).[121] Moreover, the rank and file had little interest in the business conducted at these meetings (e.g., facilities to be installed in the headquarters and new government regulations for unions). The city's workers continued to focus on "bread-and-butter" issues.

The Metalworkers' Union maintained greater distance from the Ministry of Labor structure but still had little success in attracting members at this time. Metalworkers may have avoided the union (by 1935, only 3.77 percent of the city's *metalúrgicos* were members) out of

fear. Industrialists and government officials opposed this more independent body. The state Department of Labor and the DOPS harassed the
unionists because they maintained their distance from the Ministry of
Labor and continued the anarchist tradition of denouncing the government's role in industrial relations.[122] With some unionists tied to the
government and those in opposition facing police repression, São
Paulo's industrial workers had few incentives to join the sindicatos
Vargas and Salgado Filho so vigorously supported.[123] Instead, textile
and metallurgical workers continued to rely on their factory commissions to bargain with employers over conditions and wages. These
commissions even initiated forms of direct action, such as work slowdowns and breaking equipment in the factories.[124]

Workers turned to their commissions in 1934 and 1935 for help with
the steadily deteriorating conditions at work and in their neighborhoods. In the factories, textile workers faced new speedups as mill
owners operated their factories at near capacity. At home, workers
faced rents that rose 30 to 40 percent after increases in municipal and
state taxes in 1934 and 1935. Prices of rice, beans, bread, and other
foodstuffs increased dramatically at the same time.[125] Textile workers
attempted to discuss these problems with the unionists but were repeatedly rebuffed. And when workers tried to discuss these conditions with
their employers, they were arrested for "subversive activities"; for example, a group of girls—some only thirteen years old—was arrested for
attempting to discuss their "common work interests."[126]

Events in May and June 1935 demonstrated to unionists, industrialists, and government officials how closely workers identified with their
factory commissions. Commissions of women workers from the Italo-
Brasileira mill pressed their bosses to reinstitute their old wage scales,
which had been reduced by 20 percent. More than one hundred
weavers who had also suffered wage reductions in the Crespi mills
quickly followed the Italo-Brasileira workers and declared themselves
on strike. Soon, workers from Moinho Santista, Armênia, and Matarazzo's Mariangela mills struck to recover lost wages.[127] Rotta and other
members of the Textile Workers' Union directorate thought they could
use the strike to increase their membership. For the first time since the
Ministry of Labor–approved union had been founded, striking factory
commission members met to plan strategy in the union's headquarters.
Above all else, Rotta and the other unionists wanted to co-opt the
strikers. In general assembly meetings Rotta spoke of the need to help

the strikers; when the union's directorate met in private, however, he refused to negotiate on their behalf and blocked any attempt to instigate sympathy strikes in other mills.[128]

The Italo-Brasileira management refused to reinstitute the old (i.e., the one that had been in effect at the beginning of the year) wage scale, but Crespi and other mills increased piece rates in order to resume production. Strikers from the Italo-Brasileira mill became a symbol of independent worker protest to many in São Paulo. Metallurgical and bank workers, among others, created a special fund to help the striking weavers survive without pay. Throughout the city, elites began to worry that the mill owner's intransigence might lead to a general strike. Such a strike would not only demonstrate workers' ability to unite in a common protest, it would reveal the inherent weakness of Vargas's government union structure. Interestingly, within days of the first rumors of a general strike, state Department of Labor officials pressed the Italo-Brasileira management away from its offer of keeping wage reductions at 6 percent and convinced the mill's owner (Francisco Matarazzo Junior) to offer his workers a 10 percent increase over their original wages.[129]

Ultimately, workers in the Italo-Brasileira mills received the same wages as other textile workers in the city. The significance of the strike and its settlement lay not in the final agreement but in how the strikers behaved and what that behavior represented to unionists, industrialists, and state policymakers. Rotta and his fellow unionists saw how little control they had over the rank and file. They soon attempted— unsuccessfully—to create their own factory commission structure that would tie into the union.[130] Industrialists and government officials feared not only the independent factory commissions but how those commissions built ties to other workers in the city, and to the recently created National Liberation Alliance (Aliança Nacional Libertadora, ANL), which was run by the Communist party.[131]

Industrialists and government officials, after finally meeting the strikers' demands, moved to crush the threat posed by a unified workers' movement in São Paulo. Although they had only tenuous ties to the factory commissions, editors of leftist newspapers such as A Platéia and A Plebe were arrested in mid-July, and leaders of the ANL in São Paulo were placed under "protective custody." A judge in the city ruled that these arrests were illegal and freed the activists, but industrialists and government officials had demonstrated quite clearly how they would react in the future to such "subversives."[132]

It is important to recognize how unpopular the new state-sanctioned sindicatos were among São Paulo's workers. The city's rank and file simply did not trust institutions that were tied to the government. Indeed, in 1931 and 1932, the Ministry of Labor recognized forty-six sindicatos in the city of Rio de Janeiro but only eight for the entire state of São Paulo. It was not until 1933, when unionists tied to the state Department of Labor and federal Ministry of Labor began seeking recognition for sindicatos that had tiny memberships, that the state of São Paulo outpaced the Federal District (Rio) in unions recognized in one year (fifty-two for São Paulo and twenty for Rio).[133] The key to understanding workers' views of the new government industrial relations system lay in the historical development of ideas about unions and the state. Although the anarchist movement had been a force among Rio's workers, the city's labor movement never completely shed the traditions related to less radical mutual aid societies and voluntary associations. Indeed, Carioca anarchist, socialist, and communist labor discourses shared this perspective. Moreover, both voluntary associations and anarchist and other leftist unions had a tradition of working within municipal and even federal institutions to fight for improved conditions and wages.[134]

São Paulo's version of anarcho-syndicalism, which had been socially constructed through the combination of anarchist ideology and worker praxis over the course of the late 1910s and 1920s, was the reason many Paulistanos rejected Vargas's new industrial relations system. This tradition of local organizational forms loosely tied to independent political movements was not unique to the city's textile and metallurgical workers; it was fundamental in São Paulo labor practices by the early 1930s. A comparison of printers from Rio and São Paulo reveals the two cities' divergent labor traditions. In 1932, Paulistano printers denounced Vargas's unionization law as something that "at the same time, destroys the working-class spirit of struggle, and places workers' organizations under the control of the State." Rio's printers, on the other hand, followed the Ministry of Labor's regulations and became an official sindicato; the Paulistano printers harshly criticized the Cariocas for caving in.[135] Such differences between workers in the same industry but in different cities were not limited to printers.[136] Vargas's labor rhetoric and policies would continue to resonate more among Rio's workers than among those in São Paulo because Paulistano workers' experiences had taught them to value their own local forms of organizing.[137] Moreover, the city's workers—including the female rank and file who avoided formal participation in anarchist unions and study groups—had come to accept the anarcho-syndicalist distrust of the state and politicians.[138]

When textile and metallurgical workers struck briefly in late July, they received slight wage increases but also witnessed the arrests of factory commission leaders.[139] At the same time, the leaders of Brazil's Communist party—which had no real ties to the factory commissions—decided to instigate a military putsch to overthrow the Vargas regime. This uprising (known as the Intentona) was based more on politics in Moscow than on those in Brazil. The plotters did not even attempt to organize working-class support in São Paulo; instead they concentrated their efforts on military men in Natal and Recife in the northeast. The uprising was a miserable failure. The plotters were quickly arrested and then tortured. Vargas's punishment of the activists took on a grisly tone when he arranged the extradition of Olga Benário Prestes, a German Jew (and the wife of PCB leader Luís Carlos Prestes) who was pregnant at the time, to Nazi Germany. She died in the Ravensbruck concentration camp.[140]

The PCB's attempted putsch did little more than offer Vargas and his allies a good excuse for cracking down on all labor and leftist activists. The repression in São Paulo seems to have had no connection to the uprising in the northeast. Like the police intervention in unions after the 1924 tenente uprising, the 1935 crackdown had more to do with workers' organizing and protest activities than it did with the rebellion. No matter, the Intentona would serve as a convenient excuse for Vargas to repress independent labor groups (i.e., those not tied to the state structure) and try to force São Paulo's workers into his government industrial relations system.[141] Because the grass-roots workers' movement was made up of an informal collection of factory commissions, Vargas would have a difficult time repressing it. And while Vargas attacked his opponents, the city's workers continued to rely on their own institutions and had little interest in the government-sponsored labor structure. On the other hand, the Federation of Industries began to support Vargas's system of unionization, for São Paulo's industrialists had learned through their own experiences in the early 1930s—especially during the 1932 civil war—how a comprehensive welfare system could foster social peace. By the mid-1930s, they no longer feared the Ministry of Labor; FIESP members realized that Vargas's plans and their own had much in common. Moreover, a FIESP member and staunch supporter of Fordism—Jorge Street—was now in charge of implementing Vargas's labor policies through the state Department of Labor. This arrangement created a type of corporatism São Paulo's industrialists could support, for it did not significantly challenge their control over their workers or the industrial relations system.

Class Struggle versus Conciliação:

The Estado Novo, 1935–1942

In our system, the State carries out the role of judge in relations between employees and employers. It sees that . . . clashes are avoided, excesses are corrected, and benefits are equitably distributed.

—Getúlio Vargas,
Cultura Política

Vargas, oh he was the "father of the poor," as they used to say on the radio, but of course he was truly the mother of the rich!

—Textile worker Odette Pasquini,
interview, 17 September 1987

Getúlio Vargas initiated the Estado Novo (New State) dictatorship on 10 November 1937. For São Paulo's workers, the dictatorship had begun two years earlier in the aftermath of the Communist party's quixotic putsch of November 1935. After quickly suppressing the uprising, Vargas clamped down on his political opponents. Vargas's military and industrialist allies moved against labor, using the opportunity afforded by the failed putsch to press their plans for national unification and industrialization. Paulistano industrialists and the military convinced Vargas to use the federal government's new role in industrial relations to increase control over workers and their organizations. The state could, these "modernizers" argued, accelerate industrialization, guarantee the well-being of Brazil's working people, and end class conflict.[1] The preceding twenty years of protests and organizing by São Paulo's industrial working class, however, meant that that peace would be achieved only with tight control over workers and their organizations. Accordingly, Vargas and his allies first moved to co-opt working-class movements in Brazil's most strategic industries in its most important industrial center. This, then, is the story of the implementation of the Estado Novo in São Paulo and its impact on textile and metallurgical workers.

The Making of "Modern" Brazil: The Ideology of the Estado Novo

From the declaration of the Republic in 1889, and continuing through the 1930s, the military and segments of the civilian elite struggled to recast their agrarian, multiracial society into an industrialized and unified (racially and geographically) nation. Popular mobilizations by peasants and workers especially worried these elites. Indeed, the military soon came to view itself as "presiding over the remaking of the Motherland."[2] The political crisis of the mid-1930s provided the military and its allies with the perfect opportunity to push their goal of refashioning Brazil through industrialization and by marshaling the civilian population.[3]

In speech after speech, Vargas called for all Brazilians to eschew class conflict and act in the spirit of conciliação for the greater good.[4] He told his radio and live audiences that only a strong central state could fight foreign subversion, aid in the industrialization of Brazil, and provide real social justice for all. In São Paulo on 22 July 1938, Vargas admonished a crowd, "All of us will march together united in one view for only one common effort; we shall work, without limits, for the prosperity and greatness of Brazil."[5] Creating the strong central state would, however, necessitate remaking the Brazilian population. The writings of Francisco Campos, Antônio José Azevedo Amaral, Francisco José de Oliveira Viana, and other nationalist ideologues provided the intellectual underpinnings for a program of "militarizing the nation." Their writings combined racist, fascist, and Catholic theories of the state and national development. Many of their ideas never moved beyond the printed page, but Vargas and his military and industrialist allies did implement their general corporatist framework for Brazil.[6]

No other segment of Brazilian society felt the impact of this ideology more than the industrial working class. Not only did the military wish to reshape the "dangerous classes," but São Paulo's industrialists eagerly sought to rationalize capitalist production by marshaling their workers through Fordist policies; in the wake of the 1932 civil war, the state's industrialists also relied on the federal government's intervention to co-opt and repress their workers.[7] When Vargas officially proclaimed the dictatorship in November 1937, he called for social peace during this period of "profound political and social disorder." Six months later, on May Day 1938, the dictator assured Brazilians that he understood that "order and work" were their highest aspirations. He continued his address to the country's workers by imploring, "A country is not just the conglomeration of individuals in a territory, it is, principally, a unity of race, a unity of language, a unity of national thinking. To achieve this supreme ideal, it is necessary, therefore, that all must march together in a prodigious ascent . . . to prosperity and for the greatness of Brazil."[8]

The Revolution of 1930 and the 1934 Constitution implicitly guaranteed workers improved living conditions and greater access to social justice through state intervention in return for their support of the state. Vargas made that arrangement explicit through the Estado Novo's labor and social policies. According to Helvécio Xavier Lopes of the Ministry of Labor, for example, "Unions in the Estado Novo have a dual representative function, in that they conform to the old role as professional associations, and they [also] are bodies vested with duties as representatives of the State." Ari Pitombo, of the Alagoas state government, wrote in the Ministry of Labor's *Boletim* that workers' sindicatos should act as "schools for unity and discipline."[9] Vargas publicly guaranteed the working class continued benefits such as the eight-hour day and state-run social services if they eschewed "exotic and subversive dogmas" and instead supported his government. He also promised to create a minimum wage, which he termed the "imposition of social justice."[10]

Vargas and the Ministry of Labor spoke also of improving workers' living conditions. After all, they reasoned, well-fed and properly housed workers would operate efficiently in the factories and avoid "dangerous" ideologies. Jorge Queiroz de Morais wrote that "it is the obligation of each [industrialist] to elevate the physical and moral level of the people."[11] Paulistano industrialists funded the Institute for the Rational Organization of Work (Instituto de Organização Racional do Trabalho, IDORT) to study how improvements in living and working conditions would produce laborers who acted "objectively" in the factories. The IDORT frequently reported on the need for industry to provide adequate nutrition for workers in order to receive optimal performance in return.[12]

While the Estado Novo encouraged changes in the industrial relations system it also sought to reinforce traditional gender roles. Vargas and officials in the Ministry of Labor appealed to the gender anxieties many felt at this time.[13] Indeed, the Estado Novo's corporatist structure, at least as it applied to workers, was supposed to grow out of an extended family structure, with Vargas acting as the "Father of the Poor."[14] The Estado Novo therefore included a series of regulations to bolster "traditional" families. In 1939, Vargas proposed funding special programs for the "health of mothers and children" by placing a tax on single adults and married couples without children.[15] The regime even sought to regulate gender roles. A March 1940 law called for a system of public education that would teach boys and girls distinct perspectives: "Boys and young men . . . should develop a sense of obligation to render military service to the country and special interest and affection for the life of the soldier and all that will enable youth to prepare for national defense. Home making instincts and appreciation of the opportunities and responsibilities of domestic management should be inculcated in girls, especially with regard to the bearing and rearing of children."[16] By extolling traditional gender roles, government officials hoped to encourage men to join the official unions, because it was the sindicatos that were fighting against "the ridiculous spectacle [of] the woman at work in the factory and the husband at home taking care of the domestic chores."[17] The Ministry of Labor did not encourage women to be active workers or union members. Instead, the government proudly proclaimed its interest in "protecting women, morally and physically," with special regulations. The state cared for women because they were "by nature, more fragile" than men, and because women nurtured the children and male workers of Brazil.[18] The highly gendered aspects of Estado Novo ideology meshed well with the perspectives of many male unionists and leftist activists from the early 1900s through the 1930s. Accordingly, Vargas's evolving labor policies did not necessarily represent a complete break with anarchist and other leftist ideologies, especially with regard to the role of women in society.[19]

Industrialists and other elites relied on pseudoscientific theories to support their views of women's roles in society. Maria Kiehl, a social worker in São Paulo, told Ministry of Labor officials that women did not have the physical or mental makeup for factory work. She argued in favor of strict protective regulations for women workers because "in the great majority of professions, the obligations of the wife and mother are incompatible with the obligations of that profession."[20] Ultimately, these theorists believed that capitalist development had destroyed traditional gender roles, and so threatened the cohesiveness of Brazilian families. The Estado Novo promised to restore women to their homes, where they could raise their children and provide for their mates.[21]

The various strands of Estado Novo ideology included a guarantee from government in general and Getúlio Vargas in particular that all Brazilian citizens, especially workers, would have access to true social justice. The promises of improved work conditions, increased pay, protection of women in industry, and equal representation for the popular classes through their sindicatos were linchpins in the social pact of the Estado Novo. And in speech after speech, Vargas assured Brazil's working people that all citizens were equals simply by virtue of being Brazilian.[22] In his New Year's message for 1938, Vargas explained that "when the State takes the initiative in economic assistance and supports workers' struggles, it does so to obey the imperatives of social justice." The dictator personally guaranteed such justice for all; indeed, he encouraged workers to write to him directly for his personal consideration of their problems.[23]

Implementation of the Estado Novo

The Crackdown on Labor

Even though workers in São Paulo played no role in the Communists' November 1935 putsch, they felt the full force of Vargas's violent repression of the Left. In March 1936 Vargas had the Congress declare a "state of war" and ordered police throughout Brazil to arrest labor activists.[24] Striking Paulistano textile and metallurgical workers had faced arrest throughout 1934 and 1935, but they did not have to endure a systematic offensive by industrialists and the state until early 1936.[25] Employers, with the assistance of the state Department of Labor, closely monitored the activities of workers in the city. Textile firms once again collated blacklists with information on prospective employees. The state government also stationed three battalions of its Força Pública in the city to intimidate workers in Brazil's most important industrial center.[26]

São Paulo's industrialists had explicitly requested Vargas's assistance in controlling the working class. The Federation of Industries petitioned Vargas for "social peace and tranquility" in their state. They told the federal government they would comply with its economic and social policies as long as the federal government kept workers in the factories and off picket lines.[27] Vargas readily assented, for he knew he could achieve his goal of industrialization only by controlling the city's workers, harshly, if necessary. Further, he actively sought, and received, the enthusiastic support of São Paulo's most important industrialists for his crackdown on labor.[28]

The principal feature of the Estado Novo era's control of labor was the creation of bureaucratic, government-approved unions that existed to cooperate with the state in settling disputes between workers and industrialists. The primary day-to-day functions of these new unions revolved around providing a wide range of social services, including consumer cooperatives, medical services, and schools.[29] The implementation of the imposto sindical (union tax) in 1941–42 deepened the sindicatos' reliance on the state and focus on social services. This compulsory tax was equal to one day's wages per year. Every worker paid this tax to the federal government, which then redistributed it to the unions. These funds could only be applied to government-approved activities; the Ministry of Labor could freeze a sindicato's accounts if it used any part of this money as a strike fund or in other unsanctioned ways. Thus, the administration of the tax severely restricted unions' activities and, ultimately, created unrepresentative sindicatos that received the bulk of their funding from workers who were not members. That is, with the introduction of the tax, all Paulistano textile and metallurgical workers paid mandatory dues to the unions; but without paying the additional dues (usually less than the imposto sindical) that were collected directly by the unions, those workers did not become members of the unions (i.e., they were not *sindicalizados*)[30] and were not eligible for the social services.

These arrangements fostered the creation of a new type of labor leader, whose survival depended more on the continued support of the Ministry of Labor than on that of the workers. Sometime in the late 1930s, the rank and file in São Paulo began to deride these representatives of the state by labeling them *pelegos* (a pelego is a type of sheepskin horse blanket). Workers opposed to the government-controlled union structure applied this term to the co-opted leaders, and so made the analogy of the working class as the horse, the industrial bourgeoisie as the rider, and the pelego as the saddle blanket that cushions the ride for the elites.[31] Intervention in the unions and the use of the imposto sindical therefore created a cadre of "self-interested careerists who support[ed] the current labor system and thrive[d] on it,"[32] and had little contact with the rank and file. One independent labor leader remarked that pelegos actually had an interest in maintaining small unions so they could use the large budgets derived from the imposto sindical for medical services and recreational activities for the tiny minority of workers who made up their sindicatos.[33]

Peleguismo had its origins in the federal government's interventions in the unions during this period. During the "state of war" in 1935–36, the Ministry of Labor expelled activist unionists from all of São Paulo's industrial sindicatos. The ministry then mandated that the unions notify the political police (DOPS) and the state Department of Labor of meetings so they could send observers. In 1939 the federal government outlined the official union structure and outlawed the creation of central labor organizations (i.e., unions representing multiple industries). The Ministry of Labor also retained the ultimate decision over who could run for union offices. Then, as Brazil moved closer to entering World War II, the ministry excluded German, Italian, and Japanese nationals from participation in the unions. The intimidation of foreign-born workers was further institutionalized by Article 11 of the 1942 law that mandated that unions had to "create in the spirit of their members a mentality of devotion to the Nation [*Pátria*] . . . that will lead to the highest defense of the nationality."[34]

Pelegos have traditionally had a disturbingly close relationship with industrialists and politicians. During World War II, while the vast majority of Paulistano workers faced frequent shortages of increasingly expensive foodstuffs, for example, the city's union leaders sponsored a lavish banquet in honor of Roberto Simonsen and Morvan Dias de Figueiredo, the president and vice president of the São Paulo State Federation of Industries. In their invitation the pelegos wrote that they wanted to have the banquet "to testify to the recognition and gratitude of the working class of the state [of São Paulo] for . . . [the] sincere spirit of collaboration constantly manifested . . . by Roberto Simonsen and Morvan Dias de Figueiredo."[35] Later, São Paulo's pelegos gave a smaller, less formal banquet to honor the head of the city's political police.[36] These parties demonstrate the style of industrial relations that developed during the Estado Novo: Before turning to the state bureaucracy to settle a wage issue, the pelegos in a given industry or set of industries would first publicly praise employers and the state and proclaim their loyalty to the ideal of conciliação, and then open quiet negotiations with representatives of industry.[37] Such a style of industrial relations kept the working class in an extremely weak position vis-à-vis industry.

Still, pelegos had a responsibility to mediate among the workers they technically represented, the expanding state bureaucracy, and the industrialists. While operating within the guidelines established by the

Ministry of Labor in Rio and the state Department of Labor in São Paulo, Paulistano union leaders sometimes appealed directly to Vargas to change a particular labor bureaucracy ruling. São Paulo's pelegos struggled to maintain good relations with Brazil's president, and they often couched their praise for him in personalistic terms. A letter to Vargas from twenty-five of the city's labor leaders spoke of him as "the unshakable defender of workers' demands and rights, which have been achieved by the force of your works and by your high spirit of Brazilian nationalism."[38] Then, when Vargas visited São Paulo for May Day in 1941, the city's union presidents negotiated with Minister of Labor Waldemar Falcão to provide a large turnout of union members at the ceremonies held at Pacaembu Stadium in exchange for a private audience with Vargas at which they could discuss their objections to certain ministerial actions.[39]

Peleguismo and the Textile Workers' Union

The Estado Novo's industrial relations system and its highly gendered ideology greatly exacerbated the problematic relationship between São Paulo's textile unionists and the city's female rank-and-file workers. An already weak union became little more than a state-sponsored male social club. As a result, São Paulo's women textile workers—the people who had so often led the city's labor protests and strike movements—actively avoided participation in the sindicato.

The union created by repeated ministerial interventions in the late 1930s was the model of the bureaucratic, corporatist institution envisioned by the framers of the Estado Novo. Unionists such as Melchíades dos Santos and Joaquim Teixeira, who had opposed supporting the Italo-Brasileira and other strikes in 1934 and 1935, gained their positions in the directorate (president and press and information director, respectively) when the Ministry of Labor intervened in the union in 1938. These pelegos then ran for election in 1941. Their slate received a total of seventy votes because the majority of the members did not bother to participate; indeed, the membership at the time of the election was only 1,324 workers, from 51,286 textile workers in the city (table 3.1). After taking control, Santos and Teixeira soon learned to work closely with the DOPS to purge members who threatened their hegemony within the union. Such heavy-handed tactics kept both men in leadership positions until the early 1950s.[40]

The Ministry of Labor strengthened the position of the pelegos

Table 3.1   Membership in São Paulo Textile Workers' Union, 1938–1942

Year	Members[a]	Textile workers[b]	Workers in union (%)
1938	500	—	—
1939	1,130	47,920	2.36
1940	1,071	48,209	2.22
1941	1,324	51,286	2.58
1942	995	57,950	1.72

Source: São Paulo Departamento Estadual de Estatística, Anuário Estatístico de São Paulo (1939–1943); BMTIC 86 (October 1941): 97; Flávio Rabelo Versiani, "Technical Change, Equipment Replacement, and Labor Absorption: The Case of the Brazilian Textile Industry" (Ph.D. diss., Vanderbilt University, 1971), 106; and Márcia Mendes de Almeida, "O Sindicato dos Têxteis em São Paulo: História, 1933–1957" (Tese de mestrado, Universidade de São Paulo, 1981), 73–74.

[a]Individuals who paid union dues in addition to the imposto sindical.

[b]The total number of textile workers in the city (i.e., those who paid the imposto sindical).

with a series of institutional reforms. First, it consolidated the disparate unions representing various aspects of the textile industry in the city of São Paulo and formed the Sindicato dos Trabalhadores nas Indústrias de Fiação e Tecelagam de São Paulo (hereinafter, the Textile Workers' Union) in 1941.[41] The creation of the State Federation of Textile Workers' Unions in 1942 provided yet another organization the Paulistano pelegos could use to further their financial and political ambitions. Pelegos also held key posts in important ministry institutions such as the Courts of Conciliation (Juntas de Conciliação e Julgamento) and the Industrial Workers' Retirement Pension Institute (Instituto de Aposentadores e Pensões dos Industriários, IAPI).[42]

As income from the labor tax began to swell its treasury, the union moved to fulfill its prescribed function as a bureaucratic instrument of social control. In October 1941 the union built its own headquarters building. In July and August 1942 it expanded that building and installed permanent facilities for the union's physicians and dentists. Later in 1942, it purchased land in Santos for the construction of a vacation colony. In June 1943 the union hired a lawyer and expanded its recreation department with the installation of pool tables. In August 1943 the directorate bought itself a car. In March 1944 the union hired a full-time coach for its soccer team and remodeled its stadium. Then, in April–May 1944, it built its vacation facility in Santos.[43]

The union leadership maintained close ties with industrialists as well as with Ministry of Labor functionaries. And Paulistano industrialists took advantage of this industrial relations system; indeed, they worked to bolster the unions and their leaders. Humberto Reis Costa, the president of the Textile Industrialists' Association, often praised the collaboration of Melchíades dos Santos and other pelegos. He even wrote to Vargas detailing the high degree of cooperation with which the textile unionists had negotiated the first minimum wage levels, and he published a letter in the union's newspaper, O Trabalhador Têxtil, praising Santos. Pelegos returned the compliments and honored various industrialists for their spirit of collaboration. Besides the banquets and other formal activities, the union forged closer ties with industrialists by sponsoring sporting events that included workers and foremen. Competitions, often held on factory grounds, pitted work sections against each other, with the foremen serving as captains. Some firms, such as Lanifício Santa Branca, even sponsored special medical services that were only for their employees who belonged to the union.[44]

Although Santos and Teixeira presided over a union whose membership consistently made up less than 3 percent of the total number of textile workers in São Paulo (table 3.1), they were able to maintain social peace throughout the industry by negotiating wage increases for union members and nonmembers alike. In late 1938 and early 1939, a factory commission of women at Indústria Têxteis Calfat that had no ties to the union struck against the increasingly harsh work regimes and for higher wages. This movement, which threatened the newly appointed pelegos' already weak position among the city's textile workers, prompted the union leaders to petition industry leaders and the government to improve conditions for all textile workers. Several mill owners and the state Department of Labor granted wage concessions, thus bolstering the weak position of these unionists.[45] Again in 1943, after pressure from weavers, the leaders of the Textile Workers' Union petitioned the Ministry of Labor, industrialists, and Vargas for increases in the minimum wage. When increases were granted, Santos trumpeted his role as the "defender of the workers" and tried to establish himself as an honest broker for the city's textile workers. In return for the wage adjustments, however, the union promised to push for increases in productivity among the rank and file. The pelegos attempted to accomplish this by fostering a culture that celebrated high output. They even introduced the "Song of the Brazilian Worker." Its telling refrain reveals several of the unionists' biases:

> To work is our glory
> With manly force
> To work always for victory
> And the greatness of our Brazil.[46]

The city's textile workers no doubt found a union's praise of high productivity somewhat incongruous; and the women who made up the majority of those workers considered the celebration of "manly force" typical of the male-dominated sindicato. Interestingly, the song not only embodied the Estado Novo's gendered view of work and unions, it also harked back to the anarchists' masculine discourse about work and organizing. Such a discourse—along with a very male-oriented praxis—continued to alienate women from the formal unions. Women made up about 60 percent of the city's textile workers at this time, but the directorate and the vast majority of the union's members were men.[47] Union social activities stressed male sports such as soccer and male games such as pool. Meanwhile, the union also sought to reinforce traditional female roles. It participated in the citywide Queen of Industry contest sponsored by the Federation of Industries, and members of the sindicato discussed the need to find attractive women to enter in this beauty pageant. The union also maintained a Departamento Feminino in the early 1940s. Rather than attempt to increase women's participation in the sindicato, this department sponsored cooking and hygiene classes; its basic goal was to train women to be good wives and mothers.[48]

Most women textile workers could not even join the union because of their "double duty" as factory workers and homemakers. Aracy Sanchez, a lifelong weaver, recalled that she had "too much work at home to get involved with something like the union." Another weaver, Santo Vetturuzzo, joined the sindicato to protect himself from foremen, but his wife "didn't have any reason to join. She had plenty of work to do at home." Besides, he noted, he "could take care of any problems for her."[49] Diolinda Nascimento waited until she needed help getting her full wages to join the union. "Generally, the union was not my place," she related. "But these processos (petitions) were a complex thing, so I joined to get help with one."[50] Still, industrialists had so much power over workers in those years that women who needed their jobs avoided joining the union. Many single mothers feared taking any action that might be considered suspicious by their bosses. For, while the union was supported by industry during the Estado Novo, workers remembered the many strikes of the 1920s and 1930s and the mass firings of labor activists that followed those successful movements.[51] For a wide variety of reasons—distrust of the unionists, financial considerations, and fear of employer reprisals—few female or male textile workers joined the union.

Some women who had joined the union in the early 1930s maintained their membership during the Estado Novo. Assumpta Bianchi, who began work as a weaver in the 1920s, joined in 1933 and remained in the sindicato until her retirement in 1969. Still, she never spoke at meetings because she feared the "dirty and loud men hanging around the headquarters." To her, the union hall was a dangerous place where men drank and played pool.[52] Indeed, none of the men or women workers I interviewed (see Appendix) could recall a woman speaking at a meeting during the Estado Novo years.[53] Few textile workers of either sex even attended union meetings in this period. One meeting in 1941 had 343 members present, but after that no meeting through 1944 had more than 174 people in attendance; many had fewer than 50 members present. Those who did go to meetings faced DOPS and state Department of Labor officials who asked to see the identity cards of members who spoke. And it was generally assumed that anyone who challenged the directorate would lose her or his job, and possibly go to jail.[54] Vargas and the Ministry of Labor could not even use the much-needed social services to bribe workers to join the union.[55]

Thus the union supposedly representing the largest group of workers in Brazil's leading industrial center was little more than a legal formality. It was a quasi-governmental institution with no ties to the workers' social movement—the loose network of factory commissions. The experience of São Paulo's Textile Workers' Union, therefore, reveals an important weakness of corporatism: State policymakers can fashion elaborate mechanisms to channel class struggle through formal institutions in order to foster consent, but if the objects of this manipulation refuse to participate, the corporatist strategy fails.

The Metalworkers' Union and the Estado Novo

The Ministry of Labor also intervened several times in the Sindicato dos Trabalhadores nas Indústrias Metalúrgicas, Mecânicas, e de Material Elétrico de São Paulo (hereinafter, the Metalworkers' Union) during the middle and late 1930s. Before those interventions, the sindicato leadership (many of whom had participated in the city's anarchist labor movement) had actively pursued wage and work issues and often had forced the city's metallurgy shops to obey labor legislation. These activities brought on the first intervention in January 1936, more than one year before the declaration of the Estado Novo. With state Department of Labor representatives at all their meetings, the union's leadership was forced to turn its attention to bureaucratic concerns such as maintenance of the union headquarters and the extension of social services.[56]

The union's president after this first intervention, Salvador de Lattis, was a member of the fascist Ação Integralista Brasileira. He used the sindicato's headquarters for Integralist meetings and participated in the anticommunist Union Front Against Extremists. Other members of the directorate, such as Armando Suffredini and Amilcar Castelan, had strong ties to the Ministry of Labor and were classic pelegos. These men controlled the union from 1937 to 1939, and during that time they purged members who sought to return the sindicato to its original role as a representative body of the city's metalworkers. In 1937 they even forbade any sort of political discussion within the union hall.[57]

The expanding labor bureaucracy created new opportunities for these pelegos. Access to financial resources and patronage was granted only to allies of the Vargas regime, so the federal and state governments moved to purge the Metalworkers' Union of its Integralist leaders. On 29 March 1939, Ministry of Labor representatives assumed control of the sindicato. They handed over power to Octávio Villaça of the state Department of Labor, and he installed a group of pro-Vargas unionists, who held control of the union through the Estado Novo. This new directorate of Vicente Guglielmo (president), Bernardino Silva (treasurer), and Guerino Pian (secretary) immediately took advantage of their access to funds through the IAPI and patronage that flowed from positions on the labor courts and in the state union structure. Then, when José Sanches Duran took office as the sindicato's president in May 1941, he became the first Paulistano metalworker to receive a salary for serving his companheiros.[58]

As their counterparts in the Textile Workers' Union had, these pelegos turned away from protecting workers' rights and instead concentrated on providing social services for members and fostering a culture celebrating high output on the shop floor. The union's leading pelegos filled important posts in the state Federation of Metalworkers and controlled new departments in their local sindicato, such as the

Table 3.2   Membership in the São Paulo Metalworkers' Union, 1936–1942

Year	Members[a]	Metalworkers[b]	Workers in union (%)
1936	1,689	33,060	5.10
1937	1,647	33,450	4.92
1938	1,723	33,670	5.12
1939	1,784	35,442	5.03
1940	1,708	35,800	4.77
1941	1,486	35,877	4.14
1942	1,799	36,800	4.88

Source: M. H. Simões Paes, "O Sindicato dos Metalúrgicos de São Paulo, 1932–1951" (Tese de mestrado, Universidade de São Paulo, 1979), 114, 121; O Metalúrgico, March 1943; and USDL, Monthly Labor Review 57.3 (September 1943): 581.
[a]Those individuals who paid union dues in addition to the imposto sindical.
[b]The total number of metalworkers in the city.

legal division. They also expanded medical and dental services, and then moved to buy a headquarters building with funds from the union tax. They began publishing O Metalúrgico, but used it more as a propaganda tool for the regime than as a means of drawing metalworkers together to fight for their rights. O Metalúrgico's editorials praised the hated imposto sindical and reprinted Vargas's speeches.[59] Its editorials and reports all emphasized the importance of hard work and urged São Paulo's metalúrgicos to sacrifice for the common good. One editorial proclaimed: "Metalworkers! We are the ones who make the pieces for our machines. We are the ones who forge the steel for our tools, and we are the ones who cast, adjust, and assemble all this work, so our effort must be the greatest. . . . To produce more is the best."[60] The union also editorialized that "in order to rest, it is first necessary to work. To work within the system, to work in the sense of cooperation between the workers and their employer."[61]

These policies kept potential members from joining the union, even though the industry expanded steadily during the Estado Novo years (table 3.2). São Paulo's metalworkers saw the union as a closed club where a tiny minority of the category's workers enjoyed the benefits culled from the huge labor tax. Conrado de Papa, who began work in the metal trades as a nine-year-old in 1932 and later received formal training as a fitter, saw no reason to join the union during the Vargas years: "If the state and industry supported the unions, how could those same unions fight for the workers?" He also noted that industry had a stake in keeping the union small so it could maintain close ties to the corrupt leaders.[62]

Francisco Pinto Silva remembered some union members who attempted to organize workers in the small shops throughout Brás in these years: "These opposition guys would come around during our lunch break and tell us they could help us; they worked against the pelegos." Still, neither he nor his companheiros felt they had the time to attend the meetings or get involved in politics. One of Pinto Silva's colleagues, Edson Borges, recalled, "We worked seven days a week, all day and night in those days. We didn't have any time to deal with these political issues."[63]

The structure of São Paulo's metallurgical industry had a paradoxical impact on its members' relationship with the state-sponsored sindicato. The majority of the city's metalworkers were employed in small shops (often with fewer than thirty workers) that did not have the factory-based social services offered in large textile mills, so many Paulistano metalworkers had an incentive to become sindicalizado. Yet, work relations in these small shops tended to obviate the need for a bureaucratic labor system. Roberto Unger, who began work at Fundição Higienópolis when he was twelve, saw no reason to join the union because he dealt directly with the owner. Unger and his comrades had a complex relationship with the shop's owner, for he was at once "a friend and an enemy." Waldemar Lima took a similar position; he dealt directly with his boss because that was a lot easier than going through the pelegos, whom he saw as "the government's people."[64]

São Paulo's legacy of worker protests also kept membership in the state-sponsored union low. Those older workers who had belonged to the anarchist União Operária and Associação dos Metalúrgicos in the 1920s lectured their young comrades on the necessity of independent labor organizing. Hermento Mendes Dantas remembered those older workers as being clearly anticapitalist and opposed to the Metalworkers' Union. According to David Carneiro, who had just begun working in a small metallurgy shop in Mooca in the early 1940s, "All of us younger workers listened to the older men and their stories of São Paulo in the 1920s. Sometimes an uncle or cousin would tell us about the unions back then, but mostly you heard these stories, these things about the union and politics, . . . at work or sitting around with everybody during our lunch."[65] The experiences of the people who had participated in anarchist unions in the 1920s and early 1930s, along with the historical memory of the city's metalworkers, proved to be yet another impediment to the growth of the state-sponsored sindicatos.[66]

Metalworkers who joined the union in this period did so primarily to take advantage of the growing number of services available through the sindicato.[67] But most of those who joined did not participate in the sindicato's affairs. Antônio Lombardi never attended any meetings in those years because he was not interested in politics. Geraldo Pascolato attended a few meetings, but he never spoke. "I sat and listened, it was dull, reports and those things. When there was a vote, I voted for the directorate's position. We all did, because there were DOPS there, so you didn't oppose anything."[68]

Industry and the Estado Novo

Paulistano industrialists understood well the irony of the labor relations system they had helped the state create. Small, unrepresentative unions weakened the potential collective power of the working class, but they also limited the impact of the Estado Novo's goals of national integration. Further, the industrialists' plans to use a wide variety of social services and training programs to help produce a more highly skilled and productive labor force could not be realized through the weak sindicatos. So, during 1941 and 1942, the Federation of Industries and the Rockefeller Foundation sponsored programs to provide those social services in the city's textile and metallurgy factories. The industrialists moved to improve the health conditions in the factories by installing more cafeterias and food cooperatives. This program served several purposes. First, it provided the essential nutrition many of the city's workers could not afford on their salaries. Second, it helped maintain social peace; FIESP members remembered well the many food riots before and during past strike movements, and they knew providing a steady supply of good, inexpensive foodstuffs was necessary to prevent such uprisings. Third, industrialists hoped workers who ate in factory cafeterias and in the FIESP's restaurants in the industrial districts would be less likely to organize factory commissions and plan strikes during lunch breaks than workers who gathered on their own, beyond the FIESP's control. And, fourth, industrialists wanted to buy their workers' goodwill by providing subsidized food. Antônio de Sousa Noschese, the owner of a large metallurgy establishment, told his colleagues that worker unrest was "caused by psychological factors." He said he would continue to sell discounted food "to show the workers that we want to help them. That should prevent whatever eventual uprising."[69]

In 1945, the Federation of Industries conducted a survey of its members and found these social services were widely offered by factories throughout the city. Textile industrialists began in 1937 to install cafeterias, food cooperatives, child care facilities, housing, medical facilities, recreation areas, and other services. By 1945, one-half of the industrial establishments in the city had cafeterias, and about one-third had medical and other facilities. Textile and the larger metallurgy factories (i.e., those with more than thirty workers) had more of these services available for their workers than did most other Paulistano establishments. The largest factories also created sports teams, and workers could compete against each other in soccer, volleyball, and basketball.[70]

In addition to working with the pelegos, the Federation of Industries encouraged the growth of other conservative working-class organizations. Paulistano industrialists secretly funded the Catholic Federação dos Círculos Operários. Conservative clerics involved in the Centro Dom Vidal and associated with the Catholic revival of the 1920s and 1930s founded this labor central to provide needed social services and preach anticommunism to Brazilian workers. The FIESP funded the círculos in the late 1930s and 1940s, and then increased its support when the pelegos of the textile and metallurgical workers' unions seemed to be losing control over their workers in 1944 and 1945.[71] The Federation of Industries also aided the Associação Cívica Feminina, whose members taught working-class women various domestic skills such as dressmaking, child care, and cooking. These Catholic social workers also encouraged young women to participate in the political arena in support of conservative causes.[72]

At the same time, the Federation of Industries worked closely with the federal government's propaganda machine in its efforts to engender a sense of Brazilian nationalism in the population and increase support for the Estado Novo. In 1942, the FIESP and the state government began producing films of workers in São Paulo's most advanced industrial establishments. The films not only sought to impress the Brazilian population with scenes of work in Paulistano factories, they also projected images of the "good" or "responsible" worker, who skillfully performed her or his assigned tasks, happily participated in the state-controlled union structure, and thankfully received ample compensation for a job well done.[73]

In addition to these elaborate control and propaganda mechanisms, the FIESP and the state and federal governments employed simple repression to discipline labor activists. Mid-level bureaucrats involved in implementing Estado Novo policies readily admitted that violence was a key component in the maintenance of "social peace." Feigo Machado of the São Paulo DOPS, for example, wrote to Vargas after the Estado Novo recounting his efforts to foster high levels of production in industry by breaking up strikes. Political opponents of Vargas, as well as those who supported him, noted that the state imprisoned, tortured, and generally abused the human rights of many of its opponents.[74] The U.S. consul in São Paulo observed the Brazilian government's use of violence, and at the end of the Estado Novo he concluded: "Recent experiences . . . seem to indicate that repression under the dictatorial regime was perhaps more a factor in preventing strikes than was the elaborate mechanism of reconciliation."[75]

Winners and Losers: Results of the Estado Novo

Industrialists

The Estado Novo's planners consciously set out to stimulate Brazil's industrialization. They wanted both to increase industrial production and to expand the infrastructure available for future growth. By all measures, they achieved both goals. Overall industrial production in São Paulo more than doubled between 1935 and 1942 (table 3.3). Further, those increases in output often came from expanding capacity, not from intensified use of the existing industrial sector (table 3.4). Beginning in the mid-1930s, the federal government struggled to deepen industrialization by stimulating the capital goods sector and attempting to break bottlenecks in transportation, technical training, and other areas. Ultimately, therefore, Estado Novo economic policies (along with the curtailment of imports caused by the 1930s depression) not only bolstered industrial output, they created a systematic program of industrialization for Brazil.[76]

Throughout the Vargas years, industrialists' policy recommendations received careful consideration by the federal government. At the request of textile manufacturers, Vargas adopted controls on the importation of spinning and weaving equipment (to combat "overproduction") in 1931.[77] In 1940, Paulistano industrialists enlisted the aid of the

Table 3.3   Index of Industrial Output in the State of
São Paulo, 1935–1942 (1935 = 100)

Year	Metallurgy	Textiles	Total manufacturing
1935	100.0	100.0	100.0
1936	131.9	109.1	111.5
1937	131.0	124.9	123.6
1938	183.1	115.2	135.2
1939	217.6	122.9	164.5
1940	214.4	137.0	182.1
1941	230.8	181.3	222.6
1942	239.3	206.3	210.1

Source: A. V. Villela and W. Suzigan, "Government Policy and the Economic Growth of Brazil, 1889–1945," Brazilian Economic Studies 3 (1977): 297.

state interventor, Adhemar de Barros, to petition Vargas for govern-ment assistance in maintaining high levels of production. The FIESP requested measures to maintain high output in the face of oil shortages, bottlenecks in the transportation system, and limited supplies of na-tional capital. Vargas quickly moved to address these issues.[78] His trade policy likewise furthered industrialists' interests; the government inter-vened in the foreign exchange markets during the 1930s to manage trade and balance-of-payments accounts. Through this intervention Vargas directed exchange earnings to the foreign debt and essential imports (generally capital goods).[79]

These policies, along with the strict control over workers, greatly aided industrialists during the Estado Novo. Government intervention in the economy overall, and in the industrial relations system in par-ticular, brought about the dictatorship's original goal of industrializa-tion.[80] Further, the Estado Novo fostered the economic, state, and class infrastructure needed for future industrial expansion. Capacity in-creased (table 3.4) and bottlenecks in the economy were eradicated. Along with these policies, Vargas and his allies created a powerful central state to manage this industrialization.[81] One residual effect of the Estado Novo that has received little attention, however, is the development of a nationwide industrial bourgeoisie that fought for federal policies benefiting only industry.[82] Vargas's corporatist frame-work forced industrialists throughout Brazil to organize on the state and national levels. Commercial and agrarian groups also formed such

Table 3.4   Characteristics of Manufacturing Industries in the State
of São Paulo, 1933–1939

	1933[a]	1937	1939
Number of factories	6,555	9,051	12,850
Capital invested[b]	1,906,482	3,460,452	4,679,371
Number of workers	171,667	245,715	254,721
Installed horsepower	212,108	279,573	432,650
Value of production[b]	2,060,363	3,851,878	7,107,547

Source: A. V. Villela and W. Suzigan, "Government Policy and the Economic Growth of Brazil, 1889–1945," Brazilian Economic Studies 3 (1977): 302.

[a]The numbers for 1933 and 1937 are based on the same industries; 1939's are somewhat different, but Villela and Suzigan believe that "while not strictly comparable, [they] provide a general indication of the course taken by industry" (p. 302).

[b]Contos de Réis

organizations or integrated existing federations into the new corporatist structure. These industrial, commercial, and agrarian associations became powerful institutions for their class or class fraction.

Workers and the Estado Novo

The interventions and new financial and bureaucratic controls over the unions greatly weakened São Paulo's once vibrant workers' movement. Unions and independent factory commissions that had forced employers and the state to increase wages and improve work conditions throughout the early and mid-1930s were replaced by instruments of the state and its industrialist allies.[83] The implicit bargain struck by the Estado Novo tied unions to the state in exchange for increased social justice for workers. In the final analysis, however, the Estado Novo's industrial relations system consistently supported industrialists' efforts to maintain low wages and tight discipline on the shop floor; there was little social justice for workers.

The pelegos rarely worked to improve conditions for the rank and file. When workers did convince these unionists to file processos on their behalf, they faced a hostile labor bureaucracy that supported government and industry efforts to augment production. In fall and winter 1941, the labor courts in São Paulo simply refused to judge many cases, leaving workers no avenue for redress. In 1942, when the São Paulo Regional Labor Courts functioned properly, 55.25 percent of

Table 3.5   Wages and the Cost of Living in São Paulo, 1935–1945

Year	Average factory wage[a]	Real minimum wage index	Cost-of-living index
1935	—	—	108.5
1936	—	—	124.4
1937	—	—	134.1
1938	—	—	139.5
1939	1.50	—	143.3
1940	1.05	98.02[b]	150.4
1941	1.25	89.35	166.8
1942	1.30	80.22	186.9
1943	1.50	78.78	214.8
1944	2.00	83.19	273.6
1945	2.00	67.03	319.3

Sources: São Paulo to Washington, D.C., Memo on Employment, "Employment Statistics for the State of São Paulo," SP Post 850, 18 November 1944, RG 84, NA; FIESP, *Relatório,* 1946, 4:162; Departamento Intersindical de Estatística e Estudos Sócio-Econômicos, "Objetivos e Caraterísticas do Plano Cruzado III," 17 June 1987; and Oliver Onody, *A Inflação Brasileira, 1820–1958* (Rio de Janeiro: n.p., 1960), 25.
[a]Cruzeiros per hour. In 1942 the government changed the currency from the milreis to the cruzeiro.
[b]This index begins with July 1940, which equals 100, but all years are calculated in October, so the figure for 1940 is slightly less than 100.

the cases were decided in favor of industry and 26.49 percent were thrown out of court; only 13.24 percent were settled in favor of workers, and 5.02 percent were settled through accords.[84] When bureaucratic measures failed, Paulistano industrialists used repression to circumscribe workers' protests. With little power to bargain for higher wages, industrial workers experienced a steady decline in real income (table 3.5).

Decreasing real wages are only one measure of the deteriorating conditions Paulistano workers faced during the Estado Novo. During the late 1930s, São Paulo's industrial workers continued to face shortages of essential goods; and when they could find bread, meat, fish, and produce in the markets, they were often of the lowest quality and highest price. In 1936 and 1937, Minister of Labor Agamemnon Magalhães publicly decried the power of certain "trusts" in São Paulo that limited workers' access to unadulterated bread.[85] Social services agencies in the city conducted numerous studies of working-class living conditions and found, time after time, that as São Paulo expanded in size, workers' standard of living fell. One newspaper described women workers' lives in 1940 as revolving around the question "Where will I find the cheapest food?"[86] The expanding social services made available by industrialists, the unions, and government did not yet have a significant impact on the city's workers. Only one in ten had access to free medical care; and although the city underwent a building boom in the 1930s, only 3.9 percent of all new residences in São Paulo were for workers and their families. Workers could not even afford to rent vilas operárias or buy meals at the restaurants set up by the FIESP.[87]

Several thorough studies of living conditions reveal the continuing difficulties São Paulo's workers endured during the 1930s. The 1934 study of 221 working-class families in São Paulo by North American sociologist Horace B. Davis describes how families had to combine incomes from both parents' and several children's salaries to pay rent and buy food. To escape the high cost of living in the factory districts, about one quarter of these workers lived in the city's periphery, where they could grow vegetables and raise chickens; of course, these workers also had to rely on the inefficient train system to commute to their factories. Davis also noted great differences in the quality of life among the families studied. Highly skilled metalworkers earned wages that enabled them to live more comfortable lives than those of textile and other workers.[88]

Single mothers, who were forced to accept the poorest-paying industrial employment (often in the textile sector), faced these problems on an even greater scale. One study found that about one quarter of the children in the city's "children's parks" had no fathers. These children and their single mothers were more likely to live in basements and the worst tenements in the city. The women often could not move to the periphery, for they relied on neighbors, the factories, or the few children's parks to provide day care for their children. The children of these mothers were consistently found to be in the poorest health of any working-class children studied. And if anyone had bothered to study the mothers' health, they would have found them to be in a precarious state as well.[89]

In the late 1930s and early 1940s, São Paulo's workers continued to face these same conditions. While metalworkers were able to provide better diets for their families than textile workers could, the state Department of Labor found that the city's industrial laborers, as a group, continued to earn too little to properly feed, clothe, and house

Table 3.6   Deficits in Budgets of 117 Paulistano
Working-Class Families, 1939

Expense	Families with deficit spending	Families with surplus	Families with equilibrium
Food	75	42	0
Housing	106	11	0
Clothing	79	38	0
Transportation	95	19	3
Hygiene	91	35	1
Furniture	86	31	0
Education	39	74	1
Other	85	30	2
Total expenses	87	30	0

Source: São Paulo, Secretaria da Agricultura, Indústria, e Comércio, *Aspectos do Padrão da Vida do Operário Industrial da Capital de São Paulo* (São Paulo, 1940), 48.

themselves and their families. This was the case even though more than 95 percent of the five hundred families studied had both parents and several children working outside the home.[90] Most families that provided information on their monthly budgets were not able to pay their housing, food, and other expenses (table 3.6). This situation intensified women workers' double duty, for they increased their own work loads at home to make up these deficits. That is, they cooked and canned foods that had once been bought prepared, made and mended garments rather than buying new clothes, and took in laundry and other extra work when they could.[91]

The Estado Novo did not provide the promised improvements in living conditions for the vast majority of São Paulo's industrial workers. Women, for example, could not leave their factory employment to become the sort of nurturers the regime's ideologues had envisioned. The Estado Novo's goal of national unification likewise did not come to pass. Industrialists had discriminated against black workers since the first decades of the twentieth century, and this discrimination continued during the Estado Novo. Study after study of race relations in São Paulo found that blacks faced many obstacles to gaining access to factory employment.[92] In the late 1930s and early 1940s, Paulistano blacks could not even find work as domestic servants. Postings for such positions in the *Diário Popular* often asked for "foreigners" (i.e., Italian, Spanish, and Portuguese immigrants) or "white" applicants only.[93]

In the final analysis, the Estado Novo achieved its main goal of fostering industrialization. São Paulo's industrial bourgeoisie received government assistance in eliminating economic bottlenecks such as transportation problems, shortages of domestic capital for investments, and problems with steady supplies of necessary inputs (e.g., energy and steel). Vargas further aided FIESP members by intervening in São Paulo's labor movement. Estado Novo–era labor policies reduced the unions to little more than allies of the state and employers. And when workers attempted to organize on their own, the state relied on simple repression to provide social peace. Such control helped industrialists keep wages low while production increased. The Estado Novo, perforce, served as a significant period of accumulation for industry.[94]

The complex institutional corporatist framework had one central flaw: São Paulo's workers avoided participating in the state-sponsored sindicatos.[95] São Paulo's textile and metallurgical workers avoided these unions for a variety of reasons (e.g., conflicts between women workers and male unionists, historical memory of anarchist unions that articulated an antistate ideology and were increasingly receptive to rank-and-file demands, and continued reliance upon independent forms of organizing), but in the final analysis, they did not join the unions because they recognized the Estado Novo's sindicatos as tools of the state and the industrialists. Moreover, the São Paulo state Department of Labor, the agency responsible for the implementation of Vargas's labor laws in the city, continued to be run by an industrialist. Paulistano workers understood how this system operated. They had their own legacy of organizing and protest activity—especially since the 1917 General Strike—to call upon to interpret their situation and to frame their responses to it.[96] During the 1930s and before, politicians (e.g., Vargas, leaders of the PCB and ANL, and others) and corrupt labor leaders had all promised to improve the lot of Brazil's workers. The Estado Novo proved to be yet another reminder to São Paulo's working people that they would have to organize themselves and act on their own behalf to change their lives.

World War II and the Struggle for Citizenship, 1942–1945

After the final destruction of the Nazi tyranny, [the Allied nations] hope to see established a peace which will afford to all nations the means of dwelling in safety within their own boundaries, and which will afford assurance that all the men in all the lands may live out their lives in freedom from fear and want.

—The Atlantic Charter

São Paulo's Political Prison Has Nothing in Common with the Concentration Camps of Hitlerite Germany.

—Headline in *Diário de São Paulo*,
27 September 1942

After months of German submarine attacks against their merchant marine in the fall and winter of 1942, and heavy pressure from the United States on Vargas and his military advisers to break relations with Hitler, Brazilians throughout the country called on their leaders to join the war effort. In the wake of the torpedoing of six Brazilian ships between 15 and 19 August 1942 by the Nazis, crowds attacked and demolished German- and Italian-owned businesses in Recife, Salvador, Porto Alegre, Vitória, Belém, Manaus, and Belo Horizonte. In São Paulo and Rio crowds carrying American flags attacked suspected Axis sympathizers and demanded that Vargas declare war on Germany. Finally, on 22 August, Vargas assented to all the pressure and formally declared war on the Axis.[1]

Brazil's entry into the war brought profound changes to almost every segment of its society. The twenty-five thousand soldiers of the Brazilian Expeditionary Force (Força Expedicionária Brasileira, FEB) who fought in Italy became more than just a source of great national pride; they represented Brazil's new status as an industrializing nation, even a potential world power.[2] Indeed, after the war, Brazilians lobbied the other Allies for a permanent seat on the United Nations Security Council as a symbol of their country's new status. Throughout the war,

Vargas, Minister of Labor Alexandre Marcondes Filho, Minister of War Eurico Gaspar Dutra, and other officials proudly proclaimed not only the greatness of Brazil but also the importance of each and every Brazilian in the battle against fascism. Workers and peasants alike constantly heard on the radio discussions of their importance to the international struggle for a world in which all people could live out their lives in freedom from fear and want.

While fighting fascism in Europe, Vargas maintained his Estado Novo dictatorship at home. The Ministry of Labor still manipulated the pelego-dominated unions, and industrialists continued to rely on state intervention to increase production. The war even provided new justifications for repression against workers and others who participated in "unpatriotic" behavior, such as strikes and production slowdowns. Once again, São Paulo's workers faced the irony of Vargas's rule: They constantly heard national and local leaders promise them increased social justice, but they were also told they had to work a little harder and make a few more sacrifices for the common good.

A Nation in Arms: Brazil Goes to War

From Dictatorship to "Democracy"

Even before Brazil entered the war, Vargas began preparing the population for the sacrifices ahead. He reminded Brazilians of the food shortages, inflation, and other problems the cutoff of international trade brought during World War I.[3] The dictator also recalled the great spurt of industrialization Brazil experienced during the war. No "antisocial" activities, such as strikes or "sabotage" in the factories, could be tolerated during this new war, he lectured. Vargas was especially worried about workers in São Paulo. He told the city's workers the military would guarantee laborers the right to "work peacefully and efficiently" during the war because "São Paulo's economy . . . is profoundly sensitive to . . . social disturbance."[4]

With Brazil's declaration of war, Vargas had to modify his regime's rhetoric. He could no longer rely on the quasi-fascist declarations of Francisco Campos, Antônio José Azevedo Amaral, Francisco José de Oliveira Viana, or other Estado Novo ideologues to justify his labor policies. In May 1942 Vargas called on his country's workers to maintain social peace during the struggle against international fascism. After all, the dictator told his people, they were not "slaves" like the workers in Nazi-occupied nations; Estado Novo labor policies made Brazilian workers among the freest in the world.[5]

Vargas frequently lectured the working class on his transformation from dictator to democrat. In his September 1942 Independence Day address at Rio's Vasco da Gama Stadium, Vargas assured Brazilians that their participation in the war would make them "worthy of America, a continent of free men." Two months later, on the fifth anniversary of the Estado Novo, the dictator told the country that he had brought democracy to Brazil. Vargas termed the Estado Novo a "functional democracy," in which all citizens had access to the benefits of the state. In his New Year's message, the dictator told his people they had entered the war "to defend liberty [and] the Christian traditions of family . . . [which are] the goals for which the United Nations are fighting."[6]

Included in Vargas's and Minister of Labor Marcondes Filho's appeals to workers for efficient production in the factories were explicit promises of social justice for all. The Ministry of Labor helped industrialists wage "the battle of production" in order to allow the armies in Europe to produce a "new world, more humane and just." In his weekly radio broadcasts, Marcondes Filho spoke of workers as "the producers of Brazil's wealth" and "the force [that will] produce a more tranquil and progressive union." Workers were the great defenders of Brazil; they were producing a new Brazil with "fuller [citizen] rights, social justice, and human dignity."[7]

These constant declarations of the importance of labor to the war effort worried São Paulo's industrialists, for they did not view workers as their equals.[8] Further, by entering the war, Brazil became an ally of the Soviet Union. Waldemar Clemente, the owner of a large metallurgy establishment, told his colleagues at a weekly meeting of the São Paulo state Federation of Industries that the alliance with the Soviets would bring "dangerous" consequences. He held up a copy of the book *Stalin, The Soviet Russian* that he had recently bought on the street. He told the other industrialists that "these books, once read by workers, immediately turn [the workers] into communists." Clemente assured his colleagues that such propaganda did not affect them because "we have a certain equilibrium that better controls our instincts."[9] Clemente's fears may have been a little irrational, but they demonstrate the unease São Paulo's industrialists felt as Vargas, Marcondes Filho, and other officials lauded "the producers of Brazil's wealth."

Industrialists and the War Effort

São Paulo's industrialists were already profiting handsomely from the Estado Novo's program of industrial expansion and control over labor when the exigencies of wartime production created even greater opportunities. Before Brazil's entry into the war, the Federation of Industries had petitioned Vargas for special concessions to increase output in the textile sector. First, the mill owners wanted government help with transportation problems and energy shortages.[10] Next, they petitioned Vargas and the Ministry of Labor to allow them to ignore regulations limiting women's night work and children's hours in the factories. These industrialists thought they could inexpensively increase output by intensifying their use of child and woman labor. At first, the Ministry of Labor did not want to grant Paulistano mill owners all these concessions, but Brazil's entry into the war provided a rationale for increasing production at any cost.[11]

Indeed, in September 1942 the government "mobilized" so-called strategic industries such as textiles and metalworking shops. Workers in such mobilized industries could not leave their jobs without approval from management. In November 1942 the government established fines for worker absenteeism; someone absent from work for more than twenty-four hours without "just cause" could be fined three days' pay. Those who missed work for more than eight days were considered military deserters; foreign-born workers could be prosecuted for committing "sabotage" through such an absence.[12] Factory owners could also discipline workers in these industries by deciding which men were eligible for the draft.[13] In the final analysis, although São Paulo's industrialists were unhappy with Vargas's and Marcondes Filho's rhetoric praising labor, FIESP members were quite pleased with the government's program to increase wartime production.[14] Humberto Ries Costa, president of the Textile Industry Association, assured his colleagues that "the mobilization of the textile industry is perhaps the beginning of a new phase in industrial life in Brazil . . . [because] the decree seeks to discipline the workers . . . [in whom] the love of work had disappeared."[15]

When appeals for social peace in the name of the war effort failed to control workers, industrialists once again relied on repression. After about one hundred metalworkers at General Motors do Brasil struck on the morning of 6 June 1942, for example, the political police (DOPS) immediately intervened. The DOPS arrested the leaders of the factory

Table 4.1   Index of Industrial Output in the State of
São Paulo, 1935–1945 (1935 = 100)

Year	Metallurgy	Textiles	Total manufacturing
1935	100.0	100.0	100.0
1936	131.9	109.1	111.5
1937	131.0	124.9	123.6
1938	183.1	115.2	135.2
1939	217.6	122.9	164.5
1940	214.4	137.0	182.1
1941	230.8	181.3	222.6
1942	239.3	206.3	210.1
1943	247.6	221.9	221.7
1944	261.1	163.4	220.8
1945	316.6	149.7	203.5

Source: A. V. Villela and W. Suzigan, "Government Policy and the Economic Growth of Brazil, 1889–1945," *Brazilian Economic Studies* 3 (1977): 297.

commission, and work resumed that afternoon.[16] The government also worked diligently to remind workers of its monopoly on violence. A lead article in 27 September 1942 edition of the *Diário de São Paulo* detailed the operation of one of Vargas's political prisons. The story's headline proclaimed: "São Paulo's Political Prison Has Nothing in Common with the Concentration Camps of Hitlerite Germany." The article refuted claims that the prisoners were not well fed or clothed. The story's double message was lost on no one: Brazil was an Allied country, but it maintained political prisons for those who opposed the Vargas dictatorship.[17]

Near complete control of workers' organizations and the frequent use of repression profoundly aided Paulistano industrialists' efforts to expand production. Industrial output grew at an average rate of 6.5 percent per year in the 1939–45 period, and the metallurgy sector expanded 7.5 percent per year. Textiles expanded at about 25 percent per year from 1939 to 1943, and then experienced a downturn (table 4.1).[18] The war, like the first five years of the Estado Novo, spurred an industrial expansion that laid the basis for future growth by increasing infrastructure development, the capital goods sector, and the supply of skilled and semiskilled labor.

With North American and British industry producing goods almost exclusively for their war efforts, Brazilian textile mills, led by those in São Paulo, expanded their markets, exporting to Argentina, Chile, Bolivia, South Africa, and other countries.[19] This steady expansion continued until mid-1944, and then, although production dipped, it remained well above prewar levels.[20] Industrialists ran their equipment at full capacity during the war years. This increased their dependence on workers' ability to keep the mills' older machines operating.[21] Although the state Department of Labor enforced wartime measures tying workers to their jobs, the shortage of textile workers was so acute during the war that some mill owners raided rivals' factories for the much needed semiskilled labor. Throughout the war, the FIESP studied various ways to increase the supply of skilled and semiskilled workers for the textile and other industries.[22]

Industrialists achieved growth in the textile sector by increasing the hours worked per worker rather than by increasing the number of laborers in the mills. The city of São Paulo, unlike other parts of Brazil, experienced severe shortages of skilled and semiskilled industrial workers beginning in 1936 and lasting beyond 1945. Although many people migrated to São Paulo during the war years, they made up a pool of surplus labor that was not easily employed in the city's textile mills. Many of the migrants worked as peddlers or garbage collectors, or simply returned to the rural sector. The U.S. consul in São Paulo reported in 1944, for example, that "the interesting feature of these figures [on employment levels in São Paulo] is the relatively small increase which has taken place during the war boom. The total amounts to less than 10% over the three years and accounts to a great extent for the general shortage of labor as it indicates a very small reserve even in 1941." So, throughout the war, demand for textile workers far outstripped supply.[23] Weavers had in the past taken advantage of such situations by switching mills to receive higher wages, but the wartime restrictions on mobility limited this practice.[24]

As I have explained, the metallurgy sector expanded steadily in the 1930s. Some metalworkers managed to open new small machine shops, and industrialists founded large establishments that produced metal products from steel sheets to complex machinery. The value of the metallurgy sector in general increased 48 percent, and that of machine production grew 50 percent between 1938 and 1943.[25] During the war, production was so great that the FIESP and government officials worried that many establishments would suffer shortages of skilled labor and raw materials, but the federal government managed to increase supplies of metals and began modest training programs for workers to keep machine production going through the difficult times in 1943 and 1944.[26]

Industrialists realized their production techniques were antiquated and that their products would not have survived international competition with U.S. and British goods. No matter, they demonstrated great pride in the advances in machine production during the war. The new *Revista Industrial de São Paulo* often carried a photo of some machine produced in the city on its cover, and its pages were filled with ads for the latest products from the area's machine shops.[27] A good example of São Paulo's new metallurgy establishments is Sofunge (Sociedade Técnica de Fundições Gerais). Engineers and industrialists came together in 1942 to found this company, which produced wheels and other equipment for railroad cars. They opened a factory in the Vila Anastácio neighborhood and soon began hiring skilled workers and training others. Sofunge flourished during the war and continued to supply São Paulo's growing vehicle industry in the years after 1945.[28]

The city's industrialists recognized that the Estado Novo and the war had created opportunities for future expansion as well as immediate profits. In June 1942, FIESP president Roberto Simonsen suggested that his fellow industrialists limit simple profit taking and use some of the surplus extracted from labor to reinvest in new machinery. He was not the only one to spot the huge profits (later estimated by economists at about 40 percent per year) taken by textile and other entrepreneurs. Finance Minister Artur de Souza Costa returned to Rio from a 1942 trip to São Paulo and noted that the textile industry seemed to be taking "excessive" profits.[29] Further, the U.S. consul pointed out in 1944 that the textile and metallurgy sectors were not only growing at high rates, they were producing profits of between 30 and 40 percent for industrialists at the expense of the working class. Such discussions became public by 1944. While FIESP members secretly debated what each should do with the fantastic surpluses they had recently accumulated, segments of the press editorialized against the Estado Novo's creation of such wealth through violence against labor.[30] Of course, this was one of the basic goals of the Estado Novo: the state would control the labor market so industrial development could progress. The wage squeeze and accompanying deterioration in workers' buying power would then be alleviated through the use of corporate welfare programs and social services through the co-opted unions.

Workers on the Home Front

Brazil's entry into the war created yet another context for intensifying the already harsh work regimes in the city's factories. Conrado de Papa, who began working in metallurgy as a boy in the 1930s, recalled that the sector's boom during the war required most establishments to operate nearly twenty-four hours per day, seven days a week; workers actually slept in the shops between long shifts. Papa added that when someone protested to the Ministry of Labor or state Department of Labor about having to work Saturday and Sunday, which violated the labor code, or against the great increases in the number of accidents at the factory, that person often ended up in jail for a few days.[31] Others recalled how the intense work loads of the war years kept them from any other activities. Edson Borges, who worked in a small shop in Brás, noted that he and his colleagues often talked at lunch about changing things, but they had no chance to organize: "We worked seven days a week, all day and night in those days. We didn't have any time to deal with these political issues."[32]

Industrialists increased production both by intensifying work regimes and by installing more equipment in the factories. Metalúrgicos from this era recalled how this haphazard growth made the factories even more dangerous. According to José Albertino, in order "to increase production [factory owners] installed one more machine and one more machine, and another. Then, the [work area] of each worker became much more compressed. . . . In whatever space a machine could fit, the boss put one more machine because he needed the production."[33] These conditions appeared to increase the accident rate. Geraldo Pascolato recalled that sometimes there seemed to be more accidents in the Máquinas Piratininga factory than machines built. "Guys were always being told to do their pieces too quickly. You couldn't work safely that way." According to Antônio Lombardi, "We all had something drop on us or something, but some of the companheiros were really hurt. Killed, you know."[34] Workers fought these speedups in a variety of ways (described in the next section), but during the war they often had to accept the higher production quotas. Not only was this new regime more dangerous, it robbed skilled workers of the pride they took in producing quality machines.[35]

Once again, industrialists relied on the authoritarian industrial relations system to break the bargaining power of the highly skilled

Table 4.2   Industrial Wages and the Cost of Living
in São Paulo, 1940–1945

Year	Average factory wage[a]	Real minimum wage index	Cost-of-living index
1940	1.05	98.02[b]	107[c]
1941	1.25	89.35	119
1942	1.30	80.22	132
1943	1.50	78.78	153
1944	2.00	83.19[d]	210
1945	2.00	67.03	259

Source: São Paulo to Washington, D.C., "Employment Statistics for the State of São Paulo," SP Post 850, 18 November 1944, RG 84, NA; FIESP, Relatório, 1946, 4:162; DIEESE, "Objetivos e Caraterísticas do Plano Cruzado III," 17 June 1987; and Seiti Kaneko Endo and Heron Carlos Esvael do Carmo, Breve Histórico do Indice de Preços ao Consumidor no Município de São Paulo (São Paulo: FIPE, 1985), 17.
  [a]Cruzeiros per hour. In 1942 the government changed the currency from the milreis to the cruzeiro.
  [b]This index begins with July 1940, which equals 100, but all years are calculated in October.
  [c]1939 = 100.
  [d]Vargas increased the minimum wage in 1943 for 1944.

metalúrgicos. From 1939 to 1942, employers narrowed wage differentials within this sector by granting the lower-skilled welders, smiths, and others wage gains of about 38 percent (from a low of Cr$1.27 and a high of Cr$3.20 per hour to Cr$1.75 and Cr$4.44), while skilled machinists and mechanics had quite modest wage increases of about 11 percent (Cr$1.60 and Cr$4.80 to Cr$1.77 and Cr$5.30). Increases during 1943 and 1944 averaged 10 percent for São Paulo's metalworkers.[36] Still, their wages ranked them in the top 15 percent of income for industrial workers in the city, and most factory workers not only earned less than the metalúrgicos at this time, they also suffered a severe decrease in wages in 1940, and only returned to 1939's wages in 1943. All factory workers experienced steady decreases in their real income throughout this period (table 4.2).

Many textile workers earned among the lowest wages for industrial employment in the city. Even though textile workers received nominal increases during this period (from an average of Cr$1.06 per hour in 1939 to about Cr$1.31 in 1942), their real wage rates declined during the war.[37] Foremen used their power during the dictatorship to arbitrarily reduce workers' important piece rate by finding perfect-quality cloth "flawed." When foremen chose not to exercise such control, weavers could earn wages equivalent to skilled metalworkers, but they did this through strenuous effort and long hours standing at their looms. Such work regimes led to high accident rates in the factories; in 1941, for example, São Paulo's mills reported an accident rate of 25,315 incidents per 100,000 workers. This was fifty-five times the rate suffered in Great Britain.[38] Those who produced at high levels also had to face criticism from the other weavers who sought to limit output in order to maintain some control over their work.[39]

The low average wages in the textile sector reflect the large number of women workers in the mills. Even when women gained access to traditional men's work in textiles (e.g., machinist positions in the mills), metallurgy, and other industrial establishments during the war, they continued to earn wages below those of their male counterparts. That is, regulations that forced employers to continue to pay 50 percent of workers' wages after they had been drafted (as a bonus for those who served in the armed forces) operated as an incentive for industrialists to hire women, who could not be drafted, instead of men. From 1939 to 1943, the number of women factory workers in the state of São Paulo rose from 86,745 to 213,586, and the percentage of industrial laborers who were women increased from 32.8 to 42.1 percent; this replacement of men by women increased in 1944 and 1945.[40] Even though women replaced men in many factory jobs, bosses continued to see women as auxiliary workers who were merely contributing to overall family income. Industrialists did not believe women workers needed a livable wage.[41]

These jobs were temporary, however, and women were systematically denied access to the new industrial training programs being set up by the SENAI (Serviço Nacional de Aprendizagem Industrial). Mary Cannon of the U.S. Women's Bureau noted that "the [apprenticeship] program is geared chiefly to boys, though theoretically there are opportunities for girls." Employers encouraged women workers to be ladylike at all times, Cannon explained, and "a bonus was given to a number of women [in one São Paulo city textile mill] each month for neatness and cleanliness." She added that employers maintained a structure that systematically discriminated against women workers not only by denying them advanced training but also by deliberately keeping them in the lowest-paying jobs, denying child care facilities, and having a "tendency to 'protect' women in industry with maternity and health regulations to their economic disadvantage." At the same time, these women were paid roughly 70 percent of what men received.[42] Federal regulations prohibited this practice, and many cases went to the labor courts, but no general ruling by the courts halted it. Such discrimination gravely affected the many single mothers who filled the city's factories at this time. After studying conditions in thirteen textile mills in São Paulo and Rio, Cannon sadly concluded: "There is no doubt that the large majority of women in industry work for the necessities of living—not the extras nor for economic independence. They help support the family, or are the sole wage-earners for themselves and their children. In the cotton mills especially, there was an air of indifference, of apathy; in most of these mills women and girls at the machines were poorly dressed, often barefooted."[43]

The 1936 minimum wage decree set forth a base income that was supposed to meet the necessities of food, housing, clothing, hygiene, and transportation for an individual worker (this was not a "family wage"). It also made this base equal for men and women workers. When the government finally established the first minimum wage rates in May 1940, however, it included a provision allowing employers to lower women's wages by 10 percent, which some mill owners did, supposedly to pay for nurseries and other facilities in factories. Although the Ministry of Labor closed this loophole in 1943, the minimum wage became women's wages in industry. This minimum, which was calculated by month, was Cr$220.00 for the city of São Paulo (rates varied by location according to the cost of living) in May 1940; in 1939, the average monthly income for textile workers was Cr$215.70, and metalworkers averaged about Cr$326.00. The government increased the minimum wage in January 1943 to Cr$275.00, and in May 1943 to Cr$285.00, but it continued to be a base for unskilled labor in general and semiskilled women factory workers in particular.[44] Indeed, the government did not increase the minimum wage again until January 1951. Some bosses augmented the minimum with bonuses, but these were not permanent and so did not affect the base rate used for calculating future increases.[45] Accordingly, the real minimum wage rate fell steadily in those years (table 4.2). For most workers in São Paulo, then, the only significant earnings increases during the Estado Novo came from working increased hours in the factories.

São Paulo's pelegos rarely spoke out for higher wages during the Estado Novo. The Textile Workers' Union did try to play a broker's role by privately asking Vargas for slight increases in the January 1943 minimum wage, but the directorate never attempted to mobilize its membership to push for a higher rate. Although the Metalworkers' Union discussed the rising cost of living, it actually praised the Ministry of Labor for protecting workers' earning power during the war.[46] It is perhaps appropriate that during the Estado Novo the only individuals who admitted that São Paulo's industrial workers needed higher wages were the industrialists themselves. A 1942 study of its members by the FIESP showed that 89.3 percent of those surveyed believed wages should be raised, 4.9 percent opposed increases, and 5.8 percent had no opinion.[47] It was one thing to admit that your workers needed wage increases, however, and quite another to actually grant them; these capitalists rarely increased their workers' wages. One FIESP member summed up the industrialists' denial of responsibility for their workers' predicament when he said: "I cannot understand how part of the working class can eat with the salaries they now receive. However, the increase of salaries will not resolve the situation, because, as it allows the worker to buy more food, that does not exist [in the markets], it brings an increase in prices of available goods through an increase in demand. The statistics are proving that."[48] In May 1945, FIESP president Roberto Simonsen told his colleagues that the city's workers needed immediate and significant wage increases. Simonsen understood well the problems created by the "savage capitalism" of the Estado Novo. By extracting a huge surplus from their workers with the use of the state's control over the labor market, industrialists risked destroying that labor market. Workers who did not have enough to eat certainly could not perform the rigorous duties of factory labor.[49]

With food prices climbing steadily, the city's industrialists frequently discussed workers' problems feeding themselves and their families. These industrialists knew that increases in the prices of beans, potatoes, and other basic foods had a greater impact on workers' lives than other price rises. One FIESP study showed that the average factory laborer had to work two hours just to earn enough money to pay for her or his lunch. The dangers of the lead-contaminated milk sold to workers became a public scandal in 1945.[50]

The city's industrialists had been discussing these problems since 1941, when they decided to install restaurants and food stores in their factories. They also pressured the state and federal governments to find a way to lower food costs; but prices in working-class areas continued

Table 4.3   Cost-of-Living Indexes for São Paulo,
1939–1945 (1939 = 100)

Year	Total[a]	Food	Housing	Clothing	Transportation
1939	100	100	100	100	100
1940	107	107	110	106	100
1941	119	121	114	122	100
1942	132	134	116	143	100
1943	153	153	126	183	100
1944	210	201	220	233	107
1945	259	245	270	300	115

Source: Seiti Kaneko Endo and Heron Carlos Esvael do Carmo, Breve Histórico do Índice de Preços ao Consumidor no Município de São Paulo (São Paulo: FIPE, 1985), 17–20.
[a]The total cost-of-living index was composed of thirteen areas of expenditures. The expenditures listed had the following values within the total market basket: food, 54.12%; housing, 15.33%; clothing, 10.56%; and transportation, 1.86%.

to rise (table 4.3),[51] and the city's industrialists feared the workers would rebel against these deteriorating conditions. They discussed this problem in the media and at most of their meetings during 1944 and 1945.[52] Workers, of course, talked about these price increases among themselves and sometimes complained to President Vargas about the difficulties of living on their meager wages.[53] Food prices rose so rapidly in 1944 and 1945 that even São Paulo's pelegos began to speak out against the increases. In November 1944, several of these union bosses wrote to Vargas to explain that they would not be able to control the city's industrial workers if food prices continued to rise.[54]

The physical makeup of São Paulo changed a great deal during the war, and this also affected industrial workers' lives. As the city grew, developers demolished several important working-class areas to build middle-class and luxury housing and new office complexes. This forced even more workers into basements and cortiços (tenements). Other workers had to move to the outskirts of the city, where they lived in small houses. Valêncio de Barros, who studied workers' living conditions, noted that the average worker lived in "a narrow and dark house, squeezed between neighbors, with one or two windows toward the street, filled with noise, dust, and noxious gases."[55]

FIESP members discussed the problems caused by this growth and in 1942 secured low-interest loans through the federal government for the

construction of workers' housing. The Federation of Industries estimated that ten thousand new units were needed for their workers, but
construction of that many houses during the war was impossible.
According to the U.S. consul: "The working man's housing problem, in
view of the general shortage and very high prices of construction
materials, seems to be insoluble at present or before the end of the
war . . . brings back to normal level the cost of land."[56]

These changes in housing patterns exacerbated transportation problems for the city's workers. About 900,000 Paulistanos commuted by
public transportation (600,000 by trolley and 300,000 by bus) during
the war years. Shortages of fuel and spare parts for the vehicles kept
over one-third of the buses and many of the trolleys idle. Although
public transportation remained inexpensive, it became so unreliable
that textile industrialists began providing buses for some workers.
According to one mill owner: "There are thousands of working men
living in the suburbs who . . . must get up in the early morning hours
and travel often for hours in crowded, slow, and dirty vehicles."[57] A
popular samba from 1941 illustrates how transportation problems com-
pounded the misery caused by the almost limitless power of bosses
during the Estado Novo. The samba recounts an employee's pleading
with his foreman after being fired for lateness:

> Boss, the train was late . . .
> That's why I'm getting here now
> Here is the Central's certificate
> The train was half an hour late
> You have no right
> To dismiss me!
> You must have patience
> You must understand
> I've always been obedient
> One delay is justified
> If there is reason
> I'm the head of a family
> I need the bread
> Don't say no.[58]

These problems brought on by the Estado Novo, the war, and the
industrial expansion in São Paulo had a clear and negative impact on
the lives of the city's workers, and they seem to have affected women

workers more severely than men. During the war, their homework as seamstresses increased, and the daily struggle to shelter, feed, and clothe their families forced many women weavers to take on extra work. Single mothers who worked in the mills often lived in cortiços or basements, both near the textile factories of Brás and Mooca as well as in outlying areas. Families commonly had to sleep, cook, and eat in one or two rooms, and bathing facilities were more than likely communal. One social worker in the city remarked that the inhabitants of these quarters "lead the life of animals and, at the same time, struggle in our industries, where their work is profitable [for the industrialists]."[59] Many single mothers worked unbearably long hours and then returned to the cortiços and basements to feed their waiting children: "It's common to see, near the factory exits, women workers with containers [marmitas], [buying their children's dinner] in unscrupulous establishments, that make food without any nutritional value. The question that time and again I asked, had the following answer: 'I don't have time to prepare food, so every day I buy it made,' and so thousands of workers and children pass the years eating and sleeping poorly in basements."[60] Those who escaped the dangers of these living conditions moved to the city's outlying areas, even though getting to and from the mills from there might entail leaving home at 4:00 or 5:00 in the morning, walking several miles to the suburban train stations, and arriving home around 10:00 at night.

The shortages of food most directly preoccupied women, who had the primary responsibility for feeding their families. One foreign observer noted in March 1944 that "the endless queues which one sees day after day in front of butcher shops, milk distribution depots, etc., etc., are a source of constant irritation. Housewives and servants spend hours daily standing in line, and criticism of President Vargas and the Government is so widespread that it is affecting his popularity with the masses."[61] The war also brought important changes in the system of food distribution. The public markets still operated, but chain grocery and drug stores captured an increasing portion of retail sales. While these chains sometimes charged lower prices, they also made the lives of women factory workers more difficult. Chain stores did not provide credit, which severely hampered the buying power of working-class families that traditionally depended on such arrangements. One social worker in São Paulo noted that mothers who worked in the mills had to rely on women neighbors who did not work outside the home to care for their children and do much of their shopping on accounts.[62]

Worker Survival and Resistance during the Estado Novo

Workers' Appeals to the "Father of the Poor"

From the time they first entered São Paulo's factories in the late nineteenth century, and through the mid-1930s, the city's industrial workers employed a wide variety of survival and resistance strategies to ameliorate the harsh conditions they faced. As I discussed earlier, the Estado Novo effectively destroyed the fledgling independent union movement in São Paulo; then, Brazil's entry into the war furthered the authoritarian atmosphere of the industrial relations system. Without access to independent unions, the city's workers had to rely on other tools of survival and resistance.[63] Within the world of their own culture, workers continued to write and sing protest sambas. And when frustration with life in São Paulo reached a fever pitch, workers rioted. In early February 1945, after changes in trolley schedules caused many to arrive late at work and at home, for example, hundreds of workers smashed and burned all the trolleys they could find in the Largo Sete de Setembro.[64] And finally, as they had since the first days of industrialization, workers simply left the city for the rural sector when they found the conditions in the factories intolerable.[65]

The Estado Novo and the war created several new tools for workers in their survival struggles. Women wrote directly to Vargas seeking aid for their families. Enedina Cesar de Oliveira Fernandes of the Barra Funda neighborhood wrote explaining that she had to work in the factory in order to support her children because her husband could not provide a steady income. Like many women who wrote, she specifically invoked Vargas's standing as "the protector of the poor" and requested that the federal government help her send a few of her six children to private school. Working women knew that the only way their children could avoid the mills was through such an education. Paula Martins Galvão, a single mother who lived in Bela Vista section of the city, asked Vargas to help her send the eldest of her four children to school. This, she told the dictator, was the only way to pull her family out of poverty.[66] In fact, women wrote the vast majority of the petitions for help with children's education.[67] Women workers also wrote seeking protection for their neighborhoods in the face of the great upheaval of the Estado Novo and war years. Some sought paved roads or restrictions on night work, and others denounced greedy landlords.[68]

These petitions demonstrate the complex interplay between official rhetoric and those at whom it was aimed. This is clear in the letter workers in the Bosque da Saude neighborhood wrote, complaining to Vargas that São Paulo's development was leaving them behind:

> The majority of the population of our neighborhood has few resources, Mr. President, but we are a hardworking people with the ability to earn our daily bread [and] we deserve the minimum comfort of a paved road in order to get to work.
>
> In return for the loyalty of Brazilian workers, we now have a Government that has for ten years defended and worked for those workers. . . .
>
> [And while downtown development has come at the expense of the working-class areas] . . . we don't want in any way to criticize any act of our Mayor for this! We are simply expressing our point of view. We believe in "dynamism" and "results," only we would now like to see a little more equal distribution, for example also in our neighborhood. . . .
>
> We hope Your Excellency will recognize the justice of our requests.[69]

Like others who wrote to Vargas, these residents geared their appeal to Vargas's rhetoric. They implicitly (and sometimes explicitly) offered their support to the dictator in exchange for his intervention on their behalf. Workers' children also learned to petition Vargas for help. Their teachers and parents helped them put their letters into a form that would appeal to the "father of the poor." Maria Yolanda Pugliesi of the Cambuci neighborhood, no doubt with the help of her teacher, wrote a revealing letter to the president worth quoting at length:

> I would like to present myself: I am a girl of eleven years and a Brazilian, thank God. I am in the fourth level in the Campos Sales school. . . .
>
> At the end of this year, God willing, I will finish the primary course. Last Wednesday, my teacher asked me if I wanted to continue my studies. "Naturally, yes, Dona Josefina," was my answer. She then asked me what I would want to do [with my education]. I answered I very much wanted to be a teacher, in order to teach other little girls and boys, and because I once overheard my father say that a great number of Brazilian children grow up illiterate. I think it's very bad that a girl or a boy would not know how to read or write.
>
> [Because my parents cannot afford my schooling] . . . Dona Josefina told me I should write a little letter to Dr. Getúlio Vargas, who is

considered the father of all the children of Brazil, telling him what is happening with me and asking for his support.

That is why I am writing these lines to you. Certainly, I will not be disappointed, isn't that right Senhor Getúlio? I want to be a teacher and I think that, yes, you will help me with my studies . . . [and] you will not only help me, but all of Brazil in this way. You will profit because you will have one more assistant in the fight against illiteracy. . . . Father and Mother will be very thankful, and so will I, and this way your government will have even more support.[70]

Vargas responded to these letters by ordering local authorities to investigate, and many worthy petitioners received some level of financial assistance.[71] The impact of this interplay was significant. Workers found an important resource in the president's rhetoric, and Vargas began to accumulate goodwill among Brazil's working class.[72] While such assistance reached only a handful of workers, everyone in a given neighborhood or factory heard of a neighbor's or friend's good fortune.[73]

Women workers also complained to Vargas about the police in São Paulo. Wanda Matuleonina told Vargas she was being harassed by a man in her neighborhood, but that the police would not look into this for her. Maria Rodrigues told the president that the police were harassing her. Again, these and other letters appealed to Vargas as the champion of the working class. Further, the women understood well that Vargas sought to limit the power of local institutions in his drive to integrate Brazil. They had also heard Vargas's and Minister of Labor Marcondes Filho's frequent appeals for working-class support for the war effort and their promises of an open and just society after the war. So São Paulo's workers used these letters to push the dictator to fulfill his promises of increased social justice for all Brazilians, especially since the official corporatist structure was doing so little to improve their lives.[74]

Women textile workers did not limit their protests to family and neighborhood issues. They used a variety of resources to limit the increasing exploitation forced on them by mill owners and foremen. Sometimes they operated within the official industrial relations structure and filed processos against foremen's fines or for some benefits offered by the state, but the vast majority of these women workers were not members of the Textile Workers' Union.[75] Accordingly, the most common form of resistance to the worsening life in the mills was absenteeism. Even though mill owners and the government developed harsh punishments for absent textile workers, weavers simply stayed away from the factories when they needed a break. These women also violated the wartime ban on changing jobs, which they likened to a form of slavery, and fled from low pay when they could. Rather than attempt to discipline the thousands of weavers who regularly stayed away from work or changed jobs, most textile firms offered a system of bonuses over the prevailing wage rate to workers who maintained good attendance records. Weavers used their presence in or absence from the mills as a tool for increasing their earnings.[76]

Workers who stayed in dangerous or demeaning work environments for the high wages often turned to the "father of the poor" for assistance. Workers who did not want to join the union often appealed directly to Vargas for help with bureaucratic matters.[77] A group of fourteen women glassworkers at the Campanhia Vidraria Santa Marina, for example, protested against their low pay by writing to the president. They told him that most of them were single mothers or women whose husbands were physically unable to work. So, these women reasoned, they should receive the same wages men in their factory earned.[78] Durvalina Camargo, who lived in the Lapa area, did not work outside the home, but she wrote to Vargas complaining that textile shops and the state Department of Labor were conspiring to limit the protections the president had promised to the working class. She described the sweatshops where young women she knew worked long hours at miserable wages and begged Vargas, as the protector of all workers, to intervene to guarantee that the labor laws be upheld. She further complained that state investigators were paid by industrialists to ignore code violations.[79] Durvalina Camargo knew exactly how to pique Vargas's interest. The president's concerns about Paulista elites dated back to the 1930s, and beginning with the 1932 civil war workers learned to play local industrialists and the federal government against each other.[80]

These women displayed great courage in writing their letters. They appealed directly to the president of Brazil and openly denounced powerful men, from their bosses to city and state officials. And of these women, none showed more courage than Júlia Antônia Walhiamos, a young worker in a sock factory. In early 1943 she wrote to Vargas about the sexual harassment she suffered from her foreman. She told the president that her boss often directed to her "improper proposals [that were] inconceivable for a poor girl, who is in fact honorable and moral." She added that he had threatened her job. Júlia Antônia continued: "[My boss said] I would stay in the job, if I satisfied his sexual desires just once." He also threatened to transfer her to a part of the factory where only men worked, "in jobs not fitting for a woman."[81] When she refused her foreman, he lowered her wages (Júlia Antônia sent copies of her pay envelopes to Vargas as proof of this), and then he fired her.

She first went to the state Department of Labor, but its inspectors took the word of her boss at face value. She managed to get her job back, but at the reduced rate. Moreover, she still had to work with the foreman who had harassed her and then demonstrated the full extent of his power over her. She wrote to Vargas to get some of the protection that he had promised his government would provide to workers. The president responded by ordering an investigation. Unfortunately, it was conducted by the state Department of Labor. The inspectors found that her wages did, in fact, drop from Cr$425.10 in March 1942 to Cr$301.40 in April 1942, but they found no substantive evidence that this was done as punishment by her foreman. That is, the investigators from the state Department of Labor, who were, of course, men who had regular interactions with factory owners and foremen, believed the foreman and decided that Júlia Antônia was lying. They did not, however, manage to explain why her wages dropped so dramatically (27 percent) in one month. The government did decide to pay her the cost (Cr$98.20, or about one-third of her new monthly wage) of filing an official processo against her foreman. Although she lost, Júlia Antônia's case demonstrates the lengths to which some women workers in São Paulo went to use the federal government and Vargas's rhetoric to press for social justice. Many weavers experienced sexual harassment, and the dictator's rhetoric became one more potential resource for their struggles to limit the power of foremen.

At first glance, these letters to Vargas seem to point to the atomization of São Paulo's working class: unable to go to their co-opted unions for relief, workers took matters into their own hands, one situation at a time. Such was not really the case, though. While individuals sought assistance and attempted to manipulate the Estado Novo through direct appeals to the president, women continued to organize in informal groups, many of which became clandestine factory commissions in the mills. Women felt at ease discussing sexual harassment, problems making ends meet, and other issue with their companheiras, but these were not issues they wanted to bring before the male-dominated unions. If a nursery had been installed, for example, women would meet there, where they could talk without the interference of men. Often, older women (some only in their late twenties were considered veterans) used the protection afforded by their seniority, as well as their longer experience in dealing with foremen, to put together these *comissões*.[82] In early June 1944, such groups organized a very effective consumer strike; they distributed handbills and advised workers to boycott certain stores.[83]

Further, workers' letters to Vargas clearly demonstrate that neither their rural origins nor the propaganda of the Estado Novo had obscured the consciousness of these workers.[84] When Odette Pasquini discussed Vargas and his "populist appeal," she noted that the president's policies more often than not helped industrialists, not working people: "Vargas, oh he was the 'father of the poor,' as they used to say on the radio, but of course he was truly the mother of the rich!"[85] Her comment is a perceptive one, and it demonstrates that workers did not simply accept what Vargas and his propaganda machine said about the government and its programs. The harsh realities of their lives were constant reminders that conditions had not measurably improved during the Estado Novo.

That is not to say that all Brazilian workers saw the situation perfectly clearly. Many no doubt truly believed that Vargas had their best interests in mind. Antônio Gonçalves de Andrade, who had been fired from his job as a metalworker in 1922, petitioned Vargas twenty years later for help getting his old position back.[86] Antônio Rizzo of Mooca wrote to Vargas in 1943 asking the dictator's permission to become a street vendor. An industrial accident prohibited him from heavy work, so even though selling popcorn on the street was not the sort of work Vargas spoke about men doing, he told the dictator he had to do it: "I am a man and I am ashamed of not working."[87] No one in the federal or state government could determine exactly why Rizzo had written to Vargas, for he asked for nothing from him. Rizzo, it seems, only wanted to explain why he was not living up to Vargas's expectations of "manhood," as defined by work.

The prevalence of factory commissions among workers in São Paulo's larger industrial establishments helps explain why a weaver like Odette Pasquini had such a clear view of Vargas while men such as Antônio Gonçalves de Andrade and Antônio Rizzo had more faith in Vargas's desire and ability to improve their lives. The commissions provided an important social space to articulate critiques of the industrial relations system. Older experienced workers used this social space to pass their historical memory along to new arrivals in the factories. The commissions also served as informal institutions for disciplining workers who wanted to participate in the government's industrial relations system or foremen's production speedups. So, popular opposition to the pelegos and the Estado Novo's harsh conditions did not by themselves encourage Paulistano factory workers to maintain their own independent organizations; it was the factory commissions' own internal politics that kept workers out of the sindicatos. It is important to note that at times commission members could be quite coercive. Just because all the people in a given *comissão* worked in the same section of a factory, they did not necessarily share the same perspectives on wage demands, relations with foremen, when to strike, and other issues.[88] But participation in a commission did lead its members to articulate collective positions regarding their bosses, the state, the sindicatos, and so forth. In the final analysis, then, São Paulo's legacy of independent rank-and-file factory-level organizing, along with the shared experience of increasing misery among factory workers during the Estado Novo, explains why so many of the city's industrial workers approached Vargas so skeptically at this time.[89]

Vargas responded to workers' independent organizing and letters by decreeing several wage increases and bonus schemes. In early 1942, the federal government instituted a 10 percent bonus for all textile workers. The Textile Workers' Union had not lobbied for these increases— individual weavers did with their letters to Vargas.[90] During 1943 the federal government and employers responded to workers' petitions and organizing by freezing some food prices, providing bonuses for workers supporting large families (the *abono familiar*), and twice raising the minimum wage. Thus, industrialists did increase workers' take-home pay at this time, but these hikes did not keep pace with inflation.[91]

Resistance by metalworkers likewise came to Vargas's attention. Like the weavers, they wrote directly to the president. Interestingly, metalúrgicos' letters were most often concerned with work issues and with how foremen's and employers' interference in shop-floor activities affected their lives in the factories. Male metalworkers sometimes petitioned Vargas for help with the rapidly increasing cost of living, but more often they relied on women to deal with such issues.[92] In most of their complaints about work, these metalworkers accused the state government of siding with the industrialists. They pointed out that the state Department of Labor was deliberately blocking the implementation of the dictator's labor code. This, the metalworkers reminded Vargas, kept a wedge between him and the majority of working people in São Paulo. As Antônio de Carvalho stated: "The Department of Labor of the state of São Paulo continues as only a formality, and is completely outside the program [of labor laws] for which it was created, and so it still follows the traditional system of the Old Republic. That is, it is completely at odds with . . . the wishes of Dr. Getúlio Vargas with regard to the employers and workers of São Paulo. . . . The Department of Labor of the state of São Paulo [does little] to defend your laws because the capitalists in São Paulo continue to control everything."[93] Other workers wrote of the high profits industrialists were taking at the expense of the city's workers, while still others complained about the dangerous work conditions created by greedy employers who opposed the president's labor laws.[94] Antônio Urbano, who was in the midst of a dispute with General Motors do Brasil, went so far as to tell Vargas he felt "humiliated" by his employer's treatment. This, he asserted, was not the way workers were supposed to be treated under Vargas's rule.[95]

Some metalúrgicos took this strategy one step further by specifically denouncing individual foremen and employers as Axis sympathizers and/or opponents of Vargas. Hundreds of workers, individually and in groups, used this device to harass their foremen during the war, but the denunciations by São Paulo's metalworkers seem to have caused the most extensive investigations by the DOPS and other government agencies.[96] When, for example, twenty workers at Cia Brasileira de Mineração e Metalúrgica in São Caetano (an industrial suburb of the city) wrote to Vargas complaining that the management of their firm ignored the labor code and harbored pro-Axis sympathies, the federal government immediately investigated. During the investigation, several metalworkers denounced the furnace foreman as an opponent of Vargas and a supporter of Italy. After several long visits to the factory, federal investigators determined that neither the foreman nor management was pro-Axis; indeed, they concluded the workers specifically denounced certain bosses because they had implemented speedups of the work regime. They also found that with the establishment operating twenty-four hours per day, workers slept during their breaks and seemed to live in the factory. The firm's management explained that they needed to maintain high production levels and promised the investigators they would improve work conditions soon.[97]

Other denunciations also singled out foremen who had recently intensified work regimes. Workers in a shop at São Paulo Light, which made and ran the trolleys, complained that their foreman's actions "lowered national morale and reduced [workers] to humiliating and dangerous conditions." They appealed to Vargas as nationalists who supported the Estado Novo and Brazil's participation in the war.[98] These denunciations were a powerful tool of resistance for São Paulo's metalworkers, for they brought investigations not only of the political orientation of bosses, but also of conditions in the factories. Several such denunciations even led to the imprisonment of foremen.[99] Ultimately, then, these workers learned to use the repressive tools of the regime to their advantage; they punished bosses for harsh work regimes by turning the authoritarian nature of the Estado Novo back on them.

Collective Resistance: Workers Organize Themselves

Women textile workers used factory commissions to coordinate their various survival and resistance strategies. São Paulo's metalworkers, who trusted neither Vargas nor their co-opted union, also organized independent comissões to press for higher wages and safer work conditions. Metalúrgicos met outside their factories at lunch to put together commissions and develop ties between groups from various shops. Conrado de Papa recalled, "Vargas arrived [in São Paulo] on May Day as our 'father,' but he was just working for the rich," so Papa and his colleagues organized. Hermento Mendes Dantas supported the independent comissão because it was the "first line of defense on the shop floor."[100] Only independent organizing provided a viable means for fighting the increasingly harsh work routines. Antônio Lombardi and Geraldo Pascolato recalled that several companheiros who worked as mechanics at Máquinas Piratininga would walk about the shop floor fixing equipment and talking about the commissions. They and others who belonged to the union, such as Francisco da Silva, supported the independent organizing but did not openly work with the organizers out of fear of the DOPS.[101]

The city's metalworkers had been organizing independently since the late 1910s. Paulistano metalworkers crafted and maintained a fairly representative and radical union in the 1920s and early 1930s because they did not experience the same divisions between their leadership cadre and the rank and file that the city's women textile workers had to endure. Accordingly, they did not rely as exclusively on an informal factory commission structure as did women factory workers. The pelegos' control of the Metalworkers' Union during the Estado Novo, however, encouraged them to develop such local, independent groupings. São Paulo metalworkers began to organize such factory commissions in larger factories (e.g., Sofunge, Máquinas Piratininga, Aços Finos, and others), and workers in smaller establishments organized within their shops' neighborhoods. These metalworkers chose to organize commissions not only because metalúrgicos had done so in the past, but also because they had seen and heard of the success of the women's comissões, especially those in textile mills. Many Paulistano metalworkers had started off in the textile sector or had wives, sisters, mothers, or other kin working in the mills. Male metalworkers decided to rely on factory commissions during the Estado Novo in part because they had learned of the comissões' importance through both direct experience in the mills and through kinship ties to female textile workers.[102]

Metalworkers' comissões tried to improve conditions on the shop floor by denouncing foremen and organizing slowdowns in which several key plant sections limited overall production.[103] When this failed, metalúrgicos turned to sabotage. Rather than breaking machinery, these skilled workers cleverly altered their products so that they would not function properly. Metalworkers used inferior or improper materials and passed nonworking parts and machines through the quality control sections. Waldemar Clemente's factory came to a standstill after a large number of the electric motors produced there were found to be defective because workers had substituted colored iron for the copper needed to maintain electrical conductivity. Clemente admitted that his workers could not survive on the meager wages they earned, but he offered them inexpensive foodstuffs as a solution rather than paying them more; the sabotage continued.[104] Industrialists in the city were obviously quite troubled by this, and the FIESP worked closely with the São Paulo secretary of public security and Department of Labor to combat it. They even installed a direct telephone line so owners could register acts of sabotage in the factories and call in DOPS officials to investigate. When they could determine who had performed the sabotage, the industrialists had the guilty workers jailed.[105]

While the DOPS furnished the immediate response to sabotage in the metallurgy industry, the Federation of Industries and the government also created a long-term strategy of supplying highly skilled workers who would not commit such acts. During the war they created the SENAI to train workers for the skilled trades and to indoctrinate them into being "conscientious" and "loyal" in the factories. The SENAI's purpose was to provide desperately needed workers who would use their skills according to industrialists' orders.[106]

An Experiment with "Populism"

Throughout the early 1940s, Getúlio Vargas and his closest advisers discussed their prospects for continued rule. Brazil's participation in the war against fascism in Europe, along with the regime's rhetoric about democracy and citizenship, had heightened expectations of a turn to open politics soon after the war. In 1942 and 1943, Vargas and Minister of Labor Marcondes Filho struggled to find ways to use the Estado Novo's union structure as the basis for a postdictatorship political party. They quickly realized, however, that the elaborate corporatist structure was an empty façade throughout most of Brazil and would be of limited help in mobilizing political support. Ministry of Labor research in the late 1930s revealed that there were more unionized workers in the Federal District alone than in the rest of Brazil, including the industrial heartland of São Paulo. And over 90 percent of the unionized workers throughout Brazil were men.[107]

As they considered their options for operating within a democratic framework, Vargas and Marcondes Filho moved to bolster the sindicatos. Their first step was to admit that the existing union structure was an empty shell without large-scale popular participation. Their next move was to lure workers into the state-run sindicatos by offering thorough benefits and improved work conditions.[108] Vargas attempted to accomplish this by finally creating bureaucratic institutions within the Ministry of Labor to encourage unionization and the extension of social benefits. These measures had a limited immediate impact, for the new labor bureaucrats needed time to reach rank-and-file workers; these new activists within the Ministry of Labor in Rio also recognized that the existing union leaders were an impediment to this unionization campaign. The Ministry of Labor hoped to bring workers into the sindicatos by training the government unionists to be more effective leaders and by expelling some of the pelegos. The government in Rio even convinced the National Confederation of Industries to instruct its members to hire unionized workers before those who were not sindicalizados.[109]

Vargas initiated a full-fledged "unionization campaign" in April

1943, and then released a comprehensive labor code (Consolidação das Leis do Trabalho, CLT) in May 1943 as a symbol of his commitment to the consolidation of the many types of protection he had promised the working class.[110] The Ministry of Labor encouraged pelegos to bring in as many new members as possible. Vargas's efforts to increase union membership were initially opposed by the pelegos, who had a vested interest in maintaining small, unrepresentative unions. Their opposition eventually forced Vargas to offer them cash rewards for increases in their membership. With such an incentive the Textile Workers' and Metalworkers' unions of São Paulo achieved modest gains in membership.[111]

In general, though, these changes within the labor bureaucracy had little impact in São Paulo. There were no major changes in the leadership of the textile and metallurgical workers' unions, and the state Department of Labor continued to run the industrial relations system.[112] But the rank and file in São Paulo responded to the rhetoric of a more open industrial relations system by initiating several modest strike movements. Beginning in early 1944, metalworkers pushed for higher wages; in May glassworkers struck, in September street cleaners walked out, and finally, in late 1944 and early 1945, textile workers' factory commissions demanded wage hikes and shorter hours. All these strikers received some portion of their demands through direct bargaining with employers, as both bosses and strikers ignored the elaborate industrial relations system of the Estado Novo.[113]

As the war came to an end, the political space created by Vargas grew. Editorial writers in São Paulo began to openly challenge the Estado Novo and the high profits industrialists extracted from the city's workers. They even linked such practices to the Integralists, and thus to fascism. These practices would end only with the opening of politics to all, according to the press and Vargas's elite political opponents in São Paulo.[114] Then, Brazil's representatives at the Inter-American Conference at Chapultepec, Mexico, publicly supported workers' right to strike. They admitted that this ran counter to the ideology of the Estado Novo but proclaimed that times had changed. With the end of the war in Europe, Paulistanos spoke out for freedom for all and the right to strike.[115]

Throughout 1945 Vargas continued to woo São Paulo's workers by limiting and then relaxing Ministry of Labor control over the unions. Such a tilt toward workers entailed more than simply loosening corporatist control of the unions; it also required changing the balance of power in the tripartite labor courts.[116] In the past, Ministry of Labor representatives on the court almost always sided with industry representatives in ruling against workers' processos. Vargas had great leeway in appointments to the labor courts, however, and could influence the behavior of the ministry's attorneys (procuradores da justiça do trabalho). Accordingly, the labor courts supported a higher percentage of workers' claims in 1945 than in any previous year. Indeed, several unionists who served on São Paulo's Regional Labor Tribunal confirmed that the ministry's representatives have traditionally been swayed by national political considerations.[117]

São Paulo's battered Communist party took advantage of the political openness and quickly created the United Workers' Movement (Movimento Unificador dos Trabalhadores, MUT) in April 1945 to act as an alternative to the co-opted unions. After a decade of intense repression, the Communist party had emerged as a new organization made up of young militants who concentrated their efforts on organizing workers rather than planning a quixotic revolutionary putsch.[118] Luís Firmino de Lima, a weaver who joined the partidão in 1944, recalled, "We young guys weren't concerned with party issues, we were more interested in union matters."[119] These young militants had a lot of work to do with the comissões and other workers' groups to gain their support in 1945, because the Communist party had been backing the Vargas regime (as part of the "Popular Front") and had maintained a "no strike" pledge during the war. Luís Firmino and his colleagues had a difficult time convincing textile workers to follow the MUT, which observed the PCB line of supporting Vargas and opposing strikes. The MUT even launched an antistrike push called the "Tighten Your Belt" campaign. João Amazonas, the MUT's president, appropriated the regime's and industrialists' rhetoric when he discussed the rank and file's strikes, claiming that some of them "were incited by agentes provacadores."[120] The MUT and other progressive groups did, however, organize some protests on May Day. While the pelegos, federal and state government officials, and representatives of industry gathered at the Municipal Theater to praise the Estado Novo's industrial relations system, opposition groups gathered at the Rua do Carmo off the Praça da Sé to call for freedom of the press, open elections, amnesty for political prisoners, and the right to strike.[121]

Industrial workers closely followed these and other developments, and several comissões organized successful sitdown strikes. Then, on 12 May 1945, again through their factory commissions, weavers at

Crespi struck for higher wages and improved work conditions. Workers in mill after mill throughout the city followed this lead. Soon, strikes paralyzed the textile industry. The city's glassworkers followed, and then the metalúrgicos.[122] At first, industrialists attempted to stand firm by having strikers arrested. Women, who operated through their own factory commissions, were beaten by police on picket lines and arrested.[123] In one week alone, workers at 365 firms in the city struck. The Paulistano bourgeoisie feared these strikes would evolve into a sort of class war. Many of the city's large wholesalers even took out riot insurance policies in May and June. Faced with such popular effervescence, the industrialists moved to defuse the independent organizing and bargained directly with the pelegos.[124]

The pelegos quickly recognized their tenuous position and moved to take control of the strike movement from the factory commissions. Officials from the Textile Workers' Union met with industrialists and signed an accord based on the increases bargained for by some of the city's comissões. Industrialists and the unionists met along with interventor Fernando Costa at the Palácio dos Campos Elíseos to sign the accord and praise each other for the high spirit of cooperation.[125] With more than ten thousand of the city's metalworkers out and the labor courts jammed with potential wage settlements, many industrialists in this sector negotiated directly with factory commissions. Pelegos worked with the FIESP to put together a generalized wage accord that would defuse the situation, return the strikers to work, and reclaim their leadership role of the Metalworkers' Union.[126]

The strike produced wage increases of 10 to 40 percent, depending on a worker's base wage, with the lowest paid receiving the greatest percentage gains and the highest paid the lowest percentage increases. The Federation of Industries moved to generalize these increases for glass, wood, pharmaceutical, and ceramic workers, brewers, hatters, and others who remained out.[127] Industrialists knew their workers needed significant wage increases in order to live in the inflationary São Paulo of the 1940s. The FIESP's desire to negotiate a quick settlement also demonstrated industrialists' support of the Estado Novo's industrial relations system. That is, employers feared that workers had gained too much power when individual firms signed accords with factory commissions. FIESP members therefore tried to bolster the pelegos by signing wage settlements with them like those hammered out by the comissões. They hoped this move would reinforce the industrial relations system, which had provided social peace and inexpensive labor.

They then publicly praised those pelegos as great champions of São Paulo's working class.[128] In 1946, the Federation of Industries wrote to President Dutra explaining how its members had settled the May 1945 strikes specifically to limit the power of these factory commissions and to bolster the position of the pelegos. Many factory owners even created company-controlled factory commissions in the wake of the May strike wave.[129] The industrialists took such measures in the face of continued worker mobilizations as the Estado Novo seemed to be coming to an end. Indeed, fears of further overtures by Vargas to the working class helped bring about the dictator's ouster at the hands of sectors of the military closely tied to the industrial bourgeoisie.[130]

The militance of the workers' 1945 strike movement highlights the ultimate weakness of Vargas's industrial relations system. The Estado Novo and wartime measures effectively destroyed the independent union movement in São Paulo, but they could not end workers' grassroots organizing. The factory commissions that textile and metallurgical workers had formed to fight harsh conditions on the shop floor, bargain for higher wages, and combat high rents and food costs in their neighborhoods continued to be their most effective tool for survival and resistance. Without access to sympathetic unions and with the Ministry of Labor being run in São Paulo by the state Department of Labor, workers and their comissões were forced to appeal directly to Vargas for support.

So, although the Estado Novo provided the framework for a deepening of industrial development and national integration, it did not co-opt or control all of São Paulo's industrial working class. Indeed, textile and metallurgical workers' resistance to the authoritarian and corporatist system disrupted the linear process of development envisioned by Vargas and his industrialist allies.[131] Further, workers' reactions to the Estado Novo, Brazil's participation in World War II, and the regime's rhetoric of conciliation, national integration, and social justice for all initiated a national debate—part of which would be played out with the writing of a new constitution in 1946—on the question of citizenship. Workers took Vargas's words at face value and began to demand their share of the wealth they were creating. At first, workers wrote humble requests to the dictator, and they clearly thanked Vargas for the rights he had "given" them.[132] Then, with the initial opening of the political system in 1944–45, São Paulo's industrial workers asserted themselves and struck in the face of their bosses' intransigence.

The playing out of the Estado Novo and World War II did not just push industrialization forward; it created new terms for workers' struggles for full and equal participation in Brazilian society. The expansion of the national Ministry of Labor and the government-controlled union structure, rather than co-opting and manipulating workers' consciousness, provided a new arena for this struggle. Over the course of the war São Paulo's workers had sacrificed much: they suffered long hours in their factories, declining real wages, and repressive politics. The state Department of Labor continued to represent the federal Ministry of Labor in São Paulo, and the workers' unions were still under the control of the pelegos. Paulistano workers looked forward to the promised opening up of politics and the eventual impact of Vargas's recent changes in the Ministry of Labor. Perhaps after the war São Paulo's working men and women would finally gain access to the social justice so often promised and so brutally denied during the Estado Novo.

The Industrialists' Democracy
in São Paulo, 1945–1950

We organized ourselves. After all, we fought World War II, Brazilians died for the war, we worked like slaves for the war. Good, now we had a democracy, so we organized and asked for what was ours.

—Metalworker Edson Borges,
interview, 25 September 1987

Men make their own history, but they do not make it just as they please; they do not make it under circumstances chosen by themselves, but under circumstances directly encountered, given and transmitted from the past.

—Karl Marx,
The Eighteenth Brumaire of Louis Bonaparte

On the morning of 1 August 1947, São Paulo's workers found that the Municipal Transportation Company had increased bus and trolley fares from Cr$0.60 to Cr$1.00 and Cr$0.20 to Cr$0.50, respectively. Paulistanos violently rejected the fare hikes, even though transportation costs after the increases averaged less than 2.5 percent of their total monthly expenditures. During lunch breaks, industrial workers and others who relied on mass transit began discussing the fare hikes. Workers angrily denounced the constant stream of bad news affecting them and then decided to start rocking the buses lined up in the Praça da Sé, Praça Patriarca, and Largo de São Francisco. A group of workers broke up the cobblestone streets and hurled rocks at buses and trolleys. As the crowds grew, people began shouting *"quebra-quebra"* (smash-smash). The Paulistanos broke apart and burned four hundred trolleys and forty-five buses, concentrating their efforts on the trolleys that served the factory districts. The rioters next turned their attention to Governor Adhemar de Barros and decided to punish him for betraying the city's working class. Carrying stones and planks of wood pulled from the trolleys, they marched through a cold rain to nearby city and state government buildings. There they broke windows and ransacked first-floor offices. The rioters burned everything they could pull from the buildings. By 5:00 P.M. cavalry troops had managed to regain control of the city, for most of the rioters had walked home after destroying all the trolleys and buses they could find.[1]

Paulistano workers rioted out of frustration. The promise of full citizenship in Brazil's post–Estado Novo democracy had proved false. After suffering through Vargas's dictatorial regime, São Paulo's industrial workers looked forward to exercising their rights as citizens in the democracy that began in late 1945, and to enjoying the increased social justice such citizenship promised. The years immediately following the ouster of Vargas in October 1945 held many contradictions for Brazil's working people. In politics, their new republic offered a presidential contest between two military men who had supported the dictatorship (General Eurico Dutra of the army and Partido Social Democrático [PSD] defeated Air Marshal Eduardo Gomes of the União Democrática Nacional [UDN]). At the same time, Luís Carlos Prestes of the PCB publicly embraced Vargas, the man who had deported his Jewish wife and their unborn child to Germany, where they ended up in a Nazi concentration camp. Later, politicians such as Adhemar de Barros exacerbated this frustration by abandoning the city's workers after making electoral promises of support. In the unions, pelegos maintained their close ties to industrialists and the state. Industrialists and their allies in the federal and state governments worked more closely than ever before to thwart their workers' organizing and protest activities. To São Paulo's workers, therefore, Dutra's administration represented a return to the harshest days of the Estado Novo.

The Dutra years also brought important physical changes to São Paulo. The city continued to expand, and a growing number of workers moved to outlying neighborhoods, where their dependence on the deteriorating transportation system increased.[2] Further, Paulistano industrialists rationalized production in their factories in the postwar years. The introduction of new automated machinery in the textile mills and changes in work regimes in all industries further frustrated São Paulo's workers. The quebra-quebra of August 1947 was as much a protest against the status quo in politics and changes in factory regimes as it was a protest against the fare increases. Paulistanos turned to smashing and burning trolleys and buses because the city's industrialists and their allies in the state and federal government had successfully limited their access to the political system.[3]

The Democratic Moment

For São Paulo's industrial workers, the Estado Novo effectively ended with their successful strike movement in May 1945. Although the dictatorship remained intact, the dictator, Vargas, was struggling to recast himself as a populist leader in an open society. Workers' resistance during the Estado Novo, especially during the war years, created the opportunity for Vargas to turn to Paulistano laborers for political support. The city's industrialists understood this dynamic and countered by moving to establish more open relations with various representatives of the working class. In addition to bolstering the weak position of the pelegos during the April and May strikes, FIESP members also met with female and male members of factory commissions from textile mills and metallurgy shops in the months following the strike wave. The opening of Brazilian society that accompanied the defeat of fascism in Europe further encouraged FIESP leaders to loosen the confines of the corporatist industrial relations system. Textile and metallurgy establishments negotiated directly with the comissões in May 1945, and in early 1946 Roberto Simonsen, Egon Felix Gottschalk, and other industrialists endorsed workers' right to strike.[4]

Workers' increasing confidence during the first half of 1945 forced the pelegos to open their unions a bit. After initially opposing the strike movement, leaders of both the Textile Workers' Union and the Metalworkers' Union moved to integrate the strike leaders into the sindicatos. In May, pelegos in the Metalworkers' Union recognized that the wildcat strikes were weakening their position and so offered their support in negotiations. They also increased the frequency of union meetings and encouraged opposition *militantes* to explain their strike demands. Opposition members reacted cautiously to these overtures, but in October 1945 they worked with the pelegos in a campaign for increased wages (the first the union had waged in some ten years).[5]

Women factory commission members and opposition activists in the Textile Workers' Union had asked the pelegos to support their strike efforts as early as March 1945, but the union leadership did not begin to pay attention to the rank and file until the strikes in May paralyzed industry in São Paulo. With the disintegration of the Estado Novo, the Textile Workers' Union quickly moved to bring workers from the independent comissões into the union as dues-paying members. After elections, a new directorate took over the union in June 1945. The new group included some veterans from the previous directorate and certainly did not seek to break the close ties to the Ministry of Labor or the FIESP. Still, this new leadership recognized the strength of women's independent organizing and felt they should bring these women (as well as men) into the sindicato during this period of political openness. To encourage more workers to join, these unionists decreased membership dues and permitted some limited criticism of the union and its dictatorship-era activities. During a July 1945 meeting the directorate permitted an open debate about the union's activities. New members questioned why the sindicato provided social welfare at the expense of fighting for workers' rights; this was the first open criticism of the union since 1935.[6]

At the same time, weavers' factory commissions initiated contact with the union in order to strengthen their negotiating position for future strikes. Although about 85 percent of these workers remained outside the official union structure (i.e., they did not pay dues and so were not sindicalizado), they demonstrated their willingness to integrate their local forms of organization with the union once the pelegos showed some willingness to operate a truly open union.[7] In fact, women weavers began to participate in union meetings at this time, and the union leadership moved to create new opportunities for women to serve on committees and in other activities. After witnessing the success of the factory commissions that had been organized and run solely by women outside the union structure, the directorate resolved to involve these women in some of the sindicato's affairs. While they did not offer women workers access to leadership positions in the union, they did move to create committees for women's organizing that were quite different from the earlier Departamento Feminino with its cooking and child-rearing classes.[8] These changes highlight the complexity of the rank and file's developing relationship with pelego-dominated unions in the postwar period. Workers increasingly looked to these unionists to broker their demands to industrialists and the state. No doubt many workers recognized the value of the pelegos' close ties to the FIESP and the Ministry of Labor; that is, sometimes the unionists delivered wage hikes—or claimed credit for increases actually won by factory commissions—and this influenced the rank and file's behavior.

The unions made overtures to workers in opposition to or outside the official structure while Vargas was still in office, so by the time the military and segments of the civilian political elite ousted the dictator in October 1945, many of São Paulo's industrial workers were confidently asserting their rights as full Brazilian citizens. Indeed, the city's textile and metallurgical workers increasingly called upon the Consolidated Labor Laws (CLT) in their dealings with bosses, and more and more workers joined the unions in 1945 and early 1946. Santo Vetturuzzo recalled that people from his mill joined the Textile Workers' Union then "so they could earn better wages, have protection against bosses, and enforce their rights under the law." In 1945 and 1946, Diolinda Nascimento told her companheiras about using the legal system. She had had success with a grievance, and she explained to others how they could get wages foremen had unfairly deducted from their piece rate. Luís Firmino de Lima recalled that pregnant women often sought help from women in the factory commissions to force bosses to obey laws; these shop-floor leaders then received assistance from the union's legal department.[9]

An increasing number of metalworkers also entered the union in this period specifically to protect their rights.[10] Hermento Mendes Dantas and several of his close friends joined because "we knew our rights, and so we forced the bosses, through processos, to obey the labor legislation." Lima Fereira dos Santos joined to fight for solidarity with his fellow workers. He knew the only way to improve conditions on the shop floor and to get higher wages was to act collectively. Lima was illiterate in the mid-1940s, so he had to join the union to have help filing the complicated processos.[11] These new members of the unions also had an opportunity to witness frank discussions of issues at meetings, for in October 1945 Vargas ended the practice of placing government officials at general assemblies. The entrance of new members and the increase in union autonomy combined to create an atmosphere in which the rank and file succeeded in pushing the unionists to aid them in their struggles against bosses. And the pelegos responded to this pressure in order to develop a basic level of legitimacy among the workers.[12]

Given the opportunity, some pelegos chose to work with the rank and file, attempting to act as honest brokers between workers in the commissions and their bosses or the state labor bureaucracy. Two examples of unionists who were pelegos because they benefited from the government industrial relations structure, but who also sought to represent the rank and file before the state, were Joaquim Teixeira of the Textile Workers' Union and the Metalworkers' Union's Joaquim Ferreira. Both men hoped to ride the wave of rank-and-file discontent with the status quo in the unions. So they attempted to turn the Ministry of Labor structure to their advantage in order to win increased wages and improved work conditions for their members, and at the same time bolster their positions within their unions.[13] They could not, however, refashion their unions as legitimate representative bodies for the promotion of rank-and-file interests because São Paulo's industrialists worked closely with the federal government to keep the most conservative pelegos in power in the 1940s.

The Vote: A Limited Working-Class Weapon

After Vargas's ouster, the caretaker government of José Linhares (the Chief Justice of the Supreme Court) moved to hold open elections in December 1945. The industrialists, rural oligarchs, and military men who prepared to battle for control of the presidency faced a formidable obstacle in their drive to reestablish the politics of the Old Republic: an enfranchised and assertive industrial working class. Indeed, it is essential to remember that during the war the community of textile, metallurgical, and other industrial workers in São Paulo offered their support to Vargas in return for his guarantees of full political participation for laboring people. And he or any other politician who did not further workers' goals quickly lost their support.[14] In February 1945, therefore, Vargas began to fulfill his promises by changing the election laws to permit previously disenfranchised industrial workers to vote even if they did not meet the literacy or other registration requirements. First, using his decree power, he made voting mandatory for all literate citizens except women who did not work outside the home. Then he modified the 1932 ex-officio registration system to include all factory workers, not just union members. This change in the ex-officio system (from granting registration only to union members to granting it to all factory workers) reveals Vargas's understanding of the limits of the corporatist labor relations system he imposed in the 1930s. Workers' resistance to joining official unions, along with their independent mobilizations and direct contact with the dictator (through their letters, etc.) during the Estado Novo, demonstrated to Vargas that if he hoped to benefit from workers' votes, he would have to make such a change.

Vargas's next move was to organize a political party that would represent his hoped-for labor backing, the Partido Trabalhista Brasileiro (PTB), in May 1945. Then, as Vargas continued to support workers' demands throughout 1945, he moved to test his electoral backing with the *queremista* ("We want" Vargas) campaign. During a rally commemorating the beginning of the October 1930 Revolution, Vargas told a large crowd in Rio that while he was not a candidate for the presidency, he would act as "a representative of the popular will" in the upcoming elections and the writing of the new constitution.[15] Such rhetoric, combined with Vargas's concrete actions to bolster labor, worried industrialists and their military allies. The elite's fears of a mobilized working class decisively shaped their actions from the ouster of Vargas on 29 October 1945 onward. Accordingly, Brazil's elites arranged a presidential election between two military men, and then kept as much of the Estado Novo–era corporatist control over labor as possible in the new constitution.[16]

Within the democracy of the post–Estado Novo period, São Paulo's textile and metallurgical workers still had the opportunity to use their votes as yet another resource in their overall struggle against industrialists. As the election approached, Vargas publicly endorsed General Dutra. In a "message to the people," the former dictator assured workers that only Dutra could maintain labor's recent gains, and so he gave the PTB's approval to vote for Dutra and the PSD. He ended the message by assuring the workers, "I will be on your side until the victory. After that, I will still be on the side of the people against the president, if he doesn't fulfill his campaign promises."[17] This position appealed to all those workers in São Paulo who had petitioned the dictator for some sort of assistance or knew neighbors or workmates who had.[18]

At the same time, many young PCB militantes argued against the Vargas line. Luís Firmino recalled trying to convince other textile workers to vote for the PCB's slate of candidates. He spoke to them of Vargas's late conversion to the workers' cause. His companheiros vividly remembered how Vargas had militarized the mills in 1942, and they knew well the impact of the Estado Novo's wage squeeze.[19] Assumpta Bianchi recalled that a friend in the mill used to talk to her about the partidão during breaks and assured her that anyone from the PCB would be better than a general endorsed by Vargas. Likewise, João Bonifácio did not belong to the Communist party but was willing to vote for its candidates. According to Bonifácio, "Getúlio didn't like things he couldn't completely control. We knew he wouldn't let us have a truly free union. Why would we support his guy, a general?"[20] A great number of metalworkers also supported the PCB's candidates in December 1945. The MUT organized within some of the existing comissões, and their activists frequently spoke out against Vargas, the PTB, and Dutra's campaign. Again, the young PCB activists had no problem convincing many of these workers to vote for true opposition candidates. After all, the PTB, PSD, and UDN were all parties of the political and social establishment.[21]

When they went to the polls on 2 December, São Paulo's voters gave Dutra 56 percent of their votes; Gomes received 28 percent and Fiuza 14 percent.[22] The significance of the election for São Paulo's industrial workers is hard to measure. Dutra's candidacy had Vargas's blessing, so the general might have been seen as proworker. The PCB's Fiuza, on the other hand, had no ties to workers. Indeed, the PCB nominated him in an attempt to build ties to "progressive segments of the national bourgeoisie."[23] No matter; many workers voted for the PCB candidate out of support for the party's charismatic Luís Carlos Prestes. São Paulo's working people probably voted for the PTB-endorsed Dutra and the PCB's Fiuza because once they were registered they were legally compelled to vote (they faced a fine for failing to do so) and those two candidates were seen as the least objectionable.[24]

Voting for Vargas's candidate or that of the PCB, however, had no effect on the immediate day-to-day lives of São Paulo's industrial workers. The city's textile mills, which faced renewed foreign competition in late 1945, cut production. This meant that most workers in this sector lost the overtime pay they had been earning during the war.[25] While the decreased work hours must have been a welcome break, the loss of income was quite painful, for prices continued their upward spiral. Overall inflation in São Paulo reached at least 49 percent in 1945, and in early 1946 the city's industrialists worried that inflation might increase several hundred percent during the year.[26] Output and employment in the metallurgy sector continued to expand during this period, but real wages did not keep pace with inflation. The value of the minimum wage fell 30 percent between 1944 and 1945.[27]

The increasing scarcity and high cost of foodstuffs in São Paulo further complicated workers' lives. By late December 1945 and early January 1946, working-class bairros were experiencing severe shortages of bread and other basic goods. The state government reacted quickly by creating a new set of price controls. Then, FIESP members moved to limit the availability of foodstuffs in their wealthy neighborhoods in an attempt to increase supplies for the workers. Morvan Dias de Figueiredo, the vice president of the FIESP, told his fellow industrialists they should do this not out of a sense of community or charity but because such measures were "indispensable in the defense of our society against extremist ideas that are swarming about."[28]

São Paulo's industrialists understood the resentment many workers felt toward them at this time. During the strikes in May 1945, most warehouses had been insured against riots and sackings. A cartoon in the *Folha da Manhã* captured the atmosphere well as it depicted a group of humble workers standing before a still-life painting of a bowl of fruit. In the caption, one worker says, "The painting is so cheap," and another replies, "Yes it is! [But] imagine the fortune the painter spent on models!"[29] The São Paulo press reported that the city's industries were enjoying annual profits of 37.1 percent (textiles averaged 41.2 percent and metalworking 26.5 percent, and by 1947, industrialists wanted to average 40 percent). In an effort to decrease the tensions created by food shortages, inflation, and its members' high profits the FIESP pressured newspapers in the city to stop reporting the high profits. Then, industrialists temporarily halted the construction of luxurious private homes, offices, and restaurants because they knew these projects would only increase their workers' anger. The FIESP report on this project described it as "a large-scale campaign among industrialists to restrict luxury outlays . . . for they have helped the communist effort."[30] Such tactics could not, of course, mask the reality all Paulistano workers knew well; they only postponed the latest manifestations of the exploitative relationship between workers and employers.

The Strike: A Powerful Working-Class Weapon

Throughout 1945, the textile and metallurgical workers' factory commissions grew in number and confidence. In October 1945, workers at Ford do Brasil, Companhia de Parafusos e Metalúrgica Santa Rosa, and several other large metalworking plants nominated senior workers (whose firing would lead to complex bureaucratic procedures and severance pay) to negotiate for wage hikes. When negotiations failed, the commissions looked to the union for support but were turned down. While representatives from the comissões negotiated, workers again used sabotage and other forms of shop-floor resistance.[31] Edson Borges recalled that in those days he and his companheiros argued frequently about tactics: "Some guys said let's slow up, or play with the materials. But then someone would say we could hurt the negotiations, so we waited." Waldemar Lima agreed: "We usually waited a good time, but soon we were fed up, and we would say, 'Let's slow up, then mess up, and then stop if the boss don't give in.'" David Carneiro and Edson Borges both felt they needed to work through commissions because they had left small firms for work in a large machine shop. Carneiro recalled, "We would all talk at lunch, outside the factory where there weren't company people, and we all wanted to organize." He continued, "We only talked on the street, and an older guy would represent us with the boss or union." And Borges noted, "Yes, we organized ourselves. After all, we fought World War II, Brazilians died for the war, we worked like slaves for the war. Good, now we had a democracy, so we organized and asked for what was ours."[32]

Textile workers likewise depended on their local organizations at this time. Weavers and spinners struggled to make do with less and less income as their hours dropped and the real value of their wages fell with inflation's rise. Beginning in August 1945, women from Alpagartas, Crespi, and other large mills asked the union to support their wage demands. Although the unionists wanted contact with these organizations, they were not willing to confront the industrialists on behalf of their workers. The fact that women dominated the commissions limited the support the male directorate of the Textile Workers' Union would offer. The unionists eagerly sought women members, but they were not prepared to follow the lead of women activists. This rejection forced the textile workers to rely again on independent organizing. Workers formed new factory commissions in late 1945. Women who had avoided politics during the dictatorship took advantage of the atmosphere of openness at this time and eagerly joined comissões. They felt they had sacrificed enough during the war, and now they deserved higher wages and better treatment by foremen.[33] Odette Pasquini said she joined a factory commission because her foreman intensified the work regime in the mill. Glória Salviano joined for the same reasons, and she recalled how confident some of her companheiras seemed: "They got together at lunch, and said they would change things. I thought, my God, these girls are going to strike!" Diolinda Nascimento was one of those confident young women in the mid-1940s: "We would get together in formal and informal groups, some real comissões and other informal groups, and complain about conditions. We got more and more angry, and then someone would say, 'Okay, let's stop working!'"[34]

The younger women relied on the experiences and seniority of the older women for organizing and running the factory commissions and the men in the textile mills also relied on those women and their experiences as they formed their own commissions. Lima Fereira dos Santos recalled that the women were the most active in organizing outside the union structure in those years, and he took their techniques with him when he left the mills to work as a mechanic at Cobrasma in Osasco. Luís Firmino also respected the women's factory commissions and tried to use the MUT in the textile mills in the same manner.[35] Of course, not all Paulistano workers participated in the factory commissions. Some feared retribution by bosses, others had family obligations, and still others did not like those involved in the comissões, but all workers respected the strikes called in late December 1945 and early January 1946 by not returning to the mills until settlements had been reached.[36]

Once again, the independent commissions were the focal point for the strikers because the commission leaders were truly workers' companheiros—they did not operate on behalf of the state or the unions. São Paulo's MUT activists involved with commissions placed workers' issues before the PCB's politics of national unity, and these local MUT militants explicitly rejected many of the national MUT's policies, including its absurd no-strike policy of 1945 and 1946.[37] Indeed it was only *after* São Paulo's rank and file had initiated and maintained a widespread strike movement that the national MUT and PCB organizations accepted and then endorsed these strikes.[38]

The national PCB's attitude toward São Paulo's workers and their strike movement reveals the ongoing problems the city's workers had with radical movements. Too often, the Communist party's national line reflected either the dictates of Moscow's foreign policies (e.g., the antistrike campaign that was a lingering aspect of the Popular Front strategy) or the party's desire to form a coalition with what it saw as progressive national elites. This latter line was increasingly important as the PCB adopted a strong critique of North American imperialism in the postwar period. Accordingly, the Communist party avoided censuring Brazilian industrialists and instead focused its criticism on foreign firms. Such nationalism had little impact on São Paulo's industrial workers, for their factories were owned by the very capitalists with whom the Communists sought to make ties. The PCB's nationalism was thus an impediment to building strong ties with the Paulistano industrial working class; not surprisingly, nationalism was much more successful in garnering support among workers in areas where foreign capital dominated.[39] This is not to say that the city's workers had an antagonistic or distant relationship with local Communist militants such as Roque Trevisan, Remo Forli, and Luís Firmino, or that many Paulistanos were not taken by Prestes's charisma. But it is important to recognize that workers in Brazil's leading industrial city did not see much that appealed to them in the PCB's national politics. Accordingly, São Paulo's young communist militants, as Luís Firmino noted, "weren't concerned with party issues, we were more interested in union matters," because they too were influenced by São Paulo's syndicalist legacy, which had been developing since the 1917 General Strike.[40]

As far back as the first decade of the twentieth century, São Paulo's labor discourses had taken a distinctly masculine tone. Work and organizing were male activities, and taking care of the home and raising children were to be women's work. And yet, time after time, women's labor practices—organizing locally and independently—proved to be the most effective way of marshaling Paulistano working-class resources to fight for improved conditions and wages. In the postwar years, the city's communist activists—as anarchists in the late 1910s and 1920s had—increasingly embraced Paulistano women's syndicalist tactics and traditions. This move helped the MUT militants to organize among all the city's industrial workers, because men from São Paulo's factories had also adopted women's labor practices.

São Paulo's textile workers relied upon neither the city's pelegos nor the PCB for direction. Textile strikes usually began after factory commissions met in the morning to discuss the situation at the mills. After voting for a strike, workers passed the word during lunch, and no one reentered the factories.[41] In January 1946 the commissions sought bonuses to help with rising costs. Several medium-sized mills, such as Ipiranga, São Luís, São José, and Anglo-Brasileiro, quickly granted the bonuses, and news of the payments spread throughout the city. Workers shut down all the city's textile mills and vowed not to return to work until all the owners met the strikers' demands. Paulistano metalworkers followed the lead of the senior General Motors factory commission and walked off their shop floors. Workers at Aço Paulista, Metalúrgicos Souse Noschese, and Alumínios Rochedo demanded to be paid twice a month, to have fixed and publicly posted piece rates, and to receive overtime and other payments "in accordance with Article 59 of the CLT."[42]

The city's industrialists understood that most workers needed pay hikes, but they decided to deal only with the pelegos, again attempting to strengthen the corporatist labor structure. The FIESP then directed the police to break up pickets and arrest strikers.[43] This tactic failed, however. The spectacle of the DOPS arresting striking workers days before the first truly popularly elected president in Brazilian history would take office offended São Paulo's laborers. Further, the arrests gave the strike leaders an opportunity to coordinate their activities because many of them met for the first time in jail. Antônio Ciaveletto was elected secretary for their jailhouse meetings. The jailed strikers shared tactics and information on spies and other matters. These meetings helped increase solidarity and, more important, organization among the city's hundreds of separate strike committees. Still, these gains had very real costs, for Antônio Ciaveletto and many of his companheiros suffered throughout their lives from the effects of the beatings that accompanied arrest.[44]

As the strikes spread, the workers' sense of power grew steadily. In late January, rank-and-file metalworkers resolved to seize control of the union. A large and combative meeting of São Paulo's metalúrgicos, including several hundred new members who had joined in the past year, demanded the resignations of the union's entire directorate and then replaced them with leaders from the various factory commissions. The metalworkers' assertiveness worried FIESP members, who began to fear that without the pelegos running the unions, workers could use the open political system to dismantle the Estado Novo's corporatist control mechanisms. The Federation of Industries quickly contacted Dutra, and the new president ordered the Ministry of Labor to intervene in the Metalworkers' Union and restore the pelegos to leadership roles.[45] This intervention convinced the Textile Workers' Union to act immediately, and the pelegos hastily arranged a meeting with the FIESP to demonstrate their desire to negotiate a quick settlement to the strikes. The directorate of the Metalworkers' Union installed by the Ministry of Labor telegrammed Dutra and assured him the union would act peacefully. Pelegos from both unions next traveled to Rio to show their loyalty to the new president and ask for his support for wage increases of from 10 to 30 percent. They had to negotiate for *some* wage hikes because workers from factories throughout the city continued to strike; by early February, roughly 100,000 Paulistano workers were demanding better conditions and pay increases of up to 60 percent.[46]

The attempt by rank-and-file metalworkers to take control of the union reveals their desire to institutionalize their loose workers' movement based in the factory commissions. São Paulo's metalúrgicos did not object to participating in unions per se; they were, however, opposed to the pelegos who ran their union. Had the government not stepped in, these workers might have participated in the state's industrial relations system with their own sindicato. In the aftermath of the ministerial intervention, however, São Paulo's metalworkers continued to rely on independent commissions.[47] Although the city's textile pelegos also feared a rank-and-file insurgency, Paulistano mill workers did not seem as eager to integrate with the sindicato. Weavers and spinners sought assistance from unionists in negotiating with employers, but the long legacy of women's exclusion from any sort of power in the city's Textile Workers' Union left them wary of dealing with the pelegos.

With industry in the city paralyzed, Eduardo Jafet broke ranks with Alpagartas, Crespi, and other large mills and negotiated directly with his factory's commissions. Further, Simonsen, Gottschalk, and others in the FIESP thought a de facto right to strike had been established by Brazil's support of the Chapultepec agreements and expected some right-to-strike provision in the new constitution. They therefore decided to settle with their workers and resume production. Besides, even with the downturn in the textile sector, the labor market remained quite tight. Eduardo Jafet told his fellow mill owners that he settled specifically because "there is a great lack of workers both for the rural sector and industry." With individual industrialists raising wages from 10 to 40 percent, the FIESP moved to standardize the remaining strike negotiations. The industrialists then moved to have the Regional Labor Board (Conselho Regional do Trabalho, CRT) handle the final bargaining and made sure the CRT used only the FIESP's inflation and wage statistics.[48] The final wage agreements provided 60 percent increases to the lowest paid textile and metallurgical workers, and decreasing percentages for those with higher incomes; the lowest percentage increase was 40 percent. The new work contracts, however, contained absenteeism clauses. Workers who missed more than their allotted number of absences from the factories would lose the increase for that pay period. Further, the raises were considered bonuses, so they did not affect base wage rates in future negotiations.[49]

In the end, the massive strike wave of late 1945 and early 1946 demonstrated the limited extent of Brazil's transition out of the Estado Novo. The FIESP managed to have the Ministry of Labor purge the Metalworkers' Union of its insurgent directorate in order to maintain the pelegos' power. In order to stay in the good graces of both the FIESP and the Ministry of Labor, pelegos in the Textile Workers' Union abandoned attempts to incorporate factory commission members into the sindicato. Further, industrialists granted wage increases tied to attendance and increased productivity—wage increases based on statistics from the FIESP's Department of Industrial Economics, which had an interest in underestimating the rate of inflation. Not only did the industrialists settle the strikes to resume production, they also acted to reinforce the corporatist industrial relations system. They feared that open politics would lead to a situation similar to that of Argentina, but with the MUT and PCB manipulating the workers instead of a Vargas or a Perón. FIESP members saw the strikes as essentially "political" and worried about the role of "outside agitators."[50] The industrialists were right—the strikes were political—but they misunderstood the workers' organizing and assertiveness. São Paulo's industrial workers, along with workers in Rio de Janeiro, Santos, Campinas, Porto Alegre, and other urban centers, struck to force their bosses and government to pay them a fair wage and provide them with safe working conditions.[51] They struck for the social justice they felt entitled to as Brazilian citizens.

Democracy's Limits

The solidarity, assertiveness, and independence of São Paulo's industrial workers after the ouster of Vargas in October 1945 and continuing through March 1946 greatly worried the city's industrialists, who acted quickly and decisively in the face of such popular effervescence. The FIESP enlisted the aid of President Dutra, the Ministry of Labor, and the DOPS to limit the strikers' actions and demands. Even before settling the strikes, the FIESP moved to co-opt the power of the comissões. The industrialists created their own factory commissions for workers to use to discuss everything from shop-floor safety and wages to product quality control. The Federation of Industries also moved to limit workers' efforts to publicize dangerous working conditions and poor pay. The city's industrialists paid the FIESP a tax of Cr$1.50 for each worker they employed. The money was used to fund an extensive public relations effort to downplay workers' complaints and place the blame for the strikes on the political machinations of outside agitators.[52]

Dutra aided in this effort: after intervening in the Metalworkers' Union during the strikes, he next closed the MUT. The president then moved to limit the negotiating power of the commissions by forcing them to submit all their contracts to the labor courts for final approval. After the strikes, Dutra continued to show the real face of Brazil's democracy by banning all independent commemorations of May Day. The only legal ceremony in São Paulo on 1 May 1946 was directed by the Ministry of Labor. It included a parade by members of the Catholic Círculos Operários and a speech by Dutra that highlighted the various social services that unions, the state, and industry provided. At the same time, the DOPS arrested hundreds of young activists from the comissões and the MUT.[53] Then, the Metalworkers' Union and the Textile Workers' Union severed their remaining ties to the factory commissions and moved to recapture their Estado Novo–era roles as providers of social services and allies of the state and industrialists.[54]

In 1946 the FIESP created a new ally for the pelegos: the Industrial Social Service (Serviço Social de Indústria, SESI). São Paulo's industrialists created the SESI to provide inexpensive food, entertainment, and assorted social services to their workers. They hoped such services would inculcate the city's workers with the ideal of social harmony, and they believed SESI restaurants and cooperatives would prevent future food riots. The industrialists also thought SESI-sponsored sporting and cultural events would blunt workers' class anger.[55] The SESI did increase medical services in working-class neighborhoods and provided tens of thousands of nutritious meals per day in the factory districts. Further, it sought to alleviate the double burden most women workers faced by supplying healthy and inexpensive meals that women could bring home to their families. At the same time, however, the SESI and the city's unionists sought to reinforce traditional gender ideologies by sponsoring the Queen of Industry beauty contest every year. They also produced May Days celebrating "harmony between labor and capital."[56]

While industrialists and pelegos were working to limit popular mobilization with SESI programs, politicians in Rio were writing Brazil's new constitution. This document was supposed to serve as the outline for a democratic society. In the end, however, the framers kept almost all the government's corporatist control over labor from the 1937 Constitution. While workers had some limited rights to strike, the basic organization of unions and their dependence on the union tax and the Ministry of Labor remained. Indeed, all the major political actors in the 1946 *constituinte* (constitutional convention) struggled mightily, and successfully, to perpetuate the status quo in industrial relations.[57]

Any hope São Paulo's workers had of using the new constitution and industrial relations system to their advantage ended in October, when Dutra appointed Morvan Dias de Figueiredo, the vice president of the FIESP, minister of labor. He soon became known to his fellow industrialists as the "minister of social peace," for he did not hesitate to use all the government's power against strikes and to fight all forms of independent organizing. Morvan Dias allowed industrialists to ignore many labor court decisions granting wage increases or protection to activists. At about the same time, former DOPS head Eduardo Gabriel Saad took over as the director of the São Paulo state Department of Labor. These appointments reinstituted the status quo for São Paulo's workers and industrialists. The federal Ministry of Labor again delegated responsibility for management of the industrial relations system to São Paulo's industrialists—this time quite directly through a FIESP officer—and their allies in the state Department of Labor. Vargas's brief flirtation with populist politics had slightly altered the political calculus in the state. The Dutra administration quickly changed that, however, by returning power to the state Department of Labor and by handing control over the Ministry of Labor to one of São Paulo's most conservative industrialists.[58]

North American business groups, through the Inter-American Council for Commerce and Production, helped the FIESP with this offensive against labor. They advised Paulistano industrialists on ways to limit labor mobilizations and fight the Left.[59] The pelego-led unions also followed Dutra's lead by calling fewer general assemblies and by trying to undermine the factory commissions. The Metalworkers' Union even began to lobby the federal government on behalf of the city's industrialists when they called for protection for national metallurgical concerns. While such measures would also protect their jobs, the unionists' pleas widely praised their employers as national heroes.[60]

Brazil was still formally a democracy at this time, and many on the Left prepared for the gubernatorial and state assembly elections of January 1947. The MUT militants, now using the newly formed General Workers' Confederation of Brazil (Confederação Geral dos Trabalhadores do Brasil, CGTB), maintained their ties with workers through the factory commissions. The PCB continued to rely on coalitions with nationalist elements of the industrial bourgeoisie and formed an alliance with the former São Paulo interventor, Adhemar de Barros, and his Social Progressive party (Partido Social Progressista, PSP) against Hugo Borghi of the PTB and two conservative candidates from the PSD and UDN in the gubernatorial race. Adhemar narrowly beat Borghi and became governor on the strength of his alliance with the Communists.[61] Once again, however, electoral politics proved to be no help to São Paulo's industrial workers. Adhemar had learned the importance of the working-class vote as one of Vargas's interventores, but he quickly distanced himself from those workers after the election.[62] Within a month and a half of his inauguration, Adhemar helped the federal government crush the Left and further its control of the unions.[63]

São Paulo's workers had not placed much faith in these elections, so they continued to rely on a wide variety of resistance strategies during the unraveling of Brazil's democratic moment. Those workers who maintained membership in the unions used every legal means possible to ameliorate the harsh factory conditions. Metalworkers throughout the city increasingly filed grievances to force their bosses to obey work rules and wage scales.[64] Textile workers likewise followed a dual strategy of maintaining their factory commissions and using the union's legal department to file complaints through the labor bureaucracy when necessary. Workers also took advantage of the continued shortage of factory labor and employed slowdowns to limit production; their commissions then bargained for higher wages.[65]

When all these examples failed, the factory commissions initiated strikes. Workers at Metalúrgicos Atlas, for example, negotiated during February 1947 through their comissões in order to force management to obey a series of labor court rulings on wages and work schedules. These workers had to meet at the Bank Workers' Union headquarters because their own sindicato opposed their efforts. Still, their unity closed the plant and eventually forced management to follow the court rulings. Workers at Aços Finos staged and won a similar strike. After winning, though, both groups of strikers faced retribution in the form of shift changes and firings.[66] Textile workers' commissions also struck in early 1947 for increased wages, the incorporation of all bonuses into the base wage, and the increasing of women's and children's wages to the level of men's. These walkouts failed, however, when the labor courts ruled against them, claiming inflation had slowed. The judges used FIESP statistics that greatly underestimated the upward spiral of prices for 1946 (inflation for the period between February 1946 and February 1947 reached 118 percent). Changes in the textile industry in 1947, as well as the government's and pelegos' offensive against the factory commissions, weakened the strikers' position, so they were forced to accept the rulings of the hostile labor courts.[67]

Repression and the Rationalization of Work

Intervention in the Unions

The Ministry of Labor sponsored the official 1947 May Day celebration at the Pacaembu Stadium. The ceremonies included sporting events between different groups of workers and speeches on social peace. Later that day, Governor Adhemar de Barros appeared at the protest demonstrations staged by unionists and leftist activists in the Anhangabaú Valley. Adhemar was there to try to blunt the increasing opposition sentiment among the rank and file in São Paulo. The governor spoke on workers' responsibilities to support the state's role in managing industrial relations. He called all activities by the pelegos' opponents "sabotage" and encouraged the city's industrial working people to follow the lead of ministry-approved unionists. Pelegos in the Metalworkers' Union later referred to Adhemar's performance as "a brilliant speech . . . [reminding the workers] of his support in the fight for the defense of the Federal Constitution and against high prices and unemployment." Industrialists, pelegos, and the state continued to worry about popular discontent with the unions. Then, on 7 May, the Brazilian Supreme Court ruled on behalf of President Dutra that the PCB could no longer participate in electoral politics and that the CGTB was an illegal entity. All unions with ties to the CGTB would henceforth come under ministerial control. The federal government intervened in 144 workers' sindicatos throughout Brazil, 15 of them in São Paulo. The minister of labor directed these interventions in order "to harmonize the classes and to execute loyally the laws . . . with which our country will fulfill its destiny in concert with the civilized nations." The government had not so thoroughly purged the labor movement since the establishment of the Estado Novo.[68]

The Ministry of Labor moved quickly to bolster the pelegos in the Textile Workers' Union. In May 1947, Melchíades dos Santos and Joaquim Teixeira purged activists who had ties to the factory commissions and the MUT or CGTB. The union worked closely with the state Department of Labor and the DOPS to make sure opponents of the pelego-controlled directorate played no role in any aspect of official union business. In early 1948 the authorities suspended several meetings after opposition members attempted to speak. The directorate further limited participation by restricting the number of meetings; the union averaged three general assemblies per year from 1947 to 1950. During this same period the union expelled 353 rank-and-file members for participating in the comissões and other activities.[69] Melchíades dos Santos and Teixeira then decreased funding for many social services and increased the budget of the union's soccer team; they also purchased cars for all members of the directorate. They received the enthusiastic support of the city's mill owners and used their close ties to industrialists to solicit contributions to "special funds" that never seemed to find their way into the union's treasury.[70] The pelegos also began to build ties to the U.S. consulate's Brazilian-American Cultural Union (União Cultura Brasil–Estados Unidos). As strong anticommunists and practitioners of business unionism, these men were obvious candidates for the many perquisites (e.g., trips to the United States and funding for union projects) the U.S. consulate and American Federation of Labor representatives granted to friendly labor leaders.[71]

Teixeira's role in these moves is particularly noteworthy. In late 1945 and early 1946, he had attempted to take on the role of an honest broker for the rank and file within the industrial relations system, but when the state and federal governments began closely circumscribing independent and leftist organizing, Teixeira again operated like a classic pelego. Changes in the larger political scene had temporarily changed Teixeira's relationship with the members of the factory commissions and the rank and file. Unlike Melchíades dos Santos and the Metalworkers' Union's Mário Sobral, who were the sort of pelegos who thrived in closed, small unions with more intimate ties to industrialists and government officials than to the rank and file, Teixeira and other moderate pelegos did take steps to expand the membership of their unions and acted as honest brokers when political conditions permitted such behavior.[72]

After the 1946 intervention the pelegos already had firm control over the Metalworkers' Union, but the May crackdown further empowered Mário Sobral and his cohort on the directorate. Like the Textile Workers' Union, the Metalworkers' Union returned to the Estado Novo era's style of industrial relations. The unionists worked for "real harmony between employees and employers, between Capital and Labor." They also opposed all strikes and sabotage in the factories and proclaimed the complete "solidarity of the Metalworkers with the Federal Government"; and Sanches Duran, the president of the State Federation of Metalworkers, moved to forbid all political discussions at union meetings. The directorate then limited the number of general assemblies to about three per year. The directorate also bought new medical equipment, expanded the legal department, and opened a consumer cooperative that sold many basic articles at below market costs. Further, the pelegos embezzled several hundred thousand cruzeiros from the union funds for these activities. The union managed to negotiate with industrialists for some modest wage increases, but it did so through close consultations with factory owners.[73]

Dutra next pressured the courts to overturn rulings for increased wages and improved conditions. The Supreme Labor Court reversed hundreds of decisions from São Paulo's Regional Labor Tribunal (TRT). Other levels of the labor bureaucracy either refused to hear workers' petitions or moved very slowly on them. One request for a wage increase weavers had forced the Textile Workers' Union to file in September 1947 was not settled until October 1949. Further, filing a processo for a grievance was dangerous; workers who did so faced arrest and the possibility of losing their jobs.[74] With the FIESP's vice president serving as the minister of labor, and President Dutra and Governor Adhemar de Barros firmly supporting them, São Paulo's industrialists enjoyed a previously unthought of degree of power over their workers. They had successfully circumscribed the democratic opening brought on by Vargas's ouster, for their workers still had to contend with an authoritarian, state-controlled industrial relations system. As 1947 came to an end, they discussed how well they had reined in the rank and file. Mariano J. M. Ferraz told his colleagues at the FIESP, "In the United States, the workers for some time have had all the rights and the employers all the responsibilities. Only after the passage of Taft-Hartley can we see a better situation for employers, before that the workers controlled everything." Aldo Mário de Azevedo seconded that sentiment and added, "The North American labor system is much worse than ours."[75]

The Rationalization of Production

The old and idiosyncratic looms and spinning equipment used in São Paulo's mills during World War II not only limited efficient production, they also empowered workers who had developed valuable factory-specific skills. These circumstances severely restricted industrialists' abilities to control their labor force, and so mitigated some aspects of the Estado Novo's harsh industrial relations system.[76] Mill owners fully understood this situation and had begun to order new equipment from various European manufacturers in the early 1940s, but the war prevented delivery. Half of all textile equipment in use in 1945 had been installed before 1915, and some of the machines dated back to the 1890s.[77]

By the end of the Estado Novo, mill owners had even more reason to rationalize production: they possessed huge surpluses extracted from their workers during the dictatorship, and they faced an assertive and restless working class. Throughout the war, the city's mill owners discussed using their 40 percent annual profits for new machinery as soon as they could. With help from the Ministry of Labor's Textile Commission (CETEX) and the FIESP, these industrialists began ordering new automated looms and spindles in mid-1945; the FIESP even investigated the possibility of the FEB helping to dismantle Italian factories for export to São Paulo. Throughout the Dutra years, mill owners imported new machines and ordered others from local metallurgy establishments. They did so explicitly to increase production and lower labor costs.[78]

Along with his offensive against labor and the Left in May 1947, Dutra moved to speed up the rationalization program, which had slowed after initial imports of consumer goods exhausted foreign exchange reserves. He aided Paulistano mill owners by drastically changing the system of exchange controls to limit imports of consumer goods and encourage, through a special licensing regime, the importation of capital goods (table 5.1).[79] In late 1947, Humberto Reis Costa, the president of the state Textile Industrialists' Association, complained that the sector had too few automated looms and spindles in place. He urged his fellow mill owners to take advantage of Dutra's aid and speed the equipment replacement process.[80] The owners of Alpagartas, Moinho Santista, Guilherme Giorgi, and several other mills followed this advice and ordered the most modern machinery available from abroad. In the eight years from 1945 to 1953, they imported more textile equipment than they had from 1913 to 1944. Other mills, such as those owned by the Crespi, Matarazzo, and Jafet families (i.e., several of the city's largest textile factories), did not modernize at this time.[81] The new automated machines went exclusively to São Paulo, and other cities' textile mills still relied on older manual machines into the 1950s. Only about 35 percent of the city's mills adopted this new technology, but all the area's textile factories, especially the large mills of Crespi and Matarazzo, rationalized production with incentives and other schemes in order to remain competitive.[82]

Table 5.1   Imports of Textile Equipment to
Brazil, 1940–1952

Year	Tons	U.S. $1,000
1940	3,531	2,316
1941	3,138	1,844
1942	2,397	1,854
1943	1,030	1,142
1944	794	1,021
1945	26,021	19,868
1946	6,205	6,922
1947	15,697	22,552
1948	18,265	28,939
1949	19,573	30,615
1950	15,356	25,314
1951	26,912	48,949
1952	31,107	53,499

Source: F. R. Versiani, "Technical Change, Equipment Replacement, and Labor Absorption: The Case of the Brazilian Textile Industry" (Ph.D. diss., Vanderbilt University, 1971), 70.

Many smaller and older mills could not rationalize production with new machinery or intensified work regimes and were forced to close. Mill owners spoke of a "crisis" in the textile sector as production dropped off in late 1946 and early 1947, but by mid-1947 they saw that the sector had simply gone through a period of readjustment.[83] Competition for the export markets established during the war and the introduction of new production techniques forced inefficient producers out of business, but many of their workers quickly found employment in other mills. Industrialists who were modernizing production recruited new workers among the recently unemployed. Even though the mill owners were installing automated equipment that required fewer workers per machine, they did not decrease their work forces; in fact, employment in the textile sector expanded—although very slightly at first—throughout the Dutra years (table 5.2).[84]

The recent purges of the factory commissions from the Textile Workers' Union, as well as the overall offensive against activists in the mills, coincided perfectly with the implementation of the industrialists'

Table 5.2   Production and Employment in the
Textiles Industry, 1945–1952

Year	Production of cotton cloth in Brazil (1,000 meters)	Index of textile production in Brazil (1939 = 100)	Number of workers in São Paulo mills
1945	1,085,429	143	—
1946	1,142,151	153	83,656
1947	1,063,426	143	83,712
1948	1,119,738	152	83,947
1949	1,137,000	160	96,947
1950	—	175	100,325
1951	—	—	105,252
1952	—	—	91,167

Source: F. R. Versiani, "Technical Change, Equipment Replacement and Labor Absorption: The Case of the Brazilian Textile Industry" (Ph.D. diss., Vanderbilt University, 1971); Institute for Inter-American Affairs, Brazilian Technical Studies (Washington, D.C.: Government Printing Office, 1955), 372; Diário de São Paulo, 11 March 1953.

rationalization schemes. With the assertive factory commission members restrained by this repression, mill owners easily reduced piece rates and used the absenteeism clauses in work contracts to increase output per worker. The labor courts, at the request of the FIESP, modified wage agreements in middle and late 1947 to make wages more dependent on attendance. In 1949, the courts acted to tie workers' wage increases even more closely to attendance.[85] These measures, along with the automated equipment that was arriving daily in São Paulo, effectively increased productivity per worker. The SENAI noted these increases, and a United Nations study found that the modern mills in São Paulo were more than four times more efficient in their use of labor than older mills in Rio.[86]

The SENAI in São Paulo worked vigorously during the postwar period both to increase efficiency in textile and metallurgy establishments and to produce "loyal" and "good" workers. It ran industrial training schools in the main factory districts (Lapa, Mooca, Brás, Ipiranga, Barra Funda, Belemzinho, and Cambuci) and set out to train young men and women to be "ideal" textile and metallurgical workers. Along with their training on industrial equipment, students took citizenship classes that covered workers' rights and responsibilities. The courses reinforced traditional divisions of labor by sex in the factories and homes.

The SENAI's social workers also investigated workers' home lives. In exchange for these intrusions, workers were promised steady employment and higher than average wages after graduating from SENAI courses.[87] The rationalization program necessitated training on advanced textile machinery, and the SENAI, which was funded by the Federation of Industries, consulted closely with the city's mill owners to find ideal workers.[88]

To the "developmentalists" of the United Nations' Economic Commission for Latin America, as well as to the leaders of Brazil's Communist party, the increases in productivity per worker were seen as great gains for Latin American industry.[89] To São Paulo's textile workers, those increases represented great losses. Weavers who had tended two looms were forced to manage ten or twelve at once. New spindles required one person to operate both sides of a large machine and tend two hundred spools at once rather than just one hundred. The new automatic shutoff feature on the spinning equipment forced workers to run about replacing broken threads in order to restart the machines. The looms also had shutoff switches that prevented imperfect cloth from getting through. This feature made weavers move quickly around their ten or twelve machines.[90] Glória Salviano recalled that the new work regime at Alpagartas was very strict: "We had to produce ten times more with almost no wage increase." She went from earning about Cr$150 per week between her base wage and piece rate with two looms to Cr$170 with twelve looms. Odette Pasquini remembered the foremen had the right, using the absenteeism clause, to deduct wages from days she worked if she did not maintain a perfect attendance record.[91]

Economic factors such as the desire to increase profits through the use of efficient new technologies played a key role in encouraging Paulistano mill owners to rationalize production. This should not obscure the fact that social factors such as the preponderance of women in these textile factories also played an important part in fostering rationalization. Because mill owners—like most Brazilians—tended to view women's abilities to operate looms efficiently as part of their "natural" female dexterity rather than a learned skill, they no doubt looked at the new automated machinery as a way to take advantage of their workers' innate aptitudes.[92] Further, the rationalization program offered mill owners the possibility of decreasing their total number of workers. Not only could such a development increase profits, it could also help industrialists in their ongoing offensive against textile workers' factory commissions.[93]

Metalworkers with a furnace, circa 1940s. (*Courtesy Arquivo Edgard Leuenroth, State University of São Paulo, Campinas* [UNICAMP])

In addition to the automated equipment and new wage system, mill owners used speedups and other "efficiency" measures to increase productivity. They limited the time workers were given to use bathrooms and forbade talking on the shop floor. Foremen could not completely control workers' routines in the factories, but their power increased steadily during the Dutra years, for with their unions firmly controlled by pelegos, workers had no legal avenue for redress.[94] Maria Pavone recalled that her foreman initiated a competition among the youngest weavers, who received bonuses for producing the greatest amount of cloth without any flaws. She and a friend were proud when they came in first and second, but when they met with women in the informal commission with which they associated, the older women let them know participation in such competitions was not good for one's standing among her companheiras. This episode not only highlights workers' resistance to changes in their work regimes, it also reveals important features of the informal commissions: they continued to be a social space in which young members were initiated into the existing work culture. Moreover, as Maria Pavone's story indicates, the commission

Table 5.3   Importation of Capital Goods and Production of
Machines in Brazil, 1944–1950

Year	Value of machine production imports (Cr$1,000)	Index of machine production imports (1939 = 100)	Index of Brazilian machine production (1939 = 100)
1944	1,208,174	91.9	132.6
1945	1,465,767	101.1	117.0
1946	2,777,119	168.2	169.6
1947	5,310,190	272.5	235.9
1948	4,772,260	233.2	200.8
1949	5,362,698	271.0	243.2
1950	5,846,338	280.4	271.0

Source: Luís A. Corrêa do Lago et al., A Indústria Brasileira de Bens de Capital: Origens, Situação Recente, Perspectivas (Rio de Janeiro: Editora da Fundição Getúlio Vargas, 1979), 90–93.

members did not hesitate to discipline workers who went along with their foremen's and employers' speedups. Relations within the commissions were not always harmonious.[95]

Owners of metallurgical establishments, like mill owners, used their Estado Novo–era profits to invest in new capital equipment. They expanded the size and scope of their plants and imported new equipment for the machine shops (table 5.3). In 1945 and 1946, the FIESP called on industrialists to rationalize production in order to increase efficiency and to limit the growing power of the limited number of skilled metalworkers. Metalúrgicos often worked with attendance clauses in their contracts, and labor court decisions on productivity affected them and all workers in São Paulo; but the city's machine shops did not initiate the same sort of efficiency campaigns that operated in the mills, nor did they change production techniques. Máquinas Piratininga, one of South America's most advanced metalworking concerns in the 1940s, built many machines under license from North American companies and exported them throughout Latin America and Africa. It also fabricated automated looms for São Paulo's textile mills. Even though its workers made advanced machinery, they did not do so under a highly regimented work regime or with Tayloristic production methods. Other large factories, such as Elevadores Atlas and Indústria Bardella, had clear divisions among various production departments, but the division of labor among workers did not effectively diminish the power of skilled metalworkers. Sofunge, Cobrasma, and other large plants that opened during the war expanded through the Dutra years; but even these new establishments maintained the traditional division of labor on the shop floors.[96] Machine shops did not have assembly lines, and workers fashioned individual components at their own pace without much supervision. Those shops with quotas did not vigorously enforce them, and workers organized to keep the entire plant operating at a pace they more or less set. Edson Borges remembered telling the foreman he would have produced more if only the motor assemblies came to him more rapidly. He also recalled telling his companheiros in the electric motor assembly sector that they dare not send the motors over any faster![97]

Worker Resistance

When São Paulo workers smashed and burned trolleys and buses in August 1947, they were not protesting against the subtly antilabor nature of the 1946 Constitution. Rather, these workers opposed the high prices and limited supplies of food in the markets, as well as the changes in their factories brought on by the rationalization schemes. The quebra-quebra was only the most public and assertive face of workers' complex opposition to the realities of Brazil's new democracy. They were expressing their frustration with the false promise of an open society. Ironically, even though textile and metallurgical workers resisted the changes in their work regimes and interventions in their unions, they did not have as many resources to call upon during this period of democratic politics as they had had during the Estado Novo, when they could denounce foremen to Vargas or petition for help with problems created by anti-Vargas São Paulo officials. During the Dutra years, the federal and state governments' industrial relations machinery was firmly controlled by Paulistano industrialists and their allies.

Still, metalworkers continued to use their skills to limit the impact of attendance clauses and attempted speedups. Metalworkers in the large plants (those with more than a hundred workers, such as Máquinas Piratininga and Aços Finos) set informal work regimes to counter those established by foremen. Their shop-floor commissions often coordinated such procedures, and workers who did not adhere to the production schedule were ostracized by the community of metalúrgicos. This could lead to tensions on the shop floor because there were always workers who wanted to earn extra money by meeting a foreman's new high production quotas. Mechanics and machinists used sabotage to slow or stop production. Mechanics, who were key organizers, repaired machinery throughout their plants and thus could change settings on lathes, drill presses, and other equipment to limit their effectiveness. When these methods failed, metalworkers left their factories in search of better conditions. Mechanics, machinists, and foundry workers had among the highest rates of job mobility in 1947 and 1948. A FIESP study found that the large plants had the highest turnover rates, while machinists in smaller shops usually succeeded in bargaining away harsh work rules.[98]

Metalworkers who did not change employers or organize shop-floor resistance tried to use legal procedures to mitigate the changes in their work regimes. Each year from 1947 to 1950, about 1,500 metal-workers joined the union specifically to file processos against their employers. The same number of members left the union each year, for once their grievances were settled they saw little reason to remain sindicalizado. After all, the Ministry of Labor had expelled the insurgent directorate and installed pelegos who ran an unrepresentative union. Throughout the Dutra years, the Metalworkers' Union continued to represent a tiny minority of the city's metalúrgicos. In 1949, for example, the union claimed it had a total of 15,207 dues-paying members, although some 85,000 metalworkers in São Paulo paid the imposto sindical.[99]

Weavers and spinners could not as readily call upon their skills to protect them against the changing work regimes. The rationalization programs diminished the importance of factory-specific skills for more than a third of the textile workers in the city. Still, those who could use their knowledge and manual dexterity to bargain for higher wages or better conditions did so as often as possible. Although the turnover rate for textile workers was half of that for metalworkers, one-third of the city's weavers and spinners managed to change jobs for better wages in 1947 and 1948.[100] Those wage increases, however, were often slight, and the cost of living in São Paulo rose steadily (table 5.4). Further, women textile workers continued to earn 67 percent of men's wages in textiles. Not only did skilled machinists and mechanics earn about twice as much as textile workers (in 1948, weavers averaged Cr$870 per month, and skilled metalworkers Cr$1,760), their wages increased at a greater rate during the Dutra years.[101]

Textile and metallurgical workers continued to meet in their factory commissions, and through them maintained some contact with the

Table 5.4   Cost-of-Living and Wages Indexes in São Paulo,
1945–1951 (1946 = 100)

Year	Cost of living	Minimum wage	Textile wage[a]	Metals wage[a]
1945	88	114	—	74.7
1946	100	100	100	100
1947	130	76.4	92	100
1948	141	70.5	99	125
1949	139	71.7	114	—
1950	147	67.7	118	—
1951	159	62.6	115	—

Source: Seiti Kaneko Endo and Heron Carlos Esvael do Carmo, *Breve Histórico do Índice de Preços ao Consumidor no Município de São Paulo* (São Paulo: Fundição Instituto de Pesquisas Econômicas, 1985), 17; DIEESE, "Objetivos e Caraterísticas do Plano Cruzado III"; *Diário de São Paulo*, 11 March 1953; memo, 6 June 1951, SP Post 560, RG 84, NA.
[a]These are industry averages.

unions. Weavers' and spinners' comissões throughout the city pressured mill owners for wage increases in late 1947. They also requested that the Textile Workers' Union negotiate on their behalf, but again industrialists granted increases that were based on attendance.[102] By February 1948, women textile workers were thoroughly frustrated by the male unionists' refusal to bargain for improved wages and working conditions for the rank and file. Weavers' and spinners' commissions at Varam, Gasparian, and other mills therefore opened direct negotiations with their bosses. They demanded significant changes in their work regimes and pay increases of at least 60 percent. Indeed, these women called for equal pay for equal work for the men and women in the mills. Earning the same wages as men would include an end to the new quota systems that affected only weavers and pay for the considerable time the weavers spent repairing equipment (normally the work of male mechanics). This became a key issue for all textile workers in São Paulo because both the old and the new equipment had high maintenance requirements, short of total breakdown, for which weavers and spinners received no pay. Textile workers also worried about the high accident rate that resulted from running both old and new equipment at the high speeds demanded by the quotas. Once the women's commissions initiated direct negotiations with bosses, Teixeira and his allies within the union quickly moved to take over the bargaining—to try to gain some legitimacy among the rank and file—and encouraged other factory commissions to work with the union.[103]

When textile industrialists met to discuss the workers' demands, they all agreed that wages were not keeping up with inflation. Humberto Reis Costa, Antônio Devisate, and others knew their workers would not accept another increase tied to productivity or attendance, but the majority of mill owners moved to maintain this tactic. The Textile Workers' Union then sought to have the issue settled by the courts. Mill owners were confident the Regional Labor Tribunal would again support their positions, but this time it ruled that textile workers were entitled to a 51 percent increase on the December 1946 base wage.[104] Fearing that workers throughout the city would seek large wage hikes, the Federation of Industries challenged the TRT ruling in the Supreme Labor Court in Rio. The final ruling, which was issued in December 1948—almost a year after the strike had begun—called for wage increases on a sliding scale. The poorest-paid textile workers (i.e., women) received a 40 percent increase on their December 1946 base wages; others received increases of from 35 to 20 percent. This victory, however, was slight. The increases were applied to low base wages that did not take into account the various bonus schemes. Furthermore, the Textile Industrialists' Association encouraged members to avoid paying the modest increases. This strategy forced workers to rely again on the slow and bureaucratic labor court system.[105]

Metalworkers, like weavers and spinners, avoided the union and turned to their comissões to negotiate with employers. Ignoring the union leadership's opposition to their activities, factory commissions from forty metallurgy plants in São Paulo initiated direct negotiations with employers in early 1948. The union vigorously opposed these actions and published an article in O Metalúrgico entitled "It's Good to Know," detailing the illegality of the rank and file's actions. The Federation of Industries and the owners of the metallurgy establishments arranged for the police to arrest workers who protested against the slow pace of negotiations. Finally, commissions from the Companhia de Parafusos Santa Rosa, Metalúrgica Fracalanza, and Metalúrgica Amleto Riceti convinced their bosses to grant wage increases of 40 to 50 percent; those increases then became the basis for TRT settlements for other metallurgical establishments.[106]

The activities of the factory commissions were so successful in 1948 that Mário Sobral and the other pelegos from the Metalworkers' Union called for a 200 percent wage hike in early 1949 in an effort to attract workers away from the opposition based in the factory commissions. By late 1949 and early 1950, the battle between the pelegos and the opposition had become so heated that Ministry of Labor representatives threatened to close the union if Sobral and his followers could not gain complete control over the membership. The pelegos responded by expelling opposition leaders such as Remo Forli in April 1950.[107] Forli had become an important figure because he worked with and was well liked by commission members with no ties to the union, had been active in the São Paulo MUT, and had ties to members of the union who remained sindicalizado but opposed Sobral. Because the city's metalworkers were almost exclusively male, the division between factory commissions and the union was not fraught with the same problems as in the textile sector, and so a man such as Forli could rise to a position of prominence among those who opposed the pelegos.

Ultimately, Dutra's and Adhemar de Barros's administrations offered no benefits to São Paulo's industrial workers. Pelegos maintained firm control over the city's sindicatos, and the Ministry of Labor, state Department of Labor, and DOPS were all controlled by Paulista industrialists and their allies. Not surprisingly, public opinion research conducted in 1948 by the Brazilian Public Opinion and Statistics Institute (Instituto Brasileiro de Opinião Pública e Estatística, IBOPE) revealed workers' deep dissatisfaction with Brazil's democracy: 87 percent of the "lower class" and 83 percent of the "middle class" in the city had no interest in politics. A majority of Paulistanos did, however, believe they could improve their lives through their own actions.[108] Further, São Paulo's workers were quite clear in their preference of political allies in their struggles for better lives. They told IBOPE researchers that of all politicians, they overwhelmingly supported the return of Vargas to the presidency (table 5.5).[109]

The moves Vargas had initiated in 1943 to garner working-class support were finally beginning to pay off. He could not reorient the Ministry of Labor quickly enough to create a solid backing for the queremista campaign of 1945, but by 1948 Vargas was seen as workers' best hope for an ally in Rio. Vargas's great popular-class support in the late 1940s was not due so much to anything he had done; rather, he was the beneficiary of Dutra's—and in São Paulo, Adhemar's—aggressive antiworker stance. As José Soares Maciel Filho (an industrialist and owner of Rio's O Imparcial) noted in a letter to his friend Vargas, "In

Table 5.5 Paulistanos' Electoral Preferences (percentage)
by Class[a] in October 1948

Candidate	Men				Women				Total			
	A	B	C	Total	A	B	C	Total	A	B	C	Total
Vargas (PTB)	17	21	53	37	—	19	44	31	8	20	48	35
Gomes (UDN)	17	28	8	17	17	19	3	11	17	24	5	14
Adhemar (PSP)	—	10	4	7	—	4	5	5	—	8	5	6
Campos (UDN)	17	6	3	5								
Dutra (PSD)					—	16	3	9	—	10	3	6
Other[b]	49	35	32	34	83	42	45	44	75	38	39	39

Source: Arquivo de IBOPE, "Pesquisa—São Paulo," October 1948.
[a]A is upper class, B is middle class, and C is lower class.
[b]No preference or a statistically insignificant one.

terms of working to increase your popularity among workers, nobody is doing more than General Dutra, helped by the members of his administration."[110] Vargas could finally adopt the mantle of populist leader by running against the government in Rio rather than trying to defend it, as he had had to do in 1945.[111]

The Dutra years deepened workers' distrust of politicians, pelegos, and employers. Workers' experiences in their neighborhoods and factories, as well as the remembrances of past struggles handed down by older relatives and friends, shaped the workers' critiques of the political and industrial relations systems. By the middle to late 1940s, however, workers no longer relied only on street serenaders or storytellers to spread the folklore of resistance. Popular radio shows on São Paulo's ten stations broadcast traditional working-class ideas throughout the city's many bairros. Shows such as "A Casa da Sogra" (The mother-in-law's house) and, later, "Histórias das Malocas" (Rogues' stories) struck a chord with workers, for they reproduced their lives in São Paulo in humorous but politically sensitive ways. Adoniran Barbosa, a child of Italian colonos who had worked as a weaver and later a skilled metalworker before becoming a performer, starred in many of these shows and called on his experiences to write and perform characters with whom São Paulo's working people could identify.

One of Barbosa's enduring themes was the racism blacks faced both from elites and from their fellow workers. As Zé Cunversa in "A Casa da

Sogra," he asserted the rights of even the most discriminated against to full participation in Brazilian society. In one episode, Zé shouts, "They [elite whites] want to fool me into thinking Rua Direita is theirs! No, it isn't . . . the street is free . . . I'm black, I'm Brazilian, and I'll walk on R. Direita when I want!" And, in "Histórias das Malocas" Barbosa played an old black worker, Charutinho, who lived in the fictitious working-class neighborhood of Morro Piolho (Louse Hill). Charutinho was best known for comments such as "Many people work . . . and the others live," and "The rich only know the poor on election day!"[112] Not all the technological changes in this period worsened workers' lives. Rather than atomizing workers and creating "false consciousness," the radio brought people together. Throughout the 1940s and 1950s, workers in São Paulo gathered around the radio at neighbors' houses or in barzinhos to listen to and laugh at the social commentary of the characters Barbosa and other popular actors portrayed.[113]

Rather than initiating an open society in which São Paulo's workers could exercise their full citizenship rights, the Dutra years marked a return to the Estado Novo's style of industrial relations. When Brazil moved to create a democracy, São Paulo's industrial workers rushed to press bosses and politicians to provide the social justice they associated with the democratic opening. They called upon all the resources they had developed during the dictatorship (their factory commissions, strategic participation in the unions, manipulation of the labor bureaucracy, and appeals to politicians) in their struggles for higher wages and better working conditions. Further, male textile and metallurgical workers increasingly adopted women workers' organizational techniques (i.e., reliance on independent factory commissions) during the Dutra years.

Ultimately, the intensity of Paulistano workers' participation in Brazil's democracy helped to bring an end to open politics. Dutra intervened in the unions, closed the MUT, CGTB, and PCB, and pressured the labor courts to fight workers' commissions. Moreover, the city's industrialists and their allies controlled the federal and state labor bureaucracies, through which they could limit wages in a period of intense inflation and at the same time implement rationalization schemes with limited opposition from workers. Once again, São Paulo's industrial workers resisted such dictatorial control; they relied on their own organizations and culture because the pelegos continued to run the unions. By the end of the 1940s São Paulo's industrial workers—men and women—had organized separate factory commissions that struggled for the same goals: social justice for all, an open political system, and independent and representative unions. Their organizing and resistance would help them achieve those lofty goals when they brought back "Vargas the dictator" as "Vargas the populist leader."

CHAPTER SIX

Factory Commissions and the Triumph of São Paulo's Working-Class Movement, 1950–1955

The São Paulo airport is the busiest in all Latin America. The streets of the city are crowded with automobiles. The traffic and brilliant electrical signs downtown remind the visitor of Chicago's North Michigan Avenue. In fact, the whole place gives the impression of a kind of Chicago rising in Brazil's tropical interior.

> —*U.S. News and World Report*,
> 10 August 1951

With your votes you can not only defend your interests, but you can influence the very destiny of the nation. As citizens your views will bear weight at the polls. As a class you can make your ballots the decisive numerical force. You constitute the majority. Today you are with the government. Tomorrow you will be the government.

> —Getúlio Vargas,
> *O Governo Trabalhista do Brasil*

The continued expansion of São Paulo praised by the foreign correspondent was part of the process of industrialization that had begun in the early 1900s. Neighborhoods such as Brás and Mooca, which had been swampy lowlands at the turn of the century, were crowded by large textile mills, metallurgy shops, and other industrial establishments. Working-class and middle-class neighborhoods dominated Bexiga, Consolação, Higienópolis, Vila Buarque, and Pinheiros, where cattle had grazed in 1900. Indeed, the *U.S. News and World Report* correspondent continued his description of São Paulo by noting that "the business district has dozens of new skyscrapers . . . [and] every few days a new factory is started in one of the sprawling industrial districts."[1]

São Paulo had experienced much more than just urban and industrial expansion since 1900. The establishment of industry brought with it the formation and transformation of the city's industrial working class and bourgeoisie. The struggles waged within and between these classes prompted national government elites to create a comprehensive industrial relations system. Both workers and industrialists attempted to use that system to their advantage in their struggles with each other. Getúlio Vargas, more than any other individual or institution, personified the government's role in São Paulo's class struggle. By 1950, his twenty years in national politics were marked by many seemingly contradictory twists and turns: He had been an ally of workers and an opponent of the Paulista elite, a friend to São Paulo's industrialists, a quasi-fascist dictator who repressed independent labor organizing, a leader in the fight against international fascism in World War II, and a "populist" politician who looked to workers for support.

When he returned to power in January 1951, Vargas again tried to maintain his complex identity by juggling the interests of workers and industrialists in an attempt to deepen Brazil's industrial development.[2] At the same time, São Paulo's workers, pelegos, and industrialists pursued their own agendas. The city's unionists and industrialists both hoped to maintain the status quo of the postwar years. Pelegos wanted to run their unions as small social clubs that financed benefits for their members through the imposto sindical. Mill owners and other industrialists attempted to expand their rationalization programs in order to increase output and lower labor costs. Rank-and-file textile and metallurgical workers continued to fight for improved wages and conditions and to resist their employers' efforts to change production techniques. As they had in the past, workers again relied on their factory commissions to wage these struggles. With the return of Vargas as a populist, however, workers in São Paulo again had an ally in the federal government. They took advantage of the president's moves to loosen the Ministry of Labor's control of sindicatos by building ties between their factory commissions and the reformers who emerged in the unions. These circumstances, in turn, created an environment of worker activism and militancy that culminated in 1953 in the most successful protest movement since the 1917 General Strike. Unlike that earlier period, activists from the factory commissions in the 1950s created their own institutions to complement the unions. Much like the late 1910s and early 1920s, however, this period provided the blueprint for industrial relations in Brazil for years to come.

Class Struggle in Latin America's "Number One Boom City"

In 1950 São Paulo was being heralded by foreign business executives as Latin America's number one boom city. Skyscrapers dominated where three-story office buildings had once stood in the downtown triangle; clear lines separated the city's neighborhoods by class. Observers even noted the differences between those areas dominated by factory workers and their families and the slums where recent migrants to the city lived. Traffic jams were common, and São Paulo expanded at a rate of one new building every fifty minutes. Real estate values climbed so high that industry increasingly opened new factories in suburbs such as Osasco, Garulhos, Santo André, São Bernardo, and São Caetano.[3] At the same time, industry prospered. The textile sector recaptured its wartime export markets, and metalworking continued to expand and diversify. In the early 1950s, São Paulo's industrial establishments enjoyed "exceedingly high" annual profits of between 29 and 60 percent.[4]

Even though São Paulo had grown into one of the world's largest cities, with a population of 2.2 million people,[5] workers continued to rely on the same sorts of informal institutions (e.g., factory commissions) their predecessors in the 1910s had used to negotiate with employers. Indeed, as real wages declined in 1949 and 1950 pelegos in the Textile Workers' and Metallurgical Workers' unions again concentrated their efforts on providing social services for their limited membership rather than bargaining with employers for higher wages or organizing strikes.[6] When workers used their factory commissions to wage a strike, as 1,500 workers at Matarazzo's Santa Celina mill did in October 1950, the police reacted quickly by beating and arresting all the strikers. One São Paulo state official summed up the industrial relations system in 1950 as a process wherein "the police intervene, down comes the club, and then the strike's over."[7]

The Return of Vargas and the "Workers' Democracy"

The Dutra years had been hard ones for São Paulo's industrial working class. The full power of the national and state governments had been used to further the goals of the city's industrialists while pelegos maintained a tight grip on the unions. Throughout this period, however, Getúlio Vargas was publicly fashioning himself the defender of Brazilian workers' rights. As Vargas's opponents dismantled the Estado Novo in 1945 and 1946, the former dictator began to position himself as the workers' benefactor in Brazil's democracy. He told workers he would be "a representative of the popular will" in the new order.[8] As early as 1947 Vargas was campaigning for popular backing for the 1950 presidential election. He moved to solidify his working-class support by criticizing Dutra's version of "capitalist democracy." In its place, Vargas called for a "socialist democracy, the democracy of the workers." During the campaign, Vargas appealed directly for popular support by contrasting his ties to workers with his opponents' (e.g., the UDN's Eduardo Gomes) elite backers. In Rio he told his audience: "If I am elected on October 3, as I take office the people will climb the steps of Catete [the presidential palace] with me. And they will remain with me in power."[9]

Brazil's working people clearly favored Vargas over all other politicians. A public opinion survey conducted in São Paulo one month before the election revealed that 83 percent of people classified as working class or poor supported Vargas. A survey conducted among Rio's workers (79 percent of whom supported the former dictator) detailed their dissatisfaction with Dutra's management of the economy. Not surprisingly, 86 percent of the respondents called on the government to regulate wages and rents more fairly; 58 percent favored government control of corporate profits.[10] These polls apparently reflected workers' actual hopes and beliefs, for on 3 October they gave Vargas a landslide victory with 48.7 percent of the vote in a three-way election that included the UDN's Gomes, who received 29.7 percent, and Christian Machado of the PSD, who received 21.5 percent.[11]

Even though Vargas represented many different things to his diverse constituency—many of São Paulo's leading industrialists, for example, had helped finance his 1950 presidential campaign—workers wasted little time in pressing their own agenda in late 1950.[12] They hoped that Vargas would support their claims and at the same time lessen Ministry of Labor control of their unions. One week after the election, while Dutra was still in office, workers at the Santa Celina mill in São Paulo used their factory commission to strike for 50 percent wage increases overall, and improvements in women's wages so that they would earn equal pay for equal work. The police broke up the strike, but the factory's managers understood that the political atmosphere was changing and so promised quick action on wage "readjustments."[13] In late November, São Paulo's workers began pushing their employers for Christmas bonuses as compensation for the wage squeeze they had been experiencing since 1947–48. Once again the city's workers relied on their factory commissions to bargain for higher wages and improved conditions, for even though Vargas was the president-elect, the pelegos continued to control the industrial unions. In the months preceding the election, for example, leaders of the Metalworkers' Union had received Ministry of Labor assistance in purging opposition members.[14]

Textile and metallurgical workers began to look to the union elections schedule for late 1950 and early 1951 as yet another opportunity in their struggle to improve wages and factory conditions. Their experiences with moderate pelegos on union directorates in the mid-1940s had demonstrated that the sindicatos could help workers in wage and other disputes. Besides, Vargas had promised during his presidential campaign that he would weaken the federal government's control over the unions. In fact, between the October election and Vargas's swearing in on 31 January 1951, the Ministry of Labor did loosen its grip on union affairs. In some states the government dropped the "ideological certification" (atestado de ideologia), which prevented Communists and other opposition candidates from running for union office, for the upcoming elections.

In São Paulo, these changes brought mixed results to the main industrial unions. In the wake of Vargas's election, hundreds of factory commission members joined the Textile Workers' Union in order to participate in the election of a new directorate. Unfortunately, the requirements for voting (e.g., the prerequisite of twenty-six months of full union membership under the terms of the 1943 CLT)[15] severely restricted the total number of voters. Of 4,200 eligible union members, 3,984 voted; that is, 4 percent of the 100,325 textile workers in the city elected the new directorate. The union stalwarts chose a slate of candidates with close ties to the Ministry of Labor but who also had tried to develop credentials as moderate pelegos: Joaquim Teixeira as president, João Ferri as first secretary, and Antônio Mendes Brazão as treasurer.[16] Even though this new directorate worked with the Ministry of Labor and its associated institutions (e.g., the IAPI and the labor courts), Teixeira, as he had during the brief period of open politics in 1946 and early 1947, fought for wage hikes to address workers' high expectations by negotiating new wage rates with mill owners and government officials throughout January and February. At the same time, workers' independent factory commissions held talks on hours and wage scales with Têxtil Assid Nassif and other firms. Teixeira mediated between the commissions and the mill owners, using employers' fears of wildcat strikes to convince them that granting some concessions, such as changes in the absenteeism clause, would ensure labor peace. By acting as an honest broker, Teixeira not only bargained for better conditions, he also increased his standing among the rank and file. Workers would still describe him as a pelego because of his close ties to the Ministry of Labor, but they increasingly differentiated between would-be moderates like Teixeira and hard-core pelegos such as Melchíades dos Santos.[17]

Textile workers throughout the city supported the union's demands, but women workers felt they did not go far enough. Women weavers and spinners continued to earn about 68 percent of men's wages for the same jobs.[18] Glória Salviano recalled how she and her companheiras complained to each other that they never seemed to earn the same wages men did, and that "the union wasn't going to upset the men by demanding we get increases. After all, most of the union was men." Hermínia Lorenzi dos Santos agreed: "We knew we had to do something ourselves to get men's wages, so we went in our commissions to talk to the bosses about increases."[19] Irene de Oliveira, who was only fourteen years old when she began in the mills in 1951, remembered that women textile workers aggressively pushed for increased wages at this time because they knew they would succeed: "The factories were going all night back then, with lots of girls, like me, on the night shifts. The foremen needed all the skilled weavers they could get, and we knew it, so we told them we would strike if we didn't get increases."[20] Indeed, strikes run by factory commissions without any ties to the Textile Workers' Union succeeded in gaining wage increases in 1951 and 1952.[21]

Elections within the Metalworkers' Union were like those textile workers had experienced, for the majority of São Paulo's metalworkers did not participate in them. Although union leaders and opposition factions had been campaigning formally and informally since April 1950, only 3,637 of the 5,521 eligible union members actually voted; that is, 4.7 percent of the city's 77,579 metallurgical workers chose the new directorate. As their counterparts in the Textile Workers' Union had, metalworkers elected a mildly reformist slate of men who were making themselves into moderate pelegos. Joaquim Ferreira was elected president, Altino Cavalaro was vice president, José Maria Ribeiro was secretary general, Carlos Passos de Andrade and Aldo Lombardi were secretaries, and José Biondi and Remo Forli were the treasurers.[22] Ferreira was not an opposition member of the union (indeed, he had been treasurer for the state Federation of Metalworkers in the 1940s), but he maintained cordial relations with representatives of the factory commissions and had worked with them during the open politics of

1946 and early 1947. Remo Forli, on the other hand, had been an active factory commission leader during the strike movement in late 1945 and early 1946. Further, Ferreira and the new directorate benefited from the appearance of being thoroughly oppositional because they ran against a slate headed by Mário Sobral, whom the rank and file considered the worst pelego in the state.[23]

The new directorate quickly distanced itself from Sobral, Sanchez Duran, and the other hard-core pelegos. Soon after the election, Ferreira revealed that members of the previous directorate had been stealing union funds. The directorate accused Mário Sobral, João Beraldo (a former treasurer), and Cezar Galducci (a former member of the fiscal commission) of spending union money on personal purchases, gambling, and other activities.[24] The June 1951 issue of O *Metalúrgico* included a lengthy denunciation of the previous directorate's association with the Dutra administration and industrialists, and concluded by calling on the city's metalworkers to participate in the union in order to guarantee that it stay independent.[25] Then, in a general assembly in December, the union's lawyer, Christovam Pinto Ferraz, denounced Sobral for maintaining close ties to the city's industrialists. He even claimed that Sobral and the other pelegos had ignored the rank and file's calls for wage hikes in order to protect their own ties with the FIESP.[26]

Through such actions Ferreira was able to refashion himself as a moderate or centrist pelego. He was still a pelego to many because he embraced the overall industrial relations structure and supported the widely hated imposto sindical as an important tool to fund his union. But through his actions, as well as through a comparison with hard-core pelegos such as Sobral, Ferreira staked out a moderate political position—as Teixeira had done in the Textile Workers' Union. These men accomplished this by using their ties to the federal Ministry of Labor to benefit the rank and file of their industries (as opposed to the small number of workers who were sindicalizado/a) and by maintaining good relations with activists within the factory commissions.[27]

The city's metalworkers immediately noticed the operating style of Ferreira and the new directorate. Roberto Unger, a lathe operator, said he did not trust Sobral and his cronies. He knew metalworkers from small shops who joined the union in the 1940s just to receive medical and other benefits. Because the large Cobrasma plant in Osasco where he worked made such benefits available, Unger avoided the union. After the new directorate took over, however, people he trusted in the factory commission convinced him and his companheiros that they should join.[28] Conrado de Papa remembered the campaign waged by commission members at Cobrasma throughout 1951: "These were the guys we trusted, and they told us we had to join the union now to keep it on our side. . . . They said the union would support our strikes now because the pelegos were gone."[29] Indeed, factory commissions throughout São Paulo (including Osasco and Garulhos, which were grouped with the município of São Paulo by the Ministry of Labor) became informal committees within the Metalworkers' Union. They maintained their autonomy but received support from the union in negotiations and strikes.[30]

Vargas had encouraged these changes by loosening the Ministry of Labor's control over the unions and changing the overall tone of relations between the federal government and workers' organizations. Although many hard-core pelegos remained in the labor federations and confederations, unions throughout Brazil elected reformist directorates like those chosen by São Paulo's Textile Workers' and Metalworkers' unions. Vargas's minister of labor, Danton Coelho, said the federal government would not intervene in unions because "the Brazilian worker is mature and ready for a free and vigorous union movement."[31] And the ways Vargas expanded the federal government's role in São Paulo's industrial relations system received enthusiastic support from the city's workers. Union leaders had complained to Coelho and Vargas that the state Department of Labor was nothing more than a tool of the city's industrialists. Its inspection service not only ignored workers' complaints, it provided employers with the names of workers who had filed "confidential" grievances. So, in early May, Vargas announced that the federal government would again manage the formal industrial relations system in São Paulo. For the first time since the July 1933, Paulista industrialists and their allies would not appoint the labor officials who decided how to apply federal labor legislation to their workers.[32]

Vargas's May Day speech at the Vasco de Gama Stadium in Rio (which was broadcast throughout Brazil) detailed clearly the new style of state-run industrial relations he hoped to foster. Vargas first thanked the workers for their key role in his election. He promised his "profound, sincere, and inexhaustible efforts in taking care of workers' demands" and continued by urging workers in the audience to join their unions. He told them, "The sindicato is your weapon, your defense, and your tool for political action."[33] The president said that his administration would fight for higher wages because "it is just that the worker have a reasonable salary . . . to sustain his family, educate his children, buy a house, and take care of all illnesses without favors or public assistance."[34] This veiled promise of a family wage,[35] like all his promises, included a plea that workers join their unions. Vargas assured his audience that unlike in the past, these unions would be completely free; they would be workers' "weapon," their "defense," and their "tool for political action." Vargas was offering the same bargain he had forced on workers during the Estado Novo: he would support their interests through the federal government if they would continue to back him.

São Paulo's industrial workers, however, had a good understanding of the limited value of politicians' promises. The brutal repression of the Estado Novo was less than ten years in the past, and over the past five years both President Dutra and Governor Adhemar de Barros had reneged on guarantees of support for labor's cause. Odette Pasquini, a lifelong weaver, summed up the workers' relationship with politicians when she said, "We were very important people when the elections were coming, but after we elected them, they didn't remember anything."[36] So São Paulo's workers pressured Vargas to meet his most recent promises. They responded to his May Day address by joining the city's main industrial unions (especially the Textile Workers' and Metalworkers' unions) at a rate of more than five hundred people per month in May and June 1951. Factory commissions took Vargas at his word and pressed their bosses for wage increases that would meet inflation. Women textile workers also pushed for an increase in the minimum wage, which had declined steadily in real value since the last increase in 1943 (table 6.1).[37]

Textile and metallurgical workers took advantage of two separate but highly significant developments in their drive for increased wages. First, industry was booming and there was a perceived shortage of labor in the factories. The FIESP complained that its members' establishments could not find enough skilled operatives, and workers bragged to each other that they could always change jobs if their bosses did not increase their pay. According to Diolinda Nascimento, "A foreman would do almost anything to keep a good worker . . . there weren't enough girls available for all the looms, so the foreman would say, 'please tell your girlfriends, sisters, neighbors, anyone that we have work for them here.'"[38] The other development that helped workers was the transfer of the Regional Labor Delegacy from state to federal control. Although Vargas stripped the Paulista state government of its authority, he did

Table 6.1   Cost of Living and Value of Minimum Wage
in São Paulo, 1944–1951

Year	Cost-of-living index	Minimum wage index
1944	100	100
1945	123	81
1946	141	71
1947	185	54
1948	200	50
1949	196	51
1950	208	45
1951	227	44

Sources: Seiti Kaneko Endo and Heron Carlos Esvael do Carmo, Breve Histórico do Indice de Preços ao Consumidor no Município de São Paulo (São Paulo: FIPE, 1987), 17; and DIEESE, "Objetivos e Caraterísticas do Plano Cruzado III."

not staff the federal São Paulo office. Instead, he ordered Enio Lepage, a Ministry of Labor official in the state of Paraná, to assume control of all wage negotiations in São Paulo.[39] Workers quickly turned this weak governmental presence to their advantage.

Representatives of metallurgy factory commissions from throughout the city met in the Metalworkers' Union headquarters during October and November to coordinate their bargaining tactics. With the union in friendly hands, activists from the commissions decided they would be better served by a collective effort. David Carneiro, who had associated only with the comissões in the past, recalled that he and his fellow workers started attending meetings in the union headquarters in late 1951: "First we would go there with the commission, but after we talked with other guys, we—I mean those of us who had never joined the union—decided to join." Hermento Mendes Dantas remembered that "we still felt the comissões were our first line of defense, but now we could also work with the union. You see, this way we would make it our union."[40]

In December the Metalworkers' Union petitioned the FIESP to increase wages by 50 percent for all metallurgical workers in São Paulo. The union told the industrialists they had two options for settling the strike: bosses and workers could either submit their demands to Enio Lepage in Paraná and wait for his ruling, or workers and employers could negotiate directly with each other. The threat of a prolonged bureaucratic review by a Vargas appointee clearly altered the balance of power between bosses and workers. São Paulo's industrialists feared both the possibility that Lepage would side with the workers for political reasons, and that the delays involved with such a process would encourage many workers to take advantage of the tight labor market and seek new employment at higher wages.[41]

The city's metalworkers held a meeting on 16 December with close to five thousand attending to discuss strategies for their wage negotiations. They overwhelmingly approved a motion to launch a twenty-four-hour work stoppage on 18 December. Eugenio Kemp, the strike coordinator, also began tentative negotiations with other sindicatos in the city to coordinate their protest activities. In response, employers accepted a labor court recommendation that they double the basic wages paid in 1945. Workers rejected this offer but returned to work with Christmas bonuses (equal to about 240 hours of work for the average metalúrgico) and their wage demands under review by Enio Lepage in Paraná.[42] The final settlement handed down by the Regional Labor Tribunal called for a doubling of the *actual* wages paid in 1945, not the basic wage rate. That is, metalworkers' new salaries would be double their 1945 pay with all bonuses added in.[43]

The city's textile workers used the same strategy. The union had been negotiating for an increase over the last general wage accord from 1948. At a meeting in late September the directorate listened to the demands of the various factory commissions. The unionists agreed to push for a 50 percent increase over 1948 wages and the abolition of all absenteeism clauses.[44] Mill owners refused to meet the workers' demands, so the union sponsored a twenty-four-hour walkout on 20 December, during which more than fifty thousand textile workers throughout the city struck. Industrialists responded by accepting the Ministry of Labor's suggested 25 percent increase and the abolition of absenteeism penalties. The union directorate wanted to accept this offer, but the rank and file objected. After doing so, the workers elected a separate strike committee (composed of factory commission leaders) to handle the negotiations and suggested that directorate members should lobby Ministry of Labor officials in Rio for help with their demands.[45]

In the midst of these negotiations, Getúlio Vargas met one of his May Day promises: he raised the minimum wage for all Brazilian workers for the first time since 1943. The increase brought the minimum wage to the same level (after being adjusted for inflation) it had been in 1944, after the 1943 wage hike went into effect.[46] The increase, announced by Vargas on 24 December, embodied the complex relationship that was developing between the president and São Paulo's industrial workers in the early 1950s. He had been lobbied by moderate pelegos and PTB activists to grant the increase, and Vargas paid close attention to strikes in São Paulo and elsewhere. He clearly hoped to seize the initiative and position himself as the benefactor of the working class by granting the wage increase on Christmas Eve. Along with the announcement of new rates, the president responded to the strikes in São Paulo by saying, "We don't need strikes or calls for extreme measures. . . . You can be sure that the solutions to your problems are being handled by the government."[47] In the final analysis, however, workers' activism and militancy had clearly forced the president's hand; Vargas was no longer the "father of the poor," he was now just another politician beholden to an important and active constituency.[48]

In the wake of the minimum wage increase, the textile strike brought mixed results. On the one hand, the strikers ended up accepting the 25 percent increase (which was in general only a slight increase over the new minimum wage, especially for women workers) and the abolition of all absenteeism clauses. On the other hand, this strike movement led to a new division of labor within the union. Directorate members took on roles as lobbyists with the Ministry of Labor while the factory commissions ran the strike movement through a committee elected by the rank and file.[49] The December 1951 strike, then, was the first time in the history of São Paulo's textile industry that the rank and file directed the union's activities. This new union openness takes on a further significance given the fact that more than 65 percent of the city's textile workers were women.[50] The union finally bargained for the actual demands put forward by the majority of the rank and file; it did not push for an end to women's night work and other protective measures opposed by the female majority. At last, the Textile Workers' Union truly represented São Paulo's industrial working class.

The divisions between the city's rank-and-file metalworkers and union leadership had frequently been significant, but they were not by nature structural. Most unionists representing this industry were, in fact, metalworkers. Only the most corrupt of the pelegos, such as Sanchez Duran and Mário Sobral, had had little experience on the shop floor. And both the rank and file and the union leadership were overwhelmingly male. The relationship between São Paulo's textile workers and their union activists had been much more complex and confrontational since the 1910s. Although women workers were at ease within their own informal institutions (the factory commissions), they had faced an entrenched male leadership in the union. At their best, these male unionists had been paternalistic; at their worst, they had embraced misogynist ideologies. The rank and file's activism in the 1951 strikes offered a new path for the Textile Workers' Union. As the year came to an end, São Paulo's industrial workers—especially women in the textile mills—confronted a possible watershed in their relations with unionists, bosses, and the state.

Institutionalizing Rank-and-File Power

Factory Commissions Become Union Committees

At several key conjunctures (1917–24, 1930–35, and 1945–47) São Paulo's industrial workers and the city's unionists and Left activists had come together to launch effective strikes and other protest activities. In each instance the rank and file's independent organizing convinced union and leftist leaders of the importance of work conditions and wages as issues rather than the anarchists' and Communists' political concerns or the pelegos' narrow interest in running exclusive mutual aid societies. The inability of union and left-wing activists to do more than simply react to the rank and file's demands had doomed São Paulo's working-class movement. Without the complete integration of grass-roots activists from the factory commissions into union directorates, which in the case of the textile industry would have meant the wholesale incorporation of women workers into leadership positions, union and Left activists remained out of step with the rank and file.

By late 1951 and early 1952, factory commission members, moderate pelegos, reformist union activists (i.e., those members who had been in opposition in the 1940s), and young syndicalist members of the Communist party all recognized the importance of finally bringing grass-roots leaders into the formal union structures.[51] They all realized that the election of central committees to coordinate the comissões' activities and the unions' roles during the December 1951 strike movement had been an effective strategy for mediating conflicting interests. The Textile Workers' and Metalworkers' unions therefore institutionalized the factory commissions. Leaders and rank-and-file members in both sindicatos created a series of standing committees to represent the factory commissions as parts of the formal union structure.[52]

Within the Textile Workers' Union, the Salary Committee and the Strike Committee quickly became the two most important institutions beyond the directorate. At first, only the most active factory commission members who were also formal members of the union (i.e., they were sindicalizado/a) were encouraged by directorate members to work on these committees. Those activists soon pressured the directorate, through an open confrontation at a general assembly, to allow factory commission members who were not sindicalizado/a to participate in these new union committees. One of the commissions' most outspoken allies in the union at this time was Antônio Chamorro, who had participated in factory commissions and had maintained good relations with other activists in the comissões. Chamorro had also been a vocal opponent of the hard-core pelegos since the 1940s.[53] So, popular pressure from outside the union, lobbying by unionists such as Chamorro, and Teixeira's desire to refashion himself as a moderate led to the opening of the formal union structures to the factory commission activists. Again, this opening of the union is particularly remarkable given the fact that these committees were frequently dominated by women workers. Maria Pavone remembered that the women on the Salary Committee sometimes seemed to be running the general assemblies in 1952 and 1953: "We wouldn't pay attention to the official union business, budgets, number of processos filed, that sort of thing. We waited for the report of the Salary Committee, and once they got going nobody paid attention to the directorate."[54]

In the case of metalworkers, the sex composition of the rank and file (which was practically all male) eased the integration of factory commissions into the formal union structure. Once again, the experience of the December 1951 strike movement convinced São Paulo's metalworkers to tie the comissões to the union. Not only did they create standing salary and strike committees, but activists from the larger factories (e.g., Máquinas Piratiningas, Aços Finos, and Cobrasma) put together commissions to represent workers from the smaller (i.e., those with fewer than thirty employees) establishments in Brás and Mooca.[55] Although metalworkers from those shops had been meeting during their lunch breaks and after work for years, their informal groups, which had come together to launch strikes in the past, now had a means of formalizing their position within the union. Speaking inside a small metalworking shop on the Rua Martim Burchard in Brás, José Antônio de Mendes recalled, "We needed to have a separate commission because we worked in small places, like this one here. We didn't want to talk about the problems with the company food store. Listen my son, all we have here is coffee and *mate!*"[56]

In late January and early February 1952 São Paulo's textile and metallurgical workers tested their new union structures. Metalworkers from shops throughout the city used a coordinated action by their factory commissions and the union's salary and strike committees to force employers to pay the increases promised in the last wage settlement. At the same time, members of the union directorate filed processos and lobbied Ministry of Labor officials to force São Paulo's industrialists to adhere to the wage agreement.[57] Textile factory commissions and union committees divided the labor in pretty much the same way. Workers struck Tecelagem Aziz Nader on 3 January to force their bosses to meet the new pay levels. By 12 January an estimated seven thousand workers from six more mills in the city had struck. With the union lobbying the Ministry of Labor and the factory commissions coordinating the strikers' activities, the mill owners had few options other than bracing for a general textile strike or settling. They met the workers' demands, and the strikers returned to the mills on 16 January. In early February, some mill owners attempted to pay wages below the agreed-upon scale, but the coordinated action of the factory commissions and the union brought a quick settlement: employers met their obligations and paid the proper wages.[58]

The U.S. labor attaché in São Paulo reported on the extraordinary success of the factory commissions at this time. He noted that most industrialists seemed to prefer direct negotiations with the comissões over using the labor courts. The diplomat speculated that the reasons for this change were the speed with which disputes could be settled through direct negotiations, the desire of employers to pay wages that would keep up with the rising cost of living (although this does not explain why industrialists tried to renege on the agreements from December 1951), and employers' continued apprehension about sending wage disputes to Enio Lepage, the federal labor delegate in Paraná.[59] The one key factor the attaché failed to report was the impact of the concerted actions of the factory commissions and the unions, for the unity of purpose between the rank and file and the union leadership clearly had altered the calculus of São Paulo's industrial relations system.

Vargas took note of these developments among the people he

considered his strongest supporters.[60] On May Day 1952, therefore, he placed himself on the side of the rank and file in their struggles with entrenched hard-core pelegos. He apologized for the Ministry of Labor's past support of the pelegos. He pledged his support to help the rank and file in their struggles to rid their unions of corrupt leaders and then added a criticism of politicians that many workers themselves had articulated. Brazil's workers, he said, should not be "at the mercy of those who only remember you on the eve of election day."[61] In October, his minister of labor, José de Segadas Vianna, continued these admissions by telling the pro-Vargas newspaper *Última Hora* that corruption in the unions had been an open secret since the Estado Novo. He assured Brazilians that the Ministry of Labor would do all it could to help workers expel the corrupt unionists.[62] Vargas followed these denunciations of the hard-core pelegos by abolishing once and for all the "ideological certification" for election to union office and by calling for a thorough reorganization of the Ministry of Labor.[63]

Ultimately, Vargas was denouncing the very industrial relations system he had foisted on Brazil. He tried to obscure this fact by pushing for reforms of the union structure and offering new benefits to workers, but by May Day 1952 Vargas had given up trying to coerce or gently persuade Brazil's workers into a government-manipulated union structure.[64] That is, Vargas finally abandoned the corporatist policies he had so forcefully introduced during the early 1930s and the Estado Novo dictatorship. His new perspective, however, stemmed from more than just a desire to be remembered as a democratic politician; Brazilian workers, through their refusal to join unions run by pelegos, their independent organizing and protest activities, and their direct communications with Vargas, had demonstrated that they would not be manipulated by the corporatist government structure.

São Paulo's textile and metallurgical workers continued to reveal their deep distrust of the official union structure and its representatives throughout 1952 and 1953. The rank and file in the Textile Workers' Union worked with young PCB and factory commission activists to expel hard-core pelegos through popular votes in general assemblies. Borrowing the terminology of the Estado Novo dictatorship and Dutra's crackdown on labor, the rank and file declared corrupt unionists from the past directorates *cassado* (i.e., they lost their political rights within the union).[65] Then, in elections held in August 1952, the rank and file chose outspoken critics of peleguismo to fill vacancies on the directorate. They elected Nelson Rusticci first secretary, Carlos Pinto

Ferreira second secretary, and Luís Firmino de Lima librarian. All three men had ties to the salary and strike committees, and Luís Firmino had been an activist in both the Salary Committee and the syndicalist wing of the Communist party.[66] This election took on even greater significance when, after Joaquim Teixeira died in December, the rank and file elevated Rusticci to the presidency of the union.[67]

Interestingly, the city's textile workers did not elect any women from the comissões to the directorate at this time. Although women from the factory commissions influenced the activities of the salary and strike committees, they still could not gain access to the highest leadership positions within the union. The directorate no doubt felt challenged by women's activism in the commissions and sought to limit their power within the union. The failure to include women in leadership positions demonstrates the limits of the open unions at this time: Women had a greater voice than they had had in the past, but they were again denied access to real power. Still, both textile and metallurgical workers pushed to open their unions to a wider membership. São Paulo's metalworkers replaced the last hard-core pelegos with factory commission activists in February 1953.[68] These purges affected only the most corrupt pelegos, for given the atmosphere of union openness, moderate pelegos quickly refashioned themselves as honest brokers by responding to rank-and-file demands. The city's workers took such actions because by the early 1950s they had accumulated a vast set of experiences which persuaded them that they could trust only their own institutions. Moreover, the federal government's various labor policies since the early 1940s provided factory commission members from throughout the city with various opportunities to meet (sometimes in jail, and sometimes in open union general assemblies) and map out coordinated strategies. Vargas's latest stance favoring free and open unions hastened the rise of factory commission members to positions of authority within their sindicatos. This development, in turn, helped to bring about the most important strike in Brazil since the General Strike of 1917.

The Strike of the 300,000 and the Triumph of Rank-and-File Power

At the same time that workers in São Paulo were building a strong, open union movement, industrialists—especially mill owners—were continuing their program of rationalizing production. Vargas encouraged the importation of capital equipment and even geared his exchange-rate policies in early 1953 to limit some imports (e.g., consumer goods) and to encourage the entry of others for industrial production.[69] Once again, the rationalization was uneven. A 1953 SENAI study found that only four mills in the city were completely equipped with the latest automated weaving and spinning machinery. At the same time, 35 percent of all Paulistano looms were automated because many firms had a mix of old and new machines. Further, those mills that did not have any automated equipment were forced to change their work regimes in order to keep pace with their competitors. All in all, productivity per weaver rose 80 percent from 1949 to 1959 because of the changes owners forced on work regimes.[70]

São Paulo's textile workers experienced this rationalization program through speedups, increases in the number of looms and spindles they had to tend, and a greater frequency of accidents on the shop floor. João Bonifácio recalled that the new spinning machinery had an automatic shutoff that any flaw in the thread might trigger: "What I remember is how tired we would get running around fixing the thread and restarting machines. Before the automated machines came we worked hard, but afterward we would just run around the spinning room. We just kept running all day long." Luís Firmino remembered that bosses changed both work loads and piece rates after they installed the new looms.[71] Diolinda Nascimento hated the new machines: "I was a weaver, 'first class.' But once the new looms came, I spent more time running up and down aisles switching machines on and off than I did weaving. I was still a weaver, 'first class,' but all I did was run around with the new looms."[72]

Many other weavers and spinners resented losing control over the work process when bosses installed the automated equipment. They also had to cope with increasingly harsh work regimes and decreasing real incomes. The rank and file filed thousands of processos through their union to force changes on the shop floor and to protect the piece rate system. Although the union won many of these processos, filing them was time-consuming, and each usually dealt with only one worker or shift of workers.[73] In November and December 1952, the Textile Workers' Union pressed bosses to give their workers a Christmas bonus as a sort of payment for all the changes the workers had been experiencing. Apparently, some mills granted the bonus, but no industrywide policy was adopted. The metalworkers also sought bonuses to help fight the impact of inflation, and the two unions decided to coordinate their requests for the extra pay.[74]

Shortages in raw materials for São Paulo's factories, as well as problems maintaining a steady supply of electricity in the city, allowed industrialists to shorten or stagger work shifts in early 1953.[75] The shorter shifts enabled mill owners who were installing automated machinery to fire "redundant" employees, and it helped factories with new looms or spindles to intensify work regimes while they decreased the length of each shift. With the rationing of electricity in the city, textile workers had fewer hours of work per shift (and in some cases, fewer shifts), so they had to increase their piece rate wages by speeding up their work pace. In this way, the shortage of electricity inadvertently played a key role in the rationalization of production in early 1953.[76]

São Paulo's industrial workers had faced rationalization schemes, production slowdowns, and economic recessions in the past, but they had never had well-integrated factory commissions and unions to organize collective actions against these changes; in 1953 the situation was different. Not only had the rank and file in the textile and metallurgical workers' unions gained de facto control of union policies through their strike and salary committees, they had also—with the acquiescence of the federal government—replaced hard-core pelegos with moderate pelegos and opposition activists. This process continued in February 1953 when the city's metalworkers elected Remo Forli, who began his career in the union as an opposition activist from the comissões, as their president. This election coincided with a movement among factory commission members from the textile and metallurgy establishments in Mooca to coordinate their activities. According to Conrado de Papa, the entire effort to build formal ties between activists from the two unions was initiated by weavers and metalúrgicos in Mooca during this period of open unions: "I guess it was the proximity of the mills to the metals shops. Besides, a lot of the guys I worked with had started out in the textile factories, and they still knew the factory commission people in the mills."[77] There were also important kinship ties that drew women textile and male metalworkers together in Mooca. Some were married, others were siblings or cousins, and many were paisani.

Leaders of the salary committees of the Textile Workers' and Metalworkers' unions translated these informal contacts into a formal agreement to coordinate their wage demands in January and February 1953. The two union directorates, which had worked together in their push for Christmas bonuses in late 1952, accepted this proposal. Syndicalist members of the Communist party, such as Luís Firmino, were active in coordinating the two unions' strategies, but the PCB itself played little or no role in the emerging strike movement.[78] Indeed, as factory commissions throughout the city met to discuss what tactics they would use against their employers—who were overwhelmingly Brazilians—the Communist party newspaper, *Imprensa Popular*, blamed "United States imperialism" for the problems in São Paulo's factories.[79]

The Salary Committee in the Textile Workers' Union had gathered information on wages and the cost of living from the various factory commissions during December and January. It then presented an official request to the Textile Industrialists' Association for a 60 percent increase in wages for all weavers and spinners in the city.[80] When mill owners stalled, the Strike Committee decided to hold a march from the union's headquarters on the Rua Oiapoque in Brás to the Textile Industrialists' Association in Anhangabaú. On 10 March an estimated sixty thousand textile workers paraded down the Avenida Rangel Pestana, through the Praça de Sé, and across the downtown area to Anhangabaú. The mobilization of so many workers clearly unnerved mill owners. A Ministry of Labor official even referred to the peaceful march as "a cunning form of agitation."[81] The mill owners still refused to increase wages, however.

Similar salary committees in the Bank Workers', Furniture Makers', Glassmakers', and Printers' unions contacted committee activists from the Textile Workers' and Metalworkers' unions to coordinate citywide salary demands. On 18 March, workers from all six unions held a rally in the Praça da Sé at which they demanded increased wages and action by Governor Lucas Nogueira Garcez to lower food prices in the city's markets. When no increases were offered by their bosses, factory commissions from several textile mills decided to strike on Monday, 23 March. As their predecessors had in June 1917, women from comissões in the Brás and Mooca mills agreed they would begin work in the morning and then strike after their lunch break. While workers from the hundreds of factories and small shops in these two industrial neighborhoods ate their lunches, women from commissions called on all their companheiros to join the walkout. Diolinda Nascimento recalled how women from the Matarazzo mill on Rua Dom Bosco in Mooca spread news of the walkout: "They didn't have a hard time convincing us [i.e., other women] to join them, but some of the men in the mills, who received higher salaries, didn't want to strike. I remember one man arguing with a group of girls from the comissão. He wouldn't strike, so they cornered him, and a big fight broke out. Finally, one girl took off her shoe and started beating the guy in the head.[82]

On Wednesday, 25 March, general assemblies of the Textile Workers' and Metalworkers' unions decided to call a general strike for their two industries. Textile workers still wanted a 60 percent increase, and metalworkers sought an across-the-board increase of Cr$800, which would be a 30 to 50 percent wage hike. Interestingly, although both union directorates sanctioned these walkouts, the two strike committees actually coordinated their activities in the Clube Piratininga in Mooca rather than at one of the two unions' headquarters.[83] There, with help from the two unions, they created the Central Strike Committee, which coordinated day-to-day activities and received reports directly from the factory commissions. With rank-and-file workers in control of this central committee, weavers were finally able to put a woman textile worker, Mariana Galgaitez, in as one of the directors. Young girls' and adult women's factory commissions dealt almost exclusively with Galgaitez and other women who worked with the Central Strike Committee. With the help of this committee based in Mooca, more than 100,000 textile and metallurgical workers went on strike within days. And in a meeting called by the Central Strike Committee, the two unions agreed that neither group of workers would end the strike until all the demands of both had been met.[84]

Soon, furniture makers and glassworkers joined the strike movement. By early April, some 300,000 industrial workers in São Paulo (which had a population of about 2.2 million people in 1950) were on strike. At the same time, owners of paper and candy factories quickly granted their workers increases of between 10 and 20 percent to keep them from joining the growing movement.[85] These developments, however, did not speed the settlement of the textile and metallurgical workers' wage disputes. In fact, mounted city police and the DOPS began to attack peaceful picketers. They beat the striking men and women in order, they said, to keep the factories open. The U.S. consul in São Paulo telegrammed to the embassy in Rio that the police even attacked a peaceful march to the Praça da Sé to call on Governor Nogueira Garcez to help their movement: "Crowds onlookers dispersed by mounted police, tear gas, fire hoses. . . . Reinforced police on alert patrolling affected areas. Situation disquieting."[86] These attacks were part of the Ministry of Labor's opposition to the strike movement. Enio Lepage urged workers to return to their factories and ordered the

Women textile workers who participated in the Strike of the 300,000 under arrest at the DOPS headquarters. (*Courtesy of the Centro de Memória Sindical*)

DOPS to prevent any "unauthorized" workers' meetings (i.e., any meetings by the Central Strike Committee). Minister of Labor Segadas Viana in Rio said he fully supported Lepage's activities and blamed the strike on outside agitators. He even suggested the police should crack down harder on the strikers.[87]

The opposition by the federal government only strengthened the position of the factory commission activists who were running the Central Strike Committee, for the union directorates could not accomplish much by lobbying Ministry of Labor officials.[88] Union leaders had better luck with Governor Nogueira Garcez, who worked with the TRT to put forward an offer of a 23 percent wage increase for all the strikers. Although a few unionists wanted to accept this, both the rank and file and the industrialists rejected it. At the same time, the four unions' strike committees (i.e., those for textiles, metals, furniture making, and glassworking) formalized their informal ties into the Inter-Union Unity Pact (Pacto de Unidade Intersindical, PUI) and announced publicly that no one union's workers would return to work until all the strikers settled.[89]

The city's industrialists at first reacted to the near total walkout in textiles, metallurgy, furniture making, and glassworking with bravado and threats. At a rancorous meeting in FIESP headquarters on 8 April, mill owners complained bitterly that the strike was nothing more than a "communist plot." And although they admitted that the cost of living had increased at least 23 percent since the last pay hike, they pledged not to offer higher wages.[90] As the meeting wore on, owners of metalworking shops (e.g., Aliperti and Wolff Metal) admitted that they had in fact offered their workers 20 and 23 percent increases, but the strikers had turned them down. FIESP president Antônio Devisate assured members that a favorable ruling from the TRT would force workers back to the factories and give employers the right to fire those who refused to end the strike.[91]

São Paulo's factory districts soon developed the look and atmosphere of a battlefield. Mounted police continued to attack peaceful marches by picketers, and DOPS troops set up machine-gun nests near factories. On 9 April, more than four thousand workers clashed with police in Mooca. Hundreds were wounded, and many were beaten and dragged off to jail. Factory commission members and union leaders responded by dividing their labor to speed efforts to settle the strike. Nelson Rusticci of the Textile Workers' Union negotiated with the governor and the DOPS to limit police attacks.[92] Commission members maintained pickets and worked to put together a strike fund. According to Hermínia Lorenzi dos Santos: "We all helped out during the strike, cooking and taking care of children. We didn't have a lot of money, but there was always a way, by borrowing from relatives in the interior, that sort of thing." Maria Pavone added, "The strike was hard, but we knew we could win. Sure we all helped out, because during a strike, at work, in your home you should have dignity. In everything, there should be dignity, and that's what we were fighting for."[93]

Soon after the clash in Mooca, the TRT proposed a 32 percent increase of the wages in effect on 1 January 1952 for all metalworkers in the city. A general assembly of thousands of metalworkers met in the Hipódromo de Mooca the next day and overwhelmingly rejected the offer, saying they would accept such an increase once it was offered to their companheiros in textiles, glass, and furniture making. Representatives of the unions then went to Rio to try to convince Vargas that he should support their demands. With Brás, Mooca, Ipiranga, and other factory districts paralyzed by the strike, the TRT offered textile workers a 32 percent increase on wages in effect on 15 February 1952. When this same rate was offered to glass and furniture workers, an assembly of strikers at the Mooca Hipódromo voted 7,337 to accept and 851 to stay out. The workers then voted unanimously to accept the increase and return to work, but only after all jailed strikers were freed.[94]

Remo Forli prepared a memorial thanking Governor Nogueira Garcez for his help in settling the strike and then continued with the workers' final list of demands: strikers would return to work only after the prisoners were freed, employers would pledge that no factory commission leaders would be fired, and the 32 percent increase would be codified as a two-year contract that could be renegotiated after one year.[95] While the police stalled, the Central Strike Committee initiated a march of twenty thousand workers to the governor's palace demanding the release of their companheiros from the city's jails. By this time, many strikers were so frustrated that they actually attacked the police along the route. According to Luís Firmino, "We gave everyone special instructions to remain peaceful, but a lot of the women were so fed up with the police that they cornered a few of them and beat them!" Ultimately, the march achieved its goal; the police released jailed strikers, and the city's industrial workers returned to work on 23 April, more than six weeks after textile workers had initiated the strike.[96]

The "Strike of the 300,000," as it quickly became known, was the culmination of years of grass-roots worker organizing. The rank and file's factory commissions operated in opposition to their bosses' rationalization and wage policies, and against the closed unions run by pelegos. Vargas's loosening of the government's control of the unions and the experience many commission activists had gained during the Estado Novo and Dutra years convinced these grass-roots leaders to maintain their own comissões as autonomous entities, and also to institutionalize their power through salary and strike committees. This process opened São Paulo's unions, and in the case of the Textile Workers' Union finally provided the female majority with the opportunity to direct policy. In the final analysis, the strike also demonstrated to the rank and file their own strengths and weaknesses. They found power in open unions and the unity of the four sindicatos in the PUI. The strikers also found, however, that no matter how well organized they were, they still relied on the government for the final wage settlement. The 32 percent increase was a substantial hike, but São Paulo's workers had no way of knowing if it covered the rising cost of living. Indeed, their only inflation statistics had been compiled by the municipal authorities, who often received their data from the FIESP.[97]

Leveling the Playing Field: The Aftermath of the Strike of the 300,000

The unity among São Paulo's industrial unions, as well as the factory commissions' seizure of de facto control of the textile and metallurgical workers' unions, had clearly caught both Vargas and the city's industrialists off guard. The industrialists reacted by settling the strike;

Vargas by trying to move closer to his labor constituency. In his May Day address, Vargas not only assured Brazilian workers he supported their cause, he actually attacked the rich as "those who speculate with misery, [and] those who enrich themselves with easy profits." He concluded by claiming, "A new world is born, a world in which we begin to realize that all people, because they work, have the right to share in the common wealth they produce."[98] Vargas next moved to placate workers by appointing a young PTB activist from Rio Grande do Sul, João Goulart, minister of labor. With Goulart's appointment, Brazil's workers finally had a voice in the cabinet. Although the new minister was Vargas's protégé and not from the labor movement, he did in fact represent workers' issues within the federal bureaucracy. So, twenty-three years after it was founded, the Ministry of Labor finally functioned as an advocate for workers.[99]

In the wake of the strike, São Paulo's industrial workers continued to push for improved work conditions. Textile and metallurgical workers' factory commissions, through their unions, filed tens of thousands of processos to force employers to meet their obligations contained in the new contract, as well as those spelled out in the labor code.[100] And in the aftermath of Goulart's appointment, the U.S. labor attaché noted how workers used every possible legal mechanism to deal with bosses: "It is said that every working man in São Paulo carries a copy of the labor laws in his pocket. This, of course, is not true but what is meant is that practically every industrial worker is familiar with the wording of the labor laws and determines much of his activities by his interpretation of the laws."[101]

In addition to using the labor laws to their advantage, the rank and file in São Paulo strengthened their hold over the unions. Both the textile and metallurgical workers' unions gained thousands of new members in the months after the strike.[102] Factory commission activists also gained new authority as the unions expanded their directorates in 1953 to include these grass-roots leaders. The unions then pressured Vargas and Goulart to lessen Rio's control over them; they even told Goulart they would no longer accept funds from the imposto sindical.[103] Some unionists, including João Ferri and Nelson Rusticci of the Textile Workers' Union, attempted to regain control of their sindicatos by limiting the commissions' power. They were quickly rebuffed by the rank and file, which had become accustomed to open unions.[104]

The new structure that tied factory commissions to salary and strike committees and then to union directorates—with the unions coordinating their activities under the auspices of the PUI—altered the framework of São Paulo's industrial relations system. Workers relied on this structure for the negotiations of new minimum wage rates that began in late 1953.[105] At the same time, comissões and the unions bargained with individual firms for higher wages. So, the rank and file used the official industrial relations system, but unionists, industrialists, and government bureaucrats all knew that if workers' wage demands were not at least given serious consideration, they might face another great strike. Employers and Ministry of Labor officials responded by granting wage increases or entering into negotiations with union officials.[106]

The deliberations over the 1954 minimum wage reflected the new power of São Paulo's working-class movement. Goulart reacted to popular pressure for a substantial increase by stating in February that the minimum wage should be doubled. Vargas's civilian and military opponents forced the president to disavow Goulart's proposal; in January Vargas faced intense pressure to fire the young gaúcho, who was forced to resign in late February.[107] Still, Goulart's entreaty was hard for Vargas to ignore, and on May Day the president officially doubled the minimum wage for all Brazilian workers. He justified the increase by pointing to the great wealth workers had produced for the elite and continued by assuring workers that they had, indeed, demonstrated their power. He then pressed them to channel that power through the electoral process: "With your votes you can not only defend your interests, but you can influence the very destiny of the nation. As citizens your views will bear weight at the polls. As a class, you can make your ballots the decisive numerical force. You constitute the majority. Today you are with the government. Tomorrow you will be the government."[108]

Even with the minimum wage increase, São Paulo's workers continued to suffer the impact of inflation (table 6.2). Comissões responded by pushing for higher wages. Once again industrialists balked, so in August the strike committees of the original four unions from the Inter-Union Unity Pact along with unions representing printers, bank workers, hotel workers, commercial workers, rail porters, and journalists organized a one-day general strike for 1 September to convince employers to negotiate in good faith. The planners hoped not only to pressure bosses but also to bring Vargas, who had been equivocating on workers' issues since his dramatic May Day speech, into the negotiations. Vargas, however, was unable to keep juggling so many different interest groups, and he was under increasing pressure from his military

Table 6.2   Cost of Living and Value of Minimum Wage
in São Paulo, 1951–1957

Year	Cost-of-living index	Minimum wage index
1951	100	36.80
1952	123	98.77
1953	150	81.35
1954	177	98.88
1955	212	111.04
1956	258	112.81
1957	308	122.65

Source: Seiti Kaneko Endo and Heron Carlos Esvael do Carmo, *Breve His-tórico do Índice de Preços ao Consumidor no Município de São Paulo* (São Paulo: FIPE, 1987), 17; and DIEESE, "Objetivos e Caraterísticas do Plano Cruzado III."

and civilian opponents. When the pressure from all sides reached uncontrollable dimensions and wore down Vargas's political energy and will, he killed himself, on 24 August 1954, in his bedroom in the Catete Palace.[109]

The strike organizers had attacked Vargas viciously in their meetings and in union general assemblies. Indeed, they planned to denounce the president in speeches during a march on 1 September. When Vargas killed himself, however, leaders of the Strike Committee immediately decided to use the dead president as a martyred symbol of the working class. On 1 September, strikers paralyzed the city. Although planned as a one-day protest, the rank and file decided to stay out until all the strikers received wage hikes. And, within days, employers offered 25 percent wage increases and promised to work with the unions to help control rising food prices in the city. The September 1954 strike was not quite as dramatic as the Strike of the 300,000, but it did have the same basic effect. Workers' factory commissions articulated their demands to union salary and strike committees, which then coordinated a citywide strike through the Inter-Union Unity pact. Unions throughout the interior of the state of São Paulo also struck using similar interunion agreements.[110]

Once again, though, the only data available to the strikers to justify their wage demands had been prepared by the FIESP and the city government. Further, President João Café Filho (Vargas's vice president) had no political loyalty to the rank and file and did not support the factory commissions' demands. In fact, he had close ties to many of the hard-core pelegos who had maintained positions in the labor federations after being voted out of office by the rank and file.[111] Activists involved in the Inter-Union Unity Pact decided to create their own autonomous organization to study real wage rates, different components of the cost of living, and overall working-class conditions. As early as December 1953, members of the union salary committees had complained to their sindicatos' directorates that they simply did not have accurate information on wage rates and the cost of living. And they were convinced that the city and FIESP economists frequently manipulated statistics to cheat workers.[112]

So, in late October 1955, the unions from the PUI all contributed funds (including money from the imposto sindical) to create the Inter-Union Department of Statistics and Socioeconomic Studies (Departamento Intersindical de Estatísticas e Estudos Sócio-Econômicos, DIEESE). Although representatives of the city's major unions, which together represented more than 500,000 workers, served on the DIEESE's directorate, statisticians from the Bank Workers' Union dominated the organization in its first years; the DIEESE even installed itself in the bancários' union hall.[113] In its first years the DIEESE played three key roles. First, it provided urgently needed statistics on wages and the cost of living for all workers in the city.[114] In fact, the directors decided to conduct their first study on the living conditions of São Paulo's sanitation workers, who were among the lowest paid workers in the city. The DIEESE also functioned as a sort of umbrella organization for São Paulo's unions. Union leaders, factory commissions, and salary committee activists (from practically all the city's unions) all worked on DIEESE studies and shared information, funding, and tactics.[115] Finally, by conducting house-to-house and factory-to-factory surveys of living and work conditions, DIEESE researchers were able to gather statistical information and also encourage workers to participate in factory commissions and their unions.[116]

With the founding of the DIEESE, São Paulo's working-class movement (which by the mid-1950s was made up of factory commissions tied into unions through salary and strike committees, and unions unified in the PUI and DIEESE) had finally leveled the playing field of Brazil's complex state-run industrial relations system.[117] São Paulo's workers had created the institutions they needed to fight against their bosses and the state for higher wages and improved conditions, but they did so without sacrificing the pluralism inherent in the factory commission movement. These open institutions allowed workers to retain their separate identities—of sex, race, and industry—without diminishing their collective political power. São Paulo's working-class movement, then, had the tools necessary for its various struggles, as long as Brazil remained a democracy.

From Union Democracy to
Democratic Politics?

By the mid-1950s, São Paulo's industrial workers had managed to establish a de facto industrial relations system that barely resembled the complex corporatist structure of the CLT, which remained the law of the land. Workers' factory commissions, some of which had been transformed into formal shop-floor councils within the unions, bargained directly with employers. Indeed, unionists, employers, and rank-and-file workers all preferred avoiding the labor bureaucracy, and as the labor laws became increasingly irrelevant, politicians in Rio even debated modifying the CLT.[1] The labor laws were still a source of working-class empowerment, for they provided an official discourse of rights workers could strategically call upon, but São Paulo's day-to-day industrial relations system in the mid-1950s was unfettered by the elaborate state control mechanisms of the CLT.

The roots of this open style of industrial relations lay in the independent factory commission structure and syndicalist legacy that had been evolving since the 1917 General Strike. By the mid-1950s, rank-and-file workers had succeeded in translating the internal democracy of their comissões into a democratic union movement. The Textile Workers' and Metalworkers' unions incorporated some of the factory commissions into their formal institutional structures and became much more responsive to rank-and-file demands. Labor leaders also finally admitted that their role was to support local commissions' negotiations and strikes, and they opened their directorates to workers of every political persuasion from Communists to supporters of São Paulo's colorful Jânio Quadros.[2] Moreover, the same balance of power operated in other Paulistano unions in the mid-1950s.[3]

The Communist pary also came to recognize the importance of organizing at the grass-roots level. Since the 1920s, the national PCB leadership had vacillated between a putschist impulse and the desire to make alliances with elements they saw as the "progressive national bourgeoisie." Local communist militants in São Paulo, however, had been organizing among the factory commissions since the mid-1940s. In the mid-1950s, Luís Carlos Prestes and other members of the national PCB leadership changed course. They even openly criticized their past practice of ignoring grass-roots organizing—especially among women workers.[4] Like the anarchists before them, the national PCB leadership learned the importance of organizing locally around working-class issues from rank-and-file practices.

This acceptance of the Paulistano syndicalist tradition among workers, unionists, leftist activists, and even some industrialists and government officials represented the beginning of local, grass-roots democracy for these workers. There had been periods of open electoral politics in the past, but they were "democracy" in a narrow sense. Workers had voted for prolabor politicians at various times, but always within an exclusionary political system.[5] In São Paulo in the post–Estado Novo period, for example, workers faced a hostile state: a Paulistano industrialist served as the federal minister of labor and the head of the DOPS ran the state Department of Labor. Moreover, the corporatist industrial relations structure kept workers' unions in the hands of the hard-core pelegos. And when radicals were elected to municipal and state offices throughout the state of São Paulo in 1947, the Dutra administration erased their electoral mandates by making the PCB an illegal political party.[6]

Although São Paulo's industrial workers had not forced a change in the formal regime structure by the mid-1950s, they had managed to bring about changes in the de facto industrial relations system. More important, they had succeeded in articulating the democratic foundations of their factory commission movement to the formal state-sanctioned union structure. They moved beyond voting and other forms of participation within the circumscribed polity and began the process of the democratization of civil society.[7] By exercising their rights as Brazilian citizens through their own institutions they managed to push—perhaps only slightly—the boundaries of the limited democratic regime. By making the most restrictive aspects of the CLT largely irrelevant to their relations with employers, ending the Ministry of Labor's control over the unions, cajoling some pelegos into adopting a moderate or reformist position, and creating autonomous labor institutions such as the DIEESE, these workers had partially democratized the part of the state that most affected their lives: the industrial relations system.

That is not to say that São Paulo's working people participated in an unfettered political system in the mid-1950s, or that populist politicians such as Jânio Quadros and João Goulart consistently represented the aspirations of the working class.[8] Rather, the workers' democratic forms were a modest first step in the long process of the democratization of Brazilian society, a process that was brutally interrupted by the military *golpe* of April 1964. That first step, however, became part of the Paulistano syndicalist tradition and was no doubt called upon in workers' struggles for an independent labor movement that eventually produced the Partido dos Trabalhadores.[9] The denunciations of pelegos and the imposto sindical, along with calls for union democracy, declared in that May 1987 rally of São Paulo metalworkers were part of the ongoing syndicalist heritage that grew out of the factory commission experience.

The commissions' ongoing importance to Paulistano workers is not only demonstrated in the historical records of institutions, it is manifest in their recollections and even nostalgia for the comissões. Every worker I interviewed for this book, along with people who shared their experiences from this era with me but were not formally interviewed, spoke at length about their participation in shop-floor organizations. Some explicitly recalled the factory commissions, and others added in an offhand way that their informal shop-floor groups were a lot like the comissões that the PT maintained. In an interesting way, people recalled their experiences from the 1920s to the 1950s through the lens of the late 1980s. That is not to diminish their experiences in that previous epoch, but it is important to note that the PT's legacy from the late 1970s and 1980s provided a vocabulary for some workers to use in discussing the past. Such is the complexity of working-class consciousness and historical memory.[10]

It is also important that we do not romanticize the factory commissions. Although they were a key social space for the articulation of the workers' "hidden transcripts" (which in turn made up much of their developing syndicalism) and they provided women workers with a place where they could organize without male interference, these informal institutions sometimes served as an arena for disciplining those who wanted to participate in the pelegos' unions or in foremen's production speedups. Just because all the members of a given commission worked in the same section of a factory, they did not necessarily share the same perspectives on wage demands, relations with foremen, when to strike, and other issues. A closer analysis of individual comissões would no doubt reveal differences among their members.[11]

And yet, only after we move beyond the impulse to characterize these workers' organizations as either politically pristine or desperately flawed can we focus on the central issue: Workers organized locally around the points they considered most important to their lives. Those local organizing and protest activities in turn helped to convince Left activists (e.g., the anarchists and later the Communists) to adopt a more "bread-and-butter" perspective and to embrace workers' syndicalism. At the same time, once those labor and leftist activists concentrated their activities on the local level, they were able to broaden the rank and file's syndicalism to include macrolevel political concerns. The legacy of anarchist politics in Paulistano workers' tendency to distrust state institutions is an enduring example of this.

The complicated syndicalism that developed over the first half of the twentieth century included highly gendered and, at times, contradictory discourses of work, organizing, protest, and politics. Women workers occupied a unique position in São Paulo; they dominated the textile labor force and consistently made up between 30 and 40 percent of the workers in the clothing, chemical, and food-processing sectors. These women did not perform factory labor only during their youth; such work was their career. Semiskilled factory labor in São Paulo was women's work.[12] Moreover, women were also responsible for the daily maintenance of working-class households. This put Paulistano women in a particularly strategic position, for they were often the first to experience both changes in work regimes at the point of production (the factories) and the impact of decreasing real wages, at the point of consumption (the markets). From the 1917 General Strike through the Strike of the 300,000, the city's working women organized to push for improved work conditions, for higher wages, and for dignity and respect as workers. We should take care not to see this female perspective or discourse as "natural" to women's lives. It developed out of their experiences in the wage labor market and their neighborhoods and households.[13]

Many Paulistano men—labor and leftist activists as well as rank-and-file workers—articulated very different discourses. Work itself was seen as manly, so much so that in periods of high unemployment (e.g., in the early 1930s) the economic depression became a crisis of masculinity to some. Male activists had a tendency to ignore the sort of "bread-and-butter" issues women raised, and instead concentrated on more overtly political topics. Examples of this run the gamut from the anarchists' benign neglect of workers' issues when they concentrated instead on antiwar politics in 1914 to the Communists' absurd opposition to workers' strikes in 1945 and 1946 in order to build ties to industrialists and other elites. Anarchists, Communists, and even some pelegos did, however, adopt key aspects of women's organizing and protest activities and discourses after they saw how those activities and discourses resonated among the city's industrial workers.

São Paulo's women workers developed such labor discourses and practices because they were in a unique position to do so. They were often ignored by labor and leftist leaders, or seen as a group to be mobilized from above. As we have seen, the city's workers chose instead to organize on their own, and only after that did they form ties to labor and leftist activists and populist politicians. Once again, we must be careful not to romanticize these women's politics. Their tendency toward local, democratic forms of organizing was a response to closed, male-dominated institutions. These women could have just as easily articulated quite conservative discourses had circumstances been different.[14]

The distinctly female and male components of what eventually became São Paulo's syndicalist legacy were by-products of the ongoing interaction among the four actors studied here (the industrial working class, union and Left organization leaders, industrialists, and state policymakers) and the interactions within these groups according to their various cleavages. We must ask, therefore, how the experiences of São Paulo's industrial working class fit into the national experience. São Paulo had a consistently higher percentage of women factory workers than Rio (the other industrial center during this period), and the national capital had a deeper tradition of labor unions as mutual aid societies and of popular political participation. Further, São Paulo's industry was predominantly Brazilian owned during the first half of the twentieth century, and so Paulistano workers did not conflate labor discourses and nationalism as workers in foreign-owned enterprises sometimes did.[15]

We should be careful not to universalize the São Paulo experience for all of Brazil, but at the same time we must recognize the significance of the Paulistano case. São Paulo in the 1950s was not only the largest industrial complex in Brazil, it was also the largest in Latin America. Although we should not speak of a single Brazilian worker experience, we cannot analyze the Brazil *industrial* working class without paying close attention to São Paulo. And when we do so, we find that there was an ongoing grass-roots workers' movement that sometimes articulated to formal labor and leftist institutions and sometimes supported populist politicians. Because this informal social movement did not depend on political parties, unions, or other institutions, it was able to survive periods of violent repression. This social movement survived because the state and industrialists had a difficult time identifying, let alone repressing, it. The state could not simply close down a headquarters or arrest a few leaders, for the workers' movement was broad based and operated on the factory level.

It is only when we understand the nature of this social movement that we can begin to see workers' large-scale strike movements in the years immediately following periods of repression (e.g., 1930–35, 1945–47, 1950–54) as expressions of working-class politics rather than spontaneous outbursts. These strike movements (including the 1917 General Strike and the mobilizations that followed into the early 1920s) contained calls for "reason and justice" and for "dignity," because they were not just attempts to gain improved wages and work conditions. They were also refusals to accept the status quo. Paulistano workers' rejection of "politics as usual" has had a complicated impact on Brazilian history. São Paulo's popular classes have consistently backed political outsiders such as Adhemar de Barros in 1947 and Jânio Quadros in 1953. Indeed, they were so careful with their support of populist politicians that they did not widely embrace Getúlio Vargas until he had refashioned himself as a political outsider and opponent of Dutra and the status quo in the late 1940s.

That is, Paulistanos were not mobilized from above by politicians; they gave populists their votes in exchange for the populists' support of their demands. Democracy to São Paulo's workers was not just participating in elections, it was organizing collectively and locally to push for their demands. The metalworker Edson Borges articulated this well when he recalled that in the aftermath of the Estado Novo he and his companheiros tried to exercise their rights as Brazilians: "We organized ourselves. After all, we fought World War II, Brazilians died for the war, we worked like slaves for the war. Good, now we had a democracy, so we organized and asked for what was ours."[16] Borges and other Paulistano workers attempted to bring the democracy of their factory commissions to their unions, and then perhaps to society in general. Many events and significant changes intervened between the struggles for democracy at work and in the unions that were waged in the first half of the twentieth century and those that helped to bring the military dictatorship to an end in the 1980s, but both were popular struggles for reason, justice, and dignity.

Appendix: Interviews and Oral Histories

The following people were interviewed by the author:

Bianchi, Assumpta. Textile worker since 1920s; joined union in early 1930s; interviewed in São Paulo, S.P., 10 August 1987.

Bonifácio, João. Textile worker, opposition and factory commission activist, officially joined the union in the 1950s; interviewed in São Paulo, S.P., 3 September 1987.

Borges, Edson. Metalworker since the late 1930s, did not join the union; interviewed in São Paulo, S.P., 25 September 1987.

Carneiro, David. Metalworker since 1930s; opposed but later joined the union; interviewed in São Paulo, S.P., 24 September 1987.

Ciaveletto, Antônio. Textile worker since the 1940s, union member; interviewed in São Paulo, S.P., 3 September 1987.

Dantas, Hermento Mendes. Metalworker who first worked in 1940s in textiles; was in opposition movement and factory commission of Metalworkers' Union; active in union and its directorate in 1950s; interviewed in São Paulo, S.P., 14 September 1987.

Fereira dos Santos, Lima. Metalworker in Osasco, first participated in independent factory commissions, later joined union; interviewed in Osasco, S.P., 23 September 1987.

Firmino de Lima, Luís. Textile worker and PCB activist, played role in coordinating actions of PCB and factory commissions; elected to union directorate in 1950s; interviewed in São Paulo, S.P., 7 August and 1 September 1987.

Franco, João de. Metalworker active in factory commissions in 1940s, did not join the union until mid-1950s; interviewed in São Paulo, S.P., 25 May 1987.

Habel, Carlos. Metalworker in Osasco, active in factory commissions; interviewed in Osasco, S.P., 23 September 1987.

Lima, Enrique de. Textile worker in 1940s and 1950s; participated in the union; interviewed in São Paulo, S.P., 2 September 1987.

Lima, Waldemar. Metalworker since the 1930s, active in factory commissions; interviewed in São Paulo, S.P., 25 September 1987.

Lombardi, Antônio. Metalworker since 1930s, joined union to receive benefits; interviewed in São Paulo, S.P., 24 September 1987.

Lorenzi dos Santos, Hermínia. Textile worker since late 1930s; was first active in factory commissions, then joined union in the early 1950s; interviewed in São Paulo, S.P., 12 August 1987.

Machado, Laura S. Textile worker since early 1930s; avoided the union but participated in factory commissions; interviewed in Osasco, S.P., 8 September 1987.

Mendes, José Antônio de. Metalworker since 1940s, participated in factory commissions, and joined the union in early 1950s; interviewed in São Paulo, S.P., 25 May 1987.

Nascimento, Diolinda. Textile worker since the early 1940s who participated in factory commissions but did not join the union until she needed legal help; interviewed in São Paulo, S.P., 2 September 1987.

Neto, Angela. Textile worker since early 1930s; avoided the union but was a factory commission activist; interviewed in São Paulo, S.P., 8 August 1987.

Nogueira, Alcy. President, Federation of Chemical Workers, served on Regional Labor Tribunal; interviewed in São Paulo, S.P., 1 October 1987.

Oliveira, Irene. Textile worker starting in the early 1950s; participated in factory commissions; interviewed in São Paulo, S.P., 11 August 1987.

Oliveira, João Affonso de. Metalworker active in factory commissions and later in union; interviewed in Osasco, S.P., 23 September 1987.

Pacheco, José. Metalworker in 1940s and 1950s; active in factory commissions and a union member; interviewed in São Paulo, S.P., 15 September 1987.

Papa, Conrado de. Metalworker active in factory commissions and union in 1940s and 1950s; interviewed in Osasco, S.P., 23 September 1987.

Pascolato, Geraldo. Metalworker since late 1930s; joined union during the Estado Novo in order to receive benefits but did not participate in union affairs; interviewed in São Paulo, S.P. 24 September 1987.

Pasquini, Odette. Textile worker in 1930s, 1940s, and 1950s; did not join the union, although she was active in factory commissions; interviewed in São Paulo, S.P., 17 September 1987.

Pavone, Maria. Textile worker since the 1940s; participated in factory commissions in 1940s, joined the union in the early 1950s; interviewed in São Paulo, S.P., 12 August 1987.

Pinto Silva, Francisco. Metalworker since late 1930s; did not join the union; interviewed in São Paulo, S.P., 25 September 1987.

Riberio dos Santos Filho, Elpidio. Secretary general of the Federation of Chemical Workers and once a member of the Regional Labor Tribunal; interviewed in São Paulo, S.P., 1 October 1987.

Salviano, Glória. Textile worker since early 1940s, participated in the factory commissions; interviewed in São Paulo, S.P., 14 August 1987.

Sanchez, Aracy. Textile worker since 1940s; did not join union and did not participate in factory commissions; interviewed in São Paulo, S.P., 2 September 1987.

Silva, Francisco da. Metalworker since 1930s; joined union in 1930s and opposed pelegos from that time through the 1950s; interviewed in São Paulo, S.P., 25 May 1987.

Sobrinho, Carlos Heubel. Metalworker active in factory commissions, later served on directorate of Metalworkers' Union of Osasco; interviewed in Osasco, S.P., 23 September 1987.

Toschi, Antônio. Former president of the Metalworkers' Union of Osasco; interviewed in Osasco, S.P., 15 September 1987.

Unger, Roberto. Metalworker active in factory commission movement; joined the union in the 1950s; interviewed in Osasco, S.P., 23 September 1987.

Vetturuzzo, Santo. Textile worker who joined the union in 1940s but was never active; interviewed in São Paulo, S.P., 2 September 1987.

Other oral histories consulted include the following:

Alexander Papers. Rutgers University, New Brunswick, N.J. Notes from interviews conducted by Robert J. Alexander with the following:

José Albertino Rodrigues, director of DIEESE, São Paulo, 1956

Agildo Barata, former treasurer of the Brazilian Communist party, Rio de Janeiro, 20 August 1965

Leôncio Basbaum, historian and former member of the Brazilian Communist party, São Paulo, 18 November 1965

Paulo Corti, former official of the São Paulo Metalworkers' Union, São Paulo, 17 April 1956

Vinicius Ferraz Torres, acting regional labor delegate, São Paulo, 20 April 1956

Nivaldo Fonseca, second secretary of the São Paulo Textile Workers' Union, São Paulo, 20 April 1956

Remo Forli, president of the São Paulo Metalworkers' Union, São Paulo, 27 August 1959

Dacyr Gatto, president of the São Paulo Shoemakers' Union, São Paulo, 18 April 1956

José Carlos Graça Wagner, attorney for the State Cosmetic Makers' Union, São Paulo, 26 April 1956

Célio Dinardo L. Lacerda, head of Registration Section, Union Organization and Registration Service of the Ministry of Labor, Rio de Janeiro, 5 April 1956

Aldo Lombardi, secretary general of the São Paulo Metalworkers' Union, São Paulo, 17 April 1956

Pedro Marazagão, São Paulo regional labor delegate, São Paulo, 22 April 1956

Edgar Martins, secretary to the secretary general of the São Paulo Metalworkers' Union, São Paulo, 17 April 1956

J. M. Moreira de Moraes, secretary of the São Paulo Textile Workers' Union, São Paulo, 27 April 1956

Nestor Ortiz, United States consul in São Paulo, São Paulo, 11 April 1956

Francisco Patricio de Oliveira, attorney for the São Paulo Electrical Workers' Union, São Paulo, 14 April 1956

Olavo Previatti, president of the São Paulo State Federation of Paper Makers, São Paulo, 27 April 1956

Francisco Ribeiro de Santos, attorney for the São Paulo Electrical Workers, São Paulo, 14 April 1956

Irving Salert, United States labor attaché, Rio de Janeiro, 2 July 1954

José Segadas Viana, former minister of labor, Rio de Janeiro, 16 March 1956

Centro de Memória Sindical. "O Trabalhador e a Memória Paulistana" and "A Morte de Getúlio Vargas."

Conselho Estadual de Condição Feminina e Centro de Memória Sindical, *Mulheres Operárias*. São Paulo: Nobel, 1985.

Rocha Lima, Valentia de. *Getúlio: Uma História Oral*. Rio de Janeiro: Record, 1980.

Notes

Introduction

1. Meetings during July, August, and October 1945, February 1946, January and February 1948, December 1951, and January 1952 included such rank-and-file demands. These are discussed in chapters 4, 5, and 6 in this volume.

2. Several of the many studies on the origins and operation of the PT are Margaret E. Keck, *The Workers' Party and Democratization in Brazil* (New Haven: Yale University Press, 1992); Isabel Ribeiro de Oliveira, *Trabalho e Política: As Origens do Partido dos Trabalhadores* (Petrópolis: Vozes, 1988); and Emir Sader and Ken Silverstein, *Without Fear of Being Happy: Lula, the Workers' Party, and Brazil* (London: Verso, 1991).

3. As in many other labor histories, the concept of class formation used here owes much to E. P. Thompson's classic *The Making of the English Working Class* (New York: Vintage, 1966). Thompson's study, however, tends to err on the side of culture at the expense of the material bases of class formation and the interaction of workers with those conditions. One of the goals of this book is to integrate more fully the cultural and material factors in the process of class formation.

4. For an interesting discussion of the term *the masses* see Raymond Williams, *Key Words: A Vocabulary of Culture and Society*, rev. ed. (New York: Oxford University Press, 1983), 192–97.

5. The classic work on the Brazilian elite is Raymondo Faoro's *Os Donos de Poder: Formação do Patronato Político Brasileiro*, 2d ed., 2 vols. (São Paulo: Globo, 1975). While Faoro recognizes that elites' actions have often been reactions to popular class activities, he concentrates his analysis on the elites alone. Studies of Brazil's and São Paulo's economic and political elites have tended to follow this course; see, for example, Warren Dean, *The Industrialization of São Paulo, 1880–1945* (Austin: University of Texas Press, 1969); Eli Diniz, *Empresário, Estado, e Capitalismo no Brasil, 1930–1945* (Rio de Janeiro: Paz e Terra, 1978); and Marisa Saenz Leme, *A Ideologia dos Industriais Brasileiros, 1919–1945* (Petrópolis: Vozes, 1978).

6. The much debated topic of bureaucratic-authoritarianism in Latin America was first discussed by Guillermo A. O'Donnell; see his *Modernization and Bureaucratic-Authoritarianism: Studies in South American Politics* (Berkeley: Institute of International Studies, University of California, 1979). For a thoughtful critique

of O'Donnell's theoretical framework see Karen L. Remmer and Gilbert W. Merkx, "Bureaucratic-Authoritarianism Revisited," *LARR* 17.2 (1982): 3–40.

7. Although not the focus of this study, struggles between rural folk and their bosses, landowners, representatives of the state, and others have played a central role, along with urban popular struggles, in the establishment of Brazilian authoritarianism. See, for example, Todd A. Diacon, *Millenarian Vision, Capitalist Reality: Brazil's Contestado Rebellion, 1912–1916* (Durham: Duke University Press, 1991); Manoel Correia de Oliveira, *A Terra e o Homen no Nordeste* (São Paulo: Brasiliense, 1963); and Clifford A. Welch, "Rural Labor and the Brazilian Revolution in São Paulo, 1930–1964" (Ph.D. diss., Duke University, 1990).

8. Workers' organizing and protest activities are the focus of this book. I do not assume that formal unions are sui generis representatives of the working class. Indeed, knowing how and when workers join formal institutions is central to understanding working-class history.

9. For an outstanding and thorough synthesis of Latin American labor history that details the differing relationships to the state and level of political power of national labor movements, see Ruth Berins Collier and David Collier, *Shaping the Political Arena: Critical Junctures, the Labor Movement, and Regime Dynamics in Latin America* (Princeton: Princeton University Press, 1991).

10. Because they have not analyzed this grass-roots level, scholars have assumed that Brazilian workers were less radical than their counterparts elsewhere in Latin America, and that Brazilian workers had to be mobilized from above by Left political groups and/or the state. See, for example, Robert J. Alexander, *Labor Relations in Argentina, Brazil, and Chile* (New York: McGraw-Hill, 1962), 375–87; and Hobart Spaulding, *Organized Labor in Latin America: Historical Case Studies of Workers in Dependent Societies* (New York: Harper and Row, 1977), 178–85. Alexander argues that "Brazilian workers are undoubtedly more placid and submissive than those of [Chile and Argentina]" (381). Spaulding makes a similar point: "[Brazilian workers in the 1930s and 1940s] possessed no tradition of struggle or even significant collective work experience. Accustomed to agrarian paternalism, they slipped easily into a hierarchical system dominated by state bureaucrats" (183). John D. French has gone so far as to argue that the Estado Novo dictatorship (1937–45) laid the groundwork for the development of Brazil's labor movement; see *The Brazilian Workers' ABC: Class Conflict and Alliances in Modern São Paulo* (Chapel Hill: University of North Carolina Press, 1992), 77–99; and French, "The Origin of Corporatist State Intervention in Brazilian Industrial Relations, 1930–1934: A Critique of the Literature," *Luso-Brazilian Review* 28.2 (Winter 1991): 13–26.

11. For a historically based treatment of the tension between formal institutions and maintaining grass-roots social movements see Francis Fox Piven and Richard A. Cloward, *Poor People's Movements: Why They Succeed, How They Fail* (New York: Pantheon, 1977). A work that focuses on the highly gendered nature of the social movement—formal institution dichotomy is Elizabeth Faue,

Community of Suffering and Struggle: Women, Men, and the Labor Movement in Minneapolis, 1915–1945 (Chapel Hill: University of North Carolina Press, 1991). For examples of the new social movements literature as applied to Latin America see the various essays in Arturo Escobar and Sonia Alvarez, eds., *The Making of Social Movements in Latin America: Identity, Strategy, and Democracy* (Boulder: Westview Press, 1992).

12. On "hidden transcripts" and their significance relative to "public transcripts" see James C. Scott, *Domination and the Arts of Resistance: Hidden Transcripts* (New Haven: Yale University Press, 1990).

13. For the first two decades of the twentieth century, Rio de Janeiro had a greater industrial base than São Paulo. By the mid-1920s, however, São Paulo was the largest industrial city in Brazil. By the 1950s it was the most important industrial city in Latin America.

14. *Semiskilled* workers can be defined as those individuals who have abilities acquired in the factory, generally over the long term. They are adapt at maintaining high levels of production with older, somewhat fragile machines. Accordingly, these individuals have factory-specific skills. For an analysis of the position of such workers within a general hierarchy of skills see Charles F. Sabel, *Work and Politics: The Division of Labor in Industry* (Cambridge: Cambridge University Press, 1982), 62–71. For a historical treatment of such workers see David Montgomery's study of "factory operatives" in his *The Fall of the House of Labor: The Workplace, State, and American Labor Activism, 1865–1925* (Cambridge: Cambridge University Press, 1987), 112–70.

15. *Skilled* labor is that which involves abilities that are formally highly valued by both workers and employers. Sometimes those abilities are acquired through formal apprenticeships. What is and what is not considered skilled is historically and socially determined, and thus often changes over time. Notions of skill are also gender-bound, in that abilities women have learned in the home (e.g., the needlework trades) are rarely considered skills, although men's learned knowledge of carpentry, and so on, is seen as skilled. Moreover, some work, because its practice is dominated by women, is not seen as skilled until men take it up.

The best traditional Marxist interpretation of skill is still Harry Braverman's *Labor and Monopoly Capital* (New York: Monthly Review Press, 1974). There is a growing literature on the gendered nature of work definitions and the social construction of skill. A tiny sampling of this literature for the United States would include Ava Baron, "Contested Terrain Revisited: Technology and Gender Definitions of Work in the Printing Industry, 1850–1920," in *Women, Work, and Technology: Transformations,* ed. Barbara Wright et al. (Ann Arbor: University of Michigan Press, 1987), 58–83; Mary H. Blewett, *Men, Women, and Work: Class, Gender, and Protest in the New England Shoe Industry, 1780–1910* (Urbana: University of Illinois Press, 1988); Ruth Milkman, *Gender at Work: The Dynamics of Job Segregation by Sex during World War II* (Urbana: University of Illinois Press,

1987); and the essays by Baron, Dolores Janieswski, Blewett, Dorothy Sue Cobble, and Patricia Cooper in *Work Engendered: Toward a New History of American Labor*, ed. Ava Baron (Ithaca: Cornell University Press, 1991).

For a sociological analysis of this issue for Brazil in the 1980s see John Humphrey, *Gender and Work in the Third World: Sexual Divisions in Brazilian Industry* (London: Tavistock Publications, 1987).

16. The only other sector in São Paulo that produced unions that were more militant and representative than the metallurgical and textile workers' unions was banking, which comprises a nonindustrial group of workers. Letícia Bicalho Canêdo's two studies of the *bancários* detail their militant organizing and protest activities; see her *O Sindicalismo Bancário em São Paulo* (São Paulo: Símbolo, 1978), and *Bancários: Movimento Sindical e Participação Política* (Campinas: UNICAMP, 1986).

17. On this sort of class consciousness (i.e., when the members of a social class act as a class for itself), see V. I. Lenin, "What Is to Be Done? Burning Questions of Our Movement," in *The Lenin Anthology*, ed. Robert C. Tucker (New York: Norton, 1975), 12–114; and Georg Lukács, *History and Class Consciousness*, trans. Rodney Livingstone (Cambridge, Mass.: MIT Press, 1971).

18. The starting place for analyzing hegemony is Antonio Gramsci's *Selections from the Prison Notebooks*, ed. and trans. Quinten Hoare and Geoffrey Nowel Smith (New York: International Publishers, 1971). Later interpretations of Gramsci's basic position include Nicos Poulantzas, *State, Power, and Socialism* (London: New Left Books, 1978); and Anthony Giddens, *The Class Structure of Advanced Societies* (New York: Harper, 1975). A nuanced historical application of this perspective is provided in John Gaventa, *Power and Powerlessness: Quiescence and Rebellion in an Appalachian Valley* (Urbana: University of Illinois Press, 1980).

Rank-and-file opposition to industrialist and state policies (i.e., elite attempts to foster hegemonic ideologies) is detailed throughout the present book. For an excellent critique of the hegemony literature see Scott, *Domination and the Arts of Resistance*, 70–107.

1 Industrialization and the Birth of São Paulo's Working-Class Movement

1. Marie Robinson Wright, *The New Brazil: Its Resources and Attractions; Historical, Descriptive and Industrial* (Philadelphia: George Barriet Son, 1901), 195, 238–39; Miguel Milano, *Os Fantasmas de São Paulo Antiga: Estudo Histórico-Literário da Cidade de São Paulo* (São Paulo: Saraiva, 1949), 53, 86–87; and Célia Toledo Lucena, *Bairro do Bexiga: A Sobrevivência Cultural* (São Paulo: Brasiliense, 1984), 38–47. For a general overview of São Paulo at the turn of the century see Richard M. Morse, *From Community to Metropolis: A Biography of São Paulo, Brazil* (Gainesville: University of Florida Press, 1958), 166–98.

2. Throughout this book, the name *São Paulo* refers to the city (or *município*)

of São Paulo. All references to the state will be explicit. Further, the term *Paulistano/a* refers to someone from the capital city; *Paulista* refers to anyone from the state of São Paulo.

3. For elite views of industrialization see Nelson Werneck Sodre, *História da Burguesia Brasileira* (Rio de Janeiro: Civilização Brasileira, 1976), 176; Warren Dean, *The Industrialization of São Paulo, 1880–1945* (Austin: University of Texas Press, 1969), 34–48; Steven Topik, *The Political Economy of the Brazilian State, 1889–1930* (Austin: University of Texas Press, 1987), 147–48; and Frank D. McCann, "The Formative Period of Twentieth-Century Brazilian Army Thought, 1900–1922," *Hispanic American Historical Review* (hereinafter *HAHR*) 64 (November 1984): 737–65.

4. See Flávio Rabelo Versiani and Maria Teresa R. O. Versiani, "A Industrialização Brasileira antes de 1930: Uma Contribuição," *Estudos Econômicos* 5.1 (January–April 1975): 37–63; Wilson Cano, *Raízes da Concentração Industrial em São Paulo*, 2d ed. (São Paulo: T. A. Queiroz, 1981), 195–255; Annibal V. Villela and Wilson Suzigan, *Government Policy and the Economic Growth of Brazil, 1889–1945* (Rio de Janeiro: IPEA, 1977), 88–96; and Topik, *The Political Economy of the Brazilian State*, 129–48. The rise of Brazil's textile industry is detailed in Stanley J. Stein, *The Brazilian Cotton Manufacture: Textile Enterprise in an Underdeveloped Area, 1850–1950* (Cambridge, Mass.: Harvard University Press, 1957), 1–77.

5. Versiani and Versiani, "Industrialização Brasileira," 37–42; and Dean, *Industrialization of São Paulo*, 19–47.

6. Werner Baer, *The Brazilian Economy: Growth and Development*, 2d ed. (New York: Praeger, 1983), 32–39; Dean, *Industrialization of São Paulo*, 105. For more on the early metalworking sector see Joel W. Wolfe, "The Rise of Brazil's Industrial Working Class: Community, Work, and Politics in São Paulo, 1900–1955" (Ph.D. diss., University of Wisconsin–Madison, 1990), 40–42.

7. On racist ideologies see Thomas E. Skidmore, *Black into White: Race and Nationality in Brazilian Thought* (New York: Oxford University Press, 1974). On the impact of this ideology on São Paulo's industrial labor market see George Reid Andrews, "Black and White Workers, São Paulo, Brazil, 1888–1928," *HAHR* 68.3 (August 1988): 491–524. Migration from the rural sector and the establishment of an industrial labor market segmented by gender ideologies are described in Wolfe, "The Rise of Brazil's Industrial Working Class," 10–18.

8. Wilson Cano (*Raízes da Concentração Industrial*, 140–89) and Albert Fishlow ("Origens e Consequências da Substituição de Importações no Brasil," *Estudos Econômicos* 2.6 [1972]: 8–20), for example, argue that the wartime expansion deepened industrialization. Dean (*Industrialization of São Paulo*, 83–104) argues that the war period simply witnessed the intensified use of existing capacity and so did not further industrialization. Versiani and Versiani argue that the expansion was indeed based on the expanded capacity installed before the war, but that the war created profits later used for further industrial expansion ("Industrialização Brasileira," 37–63). For a thoughtful synthesis of the various

positions on the impact of the war on the Brazilian economy see Bill Albert, *South America and the First World War: The Impact of the War on Brazil, Argentina, Peru, and Chile* (Cambridge: Cambridge University Press, 1988), 77–94.

9. On accidents, see *Boletim do Departamento Estadual do Trabalho* (hereinafter *BDET*) 30 (1919): 25, and 22 (1920): 1917. On the work regimes, see *BDET* 37 (1920): 309; and Maram, "Anarchists, Immigrants, and the Labor Movement in Brazil" (Ph.D. diss., University of California, Santa Barbara, 1972), 155.

10. Cited in Maria Célia Paoli, "Working-Class São Paulo and Its Representations, 1900–1940," *Latin American Perspectives* 14.2 (Spring 1987): 211. For the original article see *O Estado de São Paulo*, 15 September 1917. Other descriptions of such conditions can be found in *O Estado de São Paulo*, 4, 6, and 8 June 1917. On women and children in Paulista factories and the demeaning and dangerous conditions they faced, see Esmeralda Blanco B. de Moura, *Mulheres e Menores no Trabalho Industrial: Os Fatores Sexo e Idade na Dinâmica do Capital* (Petrópolis: Vozes, 1982), 30–60; and Maria Valéria Junho Pena, *Mulheres e Trabalhadores: Presença Feminina na Constituição do Sistema Fabril* (Rio de Janeiro: Paz e Terra, 1981), 83–94.

11. G. J. Bruce, *Brazil and the Brazilians* (London: Methuen, 1915), 295–97; Gilbert Last, *Facts about the State of São Paulo, Brazil* (London: British Chamber of Commerce of São Paulo and Southern Brazil, 1926), 75; and Jorge Americano, *São Paulo Nesse Tempo, 1915–1935* (São Paulo: Melhoramento, 1962), 121–22. See also *A Plebe*, 21 June 1917; and Moniz Bandeira et al., *O Ano Vermelho: A Revolução Russa e Seus Relexos no Brasil*, 2d ed. (São Paulo: Brasiliense, 1980), 48–50.

12. *BDET* 27 (1918): 329–30.

13. *Bulletin of the Pan American Union* (hereinafter *BPAU*) (April 1919): 473.

14. Lucila Hermann, "Estudo de Desenvolvimento de São Paulo Através de Análise de Uma Radial—A Estrada do Café (1935)," *Revista do Arquivo Municipal* 99 (November–December 1944): 20–25; Ernani Silva Bruno, *História e Tradições da Cidade de São Paulo*, 3 vols. (Rio de Janeiro: José Olympio, 1954), 3:1315–23; Americano, *São Paulo Nesse Tempo*, 31–32; Bruce, *Brazil and the Brazilians*, 229; and Paoli, "Working-Class São Paulo," 204–5.

15. Hermann, "Estudo de Desenvolvimento," 13–18; *BPAU* (March 1914): 399–404; *Outlook Magazine*, 31 January, 7 and 14 February 1914; Villela and Suzigan, "Government Policy," 69–74. On the process of urban reform in general in São Paulo, see Gerald Michael Greenfield, "Privatism and Urban Development in Latin America: The Case of São Paulo, Brazil," *Journal of Urban History* 8.4 (August 1982): 397–426. For this process in Rio see Jeffrey D. Needell, "Making the Carioca Belle Époque Concrete; the Urban Reforms of Rio de Janeiro under Perrera Passos," *Journal of Urban History* 10.4 (August 1984): 384–422.

16. *BPAU* (April 1916): 554.

17. Speech by Washington Luís, quoted in Paoli, "Working-Class São

Paulo," 217. On elite programs to "cleanse" working-class life in São Paulo through public health campaigns and attempts to regulate leisure in working-class neighborhoods, see Margareth Rago, *Do Cabaré ao Lar: A Utopia da Cidade Disciplinar, Brasil 1890–1930* (Rio de Janeiro: Paz e Terra, 1985), 163–203. On attempts to regulate sexuality, especially as related to prostitution, see Rago, *Os Prazeres da Noite: Prostituição e Códigos da Sexualidade Feminina em São Paulo, 1890–1930* (Rio de Janeiro: Paz e Terra, 1991), 128–40.

18. Bruno, *História e Tradições*, 3:1145; Americano, *São Paulo Nesse Tempo*, 58; and *BDET* 13–14 (1914): 790–99, and 19 (1916): 215–18. The higher cost and lower quality of food in the working-class neighborhoods are detailed in *BDET* 3 (1912): 355, 7 (1913): 339, 10 (1914): 241–45, and 14 (1915): 38–39.

19. On exports to Europe and month-to-month price fluctuations see Boris Fausto, *Trabalho e Conflito Social* (São Paulo: DIFEL, 1976), 163, 200. On food prices and inflation see *BDET* 13–14 (1914): 478–81, and 24 (1917), charts after p. 580; *Boletim da Directoria de Indústria e Comércio* (hereinafter *BDIC*) 9.3–4 (March–April 1918): 129; *BPAU* (April 1917): 529 (June 1917): 809 (August 1917): 258 (October 1917): 539, and (November 1918): 604; and Oliver Onody, *A Inflação Brasileira, 1820–1958* (Rio de Janeiro: n.p., 1960), 25.

20. The breakdown of the São Paulo community is analyzed in Morse, *Community to Metropolis*, 200–256. A similar study of this process in Rio de Janeiro is presented in Michael L. Conniff, *Urban Politics in Brazil: The Rise of Populism, 1925–1945* (Pittsburgh: University of Pittsburgh Press, 1981), 20–34.

21. *BDIC* 9.1 (January 1918): 20–21; *BPAU* (December 1917): 818.

22. U.S. Department of Commerce, *Daily Commerce Reports*, nos. 153–228, Consul Hoover, Report from São Paulo to Washington, D.C., 2 June 1917 and 16 August 1917.

23. The sexual division of labor within Paulistano working-class households left women responsible for child rearing and maintenance of the home (including purchasing and preparing food) as well as for generating a cash income—often through factory labor. On the historical development of this sexual division of labor see Wolfe, "The Rise of Brazil's Industrial Working Class," 10–18.

24. The small Socialist party in São Paulo during this period had little contact with the city's workers. For information on the Socialists see Edgard Carone, *A República Velha: Instituições e Classes Sociais* (São Paulo: Difusão Européia do Livro, 1970), 211–36; and John W. F. Dulles, *Anarchists and Communists in Brazil, 1900–1935* (Austin: University of Texas Press, 1973), 10–20.

25. Nicolau Sevcenko, *Literatura como Missão: Tensões Sociais e Criação Cultural na Primeira República* (São Paulo: Brasiliense, 1983), 161–236; Flávio Luizetto, "O Recurso da Ficção: Um Capítulo da História do Anarquismo no Brasil," in *Libertários no Brasil: Memória, Lutas, Cultura*, ed. Antonio Arnoni Prado (São Paulo: Brasiliense, 1986), 131–61; Eric Arthur Gordon, "Anarchism in Brazil: Theory and Practice, 1890–1920" (Ph.D. diss., Tulane University, 1978), 180–225. A group of anarchists founded the Colônia Cecília in the state of Santa Catarina

to experiment with primitive communitarianism; see Newton Stadler de Sousa, *O Anarquismo da Colônia Cecília* (Rio de Janeiro: Civilização Brasileira, 1970). For a fictional account of this experiment see Afonso Schmidt, *Colônia Cecília*, 3d ed. (1942; São Paulo: Brasiliense, 1980).

26. The most complete analysis of these activities can be found in Francisco Foot Hardman's lively study of anarchist culture, *Nem Pátria, Nem Patrão: Vida Operária e Cultura Anarquista no Brasil* (São Paulo: Brasiliense, 1983); see also Mariangela Alves de Lima and Maria Thereza Vargas, "Teatro Operário em São Paulo," in *Libertários no Brasil*, 162–250.

27. Gordon, "Anarchism in Brazil," 225–31. Most Brazilians—natives as well as Italian, Portuguese, and Spanish immigrants—were Catholics. Further, religion (often popular, syncretic religion) has traditionally played a central role in popular-class resistance to changing social and economic conditions; see, for example, Euclides da Cunha, *Rebellion in the Backlands*, trans. Samuel Putnam (Chicago: University of Chicago Press, 1944), 50–169; Todd A. Diacon, *Millenarian Vision, Capitalist Reality: Brazil's Contestado Rebellion, 1912–1916* (Durham: Duke University Press, 1991); and Ralph Della Cava, *Miracle at Joaseiro* (New York: Columbia University Press, 1970). Although active in rural-sector resistance, the church did not play a key role in working-class organizing until the emergence of ecclesiastical base communities in the 1960s and 1970s.

28. This shift in outlook probably resulted from the increase in the number of tradesmen, especially printers, that accompanied São Paulo's growth in the first decade of the twentieth century. For an analysis of this period see Silvia Lang Magnani, *O Movimento Anarquista em São Paulo, 1906–1917* (São Paulo: Brasiliense, 1982), 119–26; and Morse, *Community to Metropolis*, 200–218.

29. Dulles, *Anarchists and Communists*, 20–22; and Sheldon L. Maram, "The Immigrant and the Brazilian Labor Movement," in *Essays Concerning the Socioeconomic History of Brazil and Portuguese India*, ed. Dauril Alden and Warren Dean (Gainesville: University Presses of Florida, 1977), 186–87.

30. See the articles from *A Luta Proletária* and *La Barricata* reproduced in *A Classe Operária no Brasil, 1889–1930*, vol. 1, *O Movimento Operário*, ed. Paulo Sérgio Pinheiro and Michael Hall (São Paulo: Alfa-Omega, 1979), 72–74, 127–28.

31. Railroad and other workers had struck earlier for the eight-hour day. Their actions no doubt encouraged textile workers and led the anarchists to misconstrue the political potential of the workers' protests. The overall strike movement is well documented in Magnani, *Movimento Anarquista*, 119–32; see also Maram, "Anarchists, Immigrants, and the Labor Movement," 154.

32. On workers' lack of contact with radical ideas in Europe, see Michael M. Hall, "Immigration and the Early São Paulo Working Class," *Jahrbuch für Geschichte von Staat, Wirtschaft und Gesellschaft Lateinamerikas* 12 (1975): 391–407. On their identification as an ethnic group rather than a social class, see Sheldon L. Maram, "Labor and the Left in Brazil, 1890–1921: A Movement Aborted,"

HAHR 57.2 (May 1977): 257–60; and Boris Koval, *História do Proletariado Brasileiro, 1857–1967*, trans. Clarice Lima Avierina (São Paulo: Alfa-Omega, 1982), 99–102.

33. *A Laterna*, 22 April 1911. It was not rare for women anarchists to take such a position. See Gordon, "Anarchism in Brazil," 136–39.

34. *A Voz do Trabalhador*, 20 June 1914; see also Boris Fausto, *Trabalho e Conflito Social* (São Paulo: DIFEL, 1976), 116.

35. Quoted in Gordon, "Anarchism in Brazil," 138.

36. Ibid., 136–37. Other anarchists supported feminism and even printed feminist articles openly in their newspapers; see, for example, "To the Young Seamstresses of São Paulo," reprinted from *Terra Livre*, 29 July 1906, in *Women in Latin American History: Their Lives and Views*, ed. June E. Hahner (Los Angeles: UCLA Latin American Center, 1976), 114–16. Still, Hahner finds that male anarchists' gender ideologies differed little from those of other urban Brazilian men of this time; see her *Emancipating the Female Sex: The Struggle for Women's Rights in Brazil, 1850–1940* (Durham: Duke University Press, 1990), 94–95, 109–12.

37. See Rago, *Do Carebé ao Lar*, 62–84; Pena, *Mulheres e Trabalhadores*, 175–215. Joan Scott has argued that the female-male dichotomy is as important if not more important than divisions by race or class in analyzing history; see her "Gender: A Useful Category of Historical Analysis," in Scott, *Gender and the Politics of History* (New York: Columbia University Press, 1988), 28–50.

38. See Moura, *Mulheres e Menores*, 112–21; and Maria Célia Paoli, "Os Trabalhadores Urbanos na Fala dos Outros; Tempo, Espaço e Classe na História Operária Brasileira," in *Cultura e Identidade Operária: Aspectos da Cultura da Classe Trabalhadora*, ed. José Sérgio Leite Lopes (Rio de Janeiro: UFRJ/Maco Zero, 1987), 76–84. For an excellent analysis of the gendered nature of a labor discourse in the United States see Elizabeth Faue, *Community of Suffering and Struggle: Women, Men, and the Labor Movement in Minneapolis, 1915–1945* (Chapel Hill: University of North Carolina Press), 69–99.

39. Interview, Assumpta Bianchi, São Paulo, S.P., 10 August 1987. As we shall see, most women did not have the time or inclination to join anarchist organizations because they were burdened with household and child care responsibilities. Moreover, they were often put off by the atmosphere of large meetings run by male activists. For a fascinating study of the operation of similar factory commissions among Chinese textile workers see Emily Honig, "Burning Incense, Pledging Sisterhood: Communities of Women Workers in the Shanghai Cotton Mills, 1919–1949," *Signs: Journal of Women in Culture and Society* 10.4 (Summer 1985): 700–714.

40. For more details on the segmenting of the São Paulo labor market by sex see Wolfe, "The Rise of Brazil's Industrial Working Class," 10–18, 36–42. This process seems to confirm Heidi Hartmann's general perspective on how gender relations condition a transition to capitalism; see her "Capitalism, Patriarchy, and Job Segregation by Sex," in *Capitalist Patriarchy and the Case for Socialist*

Feminism, ed. Zillah R. Eisenstein (New York: Monthly Review Press, 1979), 206–47. The segmenting of the labor market in accordance with the extant sexual division of labor in the rural sector demonstrates how gender can later be used to increase existing divisions within a working class. For an analysis that concentrates on industrialists' use of existing gender and race division—without a close analysis of the development of those divisions—see David M. Gordon et al., *Segmented Work, Divided Workers: The Historical Transformation of Labor in the United States* (Cambridge: Cambridge University Press, 1982).

41. Maram ("Labor and the Left") describes the many obstacles anarchists faced as they attempted to organize among native Brazilians and the Italian, Portuguese, and Spanish immigrants. Sidney Chalhoub's study of Rio de Janeiro in the first decades of the Republic demonstrates the hostility that existed among the various ethnicities by analyzing criminal court records see *Trabalho, Lar, e Botequim: O Cotidiano dos Trabalhadores no Rio de Janeiro da Belle Époque* (São Paulo: Brasiliense, 1986), 58–88. On racial divisions within the Paulistano working class at this time, see George Reid Andrews, "Black and White Workers: São Paulo, Brazil, 1888–1928," *HAHR* 68.3 (August 1988): 491–524.

42. *A Voz do Trabalhador,* 5 July 1914; Maram, "Anarchists, Immigrants, and the Labor Movement," 264–71; Gordon, "Anarchism in Brazil," 108–16.

43. *A Voz do Trabalhador,* 1 April 1914.

44. *Avanti!* 28 November 1914.

45. *Correio Paulistano,* 3 August 1914; *Avanti!* 8 August 1914; Hermínio Linhares, *Contribuição à História das Lutas Operárias no Brasil* (São Paulo: Alfa-Omega, 1977), 60; Boris Koval, *História do Proletariado Brasileiro,* 116. Both the conservative *Correio Paulistano* and the leftist *Avanti!* commented on the failure of Left and labor activists to speak to workers' interests and needs.

46. *A Voz do Trabalhador,* 8 June 1915; see also Linhares, *Contribuição,* 60. On Brazilian anarchists' antiwar positions see Gordon, "Anarchism in Brazil," 100–107.

47. São Paulo's largely immigrant working class had little access to the city's and state's highly exclusionary political systems and so did not find socialist electoral strategies appealing. Municipal politics in the nation's capital, Rio de Janeiro, were much more open at this time, and the city had a much higher percentage of Brazilian citizens within its working class. Socialist politics therefore found a more receptive audience in Rio. Indeed, Rio's anarchists shared some of the socialists' electoral strategies. On the continuity of anarchist and socialist thought in Rio see Angela de Castro Gomes, *A Invenção do Trabalhismo* (Rio de Janeiro: IUPERJ/Vértice, 1988), 35–137. Cf. Maria Conceição Pinto de Góes, *A Formação da Classe Trabalhadora: Movimento Anarquista no Rio de Janeiro, 1888–1911* (Rio de Janeiro: Jorge Zahar, 1988), 44–46, 57–59, 82–87.

48. On the worsening conditions in the factories in 1917 see *O Estado de São Paulo,* 31 May 1917; *Diário Popular,* 6 June 1917; *BDET* 37 (1920): 309. On

fluctuating food prices see *BDET* 24 (1917), chart between pp. 580 and 581. First mention of the women's commission is in *Diário Popular,* 28 June 1917; see also Fausto, *Trabalho e Conflito Social,* 194. Workers at the Paulicéa match factory—where two thirds of the more than 300 employees were women and girls—also formed factory commissions to bargain for improved conditions and wages, see *O Combate,* 13 July 1917.

49. *Diário Popular,* 28 and 30 June 1917. Scholars must have missed these original demands, for they refer only to the reporting in *O Estado de São Paulo* and the memoirs of anarchists; see, for example, Fausto, *Trabalho e Conflito Social,* 192–200; and Maram, "Anarchists, Immigrants, and the Labor Movement," 70–74, 169–70.

50. *A Plebe,* 18 August 1918, reported on sexual harassment in the Labor textile mill. As we shall see, the anarchist press did not often report on topics such as sexual harassment before women workers raised these issues through their factory commissions.

51. *Diário Popular,* 30 June 1917; *O Estado de São Paulo,* 20, 21, and 30 June 1917; see also Fausto, *Trabalho e Conflito Social,* 194.

52. *O Estado de São Paulo,* 27 March 1966 (reproduced in Pinheiro and Hall, *A Classe Operária,* 1:226–31).

53. Everardo Dias, *História das Lutas Sociais no Brasil* (São Paulo: Alfa-Omega, 1977), 224.

54. In her study of nineteenth-century French strikes, Michelle Perrot notes that spontaneity is in the eyes of the beholder: "The spontaneity of these strikes, which is relative, is often a result of our ignorance. We only recognize them at the moment they begin; the strikes may surprise observers and employers, but the worker . . . expects the strikes or even plans them" (*Les ouvriers en grève: France, 1871–1890,* 2 vols. [Paris: Mouton, 1974], 2:414); see also James C. Scott, *Domination and the Arts of Resistance: Hidden Transcripts* (New Haven: Yale University Press, 1990), 1–16.

55. *Diário Popular,* 2 and 3 July 1917; *O Estado de São Paulo,* 23 June, 2, 3, 4, 5, and 8 July 1917.

56. *O Estado de São Paulo,* 9 July 1917; *Diário Popular,* 9–11 July 1917.

57. This account was culled from *O Estado de São Paulo* and *Diário Popular* for 9–13 July 1917; Leuenroth's account in *O Estado de São Paulo,* 27 March 1966; and Dulles, *Anarchists and Communists,* 49–55. The sacking of food warehouses and the protests against the police presence in working-class bairros reveal the strikers' frustrations with their loss of control of their neighborhoods.

58. Perrot argues that such public demonstrations play a fundamental role in building working-class solidarity and therefore consciousness in the early phases of strikes (*Ouvriers en grève,* 2:546–87).

59. This series of events demonstrates why this and other strike movements like it should not be labeled "general strikes." They are "generalized strikes," for the actions of one group of workers airing their grievances encourage other

groups to do the same. The movement grows (through public demonstrations, etc.) until there is an overall paralysis of industry. Such a process is much different from the anarchists' concept of a coordinated "general strike" that begins with a complete or near complete work stoppage throughout industry and seeks definite political goals in addition to solutions to workers' grievances. Fausto also points out this distinction (*Trabalho e Conflito Social*, 202), but because this strike movement has been referred to as a "general strike" since 1917, I use that term—rather than "generalized strike"—throughout this book.

60. *Diário Popular*, 9–11 July 1917; *O Estado de São Paulo*, 10 and 11 July 1917. Women workers have initiated and led large-scale strikes in various countries; see, for example, Temma Kaplan, "Female Consciousness and Collective Action: The Case of Barcelona, 1910–1918," *Signs: Journal of Women in Culture and Society* 7.3 (1982): 545–66; Ardis Cameron, "Bread and Roses Revisited: Women's Culture and Working-Class Activism in the Lawrence Strike of 1912," in *Women, Work, and Protest: A Century of Women's Labor History*, ed. Ruth Milkman (Boston: Routledge and Kegan Paul, 1985), 42–61; and Dana Frank, "Housewives, Socialists, and the Politics of Food: The 1917 New York Cost-of-Living Protests," *Feminist Studies* 11.2 (Summer 1985): 255–85.

61. *O Estado de São Paulo*, 12 and 13 July 1917; *Diário Popular*, 13 July 1917. On the spread of the strike to Rio see Bandeira et al., *Ano Vermelho*, 64–71; and Dulles, *Anarchists and Communists*, 56–60. Workers in Porto Alegre initiated a similar movement in August; see Miguel Bodea, *A Greve de 1917: As Origens do Trabalhismo Gaúcho* (Porto Alegre: L & PM, 1978).

62. *O Estado de São Paulo*, 21 and 28 June 1917, reports meetings of the industrialists but makes no reference to the growing strike movement. On the meeting arranged by Chaves see Dulles, *Anarchists and Communists*, 49–50.

63. Even though Leuenroth and Dias admit in their memoirs that they played no role in initiating the strike, the anarchist press in 1917 implied that activists had helped organize the walkout. The differences between the demands presented by the Crespi workers' commissions and those presented by the anarchists (along with Leuenroth's and Dias's admissions) seem to contradict the activists' assertions; see *A Plebe*, 9, 16, and 23 June 1917. The existence of the workers' leagues has further confused the issue. Anarchist labor activists opened these neighborhood organizations to foster local worker organizing. While there is no evidence of the leagues' playing a role in the planning of the original Crespi strike, the Mooca branch's headquarters was available for later organizing.

Some scholars have conflated the rhetoric of various leftist activists with the praxis of the city's rank-and-file workers during this strike. For an analysis of this point of view see Joel Wolfe, "Anarchist Ideology, Worker Practice: The 1917 General Strike and the Formation of São Paulo's Working Class," *HAHR* 71.4 (November 1991): 810–11.

64. *O Estado de São Paulo,* 10 and 12 July 1917.

65. The original demands of the committee appear in *O Estado de São Paulo,* 10 and 12 July 1917; and *Diário Popular,* 12 July 1917. The creation of the anarchist group and how it took control of the strike and discussions of the Liga Operária de Mooca are detailed in Leuenroth's testimony in *O Estado de São Paulo,* 2 March 1966; and Dias's *História,* 229–32; see also Fausto, *Trabalho e Conflito Social,* 194–204; Maram, "Anarchists, Immigrants, and the Labor Movement," 97–98; and Dulles, *Anarchists and Communists,* 48–56.

66. There is even some controversy as to whether or not the male anarchist leadership wrote the manifestos that they published as women's documents. Several appeared in *O Estado de São Paulo,* 11 July 1917, and Leuenroth's new anarchist newspaper, *A Plebe,* 21 July 1917. Without providing evidence, Dulles claims that these women's appeals were actually written by Everardo Dias (*Anarchists and Communists,* 47–48). The appeals do seem to incorporate more anarchist rhetoric (e.g., calls to "the great popular mass") than the women's stated concerns. In the first decade of the twentieth century, Argentine women workers organized in the Unión Gremial Feminina to end night work for children but defended their own night work as necessary due to their double duties as mothers and workers. Male unionists, without the women's consent, agitated to end all night work; see Marysa Navarro, "Hidden, Silent, and Anonymous: Women Workers in the Argentine Trade Union Movement," in *The World of Women's Trade Unionism: Comparative Historical Essays,* ed. Norbert C. Soldon (Westport, Conn.: Greenwood Press, 1985), 171–72.

67. *O Combate,* 24 July 1917; *O Estado de São Paulo,* 9 and 12 July 1917. These editions also show how the state Department of Labor's policies resembled the goals of the striking workers. On the middle-class's critique of *urbanismo* and its attempts to aid workers see Wolfe, "The Rise of Brazil's Industrial Working Class," 42–47.

68. *Diário Popular,* 12–14 July 1917; *O Estado de São Paulo,* 12–15 July 1917.

69. Because there was no formal union structure, the majority of strikers did not vote to accept or reject these terms as a group. Most strikers probably accepted the settlement in the same way they had decided to strike: through local meetings of factory commissions and informal gatherings outside their factories and in their neighborhoods.

70. *Diário Popular,* 16–19 July 1917; *O Estado de São Paulo,* 16–19 July 1917; *BDET* 24 (1917): 449–50.

71. *O Estado de São Paulo,* 18, 20, 23, and 25 July 1917; *Diário Popular,* 18–19 July 1917.

72. *O Estado de São Paulo,* 20 July 1917. For more on Street's view of the social question in the 1910s and 1920s see Palmira Petratti Teixeira, *A Fábrica do Sonho: Trajetória do Industrial Jorge Street* (Rio de Janeiro: Paz e Terra, 1990).

73. On middle-class opposition to the effects of rapid industrialization on the city and its inhabitants, see *Correio Paulistano,* 16 August 1914; *BDET* 14

(1915): 33–39; and Wolfe, "The Rise of Brazil's Industrial Working Class," 42–47.

74. That is, women workers did not strike because they had a unique female consciousness centered on the maintenance of life. Rather, their position within the labor market conditioned the development of their consciousness. Although São Paulo's women workers protested against high food prices and other issues related to their roles in their households, they also presented a coherent critique of work regimes. The women in this case seem to have had a stronger focus on problems arising at the point of production than did the anarchists, who maintained their focus on larger political and cultural issues. For an analysis of "female consciousness" that takes a somewhat different view see Kaplan, "Female Consciousness," 545–47.

75. On the Labor mill see *A Plebe*, 18 August 1917; see also *O Parafuso*, 22 and 27 October 1917. On child labor see *O Combate*, 23, 24, and 30 July, 27 August, and 4 September 1917. Some anarchists had begun to campaign against child labor in the months before the general strike; see Moura, *Mulheres e Menores*, 104–11. *O Combate* had reported on food shortages and high prices in Rio but ignored the situation in São Paulo before the general strike; see *O Combate*, 1, 8, and 9 May 1917; and Maram, "Anarchists, Immigrants, and the Labor Movement," 166–70. On the flour mills see *A Plebe*, 2, 3, 6, and 13 August 1917. On government regulation of markets, *O Combate*, 26 July, 3 and 6 August 1917. On factory inspections, *O Combate*, 20, 23, 24, and 30 July, 17 August, and 4 September 1917. On anarchists chiding the state, *A Plebe*, 18 August, 1 September 1917. See also Gordon, "Anarchism in Brazil," 113–15, for early anarchist views of state inspectors in the factories.

76. Quoted in Gordon, "Anarchism in Brazil," 165. Although this may have been an extreme position, many anarchists had been ambivalent about the role of unions; see Gordon, 164–76; and Magnani, *Movimento Anarquista*, 81–85.

77. *A Plebe*, 28 July 1917; see also *A Plebe*, 4, 11, and 18 August 1917.

78. *A Plebe*, 30 September 1919; *O Combate*, 22 August 1919. Fausto (*Trabalho Urbano e Conflito Social*, 174–91) notes this shift but adds that many anarchists continued to look at workers' mobilizations as an opportunity to launch an insurrectionary movement against the state.

79. On Jafet, see *A Plebe*, 8 September 1917. On Matarazzo's mill, *O Parafuso*, 27 October 1917.

80. *A Plebe*, 21 and 28 July, 4 and 11 August 1917. I should emphasize that the reopening of the FOSP followed the strikes initiated by independent factory commissions. Several authors have viewed the 1917 General Strike as resulting from anarchist organizing, but the evidence seems to suggest that Crespi workers initiated the strike on their own. Works that posit a larger anarchist role include Cristina Hebling Campos, "O Sonhar Libertário; Movimento Operário nos Anos 1917 a 1920" (Tese de mestrado, Universidade Estadual de São Paulo–Campinas, 1983), 31–34; and John D. French, *The*

Brazilian Workers' ABC: Class Conflict and Alliances in Modern São Paulo (Chapel Hill: University of North Carolina Press, 1992), 30–35.

81. Argentine anarchists also had a complex relationship with feminist activists; see Maxime Molyneux, "No God, No Boss, No Husband: Anarchist Feminism in Nineteenth-Century Argentina," *Latin American Perspectives* 13.1 (Winter 1986): 119–45.

82. It is important to keep in mind the distinction between groups labeled "workers," "the masses," "o povo," etc., by outsiders, and individuals who view themselves as part of a group (i.e., those who see themselves as part of a "class for itself").

83. During the May 1907 General Strike, the city's textile industrialists planned to form such an organization, but they did not do so until 1919; see Pinheiro and Hall, eds., *A Classe Operária*, vol. 2, *Condições de Vida e de Trabalho, Relações com Empresários e o Estado* (São Paulo: Brasiliense, 1981), 156–62; Dean, *Industrialization,* 121–22; Fausto, *Trabalho e Conflito Social,* 188–89; Maram, *Anarquistas, Imigrantes e o Movimento Operário Brasileiro, 1890–1920,* trans. José Eduardo Ribeiro Moretzsohn (Rio de Janeiro: Paz e Terra, 1979), 142–43. Rio's industrialists relied on the national association (Centro Industrial do Brasil) located in the capital to negotiate with strikers in 1917 (Dulles, *Anarchists and Communists,* 59–60).

84. Dean, *The Industrialization of São Paulo,* 67–80; Darrell E. Levi, *The Prados of São Paulo, Brazil: An Elite Family and Social Change, 1840–1930* (Athens: University of Georgia Press, 1987), 145–48. For a theoretical analysis of how popular-class organizing spurs elite-class solidarity and the formation of elite organizations, see Claus Offe and Helmut Wiesenthal, "Two Logics of Collective Action: Theoretical Notes on Social Class and Organizational Form," *Political Power and Social Theory* 1 (1980): 67–115.

85. See *O Combate,* 17 August 1917, for a description of how São Paulo state inspectors began implementing labor laws in the wake of the general strike.

86. *BPAU* (October 1917): 540, (August 1918): 142, (May 1919): 603–4; *Monthly Labor Review* 8.6 (June 1919): 261–63. See also Angela Maria de Castro Gomes, *Burguesia e Trabalho: Política e Legislação Social no Brasil, 1917–1937* (Rio de Janeiro: Campus, 1979), 55–84; and Evaristo de Moraes Filho, *O Problema do Sindicato Único no Brasil: Seus Fundamentos Sociológicos,* 2d ed. (São Paulo: Alfa-Omega, 1978), 197–216. These efforts were further encouraged by the labor provisions of the Paris peace treaty.

87. Rui Barbosa told a British diplomat that he feared "foreign anarchists" were fomenting revolution among disaffected workers in Rio and São Paulo. Rui believed only social legislation could prevent the outbreak of a revolution. See Rio to London, Report of the Political Situation, 20 November 1918, Foreign Office (hereinafter FO), 371/3653, Public Record Office (hereinafter PRO); see also Annual Report for Brazil, 1919, June 1920, FO 371/4435, PRO; and Bandeira et al., *O Ano Vermelho,* 88–95, 220–40.

88. Sheldon L. Maram, "Labor and the Left," 260–61; see also Dias, *História das Lutas Sociais*, 55–56. Adolfo Gordo was a probusiness congressman from São Paulo. The 1907 law that bears his name allowed the federal government to expel foreign-born labor activists. It was one of the government's earliest means for fighting labor agitation.

89. Quoted in Dulles, *Anarchists and Communists*, 279.

90. *O Estado de São Paulo*, 3 and 5 May 1919; *A Plebe*, 10 May 1919. Once again, the original demands of the women workers did not include a call for the end of their night work. Men strikers sought this, but women in their factory commissions did not want it (*O Estado de São Paulo*, 3, 4, and 6 May 1919). São Paulo's workers pushed for these demands as they faced steady increases in prices and scarcity of food, clothing, and housing; see Associação Comercial de São Paulo, Centro de Comércio e Indústria, *Relatório da Diretoria de 1918*, 92–94; *BDET* 28–29 (3d and 4th trimesters 1918): 481–86; *Monthly Labor Review* 7.5 (November 1918): 106–7.

91. On police matters see *O Estado de São Paulo*, 6 and 8 May 1919. The congressman is quoted in Maram, "Anarchists, Immigrants, and the Brazilian Labor Movement," 184; the original is from *O Estado de São Paulo*, 23 May 1919. On industrialists' acceptance, *O Estado de São Paulo*, 8 May 1919; and report from British embassy, Rio to London, 6 May 1919, FO 371/3653, PRO. On the state's backing for the labor legislation suggested by the Paris peace conference see "Inquerito às Condições do Trabalho em São Paulo," *BDET* 31–32 (2d and 3d trimesters 1919): 185–202. On strike settlement, see *O Estado de São Paulo*, 9, 13, 15–18, 22, and 25 May 1919.

92. On union meetings see *O Estado de São Paulo*, 5, 16, and 18 May 1919; see also Campos, "O Sonho Libertário," 56–60. On industrialists' meetings see Associação Comercial de São Paulo, Centro do Comércio e Indústria, *Relatório da Diretoria de 1919*, 93; see also Marisa Saenz Leme, *A Ideologia dos Industriais Brasileiros, 1919–1945* (Petrópolis: Vozes, 1978), 99–107.

93. *O Estado de São Paulo*, 23–28 October, and 1 November 1919.

94. The city's establishment press and foreign observers noted the differences in the grass-roots' role in planning the general strikes of 1917 and October 1919. See *O Estado de São Paulo*, 7 December 1919; and British embassy, Rio to London, Annual Report, 1919, June 1920, FO 371/4435, PRO; see also Maram, "Anarchists, Immigrants, and the Labor Movement," 190–92, and "Labor and the Left," 267; and Dulles, *Anarchists and Communists*, 88–90, 113–18.

95. The standard view of the 1920s is of a period of elite repression against a dead or dying labor movement that had reached its apogee in 1917–19; see Fausto, *Trabalho e Conflito Social*, 233–49; Paulo Sérgio Pinheiro, *Política e Trabalho no Brasil: Dos Anos Vinte a 1930*, 2d ed. (Rio de Janeiro: Paz e Terra, 1977), pt. 2; Dulles, *Anarchists and Communists*, 101–50; Azis Simão, *Sindicato e Estado: Suas Relações na Formação do Proletariado de São Paulo* (São Paulo: Ática, 1981), 101–21; and Maram, "Labor and the Left in Brazil."

96. Rudyard Kipling, *Brazilian Sketches* (New York: Doubleday, Doran, 1940), 66.

97. *BDET* 52 (3d trimester 1924): 362–64; *Boletim do Departamento Estadual de Estatística* 5 (May 1939): 159. Because of the political upheaval in 1930, no national census was taken. The state of São Paulo conducted its own census in 1934.

98. *BDET* 52 (3d trimester 1924): 362–64. Indeed, at this time the state Department of Labor, which had been created to deal with rural labor issues, turned its attention to the problems industrial workers faced. For an analysis of the state government's creation of new institutions and use of existing ones to deal with the "social question" in the early 1920s see Joel Wolfe, "Worker Mobilization, Repression, and the Rise of the Authoritarian State: São Paulo, 1914–1924" (Paper presented to the 56th Annual Meeting of the Southern Historical Association, New Orleans, La., November 1990). For an insightful analysis of Paulista politics in the 1920s that highlights the increasing power of the industrial sector over the interests of large coffee estates see Mauricio A. Font, *Coffee, Contention, and Change in the Making of Modern Brazil* (Cambridge, Mass.: Basil Blackwell, 1990).

99. On the Week of Modern Art see Morse, *From Community to Metropolis*, 258–69; and Elizabeth Lowe, *The City in Brazilian Literature* (Rutherford, N.J.: Fairleigh Dickinson University Press, 1982), 89–100. One of Mário de Andrade's most revealing works on São Paulo is his *Paulicéia Desvairada* (Hallucinated city, 1922). António de Alcântara Machado's novel of life among Italian immigrants in the city is *Brás, Bexiga, e Barra Funda* (1927); for his reporting on the city's uneven expansion in the late 1910s and 1920s see "Rodapés: Saxofone e Cavaquihno," in *António de Alcântara Machado: Obras*, vol. 1, ed. Cecília de Lara (Rio de Janeiro: Civilização Brasileira, 1983), 169–74.

100. *Boletim da Diretoria da Indústria e Comércio* 15.12 (December 1924): 227; Hermann, "Estudo de Desenvolvimento," 20–25; Bruno, *História e Tradições da Cidade*, 1315–1523; and Kipling, *Brazilian Sketches*, 68.

101. Estado de São Paulo, *Mensagem Apresentado ao Congresso Legislativo de São Paulo pelo Presidente do Estado em 1925* (São Paulo: n.p., 1925), 37.

102. On traffic problems see *O Estado de São Paulo*, 13 February 1924; Rio to London, Annual Report for 1919, January 1920, FO 371/4435, PRO; Kipling, *Brazilian Sketches*, 68. The image of the modern but menacing automobile is prominent in Alcântara Machado's *Brás, Bexiga, e Barra Funda*. On the poor sanitary conditions see *O Estado de São Paulo*, 16 July 1922; Rio to London, Annual Report for 1920, February 1921, FO 371/5539, PRO; São Paulo to Washington, D.C., 12 August 1922, 832.124/orig., Record Group (hereinafter RG) 59, National Archives (hereinafter NA). On the impact of the international flu epidemic on São Paulo see São Paulo, Serviço Sanitário, *A Grippe Epidêmica no Brasil e Especialmente em São Paulo* (São Paulo: Duprat, 1920).

103. António de Alcântara Machado copied this and other ballads as he

heard them. He published them as "Liras Paulistanas." These lines are from Lira 1, in *António de Alcântara Machado: Obras*, vol. 1, 298–99. On the importance of the imagery of São Paulo's streets in the creation of popular music see Valter Krausche, *Adoniran Barbosa: Pelas Ruas da Cidade* (São Paulo: Brasiliense, 1985).

104. This section was gleaned from interviews conducted by researchers at the Centro de Memória Sindical (hereinafter CMS) in São Paulo; see "O Trabalhador e a Memória Paulistana, 1920–1950," 5–34, which includes the remembrances of the metalworkers José Biondi, José Albertino, and Armando Sufredini. For a description of street music in these neighborhoods see Bruno, *História e Tradições da Cidade*, 1288–89.

105. "Report on the Motion Picture Market," 27 December 1919, RG 84, São Paulo (hereinafter SP) Post, NA. Brazil did have its own film industry at this time, but U.S. movies, with their larger budgets and powerful international distribution networks, dominated the Brazilian market; see Maria Rita Eliezer Galvão, *Crônica do Cinema Paulistano* (São Paulo: Ática, 1975), 29–62. For the history of the early film industry see Vincente de Paula Araújo, *A Bela Época do Cinema Brasileiro* (São Paulo: Perspectivas, 1976).

106. Memo on Movies, 5 March 1923, RG 84, SP Post 840.6, NA; see also São Paulo to Columbus Film Co., N.Y., 21 January 1919, RG 84, SP Post 840.6, NA; and Bruno, *História e Tradições da Cidade*, 1237, 1296.

107. CMS, "O Trabalhador e a Memória," 15–21; interview, Assumpta Bianchi, São Paulo, S.P., 10 August 1987. The movies also served as a form of child care, for working mothers could send their children to spend all day Saturday at the matinee.

108. This is detailed in Alcântara Machado's *Brás, Bexiga, e Barra Funda*, and Zélia Gattai's novel based on her childhood in São Paulo, *Anarquistas, Graças a Deus* (Anarchists, thank God), 11th ed. (Rio de Janeiro: Record, 1986). The various neighborhoods' distinctive atmospheres are documented in the histories of each bairro by the São Paulo Secretaria de Educação e Cultura.

109. On elite attempts to regulate leisure and "purify" working-class neighborhoods with public health campaigns and other schemes at this time see Rago, *Do Cabaré ao Lar*, 163–203; and Maria Auxiliadora Guzzo Decca, *A Vida fora das Fábricas: Cotidiano Operário em São Paulo, 1920–1934* (Rio de Janeiro: Paz e Terra, 1987), 49–95.

110. *BDET* 31–32 (1919), 11th and 12th inserts; interview, Assumpta Bianchi, São Paulo, 10 August 1987. The 58 percent figure represents an increase in the number of men working in the mills. The great expansion of the textile sector during the war led to the increased hiring of men, although women remained the majority of mill workers.

111. *O Estado de São Paulo*, 18 May 1919.

112. *BDET* 31–32 (1919), 12th insert; Brasil, Ministério de Agricultura, Indústria, e Comércio, Directoria Geral de Estatística, *Recenseamento do Brasil Realizado em 1 de Setembro 1920* (Rio de Janeiro, 1927), 5:1, 222–23, 294–95; and

Luís A. Corrêa do Lago et al., *A Indústria Brasileira de Bens de Capital: Origens, Situação Recente, Perspectivas* (Rio de Janeiro: Instituto Brasiliero de Economia, 1979), 37–47.

113. CMS, "O Trabalhador e a Memória," 51–52, 118–20.

114. The metalworkers' walkouts are described in *O Metalúrgico*, 14 April 1920. The Textile Workers' Union struck to force mill owners to allow them to collect dues at factory gates; see U.S. embassy, Rio to Washington, D.C., 26 March 1920, RG 59, 832.5045, NA; Maram, "Anarchists, Immigrants, and the Labor Movement," 195; and Dulles, *Anarchists and Communists*, 131–33.

115. British embassy, Rio to London, Annual Report 1920, February 1921, FO 371/3539, PRO; see also British embassy, Rio to London, Report on Textiles, 15 January 1919, FO 371/3653; and British embassy, Rio to London, 6 May 1919, FO 371/3653, PRO.

116. Centro dos Industriaes de Fiação e Tecelagem de São Paulo (hereinafter CIFTSP), letter to Centro Industrial do Brasil, 4 August 1920, Biblioteca Roberto Simonsen (hereinafter BRS). For the actual blacklists, see CIFTSP, *Circulares* 59, 2 August; 65, 13 September; 67, 13 October; and 70, 9 December 1920.

117. CIFTSP, *Circulares* 73, 14 December 1920; 76, 5 January 1921; see also CIFTSP, *Circulares* 80, 22 February; and 85, 16 March 1921. It was not possible to determine if these workers eventually received the bonuses.

118. Mill owners reproduced the handbill in CIFTSP, *Circular* 78, 28 January 1921.

119. Interview, Assumpta Bianchi, 10 August 1987; interview, Hermento Mendes Dantas, 14 September 1987.

120. CIFTSP, *Circulares* 7, 28 April; and 10, 4 May 1921. Textile workers used sabotage less than did workers in other industries, for they received low hourly wages and a piece rate. The destruction of equipment would therefore bring them lower wages. Textile workers tended to rely more on theft as a form of direct action in the mills.

121. On the Luzitania, CIFTSP, *Circulares* 15, 18 May; and 19, 21 May 1921; CIFTSP, letter to Pereira, Ignácio, e Cia., 19 May 1921, BRS. On the Companhia Fabril Paulistana, CIFTSP, *Circulares* (no number), 2 June; and 26, 8 June 1921; CIFTSP, letters to Delegado Geral João Baptista de Souza, 6 and 7 June 1921; CIFTSP, letters to Companhia Fabril Paulistana, 6 and 8 June 1921. On mill owners, CIFTSP, letter to Bruno Belli, 23 July 1921; CIFTSP, letter to Indústria Reunidas Francisco Matarazzo, August 1921; CIFTSP, letter to Fábio da Silva Prado, 23 July 1921; CIFTSP, letter to Estamparia Ypiranga Jafet, 29 December 1921, BRS. See also CIFTSP, *Boletim de Informações*, 7–13 August 1921; CIFTSP, *Circulares* 39, 25 July; 40, 26 July; 41, 27 July; 44, 21 August; 76, 31 December 1921; 77, 10 January 1922.

122. Interview, Assumpta Bianchi, 10 August 1987. On the mobility of labor in São Paulo at this time see U.S. consulate, São Paulo to Washington, D.C., 8 September 1921, RG 59, 832.504/5, NA.

123. CIFTSP, letters to Cotonfício Rodolfo Crespi, 6 September 1921, and 2 May 1922; Fabril Pinotti Gamba, letter to CIFTSP, 19 April 1922, BRS; and CIFTSP, *Circulares* 93, 12 April; and 118, 5 July 1922.

124. *A Plebe*, 18 March 1922; interview, Hermento Mendes Dantas, 14 September 1987.

125. On the absence of union activity see British embassy, Rio to London, Annual Report 1922, February 1923, FO 371/8431, PRO; British consulate, São Paulo to Rio and London, Monthly Consular Report, 1 February 1922, FO 371/7189, PRO; U.S. consulate, São Paulo to Washington, D.C., 19 July 1922, RG 59, 832.504/6, NA; *Fanfulla*, 5 May 1922; see also Dulles, *Anarchists and Communists*, 186–87.

126. CIFTSP, *Relatório*, 1922; CIFTSP, *Circular* 161, 16 December 1922; *A Plebe*, 13 May 1922.

127. *Fanfulla*, 5 May 1922.

128. On the paucity of working-class support for the PCB in São Paulo, see U.S. embassy, Rio to Washington, D.C., 6 August 1926, 832.00b/orig., NA; U.S. consulate, São Paulo to Washington, D.C., 18 December 1926, 832.00b/2, NA; Edgard Carone, *Classes Sociais e Movimento Operário* (São Paulo: Ática, 1989), 147–48, 166; Dulles, *Anarchists and Communists*, 186–87, 209.

129. For a thoughtful and detailed analysis of the PCB's policies in the 1920s and their negative impact on rank-and-file Brazilian workers, see Paulo Sérgio Pinheiro, *Estratégias da Ilusão: A Revolução Mundial e o Brasil, 1922–1935* (São Paulo: Companhia das Letras, 1991), 87–131.

130. U.S. embassy, Rio to Washington, D.C., 27 January 1921, RG 59, 832.108/1, NA; U.S. embassy, Rio to Washington, D.C., 14 March 1924, RG 59, 832.5043/1, NA. The anarchist movement in Chile had a similar position in the late 1910s and 1920s. Although more organized than the loose collection of factory commissions in São Paulo, Chile's anarchists, while not abandoning revolutionary goals, concentrated on bread-and-butter issues while the Communist party paid more attention to political questions; see Peter DeShazo, *Urban Workers and Labor Unions in Chile, 1902–1927* (Madison: University of Wisconsin Press, 1983), 146–242.

131. *A Plebe*, 4 August and 21 April 1923.

132. *Gazeta de Noticias*, 17 October 1923. For more on the rationalization of production see Wolfe, "The Rise of Brazil's Industrial Working Class," 78–92; and Flávio Rabelo Versiani, "Technical Change, Equipment Replacement, and Labor Absorption: The Case of the Brazilian Textile Industry" (Ph.D. diss., Vanderbilt University, 1971).

133. CIFTSP, *Relatório*, 1923; CIFTSP, *Circular* 187, 3 March 1923; British embassy, Rio to London, Annual Report, 1923; 14 March 1924, FO 371/9516, PRO; *A Plebe*, 27 January, 17 February, and 10 March 1923.

134. British embassy, Rio to London, Annual Report, 1923, 14 March 1924,

FO 371/9516, PRO; *A Plebe,* 27 January, 17 and 24 February, 10 and 24 March 1923.

135. CIFTSP, *Circulares* 210, 5 May; 217, 26 May; and 237, 27 July 1923. The anarchists, while pressing for bread-and-butter issues such as wage increases, had not abandoned their revolutionary goals; see *A Plebe,* 1 and 12 May, and 9 June 1923.

136. CIFTSP, *Circulares* 247, 17 September; 249, 2 October; 256, 26 October; 259, 17 November; 260, 9 November; 266, 30 November; and 269, 14 December 1923; *A Plebe,* 13 October and 22 December 1923; British consulate, São Paulo to Rio, "Events in São Paulo," 7 November 1923, FO 371/8429, PRO. Mill owners who had not purchased new equipment also valued these workers because they could operate the older machines, which tended to require frequent adjustments and quick repairs. Industrialists' reliance on these semiskilled workers for the operation of both old and new textile equipment demonstrates how notions of skill are socially constructed. At this moment of a perceived labor shortage, the women workers' skills were highly valued and so could be used to negotiate for higher wages.

137. British consulate, São Paulo to Rio, 15 January 1924, FO 371/9509, PRO; CIFTSP, *Circulares* 280, 18 January; 282, 23 January; 283, 25 January 1924; *O Estado de São Paulo,* 24 and 31 January 1924. On increasing prices see British embassy, Rio to London, Annual Report, 1924, April 1925, FO 371/10609, PRO.

138. On the industrialists' frustrations see CIFTSP, *Circulares* 286-A, 31 January; and 291, 11 February 1924. For the anarchists' complaints about the disorganized nature of the grass-roots movement see *A Plebe,* 15 March 1924.

139. *O Estado de São Paulo,* 1 and 17 February 1924; *A Plebe,* 16 February 1924.

140. On the owners' offers, CIFTSP, *Circulares* 294, 20 February 1924; 295, 296, and 298, n.d.; 299, 3 March; 300, 6 March 1924; British consulate, São Paulo to Rio, 8 March 1924, FO 371/9508, PRO; British Chamber of Commerce of São Paulo and Southern Brazil, *Bulletin* 7 (July 1924); *A Plebe,* 15 March 1924. On the blacklisted workers, CIFTSP, *Circulares* 301, 8 March; 302, 12 March; 304, 19 March; and 307, 29 March 1924. Of the workers on these blacklists, 79 percent were women. Blacklisting related to this strike movement continued into June 1924. On the arrests of activists, *A Plebe,* 15 March 1924; CIFTSP, *Relatório,* 1924, February 1925.

141. *A Plebe,* 15 and 29 March, 1 May, 14, 21, and 28 June 1924.

142. On the conflicts between the anarchists and Communists, see Dulles, *Anarchists and Communists,* 229–31. On the tenentes, *A Plebe,* 25 July 1924; U.S. consulate, São Paulo to Washington, D.C., 3 August 1924, RG 59, 832.00/409, NA; Morse, *Community to Metropolis,* 241–43. John French has gone so far as to argue that "by 1923, labor's various factions had been drawn into the military conspiracies that led to the successful tenentista seizure of the capital of São

Paulo on 5 July 1924"; see *The Brazilian Workers' ABC*, 45. French, however, provides no evidence for this assertion.

143. U.S. consulate, São Paulo to Washington, D.C., 3 August 1924, RG 59, 832.00/409, NA; U.S. embassy, Rio to Washington, D.C., 7 July 1924, RG 59, 832.00/405, NA; *A Plebe*, 25 July 1924. The attacks only on certain warehouses demonstrate the internal logic of the riots. Workers' attacks were a protest against only those industrialists who paid them low wages and charged them high prices for foodstuffs and other goods.

144. British consulate, São Paulo to London, "Report on Events," 5–10 July 1924, FO 371/9511, PRO; British embassy, Rio to London, 30 July 1924, FO 371/9511, PRO.

145. British embassy, Rio to London, 9 July 1924, FO 371/9510, PRO; British consul, Santos to Rio, 15 July 1924, FO 371/9511, PRO.

146. U.S. embassy, Rio to Washington, D.C., 9 July 1924, RG 59, 832.00/370, NA; U.S. consul, Santos to Washington, D.C., 13 July 1924, RG 59, 832.00/358, NA; U.S. consul, Santos to Washington, D.C., 23 July 1924, RG 59, 832.00/371, NA; U.S. embassy, Rio to Washington, D.C., 24 July 1924, RG 59, 832.00/405, NA; U.S. consulate, São Paulo to Washington, D.C., 31 July 1924, RG 59, 832.00/393, NA; U.S. consulate, São Paulo to Washington, D.C., 3 August 1924, RG 59, 832.00/409, NA; U.S. consul, Santos to Washington, D.C., 5 August 1924, RG 59, 832.00/411, NA.

147. On the British consul's report, British embassy, Rio to London, 30 July 1924, FO 371/9511, PRO; British embassy, Rio to London, 12 August 1924, FO 371/9511, PRO. On the center's boast, CIFTSP, *Circular* 346, 14 August 1924. On the state of siege see Dulles, *Anarchists and Communists*, 274–79, 251–66.

148. CIFTSP, *Circulares* 348, 21 August; 357, 29 September; 359, n.d.; 360, 7 October; 368, 28 October; 371, 1 November; 374, 6 November; 390, 12 December; and 393, 19 December 1924.

2   *"Order and Progress" and Revolution in Industrial São Paulo*

1. The increasing power of São Paulo's industrialists during the 1920s, especially relative to the state's large coffee interests, is discussed in Mauricio A. Font, *Coffee, Contention, and Change in the Making of Modern Brazil* (Cambridge, Mass.: Basil Blackwell, 1990). Industrialists also pushed for policies that aided the importation of machinery and helped them expand their markets, but the focus of this chapter is on labor relations. For information on these other policies see Marisa Saenz Leme, *A Ideologia dos Industriais Brasileiros, 1919–1945* (Petrópolis: Vozes, 1978), 76–91.

2. *O Jornal*, 17 May 1925.

3. Quoted in Warren Dean, *The Industrialization of São Paulo, 1880–1945* (Austin: University of Texas Press, 1969), 141–42; see also 128–29. Dean

mistakenly identifies the speaker as Francisco Matarazzo. For a discussion of Fordism see Edgar de Decca, *1930: O Silêncio dos Vencidos* (São Paulo: Brasiliense, 1981), 150–82. On the spread of Fordism in Europe, see Antonio Gramsci, "Americanism and Fordism," in *Selections from the Prison Notebooks*, 8th ed. (New York: International Publishers, 1985).

4. Nathaniel H. Leff, *The Brazilian Capital Goods Industry, 1929–1964* (Cambridge, Mass.: Harvard University Press, 1968), 17–18.

5. Décio Saes, *A Formação do Estado Burguês no Brasil, 1888–1891* (Rio de Janeiro: Paz e Terra, 1985); Richard Graham, *Britain and the Onset of Modernization in Brazil, 1850–1914* (Cambridge: Cambridge University Press, 1972), 232–51.

6. The drought hurt the rural sector and decreased available hydroelectricity. Shortages in electricity required the city's industries to curtail production several days per week; see Great Britain, Department of Overseas Trade, *Financial, Commercial, and Economic Conditions in Brazil, 1928* (London: DOT, 1929), 42–44.

7. Flávio Rabelo Versiani, "Industrialização: A Década de 20 e a Depressão," *Pesquisa e Planajamento Econômico* (April 1984): 61–63. Versiani expands his description of these cycles, arguing that the 1920s witnessed an overall industrial expansion, in his *A Década de 20 na Industrialização Brasileira* (Rio de Janeiro: IPEA/INPES, 1987).

8. Versiani, "Industrialização: A Década de 20 e a Depresso," 77–80.

9. For the traditional view see Annibal V. Villela and Wilson Suzigan, *Government Policy and the Economic Growth of Brazil, 1889–1945* (Rio de Janeiro: IPEA/INPES, 1977), 111–35; Albert Fishlow, "Origens e Consequências da Substituição de Importaçoes no Brasil," *Estudos Econômicos* 2.6 (1972): 8–20; Dean, *The Industrialization of São Paulo*, 105–27. Cf. Werner Baer, *The Brazilian Economy: Growth and Development*, 2d ed. (New York: Praeger, 1983), 40–43.

10. While production may have dipped in the textile sector, capacity increased.

11. Rio to Washington, D.C., 26 February 1929, transmitting British report, "Financial, Commercial, and Economic Conditions in Brazil, 1928," RG 59, 832.51/537, NA; *Monthly Labor Review* 22.3 (March 1926): 169. See also Flávio Versiani, "Technical Change, Equipment Replacement, and Labor Absorption: The Case of the Brazilian Textile Industry" (Ph.D. diss., Vanderbilt University, 1971), 31–50; José Tavares de Araújo and Vera Maria Candido Pereira, "Teares sem Lençadeira na Indústria Têxtil," in *Difusão de Inovações na Indústria Brasileira: Três Estudos de Caso*, ed. José Avares de Araújo (Rio de Janeiro: IPEA/INPES, 1976), 15–16.

12. São Paulo Secretaria da Agricultura, Indústria, e Comércio, *Estatística Industrial do Estado de São Paulo, 1928*, see the photos between pp. 78–79 and 88–89; Rio to London, 26 June 1926, FO 371/11118, PRO. The older equipment, through a series of belts running throughout the factory, utilized one central motor; the new machines had their own motors.

13. CIFTSP, annex to *Circular* 900, 8 May 1930; CIESP, *Circular* 66, 26 August 1929; interview, Assumpta Bianchi, São Paulo, S.P., 10 August 1987.

14. CIESP, *Circular* 66, 26 August 1929. Part of this overall plan was an increasingly sophisticated program of worker discipline. This began with the blacklisting scheme of the Textile Industrialists' Center. Although she fails to put this program into the context of the rationalization scheme, Maria Alice Rosa Ribeiro describes well the industrialists' offensive against their workers; see her *Condições de Trabalho na Indústria Têxtil Paulista, 1870–1930* (São Paulo: Hucitec, 1988), 84–95.

15. CIESP, *Circular* 76, 8 November 1929.

16. CIFTSP, annex to *Circular* 900, 8 May 1930. These reduced profits were relative to the extremely high earnings of the 1910s and early 1920s.

17. For details on the creation of this segmented labor market see Joel Wolfe, "The Rise of Brazil's Industrial Working Class: Community, Work, and Politics in São Paulo, 1900–1955" (Ph.D. diss., University of Wisconsin–Madison, 1990), 10–18. George Reid Andrews, through a careful study of two groups of factory records, demonstrates a slow shift away from industrial job discrimination by race in São Paulo in the late 1920s and early 1930s; see his *Blacks and Whites in São Paulo, Brazil, 1888–1988* (Madison: University of Wisconsin Press, 1991), 90–121.

18. Versiani, "Industrialização: A Década de 20 e a Depressão," 81–84; Versiani, "Technical Change, Equipment Replacement, and Labor Absorption," 62–63; Gilbert Last, *Facts about the State of São Paulo, Brazil* (São Paulo: n.p., 1926), 72–73; *Folha da Manhã*, 10, 17, and 24 January, 10 February 1952. Cf. Wilson Suzigan, *Indústria Brasileira: Origem e Desenvolvimento* (São Paulo: Brasiliense, 1986), 243–45.

19. *Diário da Noite*, 7 August 1925. Interestingly, the Ford factory assembled only vehicles that had been manufactured in the United States.

20. *O Jornal*, 18 March 1926; *Diário da Noite*, 13 July 1926; CIESP, *Circular* 76, 8 November 1929. During severe economic downturns, industrialists worked with the state to gain rural employment for their former workers; see CIESP, *Circular* 97, 12 July 1930; CIFTSP, *Circulares* 908, 12 July; 909, 15 July 1930. The most complete study of Paulista industrialists' strategies in the 1930s is Barbara Weinstein's "The Industrialists, the State, and the Issue of Worker Training and Social Services in Brazil, 1930–1950," *HAHR* 70.3 (August 1990): 397–404.

21. The Metalgraphica, Silex, and Atefactos de Aluminio metallurgy shops, and the Italo-Brasileira and Belemzihno mills offered some limited social services in 1919; see *BDET* 31–32 (2d and 3d trimesters 1919): 185–202.

22. *O Jornal*, 8 April 1925; *O Estado de São Paulo*, 6 and 7 March 1926; Richard M. Morse, *From Community to Metropolis: A Biography of São Paulo* (Gainesville: University of Florida Press, 1958), 223.

23. *Monthly Labor Review* 22.3 (March 1926): 169; interview, Assumpta Bianchi, São Paulo, S.P., 10 August 1987. Several mill owners established vilas

when they opened their factories; some of these were founded in the 1890s. For the most complete study of industry-owned workers' housing, including details of employers' control, see Eva Alterman Blay, *Eu não Tenho onde Morar: Vilas Operárias na Cidade de São Paulo* (São Paulo: Nobel, 1985).

24. *Monthly Labor Review* 22.3 (March 1926): 169; *BPAU* (November 1925): 1139–41; *A Plebe,* 12 April 1924; CMS, "Trabalhadores e a Memória Paulistana," interview with José Biondi, p. 21.

25. *Gazeta de Notícias,* 17 October 1923; British Chamber of Commerce of Southern Brazil and São Paulo, *Bulletin* 7 (July 1924); CIESP, *Circular* (no number), July 1930.

26. Dean (*The Industrialization of São Paulo,* 156) argues that such social services represented a form of paternalism. After conducting extensive research on Paulista industrialists and their strategies for social control, Barbara Weinstein has concluded that "one should draw a distinction between the paternalism of the earliest factories, and the Fordism of the 1920s. The latter did not necessarily emphasize the familial aspects of the factory, or personal relations and obligations between owners and workers. On the contrary, it wanted to rationalize and systematize social services, and it saw industry as providing a better life for all citizens, and therefore recruiting the population into the industrialist project"; personal communication from Barbara Weinstein, 27 March 1991.

27. Some charity work was done for more altruistic reasons. The Brazilian Confederation of Women, for example, pressed for better conditions for women workers with children in the 1920s and early 1930s; see Rio to Washington, D.C., report of meeting of the Brazilian Confederation of Women, RG 59, 832.405/–, NA.

28. This was Federal Decree 5083 of 1 December 1926.

29. For the industrialists' view of the child labor laws, which they frequently broke, see CIESP, *Circulares* 35, 13 April 1929; 85, 11 March 1930. The relationship between women's activism and state policies is discussed in Joel Wolfe, "Worker Mobilization, Repression, and the Rise of the Authoritarian State: São Paulo, 1914–1924" (Paper presented to the 56th Annual Meeting of the Southern Historical Association, New Orleans, La., November 1990). On government and industrialists' schemes to "rationalize" working-class life at this time, see Maria Auxiliadora Guzzo Decca, *A Vida fora das Fábricas: Cotidiano Operário em São Paulo, 1920–1934* (Rio de Janeiro: Paz e Terra, 1987), 49–95.

30. James A. Rowan, "Trade Union Movement and Wages in Brazil," *Monthly Labor Review* 21.3 (September 1925): 3–9. Beginning in 1925, São Paulo's industries faced up to 70 percent reductions in electricity due to a drought that reduced hydroelectric power. Later in the decade, textile workers again faced reduced hours when mill owners moved to reduce their stocks. See *Diário da Noite,* 16 January 1925; *O Jornal,* 10 July 1925, 16 June 1926; CIFTSP, *Circulares* 460, 6 May 1925; 637, 13 September 1926; 871, 24 August 1929; Great Britain,

Department of Overseas Trade, *Financial, Commercial, and Economic Conditions of Brazil, 1929* (London: E. Hambloch, 1920), 16. No complete set of data on inflation in São Paulo during the 1920s could be located. The 36 percent increase is from Rio to London, Annual Report 1925, October 1926, FO 371/11118, PRO.

31. Rio to London, Annual Report 1928, January 1929, FO 371/13468, PRO.

32. Dulles recounts how the state vigorously repressed the leadership of São Paulo's anarchist movement in the 1924–26 period. Many leaders were sent to the Clevelândia penal colony on Brazil's border with French Guiana; see *Anarchists and Communists*, 259–66.

Paulo Sérgio Pinheiro describes the increasingly repressive nature of state power in the 1920s and analyzes how the federal government came to associate the workers' movements in Rio and São Paulo with the international communist movement; see *Estratégias da Ilusão: A Revolução Mundial e o Brasil, 1922–1935* (São Paulo: Companhia das Letras, 1991), 87–131.

33. CIFTSP, *Circulares* 419, 10 February; 453, 25 April; 495, 10 July 1925; 499, 22 July; 509, 17 August; 527, 16 October; 544, 23 December 1925; 602, 12 June; 605, 19 June; 606, 21 June 1926.

34. São Paulo to Washington, D.C., transmitting report from *Anglo-Brazilian Chronicle*, 8 October 1926, RG 59, 832.504/20, NA.

35. There are no reliable data on the number of firms that installed new equipment, or on what percentage of the total number of looms were semi-automated. When industrialists were seeking government aid, they lamented the poor condition of their equipment; when they spoke of São Paulo as Brazil's leading industrial center, they bragged about their new machinery. On the lament see CIFTSP, annex to *Circular* 900, 8 May 1930; for the boast see CIESP, *Circular* 66, 26 August 1929.

36. See CIFTSP, *Circulares* 707, 15 July; 709, 20 July; 710, 21 July; 713, 29 July; 728, 21 October; 729, 24 October; 733, 3 November; 734, 7 November; 742, 28 November; 744, 9 December 1927.

37. CIFTSP, *Circular* 758, 24 January 1928.

38. CIFTSP, *Circular* 766, 7 March 1928.

39. CIFTSP, *Circular* 793, 6 October 1928. For a description of the overall discontent these changes fostered among the city's textile workers, see memorial from the União dos Operários em Fábricas de Tecidos de São Paulo to Getúlio Vargas, 3 August 1931, Secretaria de Presidente da República (hereinafter SPR), Ministério do Trabalho (hereinafter MTIC), Lata 3, August 1931, Arquivo Nacional do Brasil (hereinafter ANB).

40. On Ford, see David Gartman, *Auto Slavery: The Labor Process in the American Automobile Industry, 1897–1950* (New Brunswick, N.J.: Rutgers University Press, 1987), 193–96. Unfortunately for Paulistano workers, their employers did not implement Ford's policy of paying the highest wages in industry. For more on

this aspect of Fordism see Stephen Meyer, *The Five Dollar Day: Labor Management and Social Control in the Ford Motor Company, 1908–1921* (Albany: State University of New York Press, 1981).

41. *A Plebe*, 12 February, 12 March 1927; see also Dulles, *Anarchists and Communists*, 259–66.

42. CIFTSP, *Circular* 712, 29 July 1927; Rio to London, 24 August 1924, FO 371/11964, PRO. The provisions for closing unions and newspapers were aimed at communist organizing in Rio.

43. CIFTSP, *Circulares* 736, 12 November; 746, 9 December; 749, 26 December 1927. On industry's cooperation with the DOPS see CIESP, *Circular* 40, 29 April 1929.

44. In 1923, President Epitácio da Silva Pessoa created the National Department of Labor, but this institution had no impact on industrial relations in São Paulo. On this and other federal initiatives in the 1920s see Moises Poblete Troncoso, "Technical Organization of Labor in Brazil," *BPAU* (October 1923): 466–69; and Wolfe, "Worker Mobilization, Repression, and the Rise of the Authoritarian State." Because Rio de Janeiro was the seat of the federal government, both municipal and national authorities often dealt with labor issues (on a case-by-case basis) before this period. On Rio see Maria Conceição Pinto de Góes, *A Formação da Classe Trabalhadora: Movimento Anarquista no Rio de Janeiro, 1888–1911* (Rio de Janeiro: Jorge Zahar, 1988), 82–87; June E. Hahner, *Poverty and Politics: The Urban Poor in Brazil, 1870–1920* (Albuquerque: University of New Mexico Press, 1986), 285–86; and Michael L. Conniff, *Urban Politics in Brazil: The Rise of Populism, 1925–1945* (Pittsburgh: University of Pittsburgh Press, 1981), 35–77.

45. Rio to London, Annual Report for 1928, January 1929, FO 371/13468, PRO; Rio to London, 24 August 1927, FO 371/11964, PRO.

46. Luiz Werneck Vianna, *Liberalismo e Sindicato no Brasil* (Rio de Janeiro: Paz e Terra, 1978), 61–62; Angela Maria de Castro Gomes, *Burguesia e Trabalho: Política e Legislação Social no Brasil, 1917–1937* (Rio de Janeiro: Campus, 1979), 90–107. Castro Gomes points out that some of the legislation adopted under Washington Luís had been initiated during the Bernardes years.

47. Edgard Carone, *Classes Sociais e Movimento Operário* (São Paulo: Ática, 1989), 147–48, 158–68. See also Rio to Washington, D.C., 6 August 1926, RG 59, 832.00b/orig., NA. The PCB had somewhat more success among workers in Rio; see Angela de Castro Gomes, *A Invenção do Trabalhismo* (Rio de Janeiro: IUPERJ/Vértice, 1988), 138–75.

48. This distance from organized radical groups became particularly important for the informal workers' movement at this time because elite claims of foreign direction of the labor movement actually had some validity where the small Communist party was concerned. For a thorough analysis of how the PCB's goals and policies brought on increased state repression throughout the 1920s and 1930s see Pinheiro, *Estratégias da Ilusão*, 87–131, 269–331.

49. For details of the depression's impact on Brazil see Werner Baer, *The Brazilian Economy: Growth and Development*, 2d ed. (New York: Praeger, 1983), 43–46.

50. Great Britain, Department of Overseas Trade, *Financial, Commercial, and Economic Conditions of Brazil, 1930* (London: n.p., 1931), 10, 71; CIESP, *Circulares* 97, 12 July; 98, 15 July 1930.

51. Two notable crises in the system were the 1910 election of Marshal Hermes da Fonseca and the 1919 ascension of Epitácio da Silva Pessóa in the wake of Francisco de Paula Rodrigues Alves's death. The classic treatment of the "politics of the governors" remains José Maria Bello's *A History of Modern Brazil, 1889–1964*, trans. James L. Taylor (Stanford: Stanford University Press, 1966). For the political and military details of the Revolution of 1930 see Boris Fausto, *A Revolução de 1930* (São Paulo: Brasiliense, 1983); and Thomas E. Skidmore, *Politics in Brazil, 1930–1964: An Experiment in Democracy* (New York: Oxford University Press, 1967), 3–12. For a provocative account of how coffee interests in São Paulo worked with the conspirators to keep the Paulista Júlio Prestes from assuming office see Font, *Coffee, Contention, and Change*, 166–92.

52. São Paulo to London, 27 October 1927, FO 371/14203, PRO. On the unease felt throughout São Paulo—especially in elite neighborhoods—during the 1930 Revolution see Louis Mouralis, *Un Séjour aux États-Unis du Brésil: Impressiones et réflexions* (Paris: Presses Universitaires de France, 1934), 207–24.

53. CIFTSP, *Circular* 932, 28 October 1930; CIESP, *Circular* 113, 28 October 1930.

54. CIFTSP, *Circular* 933, 7 November 1930; CIESP, annex on industry to *Circular* 114, 7 November 1930; São Paulo to London, 18 November 1930, FO 371/14203, PRO. On the nervousness of São Paulo's elites during October and November 1930 see Rio to London, 23 December 1930, FO 371/14203, PRO.

55. CIESP, annex to *Circular* 114, 7 November 1930; Getúlio Vargas, *A Nova Política do Brasil*, 11 vols. (Rio de Janeiro: José Olympio, 1938–43), 1:26–28; John W. F. Dulles, *Vargas of Brazil: A Political Biography* (Austin: University of Texas Press, 1967), 75–77; and Mouralis, *Un Séjour aux États-Unis du Brésil*, 220–23.

56. São Paulo to London, 18 November 1930, FO 371/14200, PRO; Rio to London, 23 December 1930, FO 371/14203, PRO.

57. Petrópolis to London, 20 February 1932, FO 371/15807, PRO. Melo Franco was discussing the possibility of a civil war between the Vargas administration and certain Paulistas when he spoke of the need to placate "the great mass of the people."

58. Rio to London, 15 December 1930, FO 371/15059, PRO. Such promises were consistent with the tenentes' goals for Vargas's administration, for they alone among supporters of the Aliança Liberal consistently argued for a coherent social program; see Michael L. Conniff, "The Tenentes in Power: A

New Perspective on the Brazilian Revolution of 1930," *Journal of Latin American Studies* 10 (May 1978): 61–82.

59. Rio to London, 23 December 1930, FO 371/14203, PRO.

60. CIESP, *Circular* 123, 23 February 1930; Foreign Policy Association, *Information Service Bulletin*, March 1931, FO 371/15059, PRO. The Law of Two-thirds had an interesting impact on Paulistano workers. Blacks in the city supported Vargas's nationalism because it bolstered their position vis-à-vis the city's majority white working class, with its many immigrants. This measure was probably received with enthusiasm by Carioca workers, who had a tradition of xenophobia. The differing perspectives on the Law of Two-thirds provides a good example of how different groups of workers in different locations reacted to federal labor laws. On Paulistano blacks' support of Vargas's nationalism see Andrews, *Blacks and Whites in São Paulo*, 146–56. On xenophobia among Carioca workers see Sidney Chaloub, *Trabalho, Lar, e Botequim: O Cotidiano dos Trabalhadores no Rio de Janeiro da Belle Époque* (São Paulo: Brasiliense, 1986).

61. Guillermo O'Donnell provides a useful definition of "corporatism." O'Donnell considers " 'corporatist' those structures through which functional, nonterritorially based organizations officially represent 'private' interests before the state, formally subject for their existence and their right of representation to authorization or acceptance by the state, and where such right is reserved to the formal leaders of those organizations, forbidding and excluding other legitimate channels of access to the state for the rest of its members"; see his "Corporatism and the Question of the State," in *Authoritarianism and Corporatism in Latin America*, ed. James M. Malloy (Pittsburgh: University of Pittsburgh Press, 1977); 47–87; see also Philippe Schmitter, "Still the Century of Corporatism?" *Review of Politics* 36.1 (January 1974): 85–131.

62. The mixed commissions were created by Decree 21396 of 12 May 1932. The more formal Conciliation and Judgment Boards (Juntas de Conciliação e Julgamento) were created through Decree 22132 of 25 November 1932. The industrialists' centers became their unions (sindicatos). Each city or município would have one union per industry. For example, there would be one union that represented all São Paulo city textile workers, and a separate union that represented the city's metalworkers. In this way, Brazil's corporatist structure differed from O'Donnell's model, for sindicatos were territorially based.

63. Lindolfo Collor to Getúlio Vargas, 6 March 1930, Arquivo do Lindolfo Collor (hereinafter ALC), Centro de Pesquisa e Documentação (hereinafter CPDOC), Fundição Getúlio Vargas (hereinafter FGV); see also Rosa Maria Barboza de Araújo, *O Batismo do Trabalho: A Experiência de Lindolfo Collor* (Rio de Janeiro: Civilização Brasileira, 1981), 88–95.

64. See Joan L. Bak, "Cartels, Cooperatives, and Corporatism: Getúlio Vargas in Rio Grande do Sul on the Eve of Brazil's 1930 Revolution," *HAHR* 63.2 (May 1983): 255–75. Further, as Angela Maria de Castro Gomes has

demonstrated, the Revolution of 1930 did not initiate debate on these issues; government regulation of the labor market was an important issue in national political discourse throughout the 1920s; see Castro Gomes, *Burguesia e Trabalho*, 55–195. De Decca, in *1930: O Silêncio dos Vencidos*, argues forcefully that Vargas actually implemented the industrialists' political project from the 1920s.

65. Jorge Street wrote in *O Estado de São Paulo* (20 July 1917) that "the peaceful and orderly strike should not get involved with subversive movements." See chapter 1 in this volume; see also Castro Gomes, *Burguesia e Trabalho*, 213–24; Eli Diniz, *Empresário, Estado e Capitalismo no Brasil, 1930–1945* (Rio de Janeiro: Paz e Terra, 1978), 89–109. Cf. John D. French, "Industrial Workers and the Origin of Populist Politics in the ABC Region of Greater São Paulo, Brazil, 1900–1950" (Ph.D. diss., Yale University, 1985), 113–15.

66. Specifically, the Textile Industrialists' Center opposed both João Alberto's November 1930 calls for increased hours and pay and some of Collor's May 1931 social legislation (e.g., an eight-hour day, guaranteed holidays; see CIFTSP, *Circulares* 942, 5 December 1930; 1057, 30 May 1931. In these disagreements we see the one significant difference between the Paulista industrialists' Fordism and corporatism: the role of the state. The industrialists preferred to operate in an industrial relations system with the state's role limited to providing the means of repression against workers.

67. *A Platéia*, 13 May 1931; memorial from the União dos Operários em Fábricas de Tecidos de São Paulo to Getúlio Vargas, 3 August 1931, SPR, MTIC, Lata 3, August 1931, ANB. Textile industrialists throughout Brazil believed they were suffering from overproduction at this time. In fact, they convinced Vargas to limit imports of machinery in order to stabilize output. Interestingly, they did not discuss the possibility that the problem was underconsumption, which could have been solved with increased employment. On overproduction and the restrictions see Stanley J. Stein, *The Brazilian Cotton Manufacture: Textile Enterprise in an Underdeveloped Area, 1850–1950* (Cambridge, Mass.: Harvard University Press, 1957), 136–42.

68. *A Platéia*, 26 May 1931. The Textile Factory Workers' Union was founded in November 1930 by Righetti and others who had been active in the various textile unions that had operated in São Paulo since the 1917 General Strike.

69. *Folha da Manhã*, 3 July 1931. I could not locate details of the settlement in newspaper sources.

70. *Folha da Manhã*, 5 July 1931; *A Platéia*, 22 November 1930; see also Maria Helena Simões Paes, "O Sindicato dos Metalúrgicos de São Paulo, 1931–1951" (Tese de mestrado, Universidade de São Paulo, 1979), 36–37.

71. *Folha da Manhã*, 12, 17, and 18 July 1931.

72. The Federação Operária de São Paulo was anarchist, the Federação Sindical Regional de São Paulo was tied to the Communist party, the Coligação dos Sindicatos Proletários de São Paulo was associated with the Trotskyist

movement, and the Centro Operário Catholico was tied to the church. Although quite a small group, São Paulo's Trotskyists were active labor advocates. For information on this little-studied segment of the Left in Brazil see Fúlvio Abramo and Dainis Karepovs, eds., *Na Contracorrente da História: Documentos da Liga Comunista Internacionalista, 1930–1933* (São Paulo: Brasiliense, 1987).

73. *Folha da Manhã,* 18 and 19 July 1931. The men wanted eight-hour instead of ten-hour shifts so that the total number of workers could be increased.

74. *A Platéia,* 18 July 1931.

75. *Folha da Manhã,* 19 July 1931.

76. *Folha da Manhã,* 21 July 1931.

77. FIESP/CIESP, *Circular* 161, 18 July 1931.

78. For these denials see Sindicato Patronal das Indústrias de Fiação e Tecelagem do Estado de São Paulo (formerly CIFTSP), *Relatório,* 1931, n.p.; Righetti to Vargas, 3 August 1931, SPR, MTIC 17.10, Lata 46, ANB.

79. On Vargas's initial popular support in São Paulo, see Dulles, *Vargas of Brazil,* 75–77.

80. The FOSP, Textile Workers' Union, and Metalworkers' Union refused to apply for Ministry of Labor approval; see *A Platéia,* 9 January 1933, 2 August 1934; Márcia Mendes de Almeida, "O Sindicato dos Têxteis de São Paulo: História, 1933–1957" (Tese de mestrado, Universidade de São Paulo, 1981), 29–30; Simões Paes, "O Sindicato dos Metalúrgicos de São Paulo," 36–37. Also, the mixed conciliation commissions had not yet been formally established.

81. CIFTSP, *Circular* 1099, 27 July 1931.

82. The manifesto was reprinted in FIESP/CIESP, *Circular* 163, 21 July 1931.

83. FIESP/CIESP, *Circulares* 162, 20 July; 163, 21 July; 164, 22 July; 166, 30 July; (no number), 21 August 1931; *Folha da Manhã,* 22 and 29 July 1931.

84. *Folha da Manhã,* 6 and 7 August 1931.

85. Memorial from the União dos Operários em Fábricas de Tecidos de São Paulo to Getúlio Vargas, 3 August 1931, SPR, MTIC 17.10, Lata 46, ANB; see also *Folha da Manhã,* 14 August 1931.

86. Interview, Hermento Mendes Dantas, São Paulo, S.P., 14 September 1987; *A Platéia,* 9 January 1933, 2 August 1934; Simões Paes, "O Sindicato dos Metalúrgicos de São Paulo," 36–37.

87. Interview, Laura S. Machado, Osasco, S.P., 8 September 1987; interview, Angela Neto, São Paulo, S.P., 8 August 1987; memorial from the União dos Operários em Fábricas de Tecidos de São Paulo to Getúlio Vargas, 3 August 1931, SPR, MTIC 17.10, Lata 46, ANB.

88. CIFTSP, *Circular* 1157, 19 January 1932; FIESP/CIESP, *Circular* 237, 19 January 1932; Confidential File on José Righetti, SPR, MTIC 17.10, Lata 46, ANB.

89. Memorial from the União dos Operários em Fábricas de Tecidos de São

Paulo to Getúlio Vargas, 3 August 1931, SPR, MTIC 17.10, Lata 46, ANB; interview, Assumpta Bianchi, São Paulo, S.P., 10 August 1987; interview, Laura S. Machado, Osasco, S.P., 8 September 1987.

90. For an analysis of such "traditional" gender ideologies in the 1920s and 1930s see June E. Hahner, *Emancipating the Female Sex: The Struggle for Women's Rights in Brazil, 1850–1940* (Durham: Duke University Press, 1990), 113–20, 176–80. On middle-class and elite women's struggles to recast gender ideologies and praxis see Susan Kent Besse, "Freedom and Bondage: The Impact of Capitalism on Women in São Paulo, Brazil, 1917–1937" (Ph.D. diss., Yale University, 1983).

91. Confidential File on José Righetti, SPR, MTIC 17.10, Lata 46, ANB.

92. FIESP/CIESP, *Circular* 235, 14 January 1932; Rio to London, 7 May 1931, FO 371/15059, PRO; Rio to London, 9 July 1931, FO 371/15059, PRO.

93. On taxes see FIESP/CIESP, *Circular* 228, 17 December 1931. For information on machinery imports see CIESP, *Circular* 126, 13 March 1931; FIESP/CIESP, *Circular* 142, 23 May 1931; Stein, *The Brazilian Cotton Manufacture*, 138–48; and Versiani, "Technical Change, Equipment Replacement, and Labor Absorption," 57–61. On social legislation see FIESP/CIESP, *Circulares* 206, 26 October 1931; 228, 17 December 1931.

94. Indeed, João Alberto's resignation in July 1931 was one more attempt by Vargas to calm industrialists' fears; see Rio to London, 29 July 1931, FO 371/15060, PRO.

95. FIESP/CIESP, *Circulares* 253, 7 March 1932; 258, 28 March 1932; 265, 3 May 1932; 270, 16 May 1932; 284, 23 June 1932.

96. *Folha da Manhã*, 11 March 1932.

97. The industrialists' position is detailed in FIESP/CIESP, *Circulares* (no numbers), 4, 6, 9, and 12 May 1932; 268, 14 May 1932. Without access to the actual dialogue among the city's industrialists, it is impossible to know which of them had opposed the strikes all along and which had been convinced by their colleagues to oppose the strikes after the labor and leftist activists joined the workers' struggle.

98. *Folha da Manhã*, 1 and 3–9 May 1932; Rio to London, Annual Report for 1932, March 1933, FO 371/16553, PRO; Dulles, *Anarchists and Communists*, 491–95.

99. Sindicato Patronal das Indústrias Têxteis do Estado de São Paulo (formerly the CIFTSP), *Circulares* 1185-A, 10 May 1932; 1186, 13 May 1932; *Folha da Manhã*, 11 May 1932. The unionists believed that the eight-hour day would create many new positions if production levels were maintained. Male unionists had complained about the hiring of women workers over men—for jobs traditionally held by women—in 1931 as well; see Maria Célia Paoli, "Os Trabalhadores Urbanos na Fala dos Outros: Tempo, Espaço e Classe na História Operária Brasileira," in *Cultura e Identidade Operária: Aspectos da Cultura da Classe Trabalhadora*, ed. José Sérgio Leite Lopes (São Paulo: Marco Zero/UFRJ, 1987),

77. Similar male anxieties over their inability to provide for their families led to a "crisis of masculinity" among U.S. workers during these same years; see Elizabeth Faue, *Community of Suffering and Struggle: Women, Men, and the Labor Movement in Minneapolis, 1915–1945* (Chapel Hill: University of North Carolina Press, 1991), 166, 191.

100. Rio to London, 13 May 1932, FO 371/150808 PRO; *Folha da Manhã,* 12, 13, and 17 May 1932.

101. Sindicato Patronal das Indústrias Têxteis do Estado de São Paulo, *Circular* 1189, 17 May 1932; FIESP/CIESP, *Circular* 271, 17 May 1932; *Folha da Manhã,* 18 May 1932.

102. Telegram, São Paulo's Conservative Classes to Vargas, 19 May 1932, SPR, Correspondência–Entidades Representivas de Classe, Lata 7, ANB.

103. Collor to Borges de Medeiros, LC 32.05.14/2, CPDOC. Like the industrialists, Collor believed the strike was the work of extremists and Communists.

104. Collor resigned in April 1932 and was replaced by Joaquim Pedre Salgado Filho. For the settlements see *Boletim do Ministério do Trabalho, Indústria e Comércio* (hereinafter *BMTIC*) 16 (December 1935): 384–85. On the labor legislation see FIESP/CIESP, *Circular* 277, 30 May 1932; Rio to London, Annual Report for 1932, 13 March 1933, FO 371/16553, PRO; Dulles, *Anarchists and Communists,* 498–99. Salgado Filho also introduced regulations that gave pregnant factory workers special leave benefits. These policies no doubt satisfied both male and female workers.

105. For details of the unfolding of the Paulista uprising see Stanley Hilton, *A Guerra Civil Brasileira: História da Revolução Constitucionalista de 1932* (Rio de Janeiro: Nova Fronteira, 1982).

106. FIESP/CIESP, *Circulares* 292, 12 July; 293, 13 July; 295, 13 July; 302, 20 July; Rio to London, Annual Report for 1932, 13 March 1933, FO 371/16533, PRO. Vargas's aides and the military also realized that the Paulistas needed social peace to maintain industrial production. For Vargas's aides' views see Petrópolis to London, 20 February 1932, FO 371/15807, PRO; on the military see Stanley Hilton, *A Rebelião Vermelha* (Rio de Janeiro: Record, 1986), 37–38.

107. FIESP/CIESP, *Circular* 315, 28 July 1932.

108. FIESP/CIESP, *Circulares* 330, 20 September; 333, 7 October 1932; São Paulo to London, 12 October 1932, FO 371/15809, PRO.

109. Telegram, Rio to London, 9 August 1932, FO 371/15808; Rio to London, 15 August 1932, FO 371/15808; Rio to London, 13 September 1932, FO 371/15808, PRO; Góes Monteiro, Destacamento de Exército de Leste, Memória no. 6, GV (Arquivo Getúlio Vargas) 32.09.29, CPDOC; João Neves de Fontoura to Collor, GV 32.09.01/1, CPDOC, FGV.

110. For a detailed analysis of the nascent arms industry in São Paulo see Rio to London, Military Attaché's Report on the Civil War, 28 November 1932, FO 371/16548, PRO.

111. Leme, *A Ideologia dos Industriais*, 137–48; Castro Gomes, *Burguesia e Trabalho*, 224–25.

112. Rio to London, Annual Report for 1932, 13 March 1933, FO 371/16553, PRO. John D. French has mistakenly argued that Vargas first used such ex-officio voter registration to gain workers' electoral support in 1945; see *The Brazilian Workers' ABC: Class Conflict and Alliances in Modern São Paulo* (Chapel Hill: University of North Carolina Press, 1992), 112–13. The differences between the 1932 and 1945 regulations and what they tell us about the relationship between Vargas and Brazilian industrial workers are analyzed in chapter 5 in this volume.

113. *O Trabalhador Têxtil*, May 1945; *BMTIC* 15 (November 1935): 370; Mendes de Almeida, "O Sindicato dos Têxteis em São Paulo," 30–36.

114. Simões Paes, "O Sindicato dos Metalúrgicos de São Paulo," 39–41; *BMTIC* 15 (November 1935): 370.

115. See São Paulo to London, 26 May 1933, FO 371/16549; São Paulo to London, 8 September 1933, FO 371/16549, PRO.

116. The Ministry of Labor in Rio relied on state departments of labor to implement its programs. Briefly, in the early 1930s, the São Paulo Department of Labor mediated disputes between the new state-sponsored sindicatos and industrialists. FIESP members complained bitterly to Vargas that this agency sided too often with the unions; see CIESP/FIESP, *Circular* 416, 8 June 1933; Sindicato Patronal das Indústrias Têxtil do Estado de São Paulo, *Circulares* 1273, 8 June 1933; 1324, 11 November 1933; 1324, 22 November 1933; 1325, 23 November 1933; and 1332, 6 December 1933.

117. See, for example, their objection to the naming of Waldemar Lima as interventor, in telegram, Mario Rotta and Rodolfo Mantorani to Vargas, SPR, SP 14.21, Lata 26, ANB. For Mantorani's and others' protests against the quasi-fascist Integralist movement in São Paulo see telegram, São Paulo Union Leaders to Vargas, 13 December 1933, SPR, Correspondência–Entidades Representivas de Classe, Lata 7, ANB. They did once protest the deporting of several activists; see telegram from the Metalworkers' Union of São Paulo to Vargas, 6 September 1934, SPR, Correspondência–Entidades Representivas de Classe, Lata 7, ANB.

118. FIESP/CIESP, *Circulares* 416, 8 June; 449, 5 October; 450, 9 October 1933; 507, 24 April; 573, 13 November 1934; also see Sindicato Patronal das Indústrias Têxtil do Estado de São Paulo, *Circulares* 1273, 8 June; 1324, 11 November 1933; 1372, 24 April 1934. Even before Street took over, the DET passed information to the FIESP on which workers had filed complaints about their employers, but the state's industrialists wanted complete control of the industrial relations system; Vargas acceded as a way to maintain peace with the Paulista industrialists. On Vargas's political maneuvering in São Paulo in the early 1930s and his need to appease the state's elites in the aftermath of the 1932 civil war, see Angela Maria de Castro Gomes et al., "Revolução e Restau-

ração: A Experiência Paulista no Período da Constitucionalização," in *Regionalismo e Centralização Política: Partidos e Constituinte nos Anos 30,* ed. Castro Gomes (Rio de Janeiro: Nova Fronteira, 1980), 239–337.

119. As late as 1944, the Ministry of Labor focused almost exclusively on Rio. Work outside the national capital by the Departamento Nacional do Trabalho (the branch of the Ministry of Labor most responsible for workers' and union affairs) was considered extraordinary; see Ministério do Trabalho, Indústria, e Comércio, *Relatório do Departamento Nacional do Trabalho, 1944,* Arquivo Alexandre de Marcondes Filho (hereinafter AMF) 45.01(?).00, CPDOC, FGV. For a thoughtful analysis of the Ministry of Labor in Rio see Castro Gomes, *A Invenção do Trabalhismo,* 257–87.

120. Sindicato dos Operários em Fábricas de Tecidos de São Paulo (hereinafter SOFTSP), Assembléias Gerais, 13 May, 8 July, 2 September 1934; 6 January, 13 January 1935; SOFTSP, Reunião de Diretoria, 23 December 1934; see also *A Platéia,* 18, 19, and 21 July, 10 September 1934; Mendes de Almeida, "O Sindicato dos Têxteis em São Paulo," 30–36.

121. Mendes de Almeida, "O Sindicatos dos Têxteis em São Paulo," 33.

122. *A Plebe,* 1 July and 21 October 1933; *A Platéia,* 2 August 1934; Simões Paes, "O Sindicato dos Metalúrgicos de São Paulo," 56–57; telegram to Vargas, 9 January 1935, SPR, SP 14.21, Lata 26, ANB.

123. This process of ousting independent unionists and replacing them with individuals close to the Ministry of Labor and state Department of Labor was not unique to the textile and metallurgical sectors. The city's shoemakers increasingly participated in an anarchist union during the late 1920s and early 1930s. In 1933 unionists tied to the Ministry of Labor took control, and the rank and file avoided the sindicato; see interviews with Horácio Pereira Frade, president of the São Paulo Shoemakers' Union, and with Alcides Ribeiro de Almeida, secretary of the São Paulo Shoemakers' Union, São Paulo, S.P., 18 April 1956, Alexander Papers, Rutgers University, Coll. 1957, Box 2.

124. Interview, Angela Neto, São Paulo, S.P., 3 September 1987; interview, Waldemar Lima, São Paulo, S.P., 25 September 1987; FIESP/CIESP, *Circular* (no number), 2 June 1934. Metalworkers tended to tamper with machinery more often than textile workers, for textile workers depended on well-functioning machines to gain the piece rate portion of their wages.

125. FIESP/CIESP, *Circular* 617, 3 April 1935; *A Plebe,* 8 June 1935.

126. SOFTSP, Assembléias Gerais, 3 February, 7 April 1935; SOFTSP, Reunião de Diretoria, 8 March 1935; *A Plebe,* 16 February 1935.

127. *Folha da Manhã,* 7 and 8 June 1935; *O Trabalhador Têxtil,* May 1945.

128. SOFTSP, Assembléias Gerais, 7, 10, and 18 June 1935; SOFTSP, Reunião de Diretoria, 26 June 1935; Mendes de Almeida, "O Sindicato dos Têxteis em São Paulo," 53–54.

129. *Folha da Manhã,* 11, 12, 13, 15, 16, 18, 19, 20, 25, 27, 28, 29, and 30 June, and 2 and 3 July 1935.

130. SOFTSP, Assembléias Gerais, 10 and 23 November 1935.

131. *Folha da Manhã*, 4, 5, 6, 22, and 12 July 1935. For information on the ANL see Ricardo Antunes, *Classe Operária, Sindicatos, e Partido no Brasil: Da Revolução de 30 até a Aliança Nacional Libertadora* (São Paulo: Cortez, 1982), 137–66; Robert M. Levine, *The Vargas Regime: The Critical Years, 1934–1938* (New York: Columbia University Press, 1970), 58–80; and Dulles, *Anarchists and Communists*, 517–22.

132. *Folha da Manhã*, 14, 16, 19, 21, 23, and 24 July 1935.

133. These numbers are from Werneck Vianna, *Liberalismo e Sindicato*, 144.

134. On the similarities among anarchists, socialists, and Communists in Rio see Castro Gomes, *A Invenção do Trabalhismo*, 35–175. The most complete work on the associations is Michael L. Conniff, "Voluntary Associations in Rio de Janeiro, 1870–1945; A New Approach to Urban Social Dynamics," *Journal of Interamerican Studies* 17 (1975): 64–81. On the connections between Carioca urban politics in the 1910s and 1920s and Vargas's program see Conniff, *Urban Politics in Brazil*, 35–134.

135. The quote and information on the two unions are from Antunes, *Classe Operária, Sindicatos, e Partido*, 89–93; the quote is from p. 90.

136. Railroad workers, trolley operators, and hotel and commercial workers joined textile and metallurgical workers and printers in the state of São Paulo in opposing Vargas's unionization law; see Antunes, *Classe Operária, Sindicatos, e Partido*, 87–115.

137. The continuity between previous labor discourses from Rio and Vargas's is the central theme of Castro Gomes, *A Invenção do Trabalhismo*. French (*The Brazilian Workers' ABC*, 35–40) argues that workers in the state of São Paulo quickly turned to the state-sanctioned unions, but he does so without reference to any archival materials. He universalizes the experiences of the Paulista bank workers (a group that had little in common with industrial workers and who did seek Ministry of Labor recognition for their union) for all the state's workers.

138. It is important to note how contemporary experiences reinforced historical memory. The city's workers had never had a mayor or other government official on any level representing their interests—except the brief tenure of the interventor, João Alberto. Then, when Vargas handed control of the industrial relations system to the state's industrialists, workers had yet more evidence of the validity of this aspect of anarchist discourse to their experience. José Sérgio Leite Lopes, in his study of an industrial suburb of Recife in the northeastern state of Pernambuco, also argues that local political conditions were the key factor in determining workers' relationship to the new industrial relations system; see his *A Tecelagem dos Conflitos de Classe na Cidade das Chaminés* (São Paulo: Universidade de Brasília/Marco Zero, 1988), 205–62.

139. *Folha da Manhã*, 18 July 1935; *A Plebe*, 31 August 1935.

140. One of the most detailed accounts of the Intentona is Stanley Hilton's *A Rebelião Vermelha*. Paulo Sérgio Pinheiro puts this uprising into the context of the PCB's history of preferring military solutions to long-term popular organizing in *Estratégias da Ilusão*, 269–331. On Stalin's reasons for sending German Communists such as Olga Benário on such a mission, see Fernando Morais, *Olga*, 11th ed. (São Paulo: Alfa-Omega, 1986).

141. See Pinheiro, *Estratégias da Ilusão*, 308–31.

3 Class Struggle versus Conciliação: The Estado Novo

1. For analyses of the industrial bourgeoisie and the creation of a new centralized state in response to the political crisis of the early 1930s see Francisco Weffort, *O Populismo na Política Brasileira* (Rio de Janeiro: Paz e Terra, 1986), 105–64; Borris Fausto, *A Revolução de 1930: Historiografia e História* (São Paulo: Brasiliense, 1986), 86–111; Edgar de Decca, *1930: O Selêncio dos Vencidos* (São Paulo: Brasiliense, 1983), 135–82; and Edgard Carone, *A República Nova: 1930–1937* (Rio de Janeiro: DIFEL, 1974), 81–95.

2. Frank D. McCann, "The Formative Period of Twentieth-Century Brazilian Army Thought, 1900–1922," *HAHR* 64.4 (November 1984): 737–65.

3. On politics in the mid-1930s see Robert M. Levine, "Perspectives on the Mid-Vargas Years, 1934–1937," *Journal of Inter-American Studies and World Affairs* 22.1 (February 1980): 57–80; and Thomas E. Skidmore, *Politics in Brazil: An Experiment in Democracy* (New York: Oxford University Press, 1967), 12–29. On the military see Stanley E. Hilton, "The Armed Forces and Industrialists in Modern Brazil: The Drive for Military Autonomy, 1889–1954," *HAHR* 62 (November 1982): 629–73; Hilton, "Military Influence on Brazilian Economic Policy, 1930–1945," *HAHR* 53 (February 1973): 71–91; and Hilton, "Vargas and Brazilian Economic Development, 1930–1945; A Reappraisal of His Attitude toward Industrialization and Planning," *Journal of Economic History* 35 (December 1975): 754–78. For an analysis of the radical elements within the military see Michael L. Conniff, "The *Tenentes* in Power: A New Perspective on the Brazilian Revolution of 1930," *Journal of Latin American Studies* (hereinafter *JLAS*) 10 (May 1978): 61–82. Ludwig Lauerhauss, Jr., studied the long-term development of a "modernizing" elite; see his "Getúlio Vargas and the Triumph of Brazilian Nationalism: A Study of the Rise of the Nationalist Generation of 1930" (Ph.D. diss., University of California, Los Angeles, 1972).

4. The notion that Brazil is an essentially peaceful society (especially relative to its Spanish-American neighbors) was a fiercely held national myth during the nineteenth and much of the twentieth centuries. This concept was first challenged by José Honório Rodrigues in his *Conciliação e Reforma no Brasil: Uma Desafio Histórico-Cultural* (Rio de Janeiro: Civilização Brasileira, 1965). On

the importance of national myths in Brazilian history see Emília Viotti da Costa, *The Brazilian Empire: Myths and Histories* (Chicago: University of Chicago Press, 1985).

5. Getúlio Vargas, *A Nova Política do Brasil*, 11 vols. (Rio de Janeiro: José Olympio, 1938–43), 5:300, also see 4:139–44, 151–56, 181–87, and 5:121–27, 163–72.

6. The most complete analysis of this ideology is presented in Alcir Lenharo, *A Sacralização da Política* (Campinas: Papirus, 1986). Interestingly, the nationalist component of Estado Novo rhetoric appealed to middle-class blacks in São Paulo, for Vargas was seen as a potential ally in their struggles against the power of immigrant and first-generation Brazilian political interests in the state; see George Reid Andrews, *Blacks and Whites in São Paulo, Brazil, 1888–1988* (Madison: University of Wisconsin Press, 1991), 125–56.

7. For the military's fear of Paulistano workers' activities see Stanley E. Hilton, *A Rebelião Vermelha* (Rio de Janeiro: Record, 1986), 37–50. On industrialists' support for these measures see Marisa Saenz Leme, *A Ideologia dos Industriais Brasileiros: 1919–1945* (Petrópolis: Vozes, 1978), 137–51; Eli Diniz, *Empresário, Estado e Capitalismo no Brasil: 1930–1945* (Rio de Janeiro: Paz e Terra, 1978), 89–94; and Robert W. Howe, "Progressive Conservatism in Brazil: Oliveira Viana, Roberto Simonsen, and the Social Legislation of the Vargas Regime, 1930–1945" (Ph.D. diss., Cambridge University, 1975). Cf. Warren Dean, *The Industrialization of São Paulo, 1880–1945* (Austin: University of Texas Press, 1969), 206–33.

Similar perceptions of the Argentine working class convinced Juan Perón and his allies to initiate a corporatist labor system; see Carlos H. Waisman, *Reversal of Development in Argentina: Postwar Counterrevolutionary Policies and Their Structural Consequences* (Princeton: Princeton University Press, 1987), 164–252. For a comparative perspective see Thomas E. Skidmore, "Workers and Soldiers: Urban Labor Movements and Elite Responses in Twentieth-Century Latin America," in *Elites, Masses, and Modernization in Latin America, 1850–1930*, ed. Virginia Bernhard (Austin: University of Texas Press, 1979).

8. Vargas, *A Nova Política*, 4:205, 5:19–32; and *BMTIC* 45 (May 1938). This speech closely mirrors Benedict Anderson's analysis of "official nationalism"; see his *Imagined Communities: Reflections on the Origin and Spread of Nationalism* (London: Verso, 1983), 80–103.

9. *BMTIC* 88 (December 1941): 82; Ari Pitombo, "A Legislação Trabalhista e o Momento Atual," *BMTIC* 112 (December 1943): 151; and Lenharo, *A Sacralização da Política*, 37.

10. Vargas, *A Nova Política*, 4:144, 5:172. Some Paulistano industrialists also supported the creation of a minimum wage as a means to limit the appeal of leftist ideologies and to deepen capitalist development by increasing demand for domestically produced goods; see O. Pupo Nogueira, "O Repercussões Econômicos do Salário Mínimo," *BMTIC* 61 (September 1939): 135–52.

11. "O Problema Alimentar em São Paulo," *BMTIC* 83 (July 1941): 210; see also Vargas, *A Nova Política,* 7:55–134, 165–68.

12. Robert Mange, "O Fator Humano na Organização Científica do Trabalho," *BMTIC* 93 (July 1941): 203–10; Francisco Pompeo do Amaral, "Consequência da Má Alimentação no Operário," *BMTIC* 97 (September 1942): 251–65; "A Alimentação da População Paulistana," *Revista do Arquivo Municipal* (hereinafter *RAM*) 90 (May–June 1943): 55–87; and Numa Pereira do Valle, "A Habitação Econômica sob o Ponto de Vista Político e Sociológico," *RAM* 90 (May–June 1943): 89–104.

13. It is beyond the scope of this book to document gender anxieties throughout Brazil, but I should note that women's activism in different social strata created an atmosphere of fear among men. Women workers' leadership roles in strikes as well as their continued prominence in industry during the early years of the depression have already been discussed. Middle-class and elite women's activism in pushing for expanded social standing and political rights are analyzed in June E. Hahner, *Emancipating the Female Sex: The Struggle for Women's Rights in Brazil, 1850–1940* (Durham: Duke University Press, 1990), 121–80; and Susan Kent Besse, "Freedom and Bondage: The Impact of Capitalism on Women in São Paulo, Brazil, 1917–1937" (Ph.D. diss., Yale University, 1983).

14. On the relationship between families and the state structure see Romeu Rodrigues Silva, "O Problema Social no Brasil Contemporâneo," *BMTIC* 82 (June 1941): 343–51. See *BMTIC* 68 (April 1940): 71–72 for speeches by Vargas and Minister of Labor Waldemar Falcão on the role of families and the state's obligation to protect the traditional family structure.

15. Vargas, *A Nova Política,* 7:157–60; see also Ernesto Galarza, *Labor Trends and Social Welfare in Latin America, 1939–1940* (Washington, D.C.: Pan American Union, Division of Labor and Social Information, 1941), 18. No other details of this proposed tax were located.

16. The quote is from Galarza, *Labor Trends and Social Welfare,* 49. For the complete text of the law see *BMTIC* 68 (April 1940): 60–65.

17. Memorial from the União dos Operários em Fábricas de Tecidos de São Paulo to Getúlio Vargas, 3 August 1931, SPR, MTIC 17.10, Lata 46, ANB.

18. Maria Sophia Bulcão Vianna, "A Evolução do Trabalho da Mulher," *BMTIC* 37 (September 1937): 103–8; "Speech by Minister of Labor Falcão," 12 November 1937, Arquivo do Waldemar Falcão (hereinafter AWF) 37.11.12, Pasta 8, FGV, CPDOC; Vargas, *A Nova Política,* 7:157–60; and Lenharo, *A Sacralização da Política,* 44–46.

19. Angela de Castro Gomes closely analyzes the roots of Vargas's labor ideology and finds important continuities between Vargas's rhetoric and that of the Rio labor movement from the early 1900s through the 1930s; see her *A Invenção do Trabalhismo* (Rio de Janeiro: IUPERJ/Vértice, 1988). She does not, however, discuss either labor's or Vargas's gender ideologies.

20. Maria Kiehl, "O Trabalho da Mulher fora do Lar," pt. 2, *BMTIC* 97 (September 1942): 127. See also part 1 of this article in *BMTIC* 96 (August 1942): 83–95.

21. Milena Mallet, *Almas Desnudas: A Tragédia Sexual da Mulher Brasileira* (Rio de Janeiro: Victor, 1945). The Nazis used a similar gender ideology couched in nationalistic terms during this period; see Claudia Koonz, *Mothers in the Fatherland: Women, the Family and Nazi Politics* (New York: St. Martin's Press, 1987), 177–219.

22. See Vargas, *A Nova Política,* 4:144, 181–87, 5:121–28, 6:117–20, 339–49, 7:55–126; 281–85, 291–95, 8:45–47, 259–63.

23. Vargas, *A Nova Política,* 5:126–27, 167. Juan Perón also appealed, quite successfully, to Argentine workers' sense of social justice and citizenship; see Daniel James, *Resistance and Integration: Peronism and the Argentine Working Class* (Cambridge: Cambridge University Press, 1988), 14–33.

24. Carone, *A República Nova,* 342–50; Boris Koval, *História do Proletariado Brasileiro, 1857–1967,* trans. Clarice Lima Avierina (São Paulo: Alfa-Omega, 1982), 326–35; and John W. F. Dulles, *Brazilian Communism, 1935–1945: Repression during World Upheaval* (Austin: University of Texas Press, 1983), 7–42.

25. On the 1934 and 1935 strikes see chapter 2 in this volume; and telegram to Vargas, 9 January 1935, SPR, SP 14.21, Lata 26, Processo (hereinafter PR) 110/35, ANB.

26. CIESP/FIESP, *Circular* 790, 30 November 1936; telegram, federal interventor Cardoso de Melo Neto to Vargas, 18 October 1937, SPR, SP 14.21, Lata 26, ANB; and *BMTIC* 32 (April 1937): 111–18.

27. CIESP/FIESP, *Circular* 823, 17 May 1937; and telegram, FIESP to Vargas, 22 September 1939, SPR, Correspondência–Entidades Representivas de Classe 11.2, Lata 171, ANB.

28. Letter, São Paulo interventor to Vargas, 27 May 1938, SPR, SP 14.21, Lata 21, PR 2864/39, ANB; and confidential report to Vargas, "São Paulo no Momento," January 1936, AGV, 36.01.00/1, FGV, CPDOC.

29. See Luiz Werneck Vianna, *Liberalismo e Sindicato no Brasil* (Rio de Janeiro: Paz e Terra, 1978), 223–35, for an analysis of the origins of these regulations and how they were implemented by the Ministry of Labor. The activities of the Textile Workers' Union and Metalworkers' Union are detailed below.

30. Werneck Vianna, *Liberalismo e Sindicato no Brasil,* 232–33; and Kenneth Paul Erickson, *The Brazilian Corporative State and Working-Class Politics* (Berkeley: University of California Press, 1977), 36–37. When a worker was sindicalizado/a he or she paid the labor tax and union dues. That worker was also officially registered as a union member with the Ministry of Labor. The actual percentages of textile and metallurgical workers in the São Paulo unions are given below.

31. The *Novo Dicionário de Língua Portuguesa,* 15th ed., defines *pelego* as "a

common designation of the agents, more or less disguised, of the Ministry of Labor in the workers' unions," s.v. "pelego."

32. Kenneth Scott Mericle, "Conflict Resolution in the Brazilian Industrial Relations System" (Ph.D. diss., University of Wisconsin–Madison, 1974), 137.

33. Interview, Antônio Toschi (former president of the Osasco Metalworkers' Union), Osasco, S.P., 15 September 1987. A detailed discussion of the rise of bureaucratic union functionaries is presented in José Albertino Rodrigues, *Sindicato e Desenvolvimento no Brasil* (São Paulo: Difusão Européia do Livro, 1968), 146–51.

34. Interview, Luís Firmino de Lima, São Paulo, S.P., 7 August 1987; interview with Antônio Chamorro, "A Morte de Getúlio Vargas," CMS; U.S. Department of Labor (hereinafter USDL), *Monthly Labor Review* 64.3 (March 1947): 434; and CIESP/FIESP, *Circular* 162/42, 9 September 1942. These regulations were added to the Constitution of 1937, which outlawed strikes and all independent forms of organizing and mobilization; see Werneck Vianna, *Liberalismo e Sindicato no Brasil*, 211–23. Brazil's participation in World War II is described in chapter 4 in this volume.

35. FIESP Reunião Semanal, 24 June 1942; FIESP, *Relatório*, 1942, 1:110–13.

36. Sindicato dos Trabalhadores em Fiação e Tecelagem de São Paulo (hereinafter STFTSP) Reunião da Diretoria, 14 May 1942; STFTSP, Assembléias Gerais, 30 May and 21 June 1942. Cross, São Paulo to Washington, D.C., 16 July 1942, 832.504/101, RG 59, NA.

37. FIESP Reuniões Semanais, 17 June and 1 July 1942, 27 December 1944. These negotiations did not take place within a codified system of collective bargaining; rather, they were informal talks that resulted in changes in pay scales and/or work conditions but did not produce written work contracts.

38. SPR, SP 14.21, Lata 101, PR 26,595/38, ANB.

39. Interviews with José Albertino da Costa Filho and Ernesto Escames Sanchez, CMS, "O Trabalhador e a Memória Paulistana, 1920–1950." The small Pacaembu Stadium could be filled for such events only when unionists from all of the metropolitan area's sindicatos convinced their members to attend.

40. STFTSP Reuniões da Diretoria, 12 February 1937, 3 February, 30 March, and 28 December 1939; STFTSP, Assembléias Gerais, 21 and 28 September 1941; *O Trabalhador Têxtil*, May 1945; and Márcia Mendes de Almeida, "O Sindicato dos Têxteis em São Paulo: História, 1933–1957" (Tese de mestrado, Universidade de São Paulo, 1981), 63–65.

41. The first fusion was attempted in July 1939, but the process was not completed until August 1941. The Sindicato dos Operários em Fiação e Tecelagem, Sindicato dos Operários em Tecidos de Juta, Sindicato dos Operários em Tecidos de Seda, and Sindicato dos Operários em Malharia made up the new union.

42. Mendes de Almeida, "O Sindicato dos Têxteis de São Paulo," 64–68; and O Trabalhador Têxtil, May 1945.

43. Sindicato das Indústrias de Fiação e Tecelagem em Geral (hereinafter SIFTG), Circular 2169-A, 4 August 1942; Mendes de Almeida, "O Sindicato dos Têxteis em São Paulo," 68–70; O Trabalhador Têxtil, May 1945.

44. Telegram, Humberto Reis Costa to Vargas, 15 January 1943, SPR, Correspondência–Entidades Representivas de Classe 11.2, Lata 457, ANB; STFTSP Reunião da Diretoria, 17 August 1942; and, O Trabalhador Têxtil, May 1945.

45. STFTSP Reuniões da Diretoria, 3 and 27 January, 24 February 1939; Mendes de Almeida, "O Sindicato dos Têxteis em São Paulo," 64, 75–76; Maria Hermínia B. Tavares de Almeida, "Estado e Classes Trabalhadores no Brasil, 1930–1945" (Tese de doutoramento, Universidade de São Paulo, 1978), 242–73; Edgard Carone, O Estado Novo: 1937–1945 (Rio de Janeiro: DIFEL, 1976), 122–23; and Rodrigues, Sindicato e Desenvolvimento no Brasil, 153.

46. O Trabalhador Têxtil, May 1945. The rank and file's pressure on Vargas to increase the minimum wage is discussed in chapter 4 in this volume.

47. Folha da Manhã, 8 December 1942; São Paulo to Washington, D.C., 18 November 1944, RG 84, SP Post 850; and USDL, Monthly Labor Review 57.3 (September 1943): 581.

48. O Trabalhador Têxtil, May 1945; Mendes de Almeida, "O Sindicato dos Têxteis em São Paulo," 70. A similar situation existed for women clothing workers in the United States in the early 1900s. Men dominated the International Ladies Garment Workers Union, although some women served as officers. Accordingly, the union emphasized women's roles as mothers. For a detailed discussion of this union and its activities see Alice Kessler-Harris, "Where Are the Organized Women Workers?" Feminist Studies 3 (Fall 1975): 92–110.

49. Interview, Aracy Sanchez, São Paulo, S.P., 2 September 1987; and interview, Santo Vetturuzzo, São Paulo, S.P., 2 September 1987.

50. Interview, Diolinda Nascimento, São Paulo, S.P., 2 September 1987.

51. Interview, Antônio Ciaveletto, São Paulo, S.P., 3 September 1987; interview, Angela Neto, São Paulo, S.P., 8 August 1987; and interview, Laura S. Machado, Osasco, S.P., 8 September 1987.

52. Interview, Assumpta Bianchi, São Paulo, S.P., 10 August 1987.

53. The formal structure of union meetings intimidated women and thus circumscribed their participation. For a theoretical perspective on this process see Estelle Freedman, "Separatism as Strategy: Female Institution Building and American Feminism," Feminist Studies 5.3 (Fall 1979): 512–29.

54. STFTSP, Assembléias Gerais, 1941–44, show that government officials were present at all meetings. See Mendes de Almeida, "O Sindicato dos Têxteis em São Paulo," 72–74; and interview, Antônio Chamorro, "A Morte de Getúlio Vargas," CMS.

55. Workers also had access to food cooperatives, medical benefits, and other social services through their factories. Because a large number of textile mills offered such services, workers in this industry did not have the same incentive as metallurgical and other workers to join their unions. These social services are discussed below.

56. Sindicato dos Metalúrgicos de São Paulo (hereinafter SMSP) Reuniões da Diretoria, 12 February, 15 May, and 5 June 1936; and Maria Helena Simões Paes, "O Sindicato dos Metalúrgicos de São Paulo, 1932–1951" (Tese de mestrado, Universidade de São Paulo, 1979), 102–8.

57. SMSP Reuniões da Diretoria, 8 September and 18 November 1937, 28 February, 7 March, and 21 April 1938.

The Integralists were members of a nationalist movement that consciously modeled itself on German and Italian fascists; see Hélgio Trindade, *Integralismo: O Fascismo Brasileiro na Década de 30* (Rio de Janeiro: DIFEL, 1979); and Robert M. Levine, *The Vargas Regime: The Critical Years* (New York: Columbia University Press), 81–99.

58. SMSP Assembléias Gerais, 14 May 1939; SMSP Reuniões da Diretoria, 31 May, 14 September, and 21 November 1939, 28 June, 11 August, 17 and 28 September, and 16 November 1940; see also Simões Paes, "O Sindicato dos Metalúrgicos de São Paulo," 114–19.

59. SMSP Reuniões da Diretoria, 10 January, 14 June 1941, 8 and 14 March 1942; SMSP, Assembléias Gerais, 23 May 1942; and *O Metalúrgico*, February and May 1943, January and September 1944, October 1942.

60. *O Metalúrgico*, October 1942.

61. *O Metalúrgico*, September 1942.

62. Interview, Conrado de Papa, Osasco, S.P., 27 September 1987.

63. Interview, Francisco Pinto Silva, São Paulo, S.P., 25 September 1987; and interview, Edson Borges, São Paulo, S.P., 25 September 1987.

64. Interview, Roberto Unger, Osasco, S.P., 23 September 1987; and interview, Waldemar Lima, São Paulo, S.P., 25 September 1987.

65. Interview, Hermento Mendes Dantas, São Paulo, S.P., 14 September 1987; and interview, David Carneiro, São Paulo, S.P., 24 September 1987. Mendes Dantas pointed out that he and his friends often disagreed with the older workers in not completely opposing capitalism. The younger workers were more interested in safer working conditions and a more equitable distribution of the profits.

66. It is important to remember that workers in their late twenties were old enough to have participated in anarchist-oriented unions and study groups during the 1920s. This fact should serve as a reminder that just because a new historical epoch has begun (e.g., the Estado Novo), people do not forget their experiences from the previous epoch, which in this case was the very recent past. This also highlights the different experience of Carioca and Paulistano workers, for anarchism did not have the same enduring impact in Rio. Accord-

ingly, Carioca workers were less likely to eschew state-sponsored unions. See chapter 2 of this volume.

67. Interview, Antônio Lombardi, São Paulo, S.P., 24 September 1987; interview, Geraldo Pascolato, São Paulo, S.P., 24 September 1987; interview, Conrado de Papa, Osasco, S.P., 23 September 1987; and interview, Roberto Unger, Osasco, S.P., 23 September 1987. This difference, along with an absence of gender conflicts, helps to explain why the Metalworkers' Union consistently enrolled about 5 percent of the city's metalworkers while the Textile Workers' Union had less than 3 percent of its sector's workers in the union (see tables 3.1 and 3.2).

68. Interview, Geraldo Pascolato, São Paulo, S.P., 24 September 1987; interview, Antônio Lombardi, São Paulo, S.P., 24 September 1987.

69. FIESP Reuniões Semanais, 25 March, 12 May 1942, 17 January 1945; and CIESP/FIESP, Circular 91, 29 May 1942.

The creation of cafeterias and other social services in order to increase control over workers' independent organizing is a widely used tactic to limit working-class social networks; see John T. Cumbler, Working-Class Community in Industrial America: Work, Leisure, and Struggle in Two Industrial Cities (Westport, Conn.: Greenwood Press, 1979).

70. FIESP, Relatório, 1946, 6:184–290.

71. FIESP Reuniões Semanais, 15 December 1943, 10 and 24 January 1945. For an analysis of these labor groups and their opposition to the idea of class conflict see Howard Wiarda, The Brazilian Catholic Labor Movement (Amherst: University of Massachusetts Labor and Industrial Relations Center, 1969), 14–23. The círculos never attracted many Paulistano members. They were most successful in Rio Grande do Sul and Minas Gerais. Interestingly, they had their greatest impact in those areas where the Integralists were strongest. On the Catholic revival of the 1920s see Scott Mainwaring, The Catholic Church and Politics in Brazil, 1916–1985 (Stanford: Stanford University Press, 1986), 30–31.

72. FIESP Reunião Semanal, 15 December 1943; and Mary Cannon, "Women Workers in Brazil," USDL, Women's Bureau Report, no. 206 (1942), 40. According to Cannon, a large number of women workers attended the night classes offered by the associação.

73. FIESP Reuniões Semanais, 11 February, 22 July 1942.

74. Letter, Feigo Machado to Vargas, 31 December 1931, AGV 46.12.31, CPDOC; see also the interviews with Abelando de Araújo Jurema (an ally of Vargas) and José Bonifácio and José Américo (opponents of the Estado Novo) in Valentia da Rocha Lima, ed., Getúlio: Uma História Oral (Rio de Janeiro: Record, 1986), 136–39.

75. Cross, São Paulo to Washington, D.C., "The Machinery for Settling Disputes Between Capital and Labor in São Paulo," 20 July 1945, RG 84, SP Post 850.4, NA.

76. Liana Maria Aureliano, No Limiar da Industrialização (São Paulo: Brasil-

iense, 1981), 91–134; Pedro S. Malan et al., *Política Econômica Externa e Indus-trialização no Brasil: 1939–1952* (Rio de Janeiro: IPEA/INPES, 1977), 265–351; Annibal V. Villela and Wilson Suzigan, "Government Policy and the Economic Growth of Brazil, 1889–1945," *Brazilian Economic Studies* 3 (1977): 163–71; Werner Baer, *The Brazilian Economy: Growth and Development* (New York: Praeger, 1983), 44–53; Francisco Iglésias, "Aspectos Políticos e Econômicos do Estado Novo," in *Getúlio Vargas e a Economia Contemporânea*, ed. Tamás Szmrecsányi and Rui G. Granziera (Campinas: Editora da UNICAMP, 1986), 69–86; and John D. Wirth, *The Politics of Brazilian Development: 1930–1954* (Stanford: Stanford University Press, 1970), 71–129.

77. Stanley J. Stein, *The Brazilian Cotton Manufacture: Textile Enterprise in an Underdeveloped Area, 1850–1950* (Cambridge, Mass: Harvard University Press, 1957), 135–64. Vargas let the restrictions expire in 1937 because the textile industry was divided on this issue by that time.

78. Telegram, Adhemar de Barros to Vargas, 21 February 1940, SPR, SP 14.21, Lata 186, PR 4382/20, ANB; FIESP, *Relatório*, 1940, 79–80; and Villela and Suzigan, "Government Policy and Economic Growth," 317–39.

79. Vargas at first used exchange controls to bolster the export sector (especially for coffee), but after 1937 he concentrated more on stimulating industrial production with capital goods imports; see Malan et al., *Política Econômica Externa e Industrialização*, 114–24; Villela and Suzigan, "Government Policy and Economic Growth," 262–67; and Aureliano, *No Limiar da Indus-trialização*, 108–23.

80. The FIESP sometimes complained to government officials that the new industrial relations system required industrialists to expand their own bu-reaucracy in order to comply with the myriad regulations. In the final analysis, however, they had nothing but praise for the social peace fostered by the system; see telegrams, FIESP to Vargas, 22 September 1939, 11 and 12 Febru-ary 1941, SPR, Correspondência–Entidades de Classe 11.2, Lata 171 and Lata 456, ANB; and FIESP, *Relatório*, 1940, 79–80. José Segadas Viana, a Vargas supporter and minister of labor in the early 1950s, commented in 1956: "As far as the industrialists, their attitude toward Vargas varied. In 1937 they were very strongly in support of him, and indeed his regime of the Estado Novo suited them perfectly." He noted that after 1944 these industrialists began to oppose Vargas; see interview with José Segadas Viana, Rio de Janeiro, 16 March 1956, Alexander Papers, Rutgers University, Coll. 1957, Box 2.

81. The most complete analysis of government efforts to provide needed industrial inputs (e.g., steel and energy) in these years is Wirth, *The Politics of Brazilian Development*. On the centralized state see note 1 above.

82. On the development of the Paulista industrialists' political project independent of the state's agrarian interests see Mauricio A. Font, *Coffee, Contention, and Change in the Making of Modern Brazil* (Cambridge, Mass.: Basil Blackwell, 1990), 108–14. On the creation of a unified national industrial

bourgeoisie during the Estado Novo see Aureliano, *No Limiar da Industrialização*, esp. pt. 3; and Eli Diniz, *Empresário, Estado e Capitalismo no Brasil: 1930–1945* (Rio de Janeiro: Paz e Terra, 1978), chaps. 4–6.

Beginning in 1916, the Centro Industrial do Brasil did lobby the national government, but this institution really represented Rio's industrial bourgeoisie more than any national group. Further, it frequently had to work with commercial interests, for it had few legislative successes alone; see Angela Maria de Castro Gomes, *Burguesia e Trabalho: Política e Legislação Social no Brasil, 1917–1937* (Rio de Janeiro: Campus, 1979).

83. John D. French has argued that the Estado Novo actually strengthened the labor movement (*The Brazilian Workers' ABC*, 68–99). In an earlier work he asserts that "shop floor union organization had never existed in São Paulo before 1937 or even 1930 [*sic*]"; see "Industrial Workers and the Origin of Populist Politics in the ABC Region of Greater São Paulo, Brazil, 1900–1950" (Ph.D. diss., Yale University, 1985), 226–27, fn. 39.

84. Telegram, Egidio Toledo to Vargas, 21 June 1941, SPR, Correspondência–Entidades de Classe 11.2, Lata 456, ANB; FIESP Reunião Semanal, 14 April 1943; and Albert H. Berman, "Industrial Labor in Brazil" (Report to the Office of the Coordinator of Inter-American Affairs, December 1944), 22.

85. *Folha da Manhã*, 6 March 1936; *Diário de São Paulo*, 6 March 1936; and telegram to Vargas, 21 April 1937, SPR, Correspondência–Entidades de Classe 11.2, Lata 9, ANB.

86. See Gustavo Zalecki, "O Problema da Carestia do Pão em São Paulo," *RAM* 44 (February 1938): 5–113; Zalecki, "O Problema da Carne," *RAM* 46 (April 1938): 257–324; Proença de Gouveia, "A Situação Atual do Abastecimento de Carnes à População de São Paulo," *RAM* 44 (February 1938): 391–400; Clement de Bojano, "O Problema do Pescado na Cidade de São Paulo," *RAM* 48 (July 1940): 31–78; FIESP Reunião Semanal, 10 July 1940; *BMTIC* 29 (January 1937): 307–12; "São Paulo Economic, Financial, and Other Notes," 21 June 1938, RG 84, SP Post 850, NA; and *A Platéia*, 13 July 1940.

87. Samuel H. Lowrie, "A Assistência Filantrópica da Cidade de São Paulo," pt. 1, *RAM* 27 (September 1936): 208–10; "Confidential Report on IAPI," 12 July 1939, AWF 37.11.12, Pasta 11, CPDOC; FIESP, Reuniões Semanais, 18 September 1940, 11 March 1942; USDL, *Monthly Labor Review* 50.6 (June 1940): 1401–2; and *A Platéia*, 9 July 1940.

88. Horace B. Davis, "Padrão da Vida dos Operários da Cidade de São Paulo," *RAM* 13 (June 1935): 113–66. A shorter version of this study was published in English; see Horace B. Davis and Marion Rubins Davis, "Scale of Living of the Working Class in São Paulo, Brazil," *Monthly Labor Review* 44.1 (June 1937): 245–53.

89. Clorinda Guttila, "Sobre um 'Test' de Alimentação Aplicado às Crianças do Parque Infantil do Ipiranga," *RAM* 107 (March–April 1946): 95–105; Lowrie, "A Assistência Filantrópica da Cidade de São Paulo," pt. 2, *RAM* 28

(October 1936), 194–96; and São Paulo Governo Municipal, Divisão de Educação e Recreio, "Algumas Casos de Tuberculino-Reação de Pirquet e Montoux nos Parques Infantís," *RAM* 55 (May 1939), folios.

Oscar E. de Araújo's study of conditions of workers at the Usina Santa Olímpia shows that metalworkers' families had healthier diets, better housing, and generally better access to social services than textile workers and their families; see his "Uma Pesquisa de Padrão da Vida," supplement to *RAM* 80 (1941): 37–159. For an analysis of changing conditions from the 1930s to the 1970s see John Wells, "Industrial Accumulation and Living Standards in the Long Run: The São Paulo Industrial Working Class, 1930–1975," University of Cambridge, Centre of Latin American Studies, Working Paper 37, n.d.

90. Araújo found that the lower-paid metalworkers faced conditions similar to textile and other lower-wage industrial workers; see Araújo, "Uma Pesquisa de Padrão da Vida," 37–67. For the state government's studies see São Paulo Secretaria da Agricultura, Indústria, e Comércio (hereinafter SPSAIC), *Aspectos do Padrão da Vida do Operário Indústrial da Capital de São Paulo* (São Paulo: n.p., 1940), 31–48; SPSAIC, *Posição do Chefe de Família Operária em Face dos Salários Atuais* (São Paulo: n.p., 1940), 8–17; and SPSAIC, *Condições da Classe Operária na Capital Paulista: Necissidade e Possibilidade de Remediar sua Situação* (São Paulo: n.p., 1940), 4–7.

91. Ruth Milkman notes a similar situation for North American women during the depression of the 1930s; see her "Women's Work and the Economic Crisis: Some Lessons from the Great Depression," in *A Heritage of Her Own: Toward a New Social History of American Women*, ed. Nancy F. Cott and Elizabeth Pleck (New York: Touchstone, 1979), 507–41.

92. Samuel H. Lowrie, "Origem da População da Cidade de São Paulo e Diferenciação das Classes Socials," *RAM* 43 (January 1938): 195–212; Lowrie, "O Elemento Negro na População de São Paulo," *RAM* 48 (June 1938): 5–56; and Oracy Nogueira, "Atitude Desfavoravel de Alguns Anunciantes de São Paulo em Relação aos Empregados de Cor," *Sociologia* 4.4 (October 1942): 328–58. George Reid Andrews has found that blacks did not face the same level of job discrimination in the textile industry in the 1930s as they had in previous decades; see Andrews, *Blacks and Whites in São Paulo*, 90–121. Still, as the aforementioned articles suggest, people of color in the city continued to face discrimination in hiring for a wide variety of jobs.

93. Letter, Associação José do Patrocino to Vargas, 30 September 1941, SPR, Ministry of Labor, Lata 410, PR 107,839/43, ANB; and Nogueira, "Atitude Desfavoravel de Alguns Anunciantes," 328–33.

94. See chapter 5 in this volume for an analysis of how this accumulation funded a new rationalization program in the textile sector in the 1940s. Werneck Vianna terms the Estado Novo "an instrument of primitive accumulation" because the surplus extracted during this period financed later industrial development (*Liberalismo e Sindicato no Brasil*, 223).

95. Scholars often debate the impact of Estado Novo labor policies without addressing the issue of whether or not workers participated in the corporatist structure. Two recent works that do not analyze the rank and file and so misconstrue the Estado Novo as a period when workers were manipulated and/or had their consciousness raised by the state are Youssef Cohen, *The Manipulation of Consent: The State and Working-Class Consciousness in Brazil* (Pittsburgh: University of Pittsburgh Press, 1989), 118; and French, *The Brazilian Workers' ABC*, 68–99.

96. For a similar analysis of historical memory and popular culture intervening to condition workers' and peasants' responses to central state attempts at corporatist control, see Jeffrey W. Rubin, "Rethinking Post-Revolutionary Mexico: Regional History, Cultural Identity, and Radical Politics in Juchitán, Oaxaca" (Ph.D. diss., Harvard University, 1991). Ruth Berins Collier and David Collier analyze the long-term impact of Brazilian workers avoiding the corporatist structure in *Shaping the Political Arena: Critical Junctures, the Labor Movement, and Regime Dynamics in Latin America* (Princeton: Princeton University Press, 1991), 169–95. See also Ruth Berins Collier, "Popular Sector Incorporation and Political Supremacy: Regime Evolution in Brazil and Mexico," in *Brazil and Mexico: Patterns in Late Development*, ed. Sylvia Ann Hewlett and Richard S. Weinert (Philadelphia: ISHI, 1982), 57–109.

4   World War II and the Struggle for Citizenship

1. Frank D. McCann, *The Brazilian American Alliance, 1937–1945* (Princeton: Princeton University Press, 1973), 259–90.

2. The officers who served in the FEB also became key figures in Brazilian politics from the 1950s through the 1980s; see Alfred Stepan, *The Military in Politics: Changing Patterns in Brazil* (Princeton: Princeton University Press, 1971).

3. Getúlio Vargas, *A Nova Política do Brasil*, 11 vols. (Rio de Janeiro: José Olympio, 1938–43), 9:141–44.

4. Ibid., 9:163, 146.

5. Ibid., 9:215–20, 247–48, 295–97.

6. Ibid., 9:263, 311–17, 333.

7. Marcondes Filho on "Hora do Brasil," 6 and 20 July 1944, in *BMTIC* 120 (August 1944): 343–48; "Hora do Brasil," 14 and 21 December 1944, in *BMTIC* 125 (January 1945): 312–13; "Hora do Brasil," 11, 18, and 25 January 1945, in *BMTIC* 126 (February 1945): 355–62; see also Vargas, *A Nova Política*, 10:31–37, 195–201, 243–45, 299–301.

8. FIESP Reuniões Semanais, 3 January, 14 March 1945.

9. FIESP Reunião Semanal, 10 January 1945.

10. Telegram, Adhemar de Barros to Getúlio Vargas, 21 February 1940, SPR,

SP 14.21, Lata 186, PR 4382/40, ANB; FIESP, *Relatório*, 1940, 32–33, 79–80; and USDL, *Monthly Labor Review* 54.1 (January 1942): 219.

11. Report, FIESP to Vargas, SP 14.21, Lata 466, PR 37,383/41, ANB; CIESP/FIESP, *Circulares* 34/42, 6 March 1942; 66/42, 25 April 1942; SIFTC, *Circular* 2180, 4 September 1942; FIESP, *Relatório*, 1942, 1:205–6; and USDL, *Monthly Labor Review* 55.6 (December 1942): 1283.

12. CIESP/FIESP, *Circulares* 164/42, 11 September 1942; 169/42, 12 September 1942; 219/42, 17 November 1942.

13. CIESP/FIESP, *Circulares* 198/42, 23 October 1942; 211/42, 4 November 1942; and *Folha da Manhã*, 4 November 1942.

14. USDL, *Monthly Labor Review* 59.4 (October 1944): 752–53; and speech by Minister of Labor Marcondes Filho, "Inauguração de Quinta Feira Nacional das Indústrias em São Paulo," Arquivo de Alexandre Marcondes Filho (hereinafter AMF), 44.11.07, CPDOC; see also interview with José Segadas Viana, Rio de Janeiro, 16 March 1956, Alexander Papers, Rutgers University, Coll. 1957, Box 2.

15. FIESP Reunião Semanal, 19 July 1944.

16. Memo, São Paulo to Washington, D.C., 1 July 1942, RG 59, 832.5045/27, NA.

17. *Diário de São Paulo*, 27 September 1942. By publicizing such repression of "dissidents," Brazilian governments have been able to use selected torture against a few opponents to intimidate the general populace. Such public intimidation is the central theme in Ivan Angelo's frightening short story "The Tower of Glass," in *The Tower of Glass*, trans. Ellen Watson (New York: Avon Books, 1986), 119–55.

18. Werner Baer's figures for industrial output for all Brazil are slightly different. He believes total manufacturing grew at 5.2 percent per year from 1939 to 1945, textiles at 6.2 percent, and metallurgy at 9.1 percent; see his *The Brazilian Economy: Growth and Development* (New York: Praeger, 1983), 44–48. The downturn seen in Villela's and Suzigan's statistics for the state of São Paulo may have been heaviest in the mills in the interior of the state.

19. Albert H. Berman, "Industrial Labor in Brazil" (Report to the Office of the Coordinator of Inter-American Affairs, December 1944), 4; *O Estado de São Paulo*, 7 October 1942; FIESP Reunião Semanal, 5 July 1944; and Stanley J. Stein, *The Brazilian Cotton Manufacture: Textile Enterprise in an Underdeveloped Area, 1850–1950* (Cambridge, Mass.: Harvard University Press, 1957), 165–69.

20. *Revista Industrial de São Paulo* (hereinafter *RISP*), September 1945–April 1947; and Claudio L. S. Haddad, "Growth of Brazilian Real Output, 1900–1947" (Ph.D. diss., University of Chicago, 1974), 93.

21. FIESP Reunião Semanal, 27 September 1944; CIESP/FIESP, *Circular* 152/44, 4 October 1944; "A Propósito da Modernização de uma Grande Indústria," *RISP* 6 (May 1945): 16–18; and *Diário de São Paulo*, 28 January 1945.

22. FIESP Reunião Semanal, 19 July 1944; CIESP/FIESP, *Circular* 39/40, 4 April 1940; and FIESP, *Relatório*, 1942, 1:221–38. The FIESP also increased training for workers at this time and allowed some skilled workers to switch factories if employers agreed on the terms; see memo dated 6 June 1944, RG 84, SP Post 850, NA; FIESP, *Relatório*, 1944, 1:77–78; and FIESP, *Relatório*, 1942, 1:214–15.

During the Plano Cruzado of 1986–87, the author witnessed similar circumstances. A wage freeze made skilled and semiskilled metallurgical workers highly valuable in and around São Paulo, and large and medium-sized establishments sent recruiters to smaller metalworking shops in Osasco, São Bernardo, São Paulo, and other areas to entice workers to change jobs with promises of better conditions and benefits.

23. "Employment Statistics for the State of São Paulo," 18 November 1944, RG 84, SP Post 850; draft of "Comments Regarding Economic Developments of São Paulo Consular District during Year 1944," 10 January 1945, RG 84, SP Post 850; memo, Cross to Berle, 28 February 1945, RG 84, SP Post 850.4, NA; *Monthly Labor Review* 62.5 (May 1946), 748; Berman, "Industrial Labor in Brazil," 38–39; and SIFTG, *Circulares* 2556, 30 April 1945; 2576, 30 May 1945.

24. Berman, "Industrial Labor in Brazil," 38–39; interview, Assumpta Bianchi, São Paulo, S.P., 10 August 1987; and interview, Enrique de Lima, São Paulo, S.P., 2 September 1987.

25. "Indústria Mecânica; Fator Essencial do Progresso Manufatureiro do Brasil," *RISP* 11 (October 1945): 23–28; "Produção de Máquinas," *RISP* 30 (May 1947): 30–32; "Siderurgia e Metalurgia," *RISP* 39 (February 1948): 48–49; and Berman, "Industrial Labor in Brazil," 4.

26. CIESP/FIESP, *Circulares* 31/42, 2 March 1942; 213/45, 20 November 1945; SIFTG, *Circulares* 2175, 13 August 1942; 2176, 14 August 1942; São Paulo to Washington, D.C., 26 March 1943, RG 59, 832,50/138.5, NA; and FIESP, *Relatório*, 1944, 1:24.

27. "A Laminação de Ferro em São Paulo," *RISP* 6 (May 1945): 35; FIESP Reunião Semanal, 29 July 1942; FIESP, *Relatório*, 1942, 1:255–61; the March (no. 4) and October (no. 11) 1945 editions include cover photos of new machinery produced in São Paulo as well as articles on the use of these machines by Brazilian industry, especially in the textile sector. The ads in all the editions list many large and small shops and the hundreds of different machines they produced for the industrial and agrarian sectors.

28. An analysis of the rise of Sofunge is presented in "Rodas para Estradas de Ferro," *RISP* 40 (March 1948). Cobrasma in Osasco was producing various types of railroad cars and parts for trucks at this time.

29. Simonsen's remarks are in CIESP/FIESP, *Circular* 103, 13 June 1942. For a description of Souza Costa's report see O *Estado de São Paulo*, 10 June 1942; and SIFTG, *Circular* 2143, 12 June 1942. On profit rates see *Conjuntura Econômica* (April 1948): 8–9; and chapter 5 in this volume.

30. "Corporation Trading Profits in State of São Paulo Record Strong Upward Trend in 1943," 3 August 1944, RG 84, SP Post 850, NA; CIESP/FIESP, *Circulares* 2356, 24 January 1944; 37/45, 17 February 1945; and *Diário de São Paulo*, 22 February 1945.

31. Interview, Conrado de Papa, Osasco, S.P., 23 September 1987.

32. Interview, Edson Borges, São Paulo, S.P., 25 September 1987. Francisco Pinto Silva, a friend of Borges from those days, agreed that all he remembers from the war was having to work; interview, São Paulo, S.P., 25 September 1987.

33. Interview with José Albertino, "O Trabalhador e a Memória Paulistana, 1920–1950," CMS, 55–56.

34. Interview, Geraldo Pascolato, São Paulo, S.P., 24 September 1987; and interview, Antônio Lombardi, São Paulo, S.P., 24 September 1987. Both men worked at Máquinas Piratininga. During the war years they assembled smaller machines on a static assembly line. Each man was responsible for producing certain components of the machine in a given time, but they did this from a heap of pieces that were delivered by the box. They did not have to endure the misery of production on a moving assembly line.

35. Interview, Hermento Mendes Dantas, São Paulo, S.P., 14 September 1987.

36. FIESP, *Relatório*, 1946, 4:151; and USDL, *Monthly Labor Review* 57.3 (September 1943): 582. This wage policy, which was made possible by Vargas's repressive labor program, demonstrates how the value of skills is socially constructed and thus can change over time.

37. FIESP, *Relatório*, 1946, 4:151; and Berman, "Industrial Labor in Brazil," 24–25.

38. "O Problema dos Trabalhadores Idosos," *RAM* 97 (July–August 1944): 104–5. Although this article is about older industrial workers, it provides statistics on accidents for all textile workers. There are few reliable statistics on accidents for this period, so it is not possible to compare accident rates in this and earlier periods. The *Boletim do Departamento Estadual de Estatística* lists only cases where accident victims received medical treatment at city assistance stations, and these statistics are quite erratic.

39. Mary Cannon, *Women Workers in Brazil*, USDL, Women's Bureau Report, no. 206 (1942), 10–11; interview, Assumpta Bianchi, São Paulo, S.P., 10 August 1987; interview, Hermínia Lorenzi dos Santos, São Paulo, S.P., 12 August 1987; interview, Luís Firmino de Lima, São Paulo, S.P., 7 August 1987; and interview, Diolinda Nascimento, São Paulo, S.P., 2 September 1987.

40. Cannon, *Women Workers in Brazil*, 3, 17; Mary Cannon, "Women Workers in Brazil, Confidential Summary," August 1943, RG 59, 832.4055/18, NA; and "As Mulheres São Diferentes," *RAM* 91 (July 1943): 71. No statistics are available on the replacement of men by women after 1943, but a great number of men were drafted in those years.

The wartime employment of women in jobs outside their traditional gender roles again demonstrates how gender itself is socially constructed. Indeed, World War II created even greater opportunities for women to work in skilled trades in the factories of the war's primary combatants. For analyses of the muddled and often contradictory prewar, wartime, and postwar gender ideologies related to women's factory work see Ruth Milkman, *Gender at Work: The Dynamics of Job Segregation by Sex during World War II* (Urbana: University of Illinois Press, 1987); and Claudia Koonz, *Mothers in the Fatherland: Women, the Family and Nazi Politics* (New York: St. Martin's Press, 1987), 394–98.

41. Berman, "Industrial Labor in Brazil," 24–25; SIFTG, *Circular* 2205, 7 November 1942; FIESP Reuniões Semanais, 27 July 1943, 8 February 1945.

42. Cannon, *Women Workers in Brazil*, 29, 13, 23; *Conjunctura Econômica* (December 1949): 37.

43. Cannon, "Women Workers in Brazil, Confidential Summary," 3.

44. Cannon, *Women Workers in Brazil*, 9–11; FIESP Reunião Semanal, 25 April 1945; FIESP, *Relatório*, 1946, 4:151; and USDL, *Monthly Labor Review* 57.2 (August 1943): 349–50. Cf. John D. French and Mary Lynn Pedersen, "Women and Working-Class Mobilization in Postwar São Paulo, 1945–1948," *Latin American Research Review (LARR)* 24.3 (Fall 1989): 107–8.

A commission made up of government, industry, and union representatives from each region set these rates. Also, minors could be paid 50 percent of the minimum wage. For a detailed discussion of the administration of the minimum wage see João Saboia, *Salário Mínimo: A Experiência Brasileira* (Porto Alegre: L & PM Editores), 7–45.

45. Later in the 1940s and the 1950s, employers used such bonuses for all wages in order to maintain low base rates. Accordingly, increases of 40 to 60 percent on the base that industrialists bragged about during strike negotiations represented tiny increases on the wages workers were already receiving. See chapter 5 in this volume.

46. Telegram to Vargas, SPR, Correspondência–Entidades Representativas de Classe, Lata 457, ANB; and *O Metalúrgico*, October 1942, January 1944, September 1944.

47. FIESP, *Relatório*, 1942, 2:23.

48. FIESP, *Relatório*, 1944, 1:36.

49. FIESP Reunião Semanal, 16 May 1945. Simonsen detailed his vision of "rational capitalism" in hundreds of speeches and writings. Many of those are available in *A Evolução Industrial do Brasil* (São Paulo: Nacional, EDUSP, 1973), and *Ensaios Sociais, Políticos, e Econômicos* (São Paulo: FIESP, 1943). At several FIESP meetings he specifically lectured his fellow industrialists on the need to provide the appropriate mix of carbohydrates and protein in their workers' diets, for without the necessary energy they would not be able to properly perform their assigned tasks; see FIESP Reuniões Semanais, 23 August and 22 November 1944.

A good review of the literature on Brazil's brutal capitalist development is Paul Cammack's "Brazil: The Triumph of 'Savage Capitalism,'" *Bulletin of Latin American Research* 3.2 (1984): 117–30.

50. FIESP, *Relatório*, 1944, 1:35–36; *Diário da Noite*, 4 April 1945; and FIESP Reunião Semanal, 1 January 1945. The high cost and low quality of food in working-class neighborhoods in the 1910s is discussed in chapter 1 of this volume. For a discussion of this problem during the 1940s see Vicentina Ribeiro da Luz, "Habitação Ideal ao Trabalhador Manual," *RAM* 89 (March–April 1943): 141. North American workers labored less than fifteen minutes in order to buy lunch.

51. FIESP Reuniões Semanais, 25 March, 12 May 1942; FIESP, *Relatório*, 1945, 1:106–7; São Paulo to Rio, "São Paulo State Government Takes Drastic Steps toward Control of Food Prices," 5 December 1944, SP Post, 850.102; São Paulo to Rio, "State Continues Campaign against High Food Prices," 18 December 1944, SP Post 850.102; Memo, São Paulo to Rio, 5 January 1945, SP Post, 850.102; and São Paulo to Rio, 16 January 1945, SP Post 850.102, RG 84, NA.

52. *Diário de São Paulo*, 12, 13, and 27 January 1945; CIESP/FIESP, *Circulares* 4/45, 5 January 1945; 19/45, 19 January 1945; 35/45, 10 February 1945; 181/45, 25 September 1945; SIFTG, *Circulares* 2583, 13 June 1945; 2599, 11 July 1945; and FIESP Reuniões Semanais, 13 and 23 August, 4 and 18 October, 22 and 29 November, 5 and 20 December 1944, 3, 10, 17, 24, and 31 January, 8 February 1945, and at other meetings throughout 1945.

53. Interview, Assumpta Bianchi, São Paulo, S.P., 10 August 1987; interview, Glória Salviano, São Paulo, S.P., 14 August 1987; and SPR, SP 14.21, Lata 395, PR 10,113/42, ANB.

54. Clark to Washington, D.C., 1 December 1944, SP Post, 850.102, RG 84, NA. The metalworkers' union protested high food costs through *O Metalúrgico* at this time; see the February and March 1944 issues.

55. Valêncio de Barros, "São Paulo," *RAM* 105 (October–December 1945): 27–30; and SPR, Ministro do Trabalho, Lata 477-A, PR 2673/43, 7 January 1943, ANB.

56. FIESP Reunião Semanal, 11 March 1942; CIESP/FIESP, *Circulares* 134/42, 1 August 1942; 172/42, 18 September 1942; and Cross, São Paulo to Caffery, "Unrest among Employees in Textile Industry in São Paulo," 26 August 1944, SP Post 850, RG 84, NA.

57. Telegram to Vargas, 14 August 1942, SPR, Correspondência–Entidades Representativas de Classe, Lata 457, ANB; Valêncio de Barros, "São Paulo," *RAM*, 105 (October–December 1945): 36–37; FIESP Reunião Semanal, 7 June 1944; FIESP, *Relatório*, 1944, 1:119; *Relatório*, 1945, 1:115; and Cross to Caffery, "Unrest among Employees in Textile Industry in São Paulo," 26 August 1944, SP Post 850, RG 84, NA.

58. This samba was written by Arthur Vilarinho, Estenslau da Silva, and

Paquito, and was recorded by Roberto Silva. It appears in José Álvaro Moisés and Verena Stolcke, "Urban Transport and Popular Violence: The Case of Brazil," *Past and Present* 86 (February 1980): 172. The fear expressed over being late without a formal excuse highlights the authoritarian nature of the work setting, especially during the Estado Novo.

59. On the increase in homework during the war see Cannon, *Women Workers in Brazil*, 20; Ribeiro da Luz, "Habitação Ideal," 138–43; and Valêncio de Barros, "São Paulo," 28.

60. Ribeiro da Luz, "Habitação Ideal," 43.

61. Rio to Washington, D.C., 3 March 1943, RG 59, 832.00/4552, NA.

62. "Effect of Changes in Retail Trade on the Standard of Living of the Masses in São Paulo," 6 December 1942, SP Post 850, NA; and Ribeiro da Luz, "Habitação Ideal," 139.

63. Although the unions in the 1920s and early 1930s did not always represent the rank and file's demands, they served as important allies to workers in their struggles with employers and the state.

64. There are few archival materials on the sacking of the trolleys. A good press account can be found in *Diário de São Paulo*, 7 February 1945.

65. Most industrial workers in the city had relatives who still lived in the rural sector, and often these urban workers migrated to the interior of the state for harvests. Further, rural workers traveled to the city to take advantage of social services and other opportunities; see Samuel H. Lowrie, "A Assistência Filantrópica da Cidade de São Paulo," pt. 1, *RAM* 27 (September 1936): 217; Mário Neme, "Um Município Agrícola; Aspectos Sociais e Econômicos da Organização Agrária de Piracicaba," *RAM* 57 (May 1939): 54–55; and Cross to Berle, 28 February 1945, RG 84, SP Post 850.4, NA.

66. SPR, SP 14.21, Lata 467, PR 27,733/42, ANB; and SPR, SP 14.21, Lata 467, PR 4464/43, ANB. These petitions were also referred to as "processos," but they were filed by individuals without the participation of a union. Indeed, the fact that so many processos were filed outside the union structure emphasizes the weakness of the corporatist industrial relations system.

67. SPR, SP 14.21, Lata 467, PR 34,372/42, ANB, contains a letter from Manoel Dias Saraiva, who supported his three children and his sister, a widow, and her children. He asked for help sending two children to school. Another letter (SPR, SP 14.21, Lata 466, PR 34,245/41) was prepared by the friend of a family that had recently lost the father. Most of the requests came from widows, unmarried mothers, and women whose husbands could not work. Some of the many examples of this are the following: SPR, SP 14.21, Lata 328, PR 35,366/41, PR 35,427/41, PR 1383/42, PR 3708/42, PR 35,117/41, and PR 5167/42, ANB.

68. SPR, SP 14.21, Lata 328, PR 18,146/41; Lata 329, PR 13,373/41; Lata 394, PR 28,116/42; and Lata 469, PR 10,028/43, ANB.

69. SPR, SP 14.21, Lata 329, PR 13,373/41, ANB.

70. SPR, SP 14.21, Lata 466, PR 28,015/41, ANB.

71. Many requests did not include home addresses or complete names. Various government agencies attempted to locate some of the petitioners, but often they had few leads. Two of the many examples of this are SPR, MTIC, Lata 349, PR 28,213/42, and MTIC, Lata 476, PR 8188/43, ANB.

72. The disorganization of these files in the Brazilian National Archives makes it impossible to determine the total number of processos. I examined several thousand for the city and state of São Paulo, and there seemed to be many more available from the city of Rio de Janeiro. There are such documents for all regions of Brazil.

73. Interview, Hermínia Lorenzi dos Santos, São Paulo, S.P., 12 August 1987; and interview, Maria Pavone, São Paulo, S.P., 12 August 1987.

74. SPR, SP 14.21, Lata 466, PR 8653/43; Lata 466, PR 20, 138/41; Lata 466, PR 9140/42; and, Lata 186, PR 3270/40, ANB.

75. The number of processos filed increased rather steadily throughout these years; see Diário de São Paulo, 4 January, 4 and 6 March, 5 May 1945. Some women joined the union specifically to file or to participate in a collective processo; interview, Diolinda Nascimento, São Paulo, S.P., 2 September 1987.

76. Lucila Hermann, Flutuação e Mobilidade de Mão-de-Obra Fabril em São Paulo (São Paulo: Instituto de Administração, 1948), 11–45; Cannon, Women Workers in Brazil, 8, 13; Cross to Caffery, "Unrest among Employees in Textile Industry in São Paulo," 26 August 1944, RG 84, SP Post 850, NA; FIESP Reunião Semanal, 29 September 1943; FIESP, Relatório, 1944, 1:258; Relatório, 1946, 3:8–9, 18.

Hermann's study shows that men tended to change jobs for increased prestige and responsibility, and women almost always changed for income reasons. No doubt many women fled from foremen who sexually harassed them and/or their coworkers, but few would have discussed this with Hermann in the 1940s.

77. See, for example, SP 14.21, Lata 186, PR 3370/39, PR 339/40, PR 4142/40; and Lata 468, PR 34,005/42; Lata 469, PR 10,042/43, ANB.

78. SPR, SP 14.21, Lata 467, PR 7079/43, ANB. Interestingly, Vargas and the Ministry of Labor ended wage differentials by sex for the minimum wage later in 1943.

79. SPR, MTIC 17.10, Lata 411, PR 13,341/42, ANB. Vargas ordered an investigation, but the federal government relied on state Department of Labor officials in São Paulo, and those state inspectors claimed that they found no violations at the locations Camargo listed.

80. See chapter 2 in this volume.

81. SPR, MTIC 17.10, Lata 477, PR 3980/43, ANB. All the information on this case is from this file.

82. Interview, João Bonifácio, São Paulo, S.P., 3 September 1987; interview, Antônio Ciaveletto, São Paulo, S.P., 3 September 1987; interview, Hermínia

Lorenzi dos Santos, São Paulo, S.P., 12 August 1987; interview, Diolinda Nascimento, São Paulo, S.P., 2 September 1987; interview, Odette Pasquini, São Paulo, S.P., 17 September 1987; and interview, Maria Pavone, São Paulo, S.P., 12 August 1987.

83. Rio to Washington, D.C., 24 July, 1944, RG 59, 832.5045/7-2744, NA; interview, Odette Pasquini, São Paulo, S.P., 17 September 1987; interview, Laura S. Machado, Osasco, S.P., 8 September 1987; and interview, Antônio Ciaveletto, São Paulo, S.P., 3 September 1987. These comissões were most active in the factories.

84. Several scholars have argued that the influx of migrants from the rural sector to the city of São Paulo limited the overall consciousness of the working class; see José Albertino Rodrigues, *Sindicato e Desenvolvimento no Brasil* (São Paulo: Difusão Européia do Livro, 1968); Leôncio Martins Rodrigues, "Sindicalismo e Classes Operária, 1930–1964," in *História Geral da Civilização Brasileira*, vol. 10, ed. Boris Fausto (Rio de Janeiro: DIFEL, 1986), 518–20; Antônio Carlos Bernardo, *Tutela e Autonomia Sindical: Brasil, 1930–1945* (São Paulo: T. A. Queiroz, 1982), 159–69; Ricardo Antunes, *Classe Operária, Sindicatos, e Partido: Da Revolução de 30 até a Aliança Nacional Libertadora* (São Paulo: Cortez, 1982), 117–36; and Alain Touraine, "Industrialisation et conscience ouvrière à São Paulo," *Sociologie du Travail* 4.61 (October–December 1961): 77–95. These authors, though, ignore the important history of class conflict that most peasants experienced before arriving in urban environments. Although the subject has not been studied much in Brazil, Todd A. Diacon's *Millenarian Vision, Capitalist Reality: Brazil's Contestado Rebellion, 1912–1916* (Durham: Duke University Press, 1991) does discuss the effects of capitalist social relations on rural folk in Santa Catarina and Paraná. Moreover, the rural-urban dichotomy is often misleading because workers migrated to and from the rural sector according to harvests and other employment opportunities. Indeed, many people in the countryside wrote petitions to Vargas. Some colonos in the interior of São Paulo spoke to the president not only about conditions in the rural sector but also about problems their children experienced as factory workers in the capital; see SPR, SP 14.21, Lata 329, PR 15,036/41; Lata 466, PR 37,257/41, PR 23,676/41, PR 16,074/42, PR 4376/42, and PR 19,590/42, ANB.

85. Interview, Odette Pasquini, São Paulo, S.P., 17 September 1987.

86. SPR, MTIC, Lata 408, PR 34,503/42, ANB. The Ministry of Labor ruled that because no laws governing his dismissal existed in 1922, it could not act.

87. SPR, SP 14.21, Lata 466, PR 134/43, ANB.

88. Workers faced ridicule from their fellow workers for joining the union or speeding up production. This was most often articulated through the loose groupings of the factory commissions. On these issues and disagreements among commission members see interview, Assumpta Bianchi, São Paulo, S.P., 10 August 1987; interview, Hermínia Lorenzi dos Santos, São Paulo, S.P.,

12 August 1987; interview, Luís Firmino de Lima, São Paulo, S.P., 7 August 1987; and interview, Diolinda Nascimento, São Paulo, S.P., 2 September 1987.

89. Different groups of workers in different areas had their own set of relationships to the Estado Novo. Mine workers in the Morro Velho gold mine in Minas Gerais, for example, had a long legacy of common struggle (of a type perhaps unique to mining enclaves) and of independent communist organizing. So even during the harshest days of the Estado Novo, these workers maintained independent, often clandestine, labor organizations that were led by local communist militants; see Yonne de Souza Grossi, *Mina de Morro Velho: A Extração do Homen; Uma História de Experiência Operária* (Rio de Janeiro: Paz e Terra, 1982): 84–142; and Marshall C. Eakin, *British Enterprise in Brazil: The St. John d'el Rey Mining Company and the Morro Velho Gold Mine, 1830–1960* (Durham: Duke University Press, 1989), 224–29. Textile workers in Juiz de Fora, also located in Minas Gerais, had quite a different experience. The Estado Novo's labor policies contributed to the development of a union or syndicalist tradition among the workers, even though these workers recognized that the unions were tied to the state; see Maria Andréa Loyola, *Os Sindicatos e o PTB: Estudo de um Caso em Minas Gerais* (Petrópolis: Vozes, 1980), 51–57. Textile workers in an industrial suburb of Recife in the state of Pernambuco likewise saw a resurgence in union activity when later Estado Novo policies (in 1940–45) helped resuscitate a *sindicato* that had not been active since the early 1930s; see José Sérgio Leite Lopes, *A Tecelagem dos Conflitos de Classe na Cidade das Chaminés* (São Paulo: Marco Zero/Universidade de Brasília, 1988), 297–325. São Paulo continued to have a unique relationship with Vargas after the Estado Novo; see Maria Victoria Benevides, *O PTB e o Trabalhismo: Partido e Sindicato em São Paulo, 1945–1964* (São Paulo: Brasiliense, 1989). These regional and sectoral differences led Maria Célia Paoli to argue that scholars of Brazil must take into account a country's size and heterogeneity when analyzing its labor histories, for different locations have different legacies of class formation and working-class organizing and protest activities; see "Os Trabalhadores Urbanos na Fala dos Outros. Tempo, Espaço e Classe na História Operária Brasileira," in *Cultura e Identidade Operária: Aspectos da Cultura da Classe Trabalhador*, ed. José Sérgio Leite Lopes (São Paulo: Marco Zero/UFRJ, 1987), 53–101.

90. SIFTG, *Circulares* 2069-A, 16 December 1941; 2088, 16 February 1942; 2116, 4 May 1942; CIESP/FIESP, *Circular* 105/41; 20 November 1941; FIESP Reuniões Semanais, 11 February, 15 and 29 July, 12 August 1942.

91. CIESP/FIESP, *Circulares* 14/43, 18 January; 39/43, 19 February; 71/43, 3 May; 79/43, 18 May; 205/43, 28 November; 207/43, 7 December; 217/43, 20 December 1943; FIESP Reuniões Semanais, 8 and 21 September, 27 October, 1 December 1943; FIESP, *Relatório*, 1943, 1:50–60; *O Metalúrgico*, March 1943.

92. SPR, MTIC 17.10, Lata 281, PR 31,182; Lata 411, PR 13,329/42; Lata

4771, PR 4466/43; and Lata 477a, PR 2673/43, ANB. Women's concentration in this area reflected the sexual division of labor within Brazilian working-class households: women, whether or not they also worked outside their homes, were responsible for feeding and clothing their families.

93. Letter, Antônio de Carvalho to Vargas, 28 December 1938, SPR, MTIC, Lata 202, ANB. For several of the many examples of this see SPR, SP 14.12, Lata 186, PR 19,872/40; MTIC 17.10, Lata 126, PR 28,571/38; Lata 278, PR 29,983/40 and PR 28,517/40; Lata 408, PR 31,097/42; Lata 477, PR 4047/43; and Lata 475, PR 11,369/43, ANB. Interestingly, SPR, MTIC 17.10, Lata 409, PR 18,764, ANB, is from a male textile worker, Antônio Torgino Fernandes. This is the only petition from a textile worker specifically denouncing collusion between an employer and the state Department of Labor.

94. SPR, SP 14.21, Lata 467, PR 10,283/43 and PR 2432/43; Lata 512, PR 11,841/43 and PR 11,074/43, ANB. SPR, MTIC, 17.10, Lata 408, PR 34,503 and PR 133,947/43; Lata 476, PR 10,073/43; letter from Manoel Azenha Filho to Vargas, Lata 125; Lata 410, PR 30,630/42; and Lata 408, PR 33,200/42, ANB.

95. SPR, MTIC, 17.10, Lata 409, PR 19,503/43, ANB.

96. For some of the many denunciations see SPR, SP 14.21, Lata 394, PR 27,555/42, PR 26,524/42, PR 27,349/42, PR 26,357/42, PR 27,693/42, PR 28,474/42, and PR 32,479/42; Lata 466, PR 2350/43; and Lata 467, PR 23,433/42, PR 25,166/42, and PR 7248/43, ANB.

97. All this information is contained in SPR, MTIC 17.10, Lata 477, PR 3625/43, ANB.

98. SPR, SP 14.21, Lata 469, PR 5139/43, ANB.

99. SPR, SP 14.21, Lata 394, PR 28,702/42 and PR 28,761/43, ANB.

100. Interview, Conrado de Papa, Osasco, S.P., 23 September 1987; interview, Hermento Mendes Dantas, São Paulo, S.P., 14 September 1987; and interview with José Albertino, "Trabalhadores e Memória Paulistana, 1920–1950," CMS, 41–42.

101. Interview, Antônio Lombardi, São Paulo, S.P., 24 September 1987; interview, Geraldo Pascolato, São Paulo, S.P., 24 September 1987; and interview, Francisco da Silva, São Paulo, S.P., 25 May 1987.

102. Interview, David Carneiro, São Paulo, S.P., 24 September 1987; interview, João de Franco, São Paulo, S.P., 25 May 1987; interview, José Antônio de Mendes, São Paulo, S.P., 25 May 1987; interview, José Pacheco, São Paulo, S.P., 15 September 1987; and interview, Francisco Pinto Silva, São Paulo, S.P., 25 September 1987.

103. Interview, Antônio Lombardi, São Paulo, S.P., 24 September 1987; interview, Geraldo Pascolato, São Paulo, S.P., 24 September 1987; and interview with Armando Sufredini, "O Trabalhador e a Memória Paulistana, 1920–1950," CMS, 60–61.

104. FIESP Reunião Semanal, 10 January 1945; SPR, SP 14.21, Lata 468, PR 32,072/42, ANB.

105. FIESP Reuniões Semanais, 19 July 1944, 10 January 1945; FIESP, *Relatório*, 1945, 2:20; and SPR, SP 14.21, Lata 468, PR 32,992/42, ANB. Metalworkers' high skill levels empowered them to commit acts of sabotage. Even though their factory-specific skills were an important aspect of weavers' resistance, they could not sabotage work processes because any loss in production brought a decrease in wages; interview, João Bonifácio, São Paulo, S.P., 3 September 1987.

106. CIESP/FIESP, *Circulares* 47/43, 13 March 1943; 175/45, 13 September; 182/45, 25 September; 213/45, 20 November 1945; FIESP Reunião Semanal, 7 November 1945; and A. C. Pacheco e Silva, "Higiene Mental nas Fábricas," *RISP* 9 (August 1945): 21–33.

107. Angela de Castro Gomes, *A Invenção do Trabalhismo* (Rio de Janeiro: IUPERJ/Vértice, 1988), 269. There were 161,544 sindicalizados in Rio in 1936–37, and 147,657 throughout the rest of Brazil at that time. In 1937, 93.33 percent were men and 6.67 percent were women, and in 1938 the men made up 91.7 percent and the women 8.3 percent of the country's unionized workers. On the breakdown by sex, see *BMTIC* 68 (April 1940): 96.

108. This plan is discussed in a long, confidential memorandum to Vargas; see GV 43.00.00/3, AGV, FGV, CPDOC. Castro Gomes provides a detailed account of Vargas's and Marcondes Filho's plans; see *A Invenção do Trabalhismo*, 229–56.

109. Castro Gomes, *A Invenção do Trabalhismo*, 267–77; see also *BMTIC* 108 (August 1944): 335, on the arrangement with the National Confederation of Industries. This episode further highlights the acceptance by industrialists of key aspects of Vargas's labor policies.

110. Both workers' pressure on Vargas to deliver real social justice and the elite opposition's calls for a more open political system brought Vargas's first tentative steps in late 1943 toward building a populist coalition between politicians and workers; see Edgard Carone, *O Estado Novo, 1937–1945* (Rio de Janeiro: DIFEL, 1976), 303–10; and Thomas E. Skidmore, *Politics in Brazil, 1930–1964: An Experiment in Democracy* (New York: Oxford University Press, 1967), 48–60.

111. Memo from Marcondes Filho to Vargas, AMF, 45.01.00, CPDOC; Ministério do Trabalho, Indústria e Comércio, *Relatório*, 1944; CIESP/FIESP, *Circular* 59/43, 7 April 1943; Berman, "Industrial Labor in Brazil," 33–34; Evaristo de Morais Filho, *O Problema do Sindicato Único: Seus Fundamentos Sociológicos* (São Paulo: Alfa-Omega, 1952), 256–58. No reliable data on the actual number of new union members could be located.

112. The Shoemakers' Union was one in São Paulo that did have new leaders installed by the Ministry of Labor at this time; see interviews with Horácio Pereira Frade and Alcides Ribeiro de Almeida, São Paulo, S.P., 18 April 1956, Alexander Papers, Rutgers University, Coll. 1957, Box 2. John D. French (*The Brazilian Workers' ABC*, 93–99) has argued that the changes in Rio pro-

foundly affected labor in São Paulo. He reaches this conclusion without reference to any primary sources on union activity within the state. The only primary sources behind his assertion are citations from the U.S. consul, who reported that FIESP members were beginning to grow unhappy with Vargas's program.

113. Cross to Simmons (Rio), 21 January 1944, SP Post 850.4; "Symptoms of Inflation in São Paulo," 31 January 1944, SP Post 850; São Paulo to Rio, 14 May 1944, SP Post 850.4; and São Paulo to Rio, 18 September 1944, RG 84, SP Post 850.4, NA; FIESP Reunião Semanal, 3 January 1945. Press censorship continued, so the primary source of information on these wildcat strikes is the reports by U.S. diplomatic personnel in São Paulo.

114. *Diário de São Paulo*, 19, 22, 24, 25, and 28 February, 6 March 1945.

115. *Diário de São Paulo*, 6–8 March 1945; *A Noite*, 5 March 1945; and *Gazeta de Noticias*, 6 March 1945. The Brazilian representatives did not vote for a provision guaranteeing the right to strike, but they openly approved of it. Further, they voted for the final report of the conference which called for such rights.

116. The labor courts functioned with a panel of three judges: one representative of the Ministry of Labor, one from industry, and one from the unions; see Kenneth S. Mericle, "Conflict Regulation in the Brazilian Industrial Relations System" (Ph.D. diss., University of Wisconsin–Madison, 1974), 83–89.

117. Márcia Mendes de Almeida, "O Sindicato dos Têxteis em São Paulo: História, 1933–1957" (Tese de mestrado, Universidade de São Paulo, 1981), 131–33; Maria Hermínia Tavares da Almeida, "Estado e Classes Trabalhadores no Brasil, 1930–1945" (Tese de doutoramento, Universidade de São Paulo, 1978), 265–69; *O Metalúrgico*, March 1947; Robert J. Alexander, *Labor Relations in Argentina, Brazil, and Chile* (New York: McGraw-Hill, 1962), 91–96; interview, Alcy Nogueira, São Paulo, S.P., 1 October 1987; and interview, Elpídio Ribeiro dos Santos Filho, São Paulo, S.P., 1 October 1987 (both men, who were, respectively, the president and the secretary general of the Federation of Chemical and Pharmaceutical Workers of the State of São Paulo, have served as labor representatives on the Regional Labor Tribunal).

118. Vargas effectively crushed the Communist party after its failed 1935 putsch; see Carone, *O Estado Novo*, 216–32; Ronald H. Chilcote, *The Brazilian Communist Party: Conflict and Integration, 1922–1972* (New York: Oxford University Press, 1974), 41–48; and John W. F. Dulles, *Communists in Brazil, 1935–1945: Repression during World Upheaval* (Austin: University of Texas Press, 1983), 149–58.

119. Interview, Luís Firmino de Lima, São Paulo, S.P., 7 August 1987. On the rebuilding of the PCB see Carone, *O Estado Novo*, 235–49; and Dulles, *Communists in Brazil*, 165–76.

120. On the MUT's opposition to strikes and its support of Vargas, high levels of production, and the national industrial bourgeoisie, see João Ama-

zonas, *Pela Fortalecimento e Unidade Sindical* (Rio de Janeiro: Horizonte, 1945); the quote is from pp. 21–22. See also Leôncio Basbaum, *História Sincera da República de 1930–1960*, 4th ed. (São Paulo: Alfa-Omega, 1976), 182–85; and Franscisco Weffort, "Origens do Sindicalismo Populista no Brasil: A Conjuntura do Após-Guerra," *Estudos CEBRAP* 4 (1973): 82–91. French (*The Brazilian Workers ABC*, 154) defends this PCB policy: "Firm partisans of organized struggle based on careful preparation, Left/Center labor leaders believed in late 1945 that a cautious policy of methodical organization and growth would best strengthen the union, influence the employers, and facilitate success through the established bargaining procedures of existing labor legislation." Unfortunately, French provides no evidence that labor leaders thought this. By conflating the PCB's rhetoric with workers' and unionists' praxis, French fails to distinguish between the aspirations of activists in São Paulo and national Communist party leaders in Rio. These two groups, however, had very different perspectives and goals in the mid-1940s.

121. *Diário de São Paulo*, 1, 2, and 4 May 1945; *Folha da Manhã*, 3 May 1945; and *O Estado de São Paulo*, 3 May 1945. Like the anarchists of 1917, these progressive political parties (along with the MUT, the Partido Socialista Brasileiro, Frente da Resistência, Movimento Libertador do Brasil, Frente da Liberdade, Partido Socialista Revolucionário, and others sponsored the May Day event) called for freedom for themselves first and listed the right to strike as their *last* demand.

122. Port workers in Santos struck in March; tram workers in Campinas followed in April; and then São Paulo bus drivers and bakers struck. Most industrial workers struck in May. See São Paulo to Rio, 2 April 1945, SP Post 850.4, RG 84, NA; SIFTC, *Circular 2576*, 30 May 1945; FIESP, *Relatório*, 1945, 1:47; and FIESP Reunião Semanal, 16 May 1945.

123. *Folha da Manhã*, 27 May 1945; *Diário de São Paulo*, 29 May 1945; and Cross, "The Machinery for Settling Disputes Between Capital and Labor in São Paulo," 20 July 1945, SP Post 850.4, RG 84, NA.

124. FIESP members discussed how the increasing cost of living was leading to social unrest in 1944; see FIESP, *Relatório*, 1944, 1:41–42; and FIESP Reuniões Semanais, 3 and 10 January 1945; J. Henry, "Developments in Brazilian Labor Organization since V.J. Day," *Monthly Labor Review* 64.3 (March 1947): 437.

125. FIESP Reuniões Semanais, 16 and 23 May 1945; FIESP, *Relatório*, 1945, 2:136; *Folha da Manhã*, 22 May 1945; and *Diário de São Paulo*, 24 May 1945. At this time the Textile Workers' Union also issued its first strong criticism of wage policies during the Estado Novo; see *O Trabalhador Têxtil*, May 1945.

126. *Diário de São Paulo*, 19, 23, 25, and 30 May 1945; *Folha da Manhã*, 23 May 1945; and J. Henry, "Developments in Brazilian Labor Organization since V.J. Day," *Monthly Labor Review* 64.3 (March 1947): 435. Opponents of the pelegos

in the Metalworkers' Union later voiced their outrage at Sanches Duran for working with the FIESP to break the power of the factory commissions; see O Metalúrgico, February, May, and June 1947.

127. FIESP Reuniões Semanais, 23 and 30 May 1945; FIESP, Relatório, 1945, 3:7–47; SIFTG, Circular 2569, 18 May 1945; Diário de São Paulo, 22, 25, 26, 27, 29, and 30 May 1945; Folha da Manhã, 24, 25, and 26 May 1945.

128. FIESP, Relatório, 1945, 1:48–49; FIESP Reunião Semanal, 16 May 1945; and SIFTG, Circular 2576, 30 May 1945.

129. FIESP, Relatório, 1946, 4:86–87; FIESP Reunião Semanal, 23 January 1946; and interview, Conrado de Papa, Osasco, S.P., 23 September 1987.

130. FIESP, Relatório, 1945, 1:51, on São Paulo industrialists' good relations with General Eurico Dutra before the coup. On Vargas's ouster see Skidmore, Politics in Brazil, 48–62; and chapter 5 in this volume.

131. The experience of São Paulo's industrial working class calls into question the prevailing views of corporatism. The weak position of the delegitimized unions and the various resistance strategies employed by textile and metallurgical workers seem to limit the applicability of the corporatist control argument put forth by theorists such as Guillermo A. O'Donnell in "Corporatism and the Question of the State," in Authoritarianism and Corporatism in Latin America, ed. James M. Malloy (Pittsburgh: University of Pittsburgh Press, 1972), 47–87; Philippe C. Schmitter in Interest Conflict and Political Change in Brazil (Stanford: Stanford University Press, 1971); and Kenneth Paul Erickson in The Brazilian Corporative State and Working-Class Politics (Berkeley: University of California Press, 1977). Indeed, the São Paulo case seems to indicate that Brazil's corporatist system in the pre-1964 period was the more open "societal corporatism" rather than the repressive "state corporatism." Although Schmitter develops these ideal types, he places Brazil in the latter camp; see his "Still the Century of Corporatism?" Review of Politics 36.1 (January 1974): 85–121.

132. This attitude contrasts sharply with that of textile workers in the southern United States who wrote to President Roosevelt during the depression. They spoke of themselves as FDR's allies in the implementation of the New Deal and never questioned their right to full protection under the law. An excellent analysis of this is presented in Jacquelyn Dowd Hall et al., Like a Family: The Making of a Southern Cotton Mill World (Chapel Hill: University of North Carolina Press, 1987), chap. 6. Indeed, North American workers frequently invoked their rights as citizens when they protested against certain employer actions. Early expressions of this are found in the debates over the nature of the new republic detailed in Sean Wilentz, Chants Democratic: New York City and the Rise of the American Working Class, 1788–1850 (New York: Oxford University Press, 1984). This continued into the late nineteenth century, as David Montgomery points out in The Fall of the House of Labor: The Workplace, the State, and American Labor Activism, 1865–1925 (Cambridge: Cambridge University Press, 1987), 130.

5 *The Industrialists' Democracy in São Paulo*

1. *Diário de São Paulo,* 31 July, 1 and 2 August 1947; *Folha da Manhã,* 2 and 3 August 1947; telegrams, São Paulo to Rio, 1 and 2 August 1947, Rio Post, 850.4, RG 84, NA; "Monthly Labor Report, 1 August to 1 September 1947," 30 September 1947, SP Post 560, RG 84, NA. The percentage of income spent on transportation is from Arquivo do Departamento Intersindical de Estatísticas e Estudos Socio-Econômicos (hereinafter DIEESE), PLS-08, "Atualização do Salário Mínimo."

2. The city government had been planning to improve the mass transit system since 1925. For details of the extent of its deterioration by 1947 see Abraão Ribeiro, *Remodelação o do Serviço de Transporte Coletivo da Cidade de São Paulo* (São Paulo: Prefeitura Municipal, 1946); and "Modernizing Transit in Difficult Terrain," *The American City,* July 1948.

3. José Álvaro Moisés analyzes this protest in terms of workers' frustrations with the status quo in politics; see Moisés, "Protesto Urbano e Política: O Quebra-Quebra de 1947," in *Cidade, Povo, e Poder,* ed. Moisés et al. (Rio de Janeiro: CEDEC/Paz e Terra, 1982), 50–64. Similar quebra-quebras in Rio and São Paulo were initiated during the military dictatorship in the 1970s. These riots also had roots in working-class frustration with exclusionary politics and rigorous work regimes. The best account of this is provided in José Álvaro Moisés and Verena Stolcke, "Urban Transport and Popular Violence: The Case of Brazil," *Past and Present* 86 (February 1980): 174–92.

4. FIESP Reuniões Semanais, 3 and 10 January, 16 May 1945, 21 February 1946; FIESP, *Relatório,* 1945, 1:48–49.

5. *O Metalúrgico,* May and September 1945, March 1946; Maria Simões Paes, "O Sindicato dos Metalúrgicos de São Paulo, 1932–1951" (Tese de mestrado, Universidade de São Paulo, 1979), 158–61, 186.

6. Sindicato dos Trabalhadores na Indústria de Fiação e Tecelagem de São Paulo (hereinafter STIFTSP), Assembléia Geral, 11 March, 29 July 1945; interview, Luís Firmino de Lima, São Paulo, S.P., 1 September 1987; Márcia Mendes de Almeida, "O Sindicato dos Têxteis de São Paulo: História, 1933–1957" (Tese de mestrado, Universidade de São Paulo, 1981), 104.

7. STIFTSP, Reuniões de Diretoria, 17 and 24 August 1945, 12 January 1946; see also Mendes de Almeida, "O Sindicato dos Têxteis de São Paulo," 108–9; and Ricardo Maranhão, *Sindicatos e Democratização* (São Paulo: Brasiliense, 1979), 55–57. The 15 percent membership estimate is a rough one. No reliable statistics on membership were located for this period, but all accounts seem to indicate that an increasing number of Paulistano workers joined the unions during this political opening.

8. STIFTSP, Assembléias Gerais, 29 July, 16 December 1945, 24 February 1946; STIFTSP, Reuniões de Diretoria, 12 January, 27 April, 28 September 1946.

9. FIESP Reunião Semanal, 3 April 1946; interview, Santo Vetturuzzo, São Paulo, S.P., 2 September 1987; interview, Diolinda Nascimento, São Paulo, S.P., 2 September 1987; interview, Luís Firmino de Lima, São Paulo, S.P., 1 September 1987. Again, there are no reliable statistics on union membership during these years.

10. By 1949, the union claimed some 15,207 dues-paying members out of more than 85,000 metalworkers in the city who paid the imposto sindical (i.e., the union claimed a membership of about 17 percent of workers in metals); see O *Metalúrgico*, November–December 1949. As we shall see in chapter 6, however, the union had fewer than 6,000 members in 1950–51; that is, really only about 7 percent of São Paulo's metalworkers belonged to the union.

11. Interview, Hermento Mendes Dantas, São Paulo, S.P., 14 September 1987; interview, Lima Fereira dos Santos, Osasco, S.P., 23 September 1987. Once they decided the sindicatos could help them exercise their rights under the CLT, many illiterate workers must have joined to receive help filing processos and other official documents.

12. Although this period witnessed more freedom for unions, the sindicatos remained at the mercy of the Ministry of Labor, for the majority of the money in their budgets still came from the imposto sindical. This would continue to be the case as long as unions comprised only small fractions of the workers from their industries; that is, income from the imposto sindical would remain much greater than that from dues. Francisco C. Weffort emphasizes this point in his "Sindicatos e Política" (Tese de livre-doência, Universidade de São Paulo, 1972), II-31–II-33.

13. Interview, Luís Firmino de Lima, São Paulo, S.P., 1 September 1987; interview, Hermento Mendes Dantas, São Paulo, S.P., 14 September 1987; and interview, José Pacheco, São Paulo, S.P., 15 September 1987. Teixeira and Ferreira went on to play such a role in the early 1950s; see chapter 6 in this volume.

John D. French argues that most unionists in São Paulo's industrial suburb of Santo André acted on behalf of the workers in the mid-1940s. Although French provides no direct evidence of this, it is certainly possible that unionists in the Santo André and other industrial suburbs had a closer relationship to the rank and file than did São Paulo's pelegos, for the Paulistano workers had a long heritage of independent organizing that served as a focal point through which they could critique pelegos. French argues that workers in the industrial suburbs experienced their first wide-scale protests in the mid-1940s, so perhaps these workers did not have the benefit of historical memory and experience for analyzing their unionists' actions. Unfortunately, French's analysis is marred by the absence of primary sources beyond newspaper accounts and by his tendency to universalize his conclusions for all of São Paulo. In discussing groups of workers negotiating directly with bosses, for example, he asserts: "Such widespread public delegations, speaking openly and forcefully as representatives of their fellow workers, were without precedent in São Paulo (nor did they occur again on such a scale after this period)"; see French, *The Brazilian Workers' ABC: Class Conflict and Alliances in Modern São Paulo* (Chapel Hill: University of North Carolina Press, 1992), 159; on unionists in Santo André in the mid-1940s, see pp. 152–95. As we have seen, workers have been negotiating with their bosses since the 1910s. On such activities in the 1950s see chapter 6 in this volume.

14. Scholars have tended to argue that the "populist option" was created by cagey politicians who noticed that recent migrants from the rural sector experienced a sense of anomie in the industrial environments of expanding cities. These politicians then became urban *patrões* who traded protection and services for electoral support. Such a view is, ultimately, a structural analysis, for it argues that the processes of urbanization and industrialization were the bases of the populist option and ignores the role of workers' actions. One of the best works in this vein is Michael Conniff's study of Pedro Ernesto in Rio, *Urban Politics in Brazil: The Rise of Populism, 1925–1945* (Pittsburgh: University of Pittsburgh Press, 1981). For similar studies of other Latin American populists see Conniff, ed., *Latin American Populism in Comparative Perspective* (Albuquerque: University of New Mexico Press, 1982).

15. Angela de Castro Gomes, *A Invenção do Trabalhismo* (Rio de Janeiro: IUPERJ/Vértice, 1988), 303–14; and Thomas E. Skidmore, *Politics in Brazil, 1930–1964: An Experiment in Democracy* (New York: Oxford University Press, 1967), 51–52.

16. Werneck Vianna, *Liberalismo e Sindicato no Brasil*, 2d ed. (Rio de Janeiro: Paz e Terra, 1978), 246–57. The 1946 Constitution is discussed below.

17. Getúlio Vargas, *A Política Trabalhista no Brasil*, 4 (Rio de Janeiro: José Olympio, 1950), 15–16.

18. CMS, "Trabalhadores e a Memória Paulistana," interview with Laurindo Maistra, 94; CMS, "A Morte do Getúlio Vargas," interviews with José Albertino da Costa Filho, 7–8, and Adolfo Perchon, 19.

19. Interviews, Luís Firmino de Lima, São Paulo, S.P., 7 August and 1 September 1987.

20. Interview, Assumpta Bianchi, São Paulo, S.P., 10 August 1987; interview, João Bonifácio, São Paulo, S.P., 3 September 1987.

21. Interview, Waldemar Lima, São Paulo, S.P., 25 September 1987; interview, Lima Fereira dos Santos, Osasco, S.P., 23 September 1987. For a good analysis of the MUT see Ricardo Maranhão, *Sindicato e Democratização*, 57–68.

22. Yeddo Fiuza was the noncommunist former mayor of Petrópolis in the state of Rio de Janeiro. PCB leaders sought out such candidates to demonstrate their nonrevolutionary intentions. Fiuza represented the first of the group of developmentalist politicians who would dominate Brazil in the mid-1950s.

23. Timothy Harding, "The Political History of the Organized Labor Movement in Brazil" (Ph.D. diss., Stanford University, 1973), 174–77; Ronald

Chilcote, *The Brazilian Communist Party: Conflict and Integration* (New York: Oxford University Press, 1974), 51–54; John D. French, "Industrial Workers and the Origins of Populist Politics in the ABC Region of São Paulo, Brazil, 1900–1950" (Ph.D. diss., Yale University, 1985), 298–301; Skidmore, *Politics in Brazil*, 62–64.

24. On São Paulo's working-class vote and its support for the PTB and/or PCB in 1945–50, see Azis Simão, "O Voto Operário em São Paulo," *Revista Brasileira de Estudos Políticos* 1.1 (December 1956): 130–41. On Prestes's popularity as more important than the allure of the PCB in the 1940s see interview with Agildo Barata, former treasurer of the PCB, Rio de Janeiro, 20 August 1965, Alexander Papers, Rutgers University, Coll. 1957, Box 2. Interestingly, Barata describes Prestes as more of a populist than a Marxist.

25. SIFTG, *Circular* 2721, 14 January 1946; *RISP* 11 (October 1945), (March 1946); Claudio L. S. Haddad, "Growth of Brazilian Real Output, 1900–1947" (Ph.D. diss., University of Chicago, 1974), 11, 98; "Monthly Labor Report," 1 August to 1 September 1947, 30 September 1947, Rio Post 850.4, RG 84, NA.

26. The 49 percent figure is from Seiti Kaneko Endo and Carlos Heron Esvael do Carmo, *Breve Histórico do Índice de Preços ao Consumidor no Município de São Paulo* (São Paulo: FIPE, 1985), 17. Again, readers should remember that these figures traditionally underestimated the costs of goods and services in working-class bairros. For the industrialists' view of the coming price increases see FIESP Reunião Semanal, 27 February 1946.

27. *RISP* 36 (November 1947): 51–53; Haddad, "Growth of Brazilian Real Output," 147–49, 157; "Monthly Labor Report," 1 August to 1 September 1947, 30 September 1947, Rio Post 850.4, RG 84, NA. According to the figures in this report, employment in São Paulo's metalworking firms increased by 6 percent in 1946. For the value of the minimum wage see DIEESE, "Objetivos e Caraterísticas do Plano Cruzado III."

28. FIESP, *Relatório*, 1946, 1:230; 2:84; 4:97–110; FIESP Reuniões Semanais, 16 January, 21 and 27 February 1946.

29. *Folha da Manhã*, 27 February 1946.

30. *Conjuntura Econômica* (April 1948): 8–9; *Diário de São Paulo*, 3 May 1947; FIESP, *Relatório*, 1946, 4:77.

31. *O Metalúrgico*, September 1945, June 1946, March 1947; FIESP *Relatório*, 1946, 3:8–9; interview, Hermento Mendes Dantas, São Paulo, S.P., 14 September 1987. As they had during the Estado Novo, factory commissions relied on the seniority of older workers. They did so both because older workers had extensive experience in such organizing and because the CLT protected those with tenure in the factories. The Brazilian experience differed markedly from Chile's, where young workers seem to have dominated the factory commissions in the textile plants, as Peter Winn describes in *Weavers of Revolution: The Yarur Workers and Chile's Road to Socialism* (New York: Oxford University Press, 1986).

32. Interviews, Edson Borges and Waldemar Lima, 25 September 1987, São Paulo, S.P.; interview, David Carneiro, São Paulo, S.P., 24 and 25 September 1987.

33. STIFTSP, Reuniões de Diretoria, 17 and 24 August, 15 December 1945; interview, Laura S. Machado, Osasco, S.P., 8 September 1987; interview, Angelo Neto, São Paulo, S.P., 8 August 1987; interview, Maria Pavone, São Paulo, S.P., 12 August 1987; interview, Hermínia Lorenzi dos Santos, São Paulo, S.P., 12 August 1987.

34. Interview, Odette Pasquini, São Paulo, S.P., 17 September 1987; interview, Glória Salviano, São Paulo, S.P., 14 August 1987; interview, Diolinda Nascimento, São Paulo, S.P., 2 September 1987.

35. Interview, Lima Fereira dos Santos, Osasco, S.P., 23 September 1987; interviews, Luís Firmino de Lima, 7 August and 1 September 1987. Lima Fereira no doubt played an important role at Cobrasma because as a mechanic he worked throughout the large factory and could perform organizing activities in different sections without causing suspicion among the bosses.

36. Interview, Assumpta Bianchi, São Paulo, S.P., 10 August 1987; interview, Aracy Sanchez, São Paulo, S.P., 2 September 1987; interview, Antônio Ciaveletto, São Paulo, S.P., 3 September 1987; interview, Santo Vetturuzzo, São Paulo, S.P., 2 September 1987.

37. São Paulo to Rio, 15 January 1946, SP Post 850.4, RG 84, NA; interview, Luís Firmino de Lima, São Paulo, S.P., 7 August 1987; Mendes de Almeida, "O Sindicato dos Têxteis de São Paulo," 97–101; Harding, "A Political History of the Organized Labor Movement in Brazil," 181–83; Maranhão, *Sindicatos e Democratização*, 43–69. Indeed, the workers respected the leaders of the comissões because they were independent from the unions and the PCB, and that respect had long-term implications. Remo Forli and Luís Firmino led such groups of metallurgical and textile workers, respectively, and both rose to leadership positions in their unions in the 1950s. This process of opening the unions is detailed in chapter 6 in this volume.

38. French (*The Brazilian Workers' ABC*, 152–79) sees these strikes as a "spontaneous mobilization" that flourished with PCB support, but no social movement (especially one involving more than 100,000 workers) is spontaneous. Maranhão (*Sindicatos e Democratização*, 57–68) emphasizes the role of local PCB militants tied to the factory commissions in these strikes. This view tends to simplify the role of workers' commissions, for it does not recognize the importance workers placed on having organizations that were independent from political parties and the state.

Ultimately, the São Paulo case challenges Antonio Gramsci's view of the relationship between factory councils and revolutionary parties. These two entities do not have the natural affinities for each other that Gramsci identifies. Coalition building is a long process that requires a great deal of mutual respect. An excellent analysis of Gramsci's perspective can be found in Frank R.

Annunziato, "Gramsci's Theory of Trade Unionism," *Rethinking Marxism* 1.2 (Summer 1988): 142–64.

39. Studies of British-owned mining facilities in Minas Gerais detail the success of communist militants in the labor movement using nationalism as an organizing tool; see Yonne de Souza Grossi, *Mina de Morro Velho: A Extração do Homem; Uma História de Experiência Operária* (Rio de Janeiro: Paz e Terra, 1981), 166–232; and Marshall C. Eakin, *British Enterprise in Brazil: The St. John d'el Rey Mining Company and the Morro Velho Gold Mine, 1830–1960* (Durham: Duke University Press, 1989), 219–29; see also interview, Antônio Carvalho, member editorial staff *Jornal do Povo* (PCB), Belo Horizonte, M.G., 29 March 1956; and interview, Sr. Agostino, member editorial staff *Gazeta Sindical* (PCB), Rio, 21 March 1956, both from Alexander Papers, Rutgers University, Coll. 1957, Box 3. These men emphasize the role of foreign ownership in the development of Morro Velho's workers' support of the PCB. French (*The Brazilian Workers' ABC*, 180–246) details communist dominance of the labor movement in Santo André. Most of the firms he discusses were foreign owned (e.g., Firestone, Pirelli, Rhodia Química, and General Motors).

40. Interview, Luís Firmino de Lima, São Paulo, S.P., 7 August 1987. Although he does not analyze why the PCB shifted its attention to working-class organizing after the "Tighten Your Belt" campaign, French (*The Brazilian Workers' ABC*, 162) notes the change in policy after the independent worker mobilizations. On São Paulo's independence vis-à-vis both the PCB and PTB see Maria Victoria Benevides, *O PTB e o Trabalhismo: Partido e Sindicato em São Paulo, 1945–1964* (São Paulo: Brasiliense, 1989). For a fascinating analysis of the twists and turns of the Communist party's relationships with black and white workers in the U.S. South see Robin D. G. Kelley, *Hammer and Hoe: Alabama Communists during the Great Depression* (Chapel Hill: University of North Carolina Press, 1990). Kelley describes how the party appealed to blacks when it attempted to foster revolution in the South in the early 1930s. The party's analysis of African Americans as an "oppressed nation" mirrored their self-image. When the U.S. party adopted a Popular Front strategy, however, it abandoned its previous analysis and built ties to Alabama's white unions, thus alienating many of its African-American allies. Kelley's closely documented study is yet another reminder that we must analyze closely the relationship between activists' ideologies and workers' praxis.

41. FIESP, *Relatório*, 1946, 4:88; interview, Diolinda Nascimento, São Paulo, S.P., 2 September 1987; interview, Aracy Sanchez, São Paulo, S.P., 2 September 1987; interview, Antônio Ciaveletto, São Paulo, S.P., 3 September 1987; interview, Assumpta Bianchi, São Paulo, S.P., 10 August 1987.

42. *Folha da Manhã*, 1, 3, 9, 11, 15, 16, and 17 January 1946; memo, 7 January 1946, SP Post 850.4; memo, 28 January 1946, SP Post 850.4, RG 84, NA.

43. FIESP, *Relatório*, 1946, 1:86–87; FIESP Reunião Semanal, 30 January

1946; *Folha da Manhã*, 9 January 1946; CIESP/FIESP, *Circular* 42/46, 20 February 1946; São Paulo to Rio, 11 January 1946, SP Post 850.4, RG 84, NA.

44. FIESP Reunião Semanal, 30 January 1946; interview, Antônio Ciaveletto, 3 September 1987. Ciaveletto still bears scars on his forehead from police beatings.

45. FIESP Reunião Semanal, 6 February 1946; FIESP, *Relatório*, 1946, 4:73, 84–90; *Folha da Manhã*, 10 February 1946; interview, Hermento Mendes Dantas, São Paulo, S.P., 14 September 1987; interview, Lima Fereira dos Santos, Osasco, S.P., 23 September 1987.

46. *Folha da Manhã*, 9, 13, 15, 17, 20, 21, and 22 February 1946; *O Estado de São Paulo*, 24 and 27 February 1946; *Diário de São Paulo*, 21 February 1946; FIESP Reunião Semanal, 13 February 1946; CIESP/FIESP, *Circulares* 39/46, 15 February 1946; 45/46, 25 February 1946; FIESP, *Relatório*, 1946, 1:69–79.

47. Workers' continued reliance on their commissions is detailed below. A similar chain of events led to pelegos' deepening control of the unions in Juiz de Fora, Minas Gerais; see Maria Andréa Loyola, *Os Sindicatos e o PTB: Estudo de um Caso em Minas Gerais* (Petrópolis: Vozes, 1980), 57–65. José Sérgio Leite Lopes, in *A Tecelagem dos Conflitos de Classe na Cidade das Chaminés* (São Paulo: Marco Zero/Universidade de Brasília, 1988), 321–25, on the other hand, sees the sindicato as helpful to the textile workers he studied in the northeastern state of Pernambuco. Again, these differences highlight the danger of universalizing the experiences of one region's or city's workers.

48. FIESP Reuniões Semanais, 6, 21, and 27 February 1946; FIESP, *Relatório*, 1946, 3:50–52; *Folha da Manhã*, 16, 21, 24, and 28 February 1946.

49. *A Gazeta*, 6 March 1946; *Folha da Manhã*, 8 March 1946; FIESP Reuniões Semanais, 13 and 20 March 1946; FIESP, *Relatório*, 1946, 4:75–78, 115; SIFTG, *Circular* 2804, 22 April 1946. For the FIESP's view of absenteeism, see *Relatório*, 1946, 3:8–18. Metals firms, however, did not enforce the attendance clause because they feared new strikes. Textile mills relied on it to increase productivity.

50. FIESP Reuniões Semanais, 6, 13, 21, and 27 February 1946; FIESP, *Relatório*, 1946, 4:69–79, 84–90; CIESP/FIESP, *Circular* 45/46, 25 February 1946; *Folha da Manhã*, 24 February, 8 March 1946.

51. For a brief account of the strikes in other cities see Harding, "The Political History of Organized Labor in Brazil," 180–86.

52. FIESP Reuniões Semanais, 23 January, 13 March 1946; CIESP/FIESP, *Circular* 54/46, 19 March 1946; FIESP, *Relatório*, 1946, 1:76–79, 4:77–79. The public relations fee dropped to Cr$0.50 per worker after the strikes.

53. CIESP/FIESP, *Circular* 61/46, 27 March 1946; USDL, *Monthly Labor Review* 64.3 (March 1947): 438–39; *Folha da Manhã*, 1 and 3 May 1946; Mendes de Almeida, "O Sindicato dos Têxteis de São Paulo," 93–95.

54. STIFTSP, Reuniões de Diretoria, 2 and 30 March 1946; *O Metalúrgico*,

August 1946, December 1946, March 1947; Simões Paes, "O Sindicato dos Metalúrgicos de São Paulo," 169–173.

55. FIESP, *Relatório*, 1946, 1:61, 4:75; *Relatório*, 1947, 2:178; *Relatório*, 1948, 2:151; CIESP/FIESP, *Circulares* 165/46, 28 September 1946; 75/49, 23 April 1949; FIESP Reunião Semanal, 5 May 1948; SIFTG, *Circular* 3226, 5 April 1950.

56. FIESP Reuniões Semanais, 15 and 30 April 1947; *RISP* (January 1949): 24–25; STIFTSP, Reunião de Diretoria, 4 April 1950; "Labor Conditions in the São Paulo Consular District," 3 June, 14 October, 17 November, 13 December 1950, SP Post 560, RG 84, NA.

Industrialists and government officials showed an increased interest in fostering traditional gender ideologies that emphasized women's mothering and homemaking duties over working outside the home. These concerns followed women's increased participation in industry and their assertive and independent organizing and protest activities in the 1930s and 1940s. Some of these concerns are articulated in Brazil, Ministério da Educação, *Outline of Education in Brazil* (Rio de Janeiro: Imprensa Nacional, 1946). More research is needed to clarify the gender anxieties brought about by this period of political and economic transition.

57. Maria do Carmo Campello de Souza, *Estado e Partidos Políticos no Brasil, 1930–1964* (São Paulo: Alfa-Omega, 1976), 120–23; Weffort, "Origens do Sindicalismo Populista no Brasil: A Conjuntura Após-Guerra," *Estudos CEBRAP* 4 (April–June 1973): 97–98; Werneck Vianna, *Liberalismo e Sindicato*, 260–70. Not surprisingly, the military dictatorship of 1964–85 employed this labor legislation in practice and in the constitutions of 1967 and 1969; see Maria Helena Moreira Alves, *The State and Opposition in Military Brazil* (Austin: University of Texas Press, 1985), 46–53, 85–91, 182–200.

58. FIESP, *Relatório*, 1946, 1:135; "Monthly Labor Report," 1 February to 1 March 1947, Rio Post 850.4, RG 84, NA; interview, Vinicius Ferraz Torres, regional labor delegate, São Paulo, S.P., 23 April 1956, Alexander Papers, Rutgers University, Coll. 1957, Box 2.

59. "Monthly Labor Report," 1 February to 1 March 1947, Rio Post 850.4, RG 84, NA; Mendes de Almeida, "O Sindicato dos Têxteis de São Paulo," 159–65; FIESP Reuniões Semanais, 20 February 1947, 31 March 1948. The Brazilians, of course, did not need lessons on fighting labor's demands, but the U.S. efforts no doubt lent additional prestige to the hard-liners within the FIESP.

60. STIFTSP, Reuniões de Diretoria, 18 January, 3 May 1947; Mendes de Almeida, "O Sindicato dos Têxteis de São Paulo," 140; *O Metalúrgico*, April 1947.

61. On campaigning among the workers see CIESP/FIESP, *Circular* 6/47, 7 January 1947. On Adhemar's populist appeal and his ties to the PCB see John D. French, "Workers and the Rise of Adhemarista Populism in São Paulo, 1945–1947," *HAHR* 68.1 (February 1988): 1–43. French, however, seems to exaggerate the meaning of the working-class vote for Adhemar. Many workers were bitterly disappointed with the PTB and Vargas's support of Dutra and

would not vote for a PTBista without guarantees of prolabor policies. Since they had to vote anyway (a fine was levied against those who did not), they turned to Adhemar as the only viable option. Moreover, French exaggerates the importance of the PCB's support and underestimates Hugo Borghi's weakness as factors in Adhemar's victory. For a nuanced study of these events based on archival materials see Maria Victoria Benevides, *O PTB e o Trabalhismo: Partido e Sindicato em São Paulo, 1945–1964* (São Paulo: Brasiliense, 1989), 41–47.

62. The interventor's office handled all the workers' petitions during the dictatorship after they were sent to Vargas, so Adhemar probably came to understand the importance of the workers' votes at about the same time Vargas did. Adhemar later became a key civilian conspirator in the 1964 coup; see Skidmore, *The Politics of Military Rule in Brazil, 1964–1985* (New York: Oxford University Press, 1988), 14–17. The 1947 crackdown on labor is discussed below.

63. Adhemar initially paid lip service to some labor demands and met with union leaders but quickly abandoned them. French (*The Brazilian Workers' ABC*, 213–20) depicts these fifty days of his administration's prolabor rhetoric as a "government of collaboration," and even refers to the PCB as "a governing party" (p. 346, fn. 62). In a particularly unique characterization, French labels Adhemar de Barros São Paulo's "Communist/Progressive governor" (p. 214).

64. *O Metalúrgico*, January, March, and June 1947; interview, Hermento Mendes Dantas, São Paulo, S.P., 14 September 1987; interview, Lima Fereira dos Santos, Osasco, S.P., 23 September 1987; Simões Paes, "O Sindicato dos Metalúrgicos de São Paulo," 174–76.

65. STIFTSP, Reunião de Diretoria, 7 December 1946; STIFTSP, Assembléia Geral, 1 September, 27 October, 22 December 1946; FIESP, *Relatório*, 1946, 3:8–18, 4:75; *Relatório*, 1947, 2:40; FIESP Reunião Semanal, 3 April 1946; "Monthly Labor Report," 1 February to 1 March 1947, Rio Post 850.4, RG 84, NA; USDL, *Monthly Labor Review* 64.3 (March 1947): 434; interview, Assumpta Bianchi, São Paulo, S.P., 10 August 1987; interview, Glória Salviano, São Paulo, S.P., 14 August 1987; interview, Diolinda Nascimento, São Paulo, S.P., 2 September 1987.

66. "Monthly Labor Report," 1 February to 1 March 1947, 8 April 1947, Rio Post 850.4, RG 84, NA; "Labor Notes for the Week Ending 1 March," Rio Post 850.4, RG 84, NA; Maranhão, *Sindicatos e Democratização*, 49–52.

67. FIESP Reunião Semanal, 26 February 1947; FIESP, *Relatório*, 1947, 3:143–51; SIFTG, *Circular* 30310, 19 March 1947; "Labor Notes for the Week Ending 5 April," 10 April 1947, Rio Post 850.4, RG 84, NA; Endo and Esvael do Carmo, *Breve Histórico do Índice de Preços ao Consumidor*, 17. Changes in the textile sector are detailed below.

68. *Diário de São Paulo*, 1–10 May 1947; *Folha da Manhã*, 3, 7, 8, and 9 May 1947; *O Metalúrgico*, May 1947; Kenneth Paul Erickson, *The Brazilian Corporative State and Working-Class Politics* (Berkeley: University of California Press, 1977),

44–45. These moves were in concert with U.S. policies encouraging a hemispheric offensive against labor and the Left. The Truman administration rewarded Latin American regimes that moved against the Left and labor at this time, and in June 1947 the Taft-Hartley Act became law in the United States. For analyses of these policies see Kenneth Paul Erickson and Patrick V. Peppe, "Dependent Capitalist Development, U.S. Foreign Policy, and Repression of the Working Class in Chile and Brazil," *Latin American Perspectives* 8 (Winter 1976): 19–44; and Leslie Bethell and Ian Roxborough, "Latin America Between the Second World War and the Cold War: Some Reflections on the 1945–1948 Conjuncture," *JLAS* 20 (May 1988): 167–89.

69. STIFTSP, Reuniões de Diretoria, 26 May, 18 July, 5 August, 1 and 19 October 1947, 29 January, 16 February, 18 and 22 March, 1 April 1948; STIFTSP, Assembléia Geral, 18 and 22 March 1948; CMS, interview with Dante Pellacani, p. 23; Mendes de Almeida, "O Sindicato dos Têxteis de São Paulo," 131–42.

70. STIFTSP, Reuniões de Diretoria, 5 September 1947, 8 March, 27 April 1948, 8 July 1949, 9 May, 6 June 1950; STIFTSP, Assembléia Geral, 19 October, 4 August 1949; SIFTG, *Circulares* 3103, 19 November 1947; 3133, 19 January 1948; 3230, 12 April 1950.

71. STIFTSP, Reuniões de Diretoria, 8 July 1949, 19 June 1952; Mendes de Almeida, "O Sindicato dos Têxteis de São Paulo," 143. The FBI and several military attachés in the U.S. consulate maintained close contact with the DOPS, while unionists from the AFL worked with the city's pelegos; see Erickson and Peppe, "Dependent Capitalist Development," 36–40. The most complete account of the U.S. labor offensive during the Dutra years is Cliff Welch's "United States Labor Policy and the Politics of 'Ordem e Progresso' in Brazil, 1945–1950" (M.A. thesis, University of Maryland, 1987).

72. These "moderates" and their actions should not be romanticized, however. They were shrewd unionists who changed their outlook when popular pressure forced them to. For more on Teixeira's relationship with the commissions see chapter 6 in this volume.

73. *O Metalúrgico*, October, November, and December 1947, September–October and November–December 1949, July–August and September–October 1950, June 1951; SMSP, Assembléias Gerais, 28 March, 5 October 1952; Simões Paes, "O Sindicato dos Metalúrgicos de São Paulo," 156.

74. "Monthly Labor Reports," June 1947, July 1947, October 1947, Rio Post 850.4, RG 84, NA; Mendes de Almeida, "O Sindicato dos Têxteis de São Paulo," 134–35; CMS, "Trabalhadores e a Memória Paulistana," interview with Laurindo Maistro, 114–15; CMS, "A Morte de Getúlio Vargas," interview with Antônio Chamorro, 30–31; interview, Hermento Mendes Dantas, São Paulo, S.P., 14 September 1987.

75. FIESP Reunião Semanal, 16 December 1947.

76. According to Stanley Stein, industrialists in Rio managed to use un-

skilled labor in the mills, but the São Paulo data on job creation demonstrate that this was not the case in the city; see Stein, *The Brazilian Cotton Manufacture: Textile Enterprise in an Underdeveloped Area, 1850–1900* (Cambridge, Mass.: Harvard University Press, 1957), 166 for the Rio case.

77. FIESP Reuniões Semanais, 11 March, 22 April 1942, 26 February 1947; MTIC, Comissão Executiva Têxtil, *Indústria Têxtil Algodoeira* (Rio de Janeiro: Imprensa Nacional, 1946); José Tavares de Araújo and Vera Maria Candido, "Teares sem Lençadeira na Indústria Têxtil," in *Difusão de Inovações na Indústria Brasileira: Três Estudos de Caso*, ed. Araújo (Rio de Janeiro: IPEA/INPES, 1976), 16.

78. CIESP/FIESP, *Circulares* 103, 13 June 1942; 152/44, 4 October 1944; 37/45, 17 February 1945; 117/48, 4 September 1948; FIESP Reuniões Semanais, 27 September 1944, 26 February 1947; FIESP, *Relatório*, 1946, 2:61–62, 90–94; "Corporation Trading Profits in State of São Paulo Record Strong Upward Trend," 3 August 1944, SP Post 850, RG 84, NA; *Diário de São Paulo*, 28 January 1945; SIFTG, *Circulares* 2627, 22 August 1945; 3087, 24 September 1947; O. Pupo Nogueira, "A Propósito da Modernização de uma Grande Indústria," *RISP* 6 (May 1945): 16–18.

79. Baer, *The Brazilian Economy*, 64–68; Araújo and Pereira, "Teares sem Lençadeira," 17; Skidmore, *Politics in Brazil*, 69–71.

80. FIESP Reunião Semanal, 8 October 1947.

81. Flávio Rabelo Versiani, "Technical Change, Equipment Replacement, and Labor Absorption: The Case of the Brazilian Textile Industry" (Ph.D. diss., Vanderbilt University, 1971), 80–82; Stein, *The Brazilian Cotton Manufacture*, 149–50, 171; Araújo and Pereira, "Teares sem Lençadeira," 11–13.

82. United Nations Economic Commission for Latin America (ECLA), *Labor Productivity of the Cotton Textile Industry in Five Latin American Countries* (New York: UN Department of Economic Affairs, 1951), 17–30; Versiani, "Technical Change, Equipment Replacement and Labor Absorption," 66–104.

83. The readjustment had been hastened by Dutra's initial liberal trade policies in 1946 and part of 1947, which adversely affected industry; see Skidmore, *Politics in Brazil*, 69–70.

84. *Folha da Manhã*, 1 May 1947; CIESP/FIESP, *Circular* 78/47, 9 June 1947; SIFTG, *Circular* 3065, 19 July 1947; FIESP Reuniões Semanais, 28 May, 13 August, 1 October, 12 November 1947; FIESP, *Relatório*, 1947, 2:1–3; ECLA, *Productivity of the Cotton Textile Industry*, 15–38.

These data contradict those from a partial study of the employment situation made by the São Paulo State Department of Labor. By relying too heavily on statistics from the interior, the government report overestimated unemployment in textiles for the state in 1947. For the study's conclusions see "Monthly Labor Report," 1 August to 1 September 1947, 30 September 1947, Rio Post 850.4, RG 84, NA.

85. "Monthly Labor Report," 1 June to 1 July 1947 and 1 October to 1 November 1947, Rio Post 850.4, RG 84, NA; Rio to Washington, D.C., 19 January

1949, Rio Post 560, RG 84, NA; "Annual Labor Report for 1949," 8 May 1950, SP Post 560, RG 84, NA; CIESP/FIESP, *Circulares* 6/49, 8 January 1949; 16/49, 22 January 1949; 22/49, 24 January 1949; 134/49, 27 August 1949.

86. Arquivo de SENAI, SENAI and the Institute of Inter-American Affairs, "Estudo da Indústria Têxtil e Necessidades de Treinamento," 6; memo, 22 March 1950, SP Post 560, RG 84, NA; ECLA, *Productivity of the Cotton Textile Industry,* 41–48.

87. CIESP/FIESP, *Circulares* 47/43, 13 March 1943; 175/45, 13 September 1945; 213/45, 20 November 1945; FIESP Reunião Semanal, 7 November 1945; "Higiene Mental nas Fábricas," *RISP* 9 (August 1945): 21, 31; *RISP* 50 (January 1949), photos, 41–47; "Report of SENAI—National Training System for Brazilian Industrial Apprentices," 20 January 1950, SP Post 560, RG 84, NA.

In many ways the SENAI resembled Henry Ford's "Five Dollar Day" program and its sociological department. Both promised workers higher than market wages in return for good behavior at home and on the shop floor. The SENAI sought to increase skill levels, however, while Ford wanted to mitigate objections to the increasingly sophisticated division of labor on the assembly line. On the Ford program see Stephen Meyer, *The Five Dollar Day: Labor Management and Social Control in the Ford Motor Company, 1908–1921* (Albany: State University of New York Press, 1981).

88. Arquivo de SENAI, "Estudo do Indústria Têxtil," 10, 23–29; Versiani, "Technical Change, Equipment Replacement, and Labor Absorption," 131–34.

89. For critical analyses of the "developmentalist" perspective see John Sheahan, *Patterns of Development in Latin America: Poverty, Repression, and Economic Strategy* (Princeton: Princeton University Press, 1987), 179–203; and Baer, *The Brazilian Economy,* 59–91. For the PCB's support of increased productivity see Chilcote, *The Brazilian Communist Party,* 55–56.

90. Interview, Angela Neto, São Paulo, S.P., 8 August 1987; interview, Hermínia Lorenzi dos Santos, São Paulo, S.P., 12 August 1987; interview, Luís Firmino de Lima, São Paulo, S.P., 1 September 1987; interview, João Bonifácio, São Paulo, S.P., 3 September 1987.

91. Interview, Glória Salviano, São Paulo, S.P., 14 August 1987; interview, Odette Pasquini, São Paulo, S.P., 17 August 1987.

92. For a theoretical perspective on the social origins of technology in North American factories with large female work forces see Judith A. McGaw, "Women and the History of American Technology," *Signs: Journal of Women in Culture and Society* 7.4 (Summer 1982): 798–828.

93. This process closely resembles the first attempts at rationalization that were a part of the Fordist program attempted in the 1920s and that accompanied the development of the first system of "blacklisting" workers.

94. Interview, Luís Firmino de Lima, São Paulo, S.P., 1 September 1987; interview, João Bonifácio, São Paulo, S.P., 3 September 1987.

95. Interview, Maria Pavone, São Paulo, S.P., 12 August 1987.

96. "Indústria Mecânica; Fator Essencial do Progresso Manufatureiro do Brasil," *RISP* 11 (October 1945); "Produção de Máquinas," *RISP* 30 (May 1947); "Rodas para Estradas de Ferro," *RISP* 40 (March 1948); *RISP* 49 (December 1948), 51 (February 1949); FIESP Reunião Semanal, 26 February 1947; FIESP, *Relatório*, 1946, 6:130–37; *Relatório*, 1948, 2:173–74; CIESP/FIESP, *Circular* 71/47, 22 May 1947; CIESP/FIESP, *Boletim Informativo*, 14 March 1955, 99; *Diário de São Paulo*, 3 April 1952; *Folha da Manhã*, 23 December 1951, 6 January 1952, 5 and 7 September 1954; George Rad and Peter Scheier, *São Paulo: Fastest Growing City in the World* (Netherlands: Kosmos, 1954), photos, pp. 120–25.

By "Tayloristic" methods I mean attempts to rationalize production through the so-called scientific management schemes devised by Frederick Taylor and his disciples. As Daniel Nelson clearly demonstrates in his *Frederick W. Taylor and the Rise of Scientific Management* (Madison: University of Wisconsin Press, 1980), there was nothing at all scientific or exacting in Taylor's time and motion studies. For analyses of scientific management and work rationalization schemes in Latin America see Winn, *Weavers of Revolution*, 42–52; and Daniel James, "Rationalization and Working-Class Response: The Context and Limits of Factory Floor Activity in Argentina," *JLAS* 13.2 (November 1981): 375–402.

97. Interview, Edson Borges, São Paulo, S.P., 25 September 1987; interview, David Carneiro, São Paulo, S.P., 24 September; CMS, "Trabalhadores e a Memória Paulistana," interviews with Armando Suffredini and Hans Sikore, pp. 60–62.

98. Lucila Herrmann, *Flutuação e Mobilidade a Mão-de-Obra Fabril em São Paulo* (São Paulo: Instituto de Administração, 1948), 5–13; FIESP, *Relatório* 1947, 3:123; interviews, Francisco Pinto Silva, Waldemar Lima, and Edson Borges, São Paulo, S.P., 25 September 1987; interview, José Pacheco, São Paulo, S.P., 15 September 1987; interviews, Antônio Lombardi and David Carneiro, São Paulo, S.P., 24 September 1987; interview, Hermento Mendes Dantas, São Paulo, S.P., 14 September 1987.

99. *O Metalúrgico*, August–September 1948, March, April, and November–December 1949, April–May 1950; interview, David Carneiro, São Paulo, S.P., 24 and 25 September 1987; interview, Edson Borges, São Paulo, S.P., 25 September 1987. As we shall see in chapter 6, the Metalworkers' Union apparently had fewer than six thousand members in 1950–51.

100. Herrmann, *Flutuação e Mobilidade de Mão-de-Obra Fabril*, 5–7.

101. On the differences in wages for male and female textile workers see *Conjuntura Econômica* (December 1949): 37. The differences between metallurgical and textile workers are detailed in "Monthly Labor Report," 1 October to 1 November 1948, Rio Post 850.4, RG 84, NA.

102. FIESP Reuniões Semanais, 24 and 28 September 1947; SIFTG, *Circular* 3125, 13 January 1948; interview, Laura S. Machado, Osasco, S.P., 8 September 1987; interview, Angela Neto, São Paulo, S.P., 8 August 1987; interview, Maria Pavone, São Paulo, S.P., 12 August 1987.

103. Rio to Washington, D.C., 23 February 1948, Rio Post 850.4, RG 84, NA; "Monthly Labor Report," 1 January to 29 February, 9 April 1948, Rio Post 850.4, RG 84, NA; interview, Laura S. Machado, Osasco, S.P., 8 September 1987; interview, Angela Neto, São Paulo, S.P., 8 August 1987; interview, Maria Pavone, São Paulo, S.P., 12 August 1987; FIESP Reunião Semanal, 18 February 1948; *Folha da Manhã*, 25 February 1947; STIFTSP, Assembléia Geral, 22 March 1947. A 1948 study of accidents in Paulistano textile mills gave a frequency coefficient of 35.43; the rate for U.S. mills was 11.44; see *Folha da Manhã*, 20 February 1952.

104. STIFTSP, Assembléia Geral, 22 March 1948; STIFTSP, Reunião de Diretoria, 6 April 1948; FIESP Reuniões Semanais, 20 April, 19 May, 6 July 1948; CIESP/FIESP, *Circular* 62/48, 29 May 1948.

105. FIESP Reuniões Semanais, 6 July, 22 December 1948; memos, 4 May, 21 July, 11 October 1948, 20 January 1948, Rio Post, 850.4, RG 84, NA; SIFTG, *Circular* 3156, 20 January 1949.

106. *O Metalúrgico*, January–February, March, June–July, and October 1948; "Monthly Labor Reports," 1 January to 1 February and 1 May to 1 June 1948, Rio Post 850.4, RG 84, NA; Rio to Washington, D.C., 25 March, 11 October 1948, Rio Post 850.4, RG 84, NA; interview, Francisco Pinto Silva, São Paulo, S.P., 25 September 1987; interview, Antônio Lombardi, São Paulo, S.P., 24 September 1987; interview, José Pacheco, São Paulo, S.P., 15 September 1987; Simões Paes, "O Sindicato dos Metalúrgicos de São Paulo," 168.

107. *O Metalúrgico*, February 1949; "Annual Labor Report for 1949," 8 May 1950, SP Post 560, RG 84, NA; Simões Paes, "O Sindicato dos Metalúrgicos de São Paulo," 176–77.

108. Arquivo de Instituto Brasileiro de Opinião Pública e Estatística (hereinafter IBOPE), *Pesquisas Especiais*, vol. 7, "Pesquisa sobre a Matriz Política— Setembro de 1948."

109. Arquivo de IBOPE, "Pesquisa—São Paulo," October 1948. Interestingly, in a study conducted in December 1948, only 1 percent of Paulistanos of all social classes polled said they would consider supporting the PCB in elections. This extremely low number no doubt reflects some fear of supporting an illegal political party, but it also demonstrates the unpopularity of the PCB's electoral alliance with Adhemar de Barros; see Arquivo de IBOPE, "Pesquisa— São Paulo," December 1948.

110. José Soares Maciel Filho to Getúlio Vargas, Rio de Janeiro, 27 April 1948, AGV 48.04.27, FGV, CPDOC. On Maciel Filho's relationship with Vargas in the 1930s and 1940s see Conniff, *Urban Politics in Brazil*, 155, 157.

111. Francisco Campos had advised Vargas in 1945 that he would have to run against his own administration if he hoped to stay in office; see Conniff, *Urban Politics in Brazil*, 169.

112. Quoted in Valter Krausche, *Adoniran Barbosa: Pelas Ruas da Cidade* (São Paulo: Brasiliense, 1985), 34–47. Transcripts of many radio shows are available

in São Paulo's Museu Adoniran Barbosa. On the importance of the Rua Direita to the city's black population see George Reid Andrews, *Blacks and Whites in São Paulo, Brazil, 1888–1988* (Madison: University of Wisconsin Press, 1991), 179–80.

113. All the workers interviewed for this study recalled listening to popular radio shows with family and friends. On radio and popular culture see José Ramos Tinhoro, *Música Popular—do Gramofone ao Rádio e TV* (São Paulo: Ática, 1981), 57–63; and John D. French, "The Communications Revolution: Radio and Working-Class Life and Culture in Postwar São Paulo, Brazil" (Paper presented to the Third Yale Latin American Labor History Conference, April 1986).

6 Factory Commissions and the Triumph of São Paulo's Working-Class Movement

1. *U.S. News and World Report*, 10 August 1951.

2. Thomas E. Skidmore provides a comprehensive analysis of the competing ideologies and interest groups with which Vargas contended during the early 1950s; see his *Politics in Brazil, 1930–1964: An Experiment in Democracy* (New York: Oxford University Press, 1967), 81–142.

3. Even the U.S. media noted this expansion. See *Time*, 21 January 1952; *U.S. News and World Report*, 10 August 1951; P. J. L. Lebret, "Sondagem Preliminar a um Estudo sobre a Habitação em São Paulo," *RAM* 139 (April–May 1951): 7–52; Antoine Bon et al., *Brasil: 217 Photographies de A. Bon, M. Gautherot, P. Verger* (Paris: Agir, 1952), 33–35; George Rado and Peter Scheier, *São Paulo: Fastest Growing City in the World* (Netherlands: Kosmos, 1954), 22–23.

4. "Labor Conditions for the São Paulo Consular District for July 1950," 8 August 1950, SP Post 560, RG 84, NA; "Labor Conditions for the São Paulo Consular District for September 1950," 14 October 1950, SP Post 560, RG 84, NA; Institute of Inter-American Affairs, *Brazilian Technical Studies* (Washington, D.C.: Government Printing Office, 1955), 371–72.

5. Other leading industrial centers had similarly large populations in 1950: Chicago, 3.1 million; Detroit, 1.8 million; Philadelphia, 2 million; and Birmingham, England, 1.1 million.

6. Wage and price data are sketchy for this period. U.S. consular officers noted that wages for industrial workers failed to keep pace with prices in 1949 and 1950; see "Annual Labor Report on Labor Conditions in São Paulo, 1949," 8 May 1950, SP Post 560, RG 84, NA; "Annual Report on Labor Conditions in São Paulo, 1950," 18 January 1951, SP Post 560, RG 84, NA. Maria Simões Paes, "O Sindicato dos Metalúrgicos de São Paulo, 1932–1951" (Tese de mestrado, Universidade de São Paulo, 1979), 160; "Labor Conditions in the São Paulo Consular District," January 1950, 8 February 1950, SP Post 560, RG 84, NA;

"Labor Conditions in the São Paulo Consular District," November 1950, 13 December 1950, SP Post 560, RG 84, NA.

7. "Labor Conditions in the São Paulo Consular District," October 1950, 16 November 1950, SP Post 560, RG 84, NA; "Annual Report on Labor Conditions in São Paulo, 1950," 18 January 1951, SP Post 560, RG 84, NA.

8. Quoted in Skidmore, *Politics in Brazil,* 52.

9. Quoted in ibid., 79. As we have seen, Vargas was able to run against the government in Rio by the late 1940s. For more on Vargas's political strategy see Maria Celina Soares D'Araújo, *O Segundo Governo Vargas, 1951–1954: Democracia, Partidos, e Crise Política* (Rio de Janeiro: Zahar, 1982), 37–68.

10. Arquivo de IBOPE, *Pesquisas Especiais,* vol. 9, São Paulo, 6–15 September 1950; and *Pesquisas Especiais,* vol. 9, Rio de Janeiro, September 1950.

11. On the 1950 election see Skidmore, *Politics in Brazil,* 73–80; and John W. F. Dulles, *Vargas of Brazil: A Political Biography* (Austin: University of Texas Press, 1967), 292–99.

12. For a list of the industrialists who helped to fund the campaign see AGV 50.08.09.00/52, CPDOC, FGV; see also AGV 48.11.30/2, CPDOC, FGV.

13. Interview, Hermínia Lorenzi dos Santos, São Paulo, S.P., 12 August 1987; interview, Glória Salviano, São Paulo, S.P., 14 August 1987; "Labor Conditions in the São Paulo Consular District," October 1950, 17 November 1950, SP Post 560, RG 84, NA.

14. Interview, Hermento Mendes Dantas, São Paulo, S.P., 14 September 1987; "Labor Conditions in the São Paulo Consular District," November 1950, 13 December 1950, SP Post 560, RG 84, NA; "Labor Conditions in the São Paulo Consular District," December 1950, 23 January 1951, SP Post 560, RG 84, NA; Sindicato dos Metalúrgico de São Paulo (hereinafter SMSP), Assembléia Geral, 24 March 1950; *O Metalúrgico,* June 1950.

15. That is, the textile workers would have to have paid their dues in addition to the imposto sindical, and they would have to be registered with the Ministry of Labor in Rio as fully sindicalizado/a.

16. "Labor Conditions in the São Paulo Consular District," October 1950, 17 November 1950, SP Post 560, RG 84, NA; Márcia Mendes de Almeida, "O Sindicato dos Têxteis em São Paulo: História, 1933–1957" (Tese de mestrado, Universidade de São Paulo, 1981), 241.

17. STIFTSP, Reuniões de Diretoria, 16 November, 5 December 1950, 3 April 1951; "Labor Conditions in the São Paulo Consular District," First Quarter 1951, 26 April 1951, SP Post 560, RG 84, NA; interview, Luís Firmino de Lima, São Paulo, S.P., 1 September 1987; interview, Enrique de Lima, São Paulo, S.P., 2 September 1987.

18. *Conjunctura Econômico* (December 1949): 37.

19. Interview, Glória Salviano, São Paulo, S.P., 14 August 1987; interview, Hermínia Lorenzi dos Santos, São Paulo, S.P., 12 August 1987.

20. Interview, Irene de Oliveira, São Paulo, S.P., 11 August 1987.

21. Interview, Luís Firmino de Lima, São Paulo, S.P., 1 September 1987; interview, Enrique de Lima, São Paulo, S.P., 2 September 1987; interview, Diolinda Nascimento, São Paulo, S.P., 2 September 1987. Strikes waged by the factory commissions are discussed below.

22. *O Metalúrgico*, June 1950, February–March 1951. Once again, only those members of the union who had been sindicalizado/a for more than two years were eligible to vote.

23. Interview, Hermento Mendes Dantas, São Paulo, S.P., 14 September 1987; interview, Roberto Unger, Osasco, S.P., 23 September 1987; interview, Conrado de Papa, Osasco, S.P., 23 September 1987. See also Simões Paes, "O Sindicato dos Metalúrgicos de São Paulo," 177.

24. *O Metalúrgico*, June 1951; SMSP Assembléias Gerais, 28 March, 5 October 1952.

25. *O Metalúrgico*, June 1951.

26. SMSP Assembléia Geral, 30 December 1951.

27. These activities are described below. Maria Andréa Loyola identifies a similar group of unionists in Juiz de Fora in the early 1950s; see her *Os Sindicatos e o PTB: Estudo de um Caso em Minas Gerais* (Petrópolis: CEBRAP/Vozes, 1980), 65–73. José Sérgio Leite Lopes, in *A Tecelagem dos Conflitos de Classe na Cidade das Chaminés* (São Paulo: Universidade de Brasília/Marco Zero, 1988), 300–325, describes how politics in Pernambuco created an opening for such moderates in the early 1940s. On such moderates in the São Paulo Shoemakers' Union see chapter 4 in this volume. John D. French discusses what he terms the "labor Center" in Santo André in 1945 and 1946 but fails to provide much evidence of this group's ties to the rank and file. Indeed, he cites Loyola's discussion of Juiz de Fora in the early 1950s and Leite Lopes's Pernambuco study in the early 1940s as evidence of the existence of this "labor Center" in Santo André in 1945; see French, *The Brazilian Workers' ABC: Class Conflict and Alliances in Modern São Paulo* (Chapel Hill: University of North Carolina Press, 1992), 144–46.

28. Interview, Roberto Unger, Osasco, S.P., 23 September 1987.

29. Interview, Conrado de Papa, Osasco, S.P., 23 September 1987.

30. Interview, Hermento Mendes Dantas, São Paulo, S.P., 14 September 1987; interview, Conrado de Papa, Osasco, S.P., 23 September 1987; interview, Roberto Unger, Osasco, S.P., 23 September 1987.

31. Quoted in Timothy F. Harding, "The Political History of Organized Labor in Brazil" (Ph.D. diss., Stanford University, 1973), 243. This period witnessed the ascension of reformist and independent (i.e., from the PTB and PCB) labor leadership; see Robert J. Alexander, "Brazilian 'Tenentismo,'" *HAHR* 36.2 (May 1956): 240.

32. São Paulo to Rio, 8 May 1951, SP Post 560, RG 84, NA; "Labor Conditions for the São Paulo Consular District for the Second Quarter of 1951," 19 July 1951, RG 89, NA. On the formal transfer and the end of seventeen years of Paulista control of the federal industrial relations system in

São Paulo, see telegram, Lucas Nogueira Garcez (governor of São Paulo) to Getúlio Vargas, 27 July 1951, AGV 51.07.27/1, CPDOC, FGV.

33. Getúlio Vargas, *O Governo Trabalhista do Brasil*, 4 vols. (Rio de Janeiro: José Olympio, 1952–69), 1:322, 324.

34. Ibid., 1:326.

35. Promises of a family wage (i.e., a wage high enough so that the male head of a household could support his wife and children without them also working outside the home) had been a component of Vargas's initial Estado Novo ideology; see chapter 3 in this volume.

36. Interview, Odette Pasquini, São Paulo, S.P., 17 September 1987.

37. "Labor Conditions in the São Paulo Consular District for the Second Quarter of 1951," 19 July 1951, SP Post 560, RG 84, NA; interview, Hermínia Lorenzi dos Santos, São Paulo, S.P., 12 August 1987; interview, Glória Salviano, São Paulo, S.P., 14 August 1987; interview, Conrado de Papa, Osasco, S.P., 23 September 1987.

38. Interview, Diolinda Nascimento, São Paulo, S.P., 2 September 1987; see also FIESP, *Relatório*, 1951, 1:86; *U.S. News and World Report*, 10 August 1951. The key point is that mill owners thought there was a shortage of labor, even though São Paulo's population swelled with migrants from Brazil's northeast in the 1950s. This is a good example of how labor markets are segmented (i.e., mill owners did not yet want to employ *nordestinos*, just as they had once excluded black Paulistanos) and how fears of perceived shortages skew markets for labor and goods.

39. "Labor Conditions in the São Paulo Consular District for the Third Quarter of 1951," 5 October 1951, SP Post 560, RG 84, NA; Lourival Fontes to Lucas Nogueira Garcez, AGV 51.07.28/1, CPDOC, FGV.

40. Interview, David Carneiro, São Paulo, S.P., 24 September 1987; interview, Hermento Mendes Dantas, São Paulo, S.P., 14 September 1987.

41. FIESP, *Relatório*, 1951, 3:247–48; *Folha da Manhã*, 18 December 1951; "Labor Conditions in the São Paulo Consular District for the Fourth Quarter of 1951," 4 January 1952, SP Post 560, RG 84, NA; interviews, Edson Borges and Waldemar Lima, São Paulo, S.P., 25 September 1987.

42. *Folha da Manhã*, 18, 21, and 27 December 1951; *O Metalúrgico*, December 1951; "Labor Conditions in the São Paulo Consular District for the Fourth Quarter of 1951," 4 January 1951, SP Post 560, RG 84, NA.

43. "Labor Conditions in the São Paulo Consular District for the First Quarter of 1952," 24 May 1952, SP Post 560, RG 84, NA. This same report erroneously claimed that the strike movement was supported only by a minority of the rank and file.

44. Interview, João Bonifácio, São Paulo, S.P., 3 September 1987; interview, Luís Firmino de Lima, São Paulo, S.P., 7 August 1987; interview, Odette Pasquini, São Paulo, S.P., 17 September 1987; SIFTG, *Circular* 3341, 17 January 1952.

45. *Folha da Manhã,* 18–20 December 1951; SIFTG, *Circular* 3341, 17 January 1952; interview, Maria Pavone, São Paulo, S.P., 12 August 1987; interview, Laura Machado, Osasco, S.P., 8 September 1987; interview, Angela Neto, São Paulo, S.P., 8 August 1987.

46. For an analysis of the real value of the minimum wage from the 1940s through the 1980s, see Endo and Esvael do Carmo, *Breve Histórico do Índice de Preços ao Consumidor no Município de São Paulo,* 17. The increase in São Paulo was to Cr$1,190 per month. See also memo from Diretor Serviço de Estatística da Previdência e Trabalho to Presidente da Comissão de Salário Mínimo, 15 June 1951; and Despacho do MTIC, 26 September 1951, both in AGV 51.09.26/2, CPDOC, FGV.

47. *Folha da Manhã,* 25 December 1951. For examples of lobbying and Vargas's intelligence reports on labor in São Paulo, see Wladimar de Toledo Piza (S.P.) to Vargas, 14 April 1951, AGV 51.04.14/2, CPDOC, FGV; and José de Segadas Vianna to Lourival Fontes (read by Vargas), 20 December 1951, AGV 51.12.20/1, CPDOC, FGV.

48. Scholars have tended to miss this shift in Vargas's relationship with the working class, instead arguing that Vargas's years as an elected president in the 1950s witnessed a deepening of paternalistic "populist" politics. For examples of this view see Soares D'Araújo, *O Segundo Governo Vargas,* 48–50; Dulles, *Vargas of Brazil,* 306–7; Kenneth Paul Erickson, *The Brazilian Corporative State and Working-Class Politics* (Berkeley: University of California Press, 1977), 49–60; and Harding, "The Political History of Organized Labor in Brazil," 247–50.

49. *Folha da Manhã,* 21 and 25 December 1951; SIFTG, *Circular* 3342, 18 January 1952; interview, João Bonifácio, São Paulo, S.P., 10 August 1987; interview, Hermínia Lorenzi dos Santos, São Paulo, S.P., 12 August 1987.

50. SENAI report, "Distribution of Industry and Labor in the State and City of São Paulo," translated and reproduced in memo, 26 September 1951, SP Post 560, RG 84, NA.

51. As we have seen, there were important divisions between young communist activists who concentrated their energies on union and work issues (i.e., the syndicalist members of the party) and the PCB leadership, which remained out of touch with working-class issues. On the PCB's alienation from the working class (e.g., its attempts in the 1940s and 1950s to build ties to "progressive" segments of the national bourgeoisie for "national unity" and electoral gains), see Leôncio Basbaum, *História Sincera da República de 1930 a 1960,* 4th ed. (São Paulo: Alfa-Omega, 1976), 182–85; Ronald Chilcote, *The Brazilian Communist Party: Conflict and Integration, 1922–1972* (New York: Oxford University Press, 1974), 55–56; Mendes de Almeida, "O Sindicato dos Têxteis em São Paulo," 204–6; see also chapter 5 in this volume.

52. Interview, Hermento Mendes Dantas, São Paulo, S.P., 14 September 1987; interview, Roberto Unger, Osasco, S.P., 23 September 1987; interview, Carlos Heubel Sobrinho, Osasco, S.P., 23 September 1987; interview, João

Bonifácio, São Paulo, S.P., 10 August 1987; interview, Hermínia Lorenzi dos Santos, São Paulo, S.P., 12 August 1987.

53. STIFTSP, Assembléia Geral, 16 December 1951; interview, João Bonifácio, São Paulo, S.P., 10 August 1987; interview, Hermínia Lorenzi dos Santos, São Paulo, S.P., 12 August 1987; Mendes de Almeida, "O Sindicato dos Têxteis em São Paulo," 224–25.

54. Interview, Maria Pavone, São Paulo, S.P., 12 August 1987; see also Mendes de Almeida, "O Sindicato dos Têxteis em São Paulo," 224–25.

55. Interview, Hermento Mendes Dantas, São Paulo, S.P., 14 September 1987; interview, Conrado de Papa, Osasco, S.P., 23 September 1987; interview, Roberto Unger, Osasco, S.P., 23 September 1987; interview, Carlos Heubel Sobrinho, Osasco, S.P., 23 September 1987.

56. Interview, José Antônio de Mendes, São Paulo, S.P., 25 May 1987.

57. Interview, Conrado de Papa, Osasco, S.P., 23 September 1987; interview, Francisco Pinto Silva, São Paulo, S.P., 25 September 1987; O Metalúrgico, February 1952; "Labor Conditions in the São Paulo Consular District for the First Quarter of 1952," 24 May 1952, RG 84, NA. Employers often delayed paying increases they had agreed to during strike negotiations.

58. Folha da Manhã, 6, 9, 10, and 12 February 1952; "Labor Conditions in the São Paulo Consular District for the First Quarter of 1952," 24 May 1952, RG 84, NA. Indeed, Teixeira's working relationship with the city's textile industrialists, which was forged during the 1930s and 1940s, smoothed the way for the union's reformers. As late as September 1952, Humberto Reis Costa wrote to the Serviço Social de Indústria that the Textile Workers' Union was "one of the few sindicatos that is always at our disposal with good will and the desire to unite" (in possession of Barbara Weinstein). My thanks to Barbara Weinstein for the text of this letter.

59. "Labor Conditions in the São Paulo Consular District for the First Quarter of 1952," 24 May 1952, RG 84, NA.

60. For labor reporting from São Paulo that Vargas read, see Cyro Riopardense Rezende, Chefe de Polícia, DFSP, to Ministry of Labor, 13 February 1952, AGV 52.02.13, Confid., CPDOC, FGV; and José Segadas Vianna to Lourival Fontes, 7 April 1952, AGV 52.04.07/1, CPDOC, FGV. For a careful analysis of Vargas's complex and shifting relations among his enemies and allies at this time see Skidmore, Politics in Brazil, 100–112. A poll conducted by the IBOPE for Última Hora found that Brazil's working class (including workers interviewed in São Paulo, Campinas, and Riberão Preto) supported and trusted Vargas more than any other politician; see IBOPE, Pesquisas Especiais, vol. 11, May–June 1952.

61. Quoted in Harding, "The Political History of Organized Labor in Brazil," 251.

62. Última Hora, 8 October 1952.

63. *O Metalúrgico,* August 1952; Mendes de Almeida, "O Sindicato dos Têxteis em São Paulo," 201.

64. At the same time he was criticizing pelegos, Vargas pushed for the implementation of the long-forgotten profit-sharing provisions in the 1946 Constitution, improved government inspection of factories, and an increase in social services for workers. For details of these measures see FIESP, *Relatório,* 1952, 4:5–48; and "Labor Conditions in the São Paulo Consular District for the Second Quarter of 1952," 1 August 1952, SP Post 560, RG 84, NA.

65. STIFTSP, Assembléia Geral, 27 January 1952; interview, Luís Firmino de Lima, São Paulo, S.P., 1 September 1987.

66. STIFTSP, Assembléia Geral, 26 August 1952; interviews, Luís Firmino de Lima, São Paulo, S.P., 7 August and 1 September 1987; see also Mendes de Almeida, "O Sindicato dos Têxteis em São Paulo," 240–43.

67. STIFTSP, Reunião de Diretoria, 9 December 1952; *Última Hora,* 9 January 1953; interview, Luís Firmino de Lima, São Paulo, S.P., 7 August 1987; interview, João Bonifácio, São Paulo, S.P., 3 September 1987.

68. The 1953 union elections are discussed below.

69. See Werner Baer, *The Brazilian Economy: Growth and Development,* 2d ed. (New York: Praeger, 1983), 68; and Skidmore, *Politics in Brazil,* 91–97.

70. Arquivo de SENAI, SENAI and the Institute of Inter-American Affairs, "Estado de Indústria Têxtil e Necessidades de Treinamento," 1953, 25–26; ECLA, *Labor Productivity of the Cotton Textile Industry in Five Latin American Countries* (New York: UN Department of Economic Affairs, 1951), 17–20; Estanislau Fischlowitz, "Man-power Problems in Brazil," *International Labour Review* 79.4 (April 1959): 398–405; and Flávio Rabelo Versiani, "Technical Change, Equipment Replacement, and Labor Absorption: The Case of the Brazilian Textile Industry" (Ph.D. diss., Vanderbilt University, 1971), 105–30.

71. Interview, João Bonifácio, São Paulo, S.P., 3 September 1987; interview, Luís Firmino de Lima, São Paulo, S.P., 1 September 1987.

72. Interview, Diolinda Nascimento, São Paulo, S.P., 2 September 1987.

73. Interview, João Bonifácio, São Paulo, S.P., 3 September 1987; interview, Luís Firmino de Lima, São Paulo, S.P., 1 September 1987; interview, Irene de Oliveira, São Paulo, S.P., 11 August 1987; interview, Assumpta Bianchi, São Paulo, S.P., 10 August 1987; see also Mendes de Almeida, "O Sindicato dos Têxteis em São Paulo," 163–64, 185. One reliable estimate by a prolabor statistical agency put the increase in the cost of living from 1948 to 1953 at 62 percent; see Arquivo do DIEESE, "Inflação," 1957, GCN-68.

74. SIFTG, *Circular* 3441, 24 November 1952; *O Metalúrgico,* December 1952.

75. *O Estado de São Paulo,* 5 December 1952; *A Gazeta,* 5 December 1952; *Folha da Manhã,* 7, 10, and 11 March 1952; SIFTG, *Circulares* 3394, 22 July 1952; 3395, 25 July 1952; 3485, 31 March 1953; 3486, 31 March 1953; FIESP Reunião Semanal, 18 March 1953.

76. Scholars of this period have pointed out that the power shortages helped to bring on the strike, but they fail to note how rationing of electricity unintentionally aided the rationalization program for the mills; see, for example, José Álvaro Moisés, *Greve de Massa a Crise Política: Estudo da Greve dos 300 Mil em São Paulo, 1953–1954* (São Paulo: Polis, 1978); and Harding, "The Political History of Organized Labor in Brazil," 257–61.

77. Interview, Conrado de Papa, Osasco, S.P., 23 September 1987.

78. Ibid.; interview, Hermento Mendes Dantas, São Paulo, S.P., 14 September 1987; interview, João Bonifácio, São Paulo, S.P., 3 September 1987; interview, Luís Firmino de Lima, São Paulo, S.P., 1 September 1987.

79. *Imprensa Popular*, 5, 11, 12, 13, and 19 March 1953. Throughout March, reports of international reactions to Stalin's death received greater coverage than the unfolding worker unrest in São Paulo. Moisés has interpreted the work of syndicalist members of the PCB, such as Luís Firmino, as evidence that the partidão played a leading role in the strike; see *Greve de Massa*, 123–52; and "Brazil: New Questions on 'The Strike of the 300 Thousand' in São Paulo (1953)" (Paper presented at the Workshop on "Urban Working-Class Culture and Social Protest in Latin America," Woodrow Wilson International Center for Scholars, Washington, D.C., 1978), 13, 30–34.

80. Interview, Maria Pavone, São Paulo, S.P., 12 August 1987; interview, João Bonifácio, São Paulo, S.P., 10 August 1987; interview, Hermínia Lorenzi dos Santos, São Paulo, S.P., 12 August 1987; SIT⁻G, *Circulares* 3471, 22 January 1953; 3476, 20 February 1953.

81. *Folha da Manhã*, 11 March 1953; interview, João Bonifácio, São Paulo, S.P., 10 August 1987; interview, Hermínia Lorenzi dos Santos, São Paulo, S.P., 12 August 1987; interview, Maria Pavone, São Paulo, S.P., 12 August 1987.

82. Interview, Diolinda Nascimento, São Paulo, S.P., 2 September 1987; *Folha da Manhã*, 19 March 1953.

83. *Folha da Manhã*, 26 and 27 March 1953; telegram, São Paulo to Rio, 20 March 1953, SP Post 560.2, RG 84, NA; interview, Conrado de Papa, Osasco, S.P., 23 September 1987; interview, Diolinda Nascimento, São Paulo, S.P., 2 September 1953. The Textile Workers' Union is still headquartered in Brás, the Metalworkers' Union in the centro. These sources also seem to indicate that while the union directorates participated in the strikes, they initially opposed the walkouts.

84. *Folha da Manhã*, 27 and 28 March 1953; interview, Luís Firmino de Lima, São Paulo, S.P., 7 August 1987; interview, Antônio Ciaveletto, São Paulo, S.P., 3 September 1987; interview, Hermínia Lorenzi dos Santos, São Paulo, S.P., 12 August 1987; interview, Maria Pavone, São Paulo, S.P., 12 August 1987.

85. *Folha da Manhã*, 31 March, 2 April 1953; telegram, São Paulo to Rio, 31 March 1953, Rio Post 560.2, RG 84, NA. Bank workers and printers do not seem to have formally struck for higher wages at this time.

86. Telegram, São Paulo to Rio, 31 March 1953 (afternoon), Rio Post 560.2,

RG 84, NA; see also *Folha da Manhã*, 31 March 1953. See *Folha da Manhã*, 2 April 1953, for details of a police raid on the headquarters of the State Commission for the Fight Against Food Shortages.

87. *Folha da Manhã*, 26, 29, and 31 March, 1, 7, and 8 April 1953. In a peculiar assertion, John D. French claims that "the ultimate success of the 'strike of the 300,000' . . . flowed from the actions of the federal government of the populist Getúlio Vargas and his controversial Labor Minister João (Jango) Goulart. . . . Vargas sanctioned Goulart's initiatives to bring about a settlement by São Paulo's Regional Labor Tribunal favorable to the workers" ("Workers and the Rise of Adhemarista Populism in São Paulo, 1945–1947," *HAHR* 68.1 [February 1988]: 39). Apart from neglecting the rank and file's—especially women textile workers'—accomplishments in launching this grass-roots general strike, and misinterpreting the role of the Ministry of Labor in the strike, French's argument ignores the fact that Goulart did not become the minister of labor in Brazil until 15 June 1953, about three months after the end of the strike.

88. *Folha da Manhã*, 29 March, 1 April 1953; interview, Luís Firmino de Lima, São Paulo, S.P., 7 August 1987; interview, Antônio Ciaveletto, São Paulo, S.P., 3 September 1987; interview, Hermínia Lorenzi dos Santos, São Paulo, S.P., 12 August 1987. See also Segadas Vianna's comments about how he opposed the way these strikers avoided the formal industrial relations system and thus did not want to negotiate with them, in Valentina da Rocha Lima, ed., *Getúlio: Uma História Oral* (Rio de Janeiro: Record, 1986), 179–80.

89. *Folha da Manhã*, 3, 4, and 7 April 1953; interview, Luís Firmino de Lima, São Paulo, S.P., 7 August 1987. Because the *bancários* and *gráficos* were not formally on strike, they did not join the PUI at this time. Still, printers negotiated a 75 percent increase on their 1949 wages; see Jover Telles, *O Movimento Sindical no Brasil*, 2d ed. (São Paulo: Ciênicas Humanas, 1981), 54–55.

90. FIESP Reunião Semanal, 8 April 1953. It is interesting to see how São Paulo's industrialists had become captives of their own rhetoric. As recently as the mid-1940s, the FIESP had planted stories in the press to blame Communists and outside agitators for strikes they admitted were based in workers' needs for higher salaries. By April 1953, these industrialists were embracing as truth the very rhetoric they had created.

91. FIESP Reunião Semanal, 8 April 1953.

92. *Folha da Manhã*, 10 April 1953; STIFTSP, Reunião de Diretoria, 9 April 1953.

93. Interview, Hermínia Lorenzi dos Santos, São Paulo, S.P., 12 August 1987; interview, Maria Pavone, São Paulo, S.P., 12 August 1987.

94. *Folha da Manhã*, 11, 12, 14, 15, 16, 17, and 18 April 1953; interview, Conrado de Papa, Osasco, S.P., 23 September 1987; interview, João Bonifácio, São Paulo, S.P., 3 September, 1987.

95. *Diário de São Paulo*, 18 April 1953.

96. *Folha da Manhã,* 19, 21, 22, and 23 April 1953; *Folha da Tarde,* 20 April 1953; *O Estado de São Paulo,* 24 April 1953; *Última Hora,* 24 April 1953; interview, Luís Firmino de Lima, São Paulo, S.P., 7 August 1987.

97. FIESP, *Relatório,* 1946, 3:51; *Relatório,* 1948, 2:175–76; FIESP Reunião Semanal, 20 April 1948.

98. *Folha da Manhã,* 3 May 1953.

99. Harding, "The Political History of Organized Labor in Brazil," 264–76.

100. FIESP, *Relatório,* 1953, 5:4–7, 13; FIESP Reunião Semanal, 23 September 1953; interview, Luís Firmino de Lima, São Paulo, S.P., 7 August 1987; interview, Assumpta Bianchi, São Paulo, S.P., 10 August 1987; interview, Roberto Unger, Osasco, S.P., 23 September 1987.

101. "Labor Conditions in the São Paulo Consular District for the Second Quarter of 1953," 5 August 1953, RG 84, NA. Indeed, throughout Brazil workers increasingly called upon the CLT to force employers to change work conditions and provide wages that at least kept pace with inflation. The return of Vargas to the presidency, this time as a populist, enabled workers and their unions to use the federal labor ministry to their advantage in local struggles; see Telles, *O Movimento Sindical no Brasil,* 42–52; José Sérgio Leite Lopes, *A Tecelagem dos Conflitos de Classe na Cidade das Chaminés* (São Paulo: Marco Zero/ Universidade de Brasília, 1988), 328–408; and Loyola, *Os Sindicatos e o PTB,* 65–73.

102. No reliable statistics on union membership were uncovered for this period, but interviews and other sources indicate that the growth in union membership was substantial in the months after the strike; indeed, my sources estimate that both unions had well over ten thousand members in the mid-1950s; see João Amazonas, "Mass Strikes as a Weapon of Struggle," *World Trade Union Movement* 15 (August 1953): 23–24; interview, João Bonifácio, São Paulo, S.P., 3 September 1987; interview, Hermento Mendes Dantas, São Paulo, S.P., 14 September 1987.

103. *O Metalúrgico,* May 1953; *Última Hora,* 15 July 1953; interview, João Bonifácio, São Paulo, S.P., 3 September 1987; interview, Conrado de Papa, Osasco, S.P., 23 September 1987.

104. STIFTSP, Reuniões de Diretoria, 9 May, 18 June, 13 July 1953; interview, Luís Firmino de Lima, São Paulo, S.P., 7 August 1987; see also Robert J. Alexander, "General Impressions of Labor-Management Relations in São Paulo," 28 April 1956, Alexander Papers, Rutgers University, Coll. 1957, Box 6; and Alexander, "Brazilian 'Tenentismo,'" 240.

105. *O Metalúrgico,* July, October, December 1953; *Diário de São Paulo,* 13 December 1953.

106. SIFTG, *Circulares* 3620, 29 March 1954; 3625, 13 April 1954.

107. Skidmore, *Politics in Brazil,* 127–32; Harding, "The Political History of Organized Labor in Brazil," 267–69. A dockworkers' strike in Rio in late 1953 no doubt influenced Goulart as well; see Dennis Linhares Barsted, *Medição de*

Forças: O Movimento Grevista de 1953 e a Época do Operários Navais (Rio de Janeiro: Zahar, 1982).

108. For the complete May Day speech see *Folha da Manhã*, 2 May 1954. The quote is from Skidmore, *Politics in Brazil*, 133.

109. See Skidmore, *Politics in Brazil*, 131–42; and Soares D'Araújo, *O Segundo Governo Vargas*, 113–26, for details of the political pressures that led to Vargas's suicide.

110. CMS, "A Morte de Getúlio Vargas," interviews with unionists Alfonso Delillis, Luís Tenório de Lima, Adolfo Perchon, Antônio Chamorro, and José Albertino de Costa Filho, pp. 3–4, 6–7, 18, 32–35; *Folha da Manhã*, 1, 2, and 3 September 1954; *Folha da Noite*, 2 and 3 September 1954; *Diário Popular*, 3 September 1954; *Última Hora*, 31 September 1954; SIFTG, *Circular 3696*, 12 November 1954; FIESP, *Relatório*, 1954, 1:9–13.

111. Harding, "The Political History of Organized Labor in Brazil," 280–87; Mendes de Almeida, "O Sindicato dos Têxteis em São Paulo," 201.

112. Arquivo do DIEESE, unnumbered letter from Nicolau Torloni to Luís Cardia, 15 December 1953; interview, Ernesto Mendes Dantas, São Paulo, S.P., 14 September 1987.

113. Arquivo do DIEESE, DIE, unnumbered letter to Bancários, 21 October 1955; DIE, 0.5.4, Report on Executive Meeting, 22 December 1955.

114. Early DIEESE studies included analyses of unemployment, wage levels by sex, skill levels, where workers bought food, housing, transportation, etc.; see Arquivo do DIEESE, PLS-07, PLS-05, PLS-02, PLS-01, MRT-5, GCN-68.

115. Interview, Hermento Mendes Dantas, São Paulo, S.P., 14 September 1987; interview, Luís Firmino de Lima, São Paulo, S.P., 7 August 1987.

116. Interview, Hermínia Lorenzi dos Santos, São Paulo, S.P., 12 August 1987; interview, Hermento Mendes Dantas, São Paulo, S.P., 14 September 1987.

117. The DIEESE continued to represent workers' interests during the 1964–85 military dictatorship. Indeed, in 1973 the World Bank publicly backed the DIEESE's statistics that revealed a higher rate of inflation for Brazil than the military regime had claimed. During the late 1970s and the 1980s, the PT's unions relied heavily on DIEESE research to bargain for increased wages. See Margaret E. Keck, *The Workers' Party and Democratization in Brazil* (New Haven: Yale University Press, 1991), 63–64, 75.

Epilogue: From Union Democracy to Democratic Politics?

1. "Report on Brazilian Labor Laws and Work," 20 September 1955, Rio Post 560, RG 84, NA; *O Trabalhador Têxtil*, November 1956; Robert J. Alexander, "Observations on the São Paulo Textile Union," 24 April 1956, Alexander Papers, Rutgers University, Coll. 1957, Box 6; interview, Carmino Urcioti,

labor relations director, Indústrias Reunidos F. Matarazzo, São Paulo, S.P., April 1956; and interview, José Segadas Viana, former minister of labor, Rio de Janeiro, 16 March 1956, both in Alexander Papers, Rutgers University, Coll. 1956, Box 2.

2. On the unions in the mid-1950s, see interviews with Nivaldo Fonseca, second secretary of the São Paulo Textile Workers' Union, São Paulo, S.P., 20 April 1956; J. M. Moreira de Moraes, secretary of the São Paulo State Textile Industrialists' Association, São Paulo, S.P., 27 April 1956; Júlio Devichiatti, president of the São Paulo Textile Workers' Union, São Paulo, S.P., 27 April 1956; Remo Forli, president of the São Paulo Metalworkers' Union, São Paulo, S.P., 27 August 1959; Edgar Martins, secretary to the secretary general of the São Paulo Metalworkers' Union, São Paulo, S.P., 17 April 1956; and Paulo Corti, ex-official of the São Paulo Metalworkers' Union, São Paulo, S.P., 17 April 1956; all in Alexander Papers, Rutgers University, Coll. 1957, Box 2. These men did not agree on the level of popular participation in their unions or on which political orientation represented the best hope for workers in general, but they all agreed that the unions were more diverse and open than they had been before the mid-1950s.

On Jânio Quadros's rapid rise from mayor of São Paulo to president of Brazil see Thomas E. Skidmore, *Politics in Brazil: An Experiment in Democracy* (New York: Oxford University Press, 1967), 187–89; and Hélio Damante, "O Movimento de 22 de Março de 1953 em São Paulo," *Revista Brasileira de Estudos Políticos* 18 (January 1965): 105–12.

3. In addition to the interviews cited in note 2 above, see also interviews with Francisco Patrício de Oliveira, lawyer for the São Paulo Energy Workers' Union, São Paulo, S.P., 14 April 1956; and José Carlos Graça Wagner, lawyer for the São Paulo State Cosmetic Makers' Union, São Paulo, S.P., 25 April 1956, Alexander Papers, Rutgers University, Coll. 1957, Box 2. Oliveira spoke of his union's desire to develop a shop-floor delegate system. See also Robert J. Alexander, "Brazilian 'Tenentismo,'" *HAHR* 36.2 (May 1956): 240; and Ruth Berins Collier and David Collier, *Shaping the Political Arena: Critical Junctures, the Labor Movement, and Regime Dynamics in Latin America* (Princeton: Princeton University Press, 1991), 549.

4. These self-critiques were a major theme in the mid-1950s. A few of the clearest statements of the PCB's failure to organize among the grassroots can be found in Iracema Ribeiro, "O Trabalho Feminino: Dever de Todo o Partido," *Imprensa Popular,* 19 December 1954; Prestes's address to the party's Fourth Congress in 1954, *Imprensa Popular,* 21 December 1954; Prestes's report to the Central Committee, May 1956, *Imprensa Popular,* 7 June 1956; see also *Imprensa Popular,* 27 March, 3 April 1955.

5. Nicanor do Nascimento, a socialist congressman from Rio in the 1910s and early 1920s, was a constant critic of government labor practices; see John W. F. Dulles, *Anarchists and Communists in Brazil, 1900–1935* (Austin: University of

Texas Press, 1973), 83–84, 90. Pedro Ernesto, the populist mayor of Rio in the 1930s, was a vocal supporter of the city's workers; see Michael L. Conniff, *Urban Politics in Brazil: The Rise of Populism, 1925–1945* (Pittsburgh: University of Pittsburgh Press, 1981), 98–116. Indeed, in the December 1945 elections, which elevated Dutra to the presidency, Luís Carlos Prestes was elected both senator and congressman from Rio; he served as senator until the federal government canceled his and other elected Communists' electoral mandates in January 1948; see John W. F. Dulles, *Vargas of Brazil: A Political Biography* (Austin: University of Texas Press, 1967), 281.

6. Indeed, Collier and Collier (*Shaping the Political Arena*, 360–84) refer to politics at this time as "aborted populism." On the municipal elections in Santo André see John D. French, *The Brazilian Workers' ABC: Class Conflict and Alliances in Modern São Paulo* (Chapel Hill: University of North Carolina Press, 1992), 237–50.

7. For a forceful analysis of the distinction between participating in a competitive electoral system that is loosely labeled "democratic," on the one hand, and the creation of democratic forms of representation and the democratization of civil society, on the other, see Francisco Weffort, *Por que Democracia?* (São Paulo: Brasiliense, 1984), 32–47, 85–99.

8. Indeed, Quadros spoke to an interesting constituency of middle-class voters and some of the poorest Brazilians in the tertiary sector of the economy, and Goulart maintained close ties to many pelegos within the labor federations and confederations. For a detailed and nuanced account of these two men's presidential administrations see Skidmore, *Politics in Brazil*, 187–302.

9. The most complete work on the PT and its role in the transition out of military dictatorship is Margaret E. Keck's *The Workers' Party and Democratization in Brazil* (New Haven: Yale University Press, 1992). Indeed, "New Unionism" developed in the city's industrial suburbs, and we do not yet have a closely documented historical study of the PT's roots in the greater São Paulo area.

10. In her study of working-class memory, Eclea Bosi notes how present conditions served as a lens through which her informants viewed the past; see her *Memória e Sociedade: Lembranças de Velhos*, 2d ed. (São Paulo: T. A. Queiroz, 1987). For a theoretical analysis of the impact of the present on historical memory see The Popular Memory Group, "Popular Memory: Theory, Politics, Method," in *Making Histories: Studies in History-Writing and Politics*, ed. Richard Johnson et al. (London: Hutchinson/University of Birmingham Centre for Contemporary Cultural Studies, 1982), 205–52; and Joan W. Scott, "The Evidence of Experience," *Critical Inquiry* 17.4 (Summer 1991): 773–97.

11. In reviewing the "new social movements" literature Jeffrey W. Rubin points out how a focus on the relationship between these social movements and the state (or between them and employers) tends to highlight those social movements' democratic aspects and obscure their sometimes contentious internal dynamics; see Rubin, "Ambiguity and Contradiction in a Radical Popular

Movement: The Peasant-Worker Alliance in Juchitán, Mexico, 1973–1992" (Paper presented to the Ninth Annual Latin American Labor History Conference, Stony Brook, N.Y., April 1992), 1–12.

12. For a detailed statistical analysis of women's industrial labor in São Paulo, see Eva Alterman Blay, *Trabalho Domesticado: A Mulher na Indústria Paulista* (São Paulo: Ática, 1978), 135–92. All the women interviewed by the author worked in the factories until they retired in their late fifties or sixties.

13. That is, working women's class consciousness did not, as Temma Kaplan has argued, develop out of a "need to preserve life"; see Kaplan, "Female Consciousness and Collective Action: The Case of Barcelona, 1910–1918," *Signs: Journal of Women in Culture and Society* 7.3 (1982): 545–66.

14. Sonia Alvarez has described how middle-class Brazilian women in the mid-1960s "politicized motherhood" by adopting some of the dictatorship's rhetoric about the importance of women as nurturers (a discourse that closely matched that of the Estado Novo) to protest various government policies; see Alvarez, *Engendering Democracy in Brazil: Women's Movements in Transition Politics* (Princeton: Princeton University Press, 1990), 43–56. For an analysis of U.S. women's organizing to protect their families that took on a decidedly conservative perspective see Nancy Maclean, "White Women and Klan Violence in the 1920s: Agency, Complicity, and the Politics of Women's History," *Gender and History* 3.3 (Autumn 1991): 287–303.

15. Because these industries were nationally owned and produced goods primarily for domestic consumption, we should avoid applying a "dependency" perspective to the study of workers in Latin America's largest industrial complex over the course of the first half of the twentieth century. Studies that take some form of dependency theory as their theoretical framework for analyzing Latin American labor history include Hobart A. Spalding, Jr., *Organized Labor in Latin America: Historical Case Studies of Workers in Dependent Societies* (New York: Harper Torchbooks, 1977): and Charles Bergquist, *Labor in Latin America: Comparative Essays on Chile, Argentina, Venezuela, and Colombia* (Stanford: Stanford University Press, 1986).

16. Interview, Edson Borges, São Paulo, S.P., 25 September 1987.

Bibliography

Archives

Alexander Papers, Rutgers University (New Brunswick, N.J.). Collection 1957. These materials were gathered by Robert J. Alexander in Brazil throughout the 1950s.

Arquivo da Federaçao das Indústrias do Estado de São Paulo (FIESP) (São Paulo). Atas de Directoria and Atas das Reuniões Semanais, *Circulares*, and *Relatórios*. The FIESP archive includes typed minutes of weekly meetings from the 1930s, 1940s, and 1950s. All the FIESP's internal communications through its *Circulares* as well as its unpublished *Relatórios* are located in this archive.

Arquivo do Centro dos Industriaes de Fiação e Tecelagem de São Paulo (São Paulo). This archive contains the center's internal and external communications along with its *Circulares*.

Arquivo do Departamento Intersindical de Estatísticas e Estudos Sócio-Econômicos (DIEESE) (São Paulo). This archive contains the internal documents on the DIEESE's founding, along with copies of all the studies it has conducted since 1955. Some of the original data collected are also available.

Arquivo do Serviço Nacional de Aprendizagem Industrial (SENAI) (São Paulo). The internal documents on early SENAI activities, as well as studies of factory and labor market conditions, are located in this archive.

Arquivo do Sindicato dos Metalúrgicos de São Paulo (São Paulo). Atas das Assembléias Gerais and Reuniões de Diretoria. This archive contains the reports on the meetings of the union general assemblies and the directorate. The union's records include copies of various publications, including the newspaper *O Metalúrgico*.

Arquivo do Sindicato dos Têxteis de São Paulo (São Paulo). Atas das Assembléias Gerais and Reuniões de Diretoria. Like the archive of the Metalworkers' Union, the Textile Workers' Union archive includes records of meetings. It also contains some processos and various other materials.

Arquivo Nacional do Brasil (Rio de Janeiro). Secretaria de Presedência da República, 1930–47; Interventória de São Paulo (14.21). This archive contains processos filed by individuals, unions, trade associations, and so on. Each file includes original letters and reports made by various government agencies in response.

Arquivos de Instituto Brasileiro de Opinião Pública e Estatística (IBOPE) (Rio de Janeiro and São Paulo). These archives contain original polling data starting in the 1940s.

Fundição Getúlio Vargas, Centro de Pesquisa e Documentação (CPDOC) (Rio de Janeiro). Included are the Arquivo de Getúlio Vargas, the Arquivo de Lindolfo Collor, the Arquivo de Alexandre de Marcondes Filho, and the Arquivo de Waldemar Falcão.

Great Britain, Public Record Office (Microfilms, Banco do Estado de São Paulo BANESPA, São Paulo). Diplomatic records pertaining to Brazil.

United States National Archives (Washington, D.C., and Suitland, Md.). Sources from the National Archives are found in Central Decimal File, Record Group 59, and Post Records, Record Group 84.

Newspapers

Avanti!
O Combate
Correio Paulistano
Diário da Noite
Diário Popular
O Estado de São Paulo
Folha da Manhã
Gazeta de Noticias
Imprensa Popular

O Jornal
A Laterna
O Metalúrgico
O Parafuso
A Platéia
A Plebe
O Trabalhador Têxtil
Última Hora
A Voz do Trabalhador

Bulletins and Other Periodicals

Boletim da Directoria de Indústria e Comércio (BDIC)
Boletim do Departamento Estadual de Estatística (BDEE)
Boletim do Departamento Estadual do Trabalho (BDET)
Boletim do Ministério do Trabalho, Indústria, e Comércio (BMTIC)
Bulletin of the Pan American Union (BPAU)

Conjunctura Econômica
Daily Commerce Reports
Hispanic American Historical Review (HAHR)
Journal of Latin American Studies (JLAS)
Latin American Perspectives (LAP)
Monthly Labor Review
Revista do Arquivo Municipal (RAM)
Revista Industrial de São Paulo (RISP)

Primary Sources

Amaral, R. Pompêo do. "A Alimentação da População Paulistano." *RAM* (May–June 1943): 55–87.

Amazonas, João. "Mass Strikes as a Weapon of Struggle." *World Trade Union Movement* 15 (1–15 August 1953): 20–24.

———. *Pelo Fortalecimento e Unidade Sindical.* Rio de Janeiro: Horizonte, 1945.

Andrade, Celeste Souza. "Migrantes Nacionais no Estado de São Paulo." *Sociologia* 14.2 (May 1952): 111–30.

Andrews, C. C. *Brazil: Its Conditions and Prospects.* New York: D. Appleton, 1887.

Araújo, Oscar E. de. "A Alimentação da Classe Obreira de São Paulo." *RAM* (August 1940): 91–116.

———. "Estatística Predial." *RAM* (March 1935): 7–44.

———. "Habitações Econômicos." *RISP* (December 1945): 55.

———. "Padrão de Vida de Operários em São Paulo." *O Observador Econômico e Financeiro* 6.69 (October 1941): 39–54.

———. "Uma Pesquisa de Padrão de Vida." *RAM*, supplement (1941).

Bandeira Junior, Antônio Francisco. *A Indústria no Estado de São Paulo em 1901.* São Paulo: Diário Oficial, 1901.

Barros, Valêncio de. "São Paulo." *RAM* (October–December 1945): 25–39.

Berman, Albert. "Industrial Labor in Brazil." Washington, D.C.: Office of the Coordinator of Inter-American Affairs, Research Division, 1944.

Bicudo, Virgínia Leone. "Atitudes Raciais de Pretos e Mulatos em São Paulo." *Sociologia* 9.3 (1947): 195–219.

"Big Time in São Paulo." *Fortune,* July 1950.

Bojano, Clemente de. "O Problema do Pescado na Cidade de São Paulo." *RAM* (July 1940): 31–78.

Bon, Antoine, et al. *Brasil: 217 Photographies de A. Bon, M. Gautherot, P. Verger.* Paris: Agir, 1952.

Brasil, Ministério de Agricultura, Indústria, e Comércio. Directoria Geral de Estatística. *Recenseamento do Brasil Realizado em 1 Setembro de 1920.* 4 vols. Rio de Janeiro, 1927.

Brasil, Ministério da Educação. *Outline of Education in Brazil.* Rio de Janeiro: Imprensa Nacional, 1946.

Brasil, Ministério do Trabalho, Indústria, e Comércio. Comissão Executiva Têxtil. *Indústria Têxtil Algodeira.* Rio de Janeiro, 1946.

"Brazil's City of Go-Getters." *Business Week,* 13 July 1957.

British Chamber of Commerce of São Paulo and Southern Brazil. *Report on Brazil's Trade and Industry in 1918, with Special Reference to the State of São Paulo.* São Paulo, 1919.

Bruce, G. J. *Brazil and the Brazilians.* London: Methuen, 1915.

Caldeira, Branca da Cunha. "A Indústria Têxtil Paulista." *Geografia* 1.4 (1935): 50–66.

Caldeira, Nelson Mendes. "Aspectos da Evolução Urbana de São Paulo." *Boletim do Departamento Estadual de Estatística* (June 1939).

——. "O Crescimento de São Paulo." *Economia* 2.19 (December 1940).

Campos, Carlos de. "Mensagem Apresentada ao Congresso Legislativo em 14 de Julho de 1925." São Paulo, 1925.

Cannon, Mary. *Women Workers in Brazil.* U.S. Department of Labor, Women's Bureau, Bulletin no. 206, 1945.

"City of Enterprise." *Time,* 21 January 1952.

Clemenceau, Georges. *South America Today.* London: T. Fisher Unwin, 1911.

Davis, Horace B. "Padrão de Vida dos Operários da Cidade de São Paulo." *RAM* (June 1935): 113–66.

Deursen, Henri Van. "L'Emancipation Industrielle du Brésil. Caractéres et Developpement de l'Industrie dans l'État de São Paulo." *Revue Economique Internationale* 26.2 (August 1934): 275–335.

Dias, Eduardo. *Um Imigrante e a Revolução: Memórias de um Militant Operário, 1934–1951.* São Paulo: Brasiliense, 1983.

Dias, Everardo. *História das Lutas Sociais no Brasil.* São Paulo: Alfa-Omega, 1977.

"Dissolution of the Confederation of Workers of Brazil." *World Trade Union Movement Information Bulletin,* 30 June 1947.

Duarte, Paulo. "Departamento de Cultura: Vida e Morte de Mário de Andrade." *RAM* (January–February 1946): 75–86.

Duncan, Julian S. "Beef and Milk for Urban Brazil." *Inter-American Economic Affairs* 9.1 (Summer 1955): 3–16.

Fischlowitz, Estanislau. "Man-power Problems in Brazil." *International Labour Review* 79.4 (April 1959): 398–417.

Franco, João Evangelista. "O Serviço aos Menores no Estado de São Paulo." *RAM* (September–October 1944): 7–44.

Galarza, Ernesto. *Labor Trends and Social Welfare in Latin America, 1939–1940.* Washington, D.C.: Pan American Union, Division of Labor and Social Information, 1941.

Ginsberg, Aniela Meyer. "Relações Raciais entre Negros e Brancos em São Paulo." *Anhembi* 13.39 (February 1954): 443–64.

Gouveia, Proença de. "A Situação Atual do Abastecimento de Carnes a População de São Paulo." *RAM* (February 1938): 391–400.

Great Britain, Department of Overseas Trade. *Report on the Economic and Financial Conditions of Brazil.* London, 1920–55.

Guttila, Clorinda. "Sobre um *Test* de Alimentação Aplicado às Crianças do Parque Infantil do Ipiranga." *RAM* (March–April 1946): 95–105.

Henry, J. "Developments in Brazilian Labor Organizations since V.J. Day." *Monthly Labor Review* 64.3 (March 1947): 433–42.

Hermann, Lucila. "Características da Evolução do Parque Industrial do Estado de São Paulo." *Revista de Administração* 1.4 (December 1947): 87–114.

——. "Estudo de Desenvolvimento de São Paulo através de Análise de uma Radial—A Estrada do Café (1935)." *RAM* (November–December 1944): 7–44.

—— *Flutuação e Mobilidade de Mão-de-Obra Fabril em São Paulo.* São Paulo: Instituto de Administração, 1948.

"Indústria Mecânica: Fator Essencial do Progresso Manufatureiro do Brasil." *RISP* 11 (October 1945): 23–28.

Instituto de Organização Racional do Trabalho. "Jornada contra o Desperdício nos Transportes." *IDORT* 9, 97–100 (January–April 1940).

——. "Jornada da Habitação Econômica." *RAM* (March–April 1942).

——. "Jornada sobre Alimentação." *IDORT* 10, 116–20 (August–December 1941).

James, Preston E. "Rio de Janeiro and São Paulo." *Geographical Review* (April 1933): 271–98.

Kiehl, Maria. "O Trabalho da Mulher Fora do Lar." *BMTIC* 8, 96 (August 1942).

Kipling, Rudyard. *Brazilian Sketches.* New York: Doubleday, Doran, 1940.

Lanari Junior, Amaro. "A Laminação de Ferro em São Paulo." *RISP* (May 1945): 35.

Last, Gilbert A. *Facts about the State of São Paulo, Brazil.* London: British Chamber of Commerce of São Paulo and Southern Brazil, 1926.

Le Voci, Antonio. "Transporte Coletivo em São Paulo no Ano de 1934." *RAM* (March 1936): 99–107.

Lebret, P. J. L. "Sondagem Preliminar a um Estudo sobre a Habitação em São Paulo." *RAM* (April–May 1951): 7–52.

Linhares, Hermínio. *Contribuição 'a História das Lutas Operárias no Brasil.* São Paulo: Alfa-Omega, 1977.

Lloyd, Reginald. *Twentieth-Century Impression of Brazil: Its History, People, Commerce, Industry, and Resources.* London: Lloyd's Great Britain Publishing Co., 1913.

Lowrie, Samuel Harman. "A Assistência Filantropica da Cidade de São Paulo." Parts 1–3. *RAM* (September 1936): 193–238; (October 1936): 175–211; (November 1936): 23–49.

——. "Elemento Negro no População de São Paulo." *RAM* (June 1938): 5–56.

——. "Origem da População da Cidade de São Paulo e Diferenciação das Classes Sociais." *RAM* (January 1938): 195–21.

——. "Pesquisa de Padrão de Vida das Famílias dos Operários da Limpeza Pública da Municipalidade de São Paulo." *RAM* (October 1938): 183–304.

"Lucros e Perdas nas Indústrias de São Paulo." *Conjuntura Econômica* (April 1948): 8–9.

Luz, Vicentina Ribeiro de. "Habitação Ideal ao Trabalhador Manual." *RAM* (March–April 1943).

Machado, António Alcântara. *Brás, Bexiga, e Barra Funda*. 1927. Reprint. São Paulo: Imprensa Oficial do Estado de São Paulo, 1982.

――――. *Obras*. Volume 1: *Prosa Preparatória, e Cavaquinho e Saxofone*. Rio de Janeiro: Civilização Brasileira, 1983.

――――. *Obras*. Volume 2: *Path Baby e Prosa Turística: O Viajante Europeu e Platino*. Rio de Janeiro: Civilização Brasileira, 1983.

Mallet, Milena. *Almas Desnudas: A Tragédia Sexual da Mulher Brasileira*. Rio de Janeiro: Victor, 1945.

Mange, Roberto. "O SENAI." *RISP* (December 1944): 15–17.

Meireles, Cecília. "Trabalho Feminino no Brasil." *Observador Econômica e Financeira* (July 1939): 93–107.

Melo, Randolfo Homen de. "A Agua em São Paulo." *RAM* (July 1935): 164–66.

"Modernizing Transit in Difficult Terrain." *The American City* (July 1948): 121.

Monbeig, Pierre. "Aspectos Geográficos do Crescimento da Cidade de São Paulo." *Boletim Paulista de Geografia* 16 (March 1954): 3–29.

Mouralis, Louis. *Un Séjour aux Etats-Unis du Brésil*. Paris: Presses Universitaires, 1934.

Neme, Mario. "Um Município Agrícola: Aspectos Sociais e Econômicos da Organização Agraria de Piracicaba." *RAM* (May 1939).

Nogueira, O. Pupo. *A Indústria em Face das Leis do Trabalho*. São Paulo: Salesianas, 1935.

――――. "A Propósito da Modernização de uma Grande Indústria." *RISP* (May 1945): 16–18.

Nogueira, Oracy. "Atitude Desfavoravel de Alguns Anunciantes de São Paulo em Relação ao Empregados de Côr." *Sociologia* 4.4 (October 1942): 328–58.

"Number One Boom City in the Hemisphere." *U.S. News and World Report*, 10 August 1951.

Paiva Pereira, Juvenal. "O Problema Rural." Parts 1–2. *RAM* (April 1938): 325–46; (June 1938): 57–78.

Penteado, Jacob. *Belemzinho, 1910: Retrato de Uma Época*. São Paulo: Martins, 1962.

Pierson, Donald. "Um Estudo Comparativo da Habitação em São Paulo." *RAM* (March–April 1942): 241–54.

――――. "Habitações de São Paulo: Estudo Comparativo." *RAM* (January–February 1942): 199–238.

――――. "Hábitos Alimentares em São Paulo: Estudo Comparativo." *RAM* (September–October 1944): 45–79.

Poblete Troncoso, Moisés. "Labor Movement in Brazil." *Monthly Labor Review* 29.1 (July 1929): 51–61.

Prado, Antonio Arnoni, and Francisco Foot Hardman, eds. *Contos Anarquistas: Antologia da Prosa Libertária no Brasil, 1901–1935*. São Paulo: Brasiliense, 1985.

"O Problema dos Trabalhadores Idosos." *RAM* (July–August 1944).

"Produção de Maquinas." *RISP* (May 1947): 26–34.

Rado, George, and Peter Scheier. *São Paulo: Fastest Growing City in the World.* Netherlands: Kosmos, 1954.

Reis, Morel Marcondes. *A Evolução de Ensino Técnico em São Paulo.* São Paulo: Departamento de Serviço Público, 1945.

Ribeiro, Abraão. *Remodela o do Serviço de Transporte Coletivo da Cidade de São Paulo.* São Paulo: Prefeitura Municipal, 1946.

Rowan, James A. "Trade Union Movement and Wages in Brazil." *Monthly Labor Review* 21.3 (September 1925): 1–11.

Rudolfer, Bruno, and Antônio le Voci. *O Transporte Coletivo na Cidade de São Paulo.* 2 vols. São Paulo: Prefeitura do Município, 1943.

São Paulo. Departamento Estadual do Trabalho. *A Immigração e as Condições do Trabalho em São Paulo.* São Paulo: Rothschild, 1915.

São Paulo. Governo Municipal. Divisão de Educação e Recreio. "Alguns Casos de Tuberculino-Reação de Pirquet e Mantoux nos Parques Infantís." *RAM* (May 1939): 97–104.

São Paulo. Secretaria da Agricultura, Indústria, e Comércio. *Aspectos do Padrão da Vida do Operário Industrial da Capital de São Paulo.* São Paulo, 1940.

————. *Condições da Classe Operária na Capital Paulista: Necissidade e Possibilidade de Remediar sua Situação.* São Paulo, 1940.

————. *Estatística Industrial do Estado de São Paulo.* 10 vols. 1930–39. São Paulo: 1931–40.

————. *Posição do Chefe de Família Operária em Face dos Salários Atuais.* São Paulo, 1940.

SENAI and the Institute of Inter-American Affairs. "Estudo da Indústria Têxtil e Necessidades de Treinamento." Rio de Janeiro, 1953.

Simonsen, Roberto C. *As Atividades do Serviço Social da Indústria no Estado de São Paulo.* São Paulo: Siqueira, 1947.

————. *A Evolução Industrial do Brasil.* São Paulo: Nacional, EDUSP, 1973.

Souza, G. H. de Paula, et al. "Inquerito sobre Alimentação Popular em um Bairro de São Paulo." *RAM* (October 1935): 121–81.

Teles, Guiomar Urbina. "O Problema do Cortiço." *Serviço Social* 23–27 (November 1940–March 1941): 11–111.

United Nations. Economic Commission on Latin America. *Labor Productivity of the Cotton Textile Industry in Five Latin American Countries.* New York: UN Department of Economic Affairs, 1951.

United States. Department of Commerce. *Brazil: A Study of Economic Conditions since 1913.* Bureau of Foreign and Domestic Commerce Miscellaneous Series, no. 86. Washington, D.C., 1920.

United States. Institute of Inter-American Affairs. *Brazilian Technical Studies.* Washington, D.C.: Government Printing Office, 1955.

Vargas, Getúlio. *O Governo Trabalhista do Brasil.* 4 vols. Rio de Janeiro: José Olympio, 1953–69.

————. *A Nova Política do Brasil.* 11 vols. Rio de Janeiro: José Olympio, 1938–43.

————. *A Política Trabalhista no Brasil.* Rio de Janeiro: José Olympio, 1950.

Walle, Paul. *Au Pays de l'Ur Rouge: L'Etat de São Paulo.* Paris: Augustin Challenel, 1921.

Willems, Emílio. "The Structure of the Brazilian Family." *Social Forces* 31.4 (May 1953): 339–45.

Wright, Marie Robinson. *The New Brazil: Its Resources and Attractions; Historical, Descriptive, and Industrial.* Philadelphia: George Barriet Son, 1901.

Zalecki, Gustavo. "O Problema da Carestia do Pão em São Paulo." *RAM* (February 1938): 5–113.

————. "O Problema da Carne." *RAM* (April 1938): 257–324.

Secondary Sources

Albert, Bill. *South America and the First World War: The Impact of the War on Brazil, Argentina, Peru, and Chile.* Cambridge: Cambridge University Press, 1988.

Alexander, Robert J. "Brazilian 'Tenentismo.'" *HAHR* 36.2 (May 1956): 229–42.

————. *Labor Relations in Argentina, Brazil, and Chile.* New York: McGraw-Hill, 1962.

Alvarez, Sonia. *Engendering Democracy in Brazil: Women's Movements in Transition Politics.* Princeton: Princeton University Press, 1990.

Americano, Jorge. *São Paulo Atual, 1935–1962.* São Paulo: Melhoramento, 1963.

————. *São Paulo Nesse Tempo, 1915–1935.* São Paulo: Melhoramento, 1962.

Andrews, George Reid. "Black and White Workers: São Paulo, Brazil, 1888–1928." *HAHR* 68.3 (August 1988): 491–524.

————. *Blacks and Whites in São Paulo, Brazil, 1888–1988.* Madison: University of Wisconsin Press, 1991.

Annunziato, Frank R. "Gramsci's Theory and Trade Unionism." *Rethinking Marxism* 1.2 (Summer 1988): 142–64.

Antunes, Ricardo. *Classe Operária, Sindicatos, e Partido no Brasil: Da Revolução de 30 até a Aliança Nacional Libertadora.* São Paulo: Cortez, 1982.

Araújo, Rosa Maria Barbosa de. *O Batismo do Trabalho: A Experiência de Lindolfo Collor.* Rio de Janeiro: Civilização Brasileira, 1981.

Araújo, José Tavares de, and Vera Maria Candido Pereira. "Teares sem Lençadeira na Indústria Têxtil." In *Difusão de Inovações na Indústria Brasileira: Três Estudos de Caso,* ed. José Tavares de Araújo. Rio de Janeiro: IPEA/INPES, 1976.

Aureliano, Liana Maria. *No Limiar da Industrialização.* São Paulo: Brasiliense, 1981.

Baer, Werner. *The Brazilian Economy: Growth and Development.* 2d ed. New York: Praeger, 1983.

Bak, Joan L. "Cartels, Cooperatives, and Corporatism: Getúlio Vargas in Rio Grande do Sul on the Eve of Brazil's 1930 Revolution." *HAHR* 63.2 (May 1983): 255–75.

Bandeira, Moniz, et al. *O Ano Vermelho: A Revolução Russa e Seus Reflexos no Brasil.* São Paulo: Brasiliense, 1980.

Baron, Eva. "Contested Terrain Revisited: Technology and Gender Definitions of Work in the Printing Industry, 1850–1920." In *Women, Work, and Technology: Transformations,* ed. Barbara Wright et al. Ann Arbor: University of Michigan Press, 1987.

Baron, Eva, ed. *Work Engendered: Toward a New History of American Labor.* Ithaca: Cornell University Press, 1991.

Barsted, Dennis Linhares. *Medição de Forças: O Movimento Grevista de 1953 e a Época dos Operários Navais.* Rio de Janeiro: Zahar, 1982.

Basbaum, Leôncio. *História Sincera da República, 1930–1960.* 4th ed. São Paulo: Alfa-Omega, 1976.

Beiguelman, Paula. *Os Companheiros de São Paulo.* São Paulo: Símbolo, 1977.

Benevides, Maria Victoria. *O PTB e o Trabalhismo: Partido e Sindicato em São Paulo, 1945–1964.* São Paulo: Brasiliense, 1989.

Bergquist, Charles. *Labor in Latin America: Comparative Essays on Chile, Argentina, Venezuela, and Colombia.* Stanford: Stanford University Press, 1986.

Besse, Susan Kent. "Freedom and Bondage: The Impact of Capitalism on Women in São Paulo, Brazil, 1917–1937." Ph.D. diss., Yale University, 1983.

Bethell, Leslie, and Ian Roxborough. "Latin America Between the Second World War and the Cold War: Some Reflections on the 1945–1948 Conjuncture." *JLAS* 20 (May 1988): 167–89.

Bicalho, Letícia Canêdo. *Bancários: Movimento Sindical e Participação Política.* Campinas: UNICAMP, 1986.

———. *O Sindicalismo Bancário em São Paulo.* São Paulo: Símbolo, 1978.

Blay, Eva Alterman. *Eu No Tenho Onde Morar: Vilas Operárias na Cidade de São Paulo.* São Paulo: Nobel, 1985.

Bodea, Miguel. *A Greve de 1917: As Origens do Trabalhismo Gaúcho.* Porto Alegre: L & PM, 1978.

Bosi, Eclea. *Memória e Sociedade: Lembranças de Velhos.* 2d ed. São Paulo: T. A. Queiroz, 1987.

Bruno, Ernani Silva. *História e Tradições da Cidade de São Paulo.* Vol. 3. Rio de Janeiro: José Olympio, 1954.

Cammack, Paul. "Brazil: The Triumph of 'Savage Capitalism.'" *Bulletin of Latin American Research* 3.2 (1984): 117–30.

Campello de Souza, Maria do Carmo. *Estado e Partidos Políticos no Brasil, 1930–1964.* São Paulo: Alfa-Omega, 1976.

Campos, Cristina Hebling. "O Sonhar Libertário; Movimento Operário nos Anos 1917 a 1920." Tese de mestrado, Universidade Estadual de São Paulo, Campinas, 1983.

————. *O Sonhar Libertário: Movimento Operário nos Anos de 1917 a 1921*. São Paulo: UNICAMP, 1988.

Candido, Antônio. "The Brazilian Family." In *Brazil: Portrait of a Half a Continent*, ed. T. Lynn Smith and Alexander Merchant. New York: Dryden, 1951.

Cano, Wilson. *Desequilíbrios Regionais e Concentração Industrial no Brasil, 1930–1970*. São Paulo: Global, 1985.

————. *Raízes da Concentração Industrial em São Paulo*. São Paulo: T. A. Queiroz, 1983.

Carone, Edgard. *Classes Sociais e Movimento Operário*. São Paulo: Ática, 1989.

————. *O Estado Novo, 1937–1945*. Rio de Janeiro: DIFEL, 1976.

————. *A República Velha: Instituições e Classes Sociais*. São Paulo: Difusão Européia do Livro, 1970.

Castro Gomes, Angela Maria. *Burguesia e Trabalho: Política e Legislação Social no Brasil, 1917–1937*. Rio de Janeiro: Campus, 1979.

————. *A Invenção do Trabalhismo*. Rio de Janeiro: IUPERJ/Vértice, 1988.

Castro Gomes, Angela Maria, et al. "Revolução e Restauração: A Experiência Paulista no Período da Constitucionalização." In *Regionalismo e Centralização Política: Partidos e Constituinte nos Anos 30*, ed. Castro Gomes. Rio de Janeiro: Nova Fronteira, 1980.

Chalhoub, Sidney. *Trabalho, Lar, e Botequim: O Cotidiano dos Trabalhadores no Rio de Janeiro da Belle Époque*. São Paulo: Brasiliense, 1986.

Chilcote, Ronald H. *The Brazilian Communist Party: Conflict and Integration, 1922–1972*. New York: Oxford University Press, 1974.

Cohen, Youssef. *The Manipulation of Consent: The State and Working-Class Consciousness in Brazil*. Pittsburgh: University of Pittsburgh Press, 1989.

Collier, David, and Ruth Berins Collier. *Shaping the Political Arena: Critical Junctures, the Labor Movement, and Regime Dynamics in Latin America*. Princeton: Princeton University Press, 1991.

Collier, Ruth Berins. "Popular Sector Incorporation and Political Supremacy: Regime Evolution in Brazil and Mexico." In *Brazil and Mexico: Patterns in Late Development*, ed. Sylvia Ann Hewlitt and Richard S. Weinert. Philadelphia: ISHI, 1982.

Conniff, Michael L. "The *Tenentes* in Power: A New Perspective on the Brazilian Revolution of 1930." *JLAS* 10 (May 1978): 61–82.

————. *Urban Politics in Brazil: The Rise of Populism, 1925–1945*. Pittsburgh: University of Pittsburgh Press, 1981.

————. "Voluntary Associations in Rio de Janeiro, 1870–1945: A New Approach to Urban Social Dynamics." *Journal of Interamerican Studies* 17 (1975): 64–81.

Corrêa do Lago, Luís A. et al. *A Indústria Brasileira de Bens de Capital: Origens, Situação Recente, Perpectivas*. Rio de Janeiro: Editora da Fundição Getúlio Vargas, 1979.

Costa, Emília Viotti de. "Experience versus Structures: New Tendencies in the

History of Labor and the Working Class in Latin America—What Do We Gain? What Do We Lose?" *International Labor and Working-Class History* 36 (Fall 1989): 3–24.

Damante, Hélio. "O Movimento de 22 de Março de 1953 em São Paulo." *Revista Brasileira de Estudos Políticos* 18 (January 1965): 105–12.

Dean, Warren. *The Industrialization of São Paulo, 1880–1945*. Austin: University of Texas Press, 1969.

de Decca, Edgar. *1930: O Silêncio dos Vencidos*. São Paulo: Brasiliense, 1986.

DeShazo, Peter. *Urban Workers and Labor Unions in Chile, 1902–1927*. Madison: University of Wisconsin Press, 1983.

Diacon, Todd A. *Millenarian Vision, Capitalist Reality: Brazil's Contestado Rebellion, 1912–1916*. Durham: Duke University Press, 1991.

Diniz, Eli. *Empresário, Estado, e Capitalismo no Brasil, 1930–1945*. Rio de Janeiro: Paz e Terra, 1978.

Dulles, John W. F. *Anarchists and Communists in Brazil, 1900–1935*. Austin: University of Texas Press, 1973.

———. *Brazilian Communism, 1935–1945: Repression during World Upheaval*. Austin: University of Texas Press, 1983.

———. *Vargas of Brazil: A Political Biography*. Austin: University of Texas Press, 1967.

Eakin, Marshall C. *British Enterprise in Brazil: The St. John d'el Rey Mining Company and the Morro Velho Gold Mine, 1830–1960*. Durham: Duke University Press, 1989.

Endo, Seiti Kaneko, and Heron Carlos Esvael do Carmo. *Breve Histórico de Preços ao Consumidor no Município de São Paulo*. São Paulo: Fundição Instituto de Pesquisas Econômicas, 1985.

Erickson, Kenneth Paul. *The Brazilian Corporative State and Working-Class Politics*. Berkeley: University of California Press, 1977.

Erickson, Kenneth Paul, and Patrick V. Peppe. "Dependent Capitalist Development, U.S. Foreign Policy, and Repression of the Working Class in Chile and Brazil." *LAP* 8 (Winter 1976): 19–44.

Escobar, Arturo, and Sonia Alvarez, eds. *The Making of Social Movements in Latin America: Identity, Strategy, and Democracy*. Boulder: Westview Press, 1992.

Faue, Elizabeth. *Community of Suffering and Struggle: Women, Men, and the Labor Movement in Minneapolis, 1915–1945*. Chapel Hill: University of North Carolina Press, 1991.

Fausto, Boris. *A Revolução de 1930: Historiografia e História*. São Paulo: Brasiliense, 1970.

———. *Trabalho Urbano e Conflito Social*. São Paulo: DIFEL, 1976.

Fishlow, Albert. "Origens e Consequências da Substituição de Importações no Brasil." *Estudos Econômicos* 2.6 (1972): 8–20.

Font, Mauricio A. *Coffee, Contention, and Change in the Making of Modern Brazil*. Cambridge, Mass.: Basil Blackwell, 1990.

Freedman, Estelle. "Separatism as Strategy: Female Institution Building and American Feminism, 1870–1930." *Feminist Studies* 5.3 (Fall 1979): 512–29.

French, John D. *The Brazilian Workers' ABC: Class Conflict and Alliances in Modern São Paulo.* Chapel Hill: University of North Carolina Press, 1991.

———. "Industrial Workers and the Origins of Populist Politics in the ABC Region of Greater São Paulo, Brazil, 1900–1950." Ph.D. diss., Yale University, 1985.

———. "The Origin of Corporatist State Intervention in Brazilian Industrial Relations." *Luso-Brazilian Review* 28.2 (Winter 1991): 13–26.

———. "Workers and the Rise of Adhemarista Populism in São Paulo, 1945–1947." *HAHR* 68.1 (February 1988): 1–43.

French, John D., and Mary Lynn Pedersen. "Women and Working-Class Mobilization in Postwar São Paulo." *Latin American Research Review* 24.3 (1989): 99–125.

Gomes, Francisco Magalhaes. *História da Siderurgia no Brasil.* Belo Horizonte: Itatiaia, 1983.

Gordon, Eric Arthur. "Anarchism in Brazil: Theory and Practice." Ph.D. diss., Tulane University, 1978.

Gramsci, Antonio. *Selections from the Prison Notebooks.* 8th ed. New York: International Publishers, 1985.

Greenfield, Gerald Michael. "Privatism and Urban Development in Latin America." *Journal of Urban History* 8.4 (August 1982): 397–426.

Grossi, Yonne de Souza. *Mina de Morro Velho: A Extração do Homem; Uma História de Experiência Operária.* Rio de Janeiro: Paz e Terra, 1982.

Guzzo Decca, Maria Auxiliadora. *A Vida fora das Fábricas: Cotidiano Operário em São Paulo, 1920–1934.* Rio de Janeiro: Paz e Terra, 1987.

Haddad, Claudio L. S. "Growth of Brazilian Real Output, 1900–1947." Ph.D. diss., University of Chicago, 1974.

Hahner, June. *Emancipating the Female Sex: The Struggle for Women's Rights in Brazil, 1850–1940.* Durham: Duke University Press, 1990.

———. *Poverty and Politics: The Urban Poor in Brazil, 1870–1920.* Albuquerque: University of New Mexico Press, 1986.

Hahner, June, ed. *Women in Latin American History: Their Lives and Views.* Los Angeles: UCLA Latin American Center, 1976.

Hall, Jacquelyn Dowd, et al. *Like a Family: The Making of a Southern Cotton Mill World.* Chapel Hill: University of North Carolina Press, 1987.

Hall, Michael M. "Immigration and the Early São Paulo Working Class." *Jahrbuch für Geschichte von Staat, Wirtschaft und Gesellschaft Lateinamerikas* 12 (1975): 391–407.

Harding, Timothy. "The Political History of the Organized Labor Movement in Brazil." Ph.D. diss., Stanford University, 1973.

Hardman, Francisco Foot. *Nem Patria, Nem Patrão: Vida Operária e Cultura Anarquista no Brasil.* São Paulo: Brasiliense, 1983.

Hartmann, Heidi. "Capitalism, Patriarchy, and Job Segregation by Sex." In *Capitalist Patriarchy and the Case for Socialist Feminism*, ed. Zillah R. Eisenstein. New York: Monthly Review Press, 1979.

Hilton, Stanley E. "The Armed Forces and Industrialists in Modern Brazil: The Drive for Military Autonomy, 1889–1954." *HAHR* 62.4 (November 1982): 629–73.

———. "Military Influence on Brazilian Economic Policy, 1930–1945." *HAHR* 53.1 (February 1973): 71–94.

———. *1932: A Guerra Civil Brasileira*. Rio de Janeiro: Nova Fronteira, 1982.

———. *A Rebelião Vermelha*. Rio de Janeiro: Record, 1986.

———. "Vargas and Brazilian Economic Development, 1930–1945: A Reappraisal of His Attitude toward Industrialization and Planning." *Journal of Economic History* 35.4 (December 1975): 754–78.

Holloway, Thomas H. *Immigrants on the Land: Coffee and Society in São Paulo, 1886–1934*. Chapel Hill: University of North Carolina Press, 1980.

Honig, Emily. "Burning Incense, Pledging Sisterhood: Communities of Women Workers in the Shanghai Cotton Mills, 1919–1949." *Signs: Journal of Women in Culture and Society* 10.4 (Summer 1985): 700–714.

Humphrey, John. *Gender and Work in the Third World: Sexual Divisions in Brazilian Industry*. London: Tavistock Publications, 1987.

Iglésias, Francisco. "Aspectos Políticos e Econômicos do Estado Novo." In *Getúlio Vargas e a Economia Contemporânea*, ed. Tamás Szmrecsanyi and Rui G. Granziera. Campinas: UNICAMP, 1986.

James, Daniel. *Resistance and Integration: Peronism and the Argentine Working Class*. Cambridge: Cambridge University Press, 1988.

Johnson, Richard, et al., eds. *Making Histories: Studies in History-Writing and Politics*. London: Hutchinson/University of Birmingham Centre for Contemporary Studies, 1982.

Joll, James. *The Anarchists*. 2d ed. Cambridge, Mass.: Harvard University Press, 1980.

Kaplan, Temma. "Female Consciousness and Collective Action: The Case of Barcelona, 1910–1918." *Signs: Journal of Women in Culture and Society* 7.3 (1982): 545–66.

Keck, Margaret E. *The Workers' Party and Democratization in Brazil*. New Haven: Yale University Press, 1992.

Keremitsis, Eileen. "The Early Industrial Worker in Rio de Janeiro, 1870–1930." Ph.D. diss., Columbia University, 1982.

Khoury, Yara Aun. *As Greves de 1917 em São Paulo*. São Paulo: Cortez, 1981.

Koval, Boris. *História do Proletariado Brasileiro, 1857–1967*. Trans. Clarice Lima Avierina. São Paulo: Alfa-Omega, 1982.

Krausche, Valter. *Adoniran Barbosa: Pelas Ruas da Cidade*. São Paulo: Brasiliense, 1985.

Lauerhaus, Ludwig, Jr. "Getúlio Vargas and the Triumph of Brazilian Nationalism: A Study of the Rise of the Nationalist Generation of 1930." Ph.D. diss., University of California, Los Angeles, 1972.

Leff, Nathaniel H. *The Brazilian Capital Goods Industry, 1929–1964*. Cambridge, Mass.: Harvard University Press, 1968.

Leite Lopes, José Sérgio. *A Tecelagem dos Conflitos de Classe na Cidade das Chaminés*. São Paulo: Marco Zero/Universidade de Brasília, 1988.

Leite Lopes, José Sérgio, ed. *Cultura e Identidade Operária: Aspectos da Cultura da Classe Trabalhadora*. São Paulo: Marco Zero/UFRJ, 1987.

Leme, Maria Saenz. *A Ideologia dos Industriais Brasileiros, 1919–1945*. Petrópolis: Vozes, 1979.

Lenharo, Alcir. *A Sacralização da Política*. Campinas: Papirus, 1986.

Levi, Darrell E. *The Prados of São Paulo: An Elite Family and Social Change, 1840–1930*. Athens: University of Georgia Press, 1987.

Levine, Robert M. "Perspectives on the Mid-Vargas Years, 1934–1937." *Journal of Inter-American Studies and World Affairs* 22.1 (February 1980): 57–80.

————. *The Vargas Regime: The Critical Years, 1934–1938*. New York: Columbia University Press, 1970.

Love, Joseph. *São Paulo in the Brazilian Federation, 1889–1937*. Stanford: Stanford University Press, 1980.

Lowe, Elizabeth. *The City in Brazilian Literature*. Rutherford, N.J.: Fairleigh Dickinson University Press, 1982.

Loyola, Maria Andréa. *Os Sindicatos e o PTB: Estudo de um Caso em Minas Gerais*. Petrópolis: Vozes, 1980.

Lucena, Célica Toledo. *Bairro de Bexiga: A Sobrevivência Cultural*. São Paulo: Brasiliense, 1984.

McCann, Frank D. *The Brazilian American Alliance, 1937–1945*. Princeton: Princeton University Press, 1973.

————. "The Formative Period of Twentieth-Century Brazilian Army Thought, 1900–1922." *HAHR* 64.4 (November 1984): 737–65.

McConarty, James Paul. "The Defense of the Working Class in the Brazilian Chamber of Deputies, 1917–1920." Master's thesis, Tulane University, 1973.

McGaw, Judith A. "Women and the History of American Technology." *Signs: Journal of Women in Culture and Society* 7.4 (Summer 1982): 798–828.

Maclean, Nancy. "White Women and Klan Violence in the 1920s: Agency, Complicity, and the Politics of Women's History." *Gender and History* 3.3 (Autumn 1991): 287–303.

Magnani, Silvia Lang. *O Movimento Anarquista em São Paulo, 1906–1917*. São Paulo: Brasiliense, 1982.

Mainwaring, Scott. *The Catholic Church and Politics in Brazil, 1916–1985*. Stanford: Stanford University Press, 1986.

Malan, Pedro S., et al. *Política Econômica Externa e a Industrialização no Brasil, 1939–1952*. Rio de Janeiro: IPEA/INPES, 1977.

Malloy, James M. *The Politics of Social Security in Brazil*. Pittsburgh: University of Pittsburgh Press, 1979.

Maram, Sheldon L. "Anarchists, Immigrants, and the Brazilian Labor Movement." Ph.D. diss., University of California, Santa Barbara, 1972.

———. *Anarquistas, Imigrantes, e o Movimento Operário Brasileiro, 1890–1920*. Trans. José Eduardo Ribeiro Moretzsohn. Rio de Janeiro: Paz e Terra, 1979.

———. "Labor and the Left in Brazil, 1890–1921: A Movement Aborted." *HAHR* 57.2 (May 1977): 254–72.

———. "Urban Labor and Social Change in the 1920s." *Luso-Brazilian Review* 16.2 (Winter 1979): 215–23.

Maranhão, Ricardo. *Sindicato e Democratização: Brasil, 1945–1950*. São Paulo: Brasiliense, 1979.

Mendes de Almeida, Márcia. "O Sindicato dos Têxteis em São Paulo: História, 1933–1957." Tese de mestrado, Universidade de São Paulo, 1981.

Mericle, Kenneth S. "Conflict Regulation in the Brazilian Industrial Relations System." Ph.D. diss., University of Wisconsin, 1974.

Meyer, Stephen. *The Five Dollar Day: Labor Management and Social Control in the Ford Motor Company, 1908–1921*. Albany: State University of New York Press, 1981.

Milano, Miguel. *Os Fantasmas de São Paulo Antiga: Estudo Histórico-Literário da Cidade de São Paulo*. São Paulo: Saraiva, 1949.

Moisés, José Álvaro. *Greve de Massa e Crise Política: Estudo da Greve dos 300 Mil em São Paulo—1953–1954*. São Paulo: Polis, 1978.

———. "A Greve dos 300 Mil e as Comissões de Empresa." *Caderno CEDEC*. São Paulo: Brasiliense, 1977.

———. "Protesto Urbano e Política: O Quebra-Quebra de 1947." In *Cidade, Povo, e Poder*, ed. J. Á. Moisés et al. Rio de Janeiro: CEDEC/Paz e Terra, 1982.

Moisés, José Álvaro, and Verena Stolcke. "Urban Transport and Popular Violence: The Case of Brazil." *Past and Present* 86 (February 1980): 174–92.

Molyneux, Maxime. "No God, No Boss, No Husband: Anarchist Feminism in Nineteenth-Century Argentina." *LAP* 13.1 (Winter 1986): 113–45.

Moraes Filho, Evaristo de. *O Problema do Sindicato Único no Brasil: Seus Fundamentos Sociológicos*. 2d ed. São Paulo: Alfa-Omega, 1978.

Morais, Fernando. *Olga*. São Paulo: Alfa-Omega, 1986.

Moreira Alves, Maria Helena. *The State and Opposition in Military Brazil*. Austin: University of Texas Press, 1985.

Morse, Richard. *From Community to Metropolis: A Biography of São Paulo, Brazil*. Gainesville: University of Florida Press, 1958.

Moura, Esmeralda Blanco B. de. *Mulheres e Menores no Trabalho Industrial: Os Fatores Sexo e Idade na Dinâmica do Capital*. Petrópolis: Vozes, 1982.

Navarro, Marysa. "Hidden, Silent, and Anonymous: Women Workers in the Argentine Trade Union Movement." In *The World of Women's Trade Union-

ism: Comparative Historical Essays, ed. Norbert C. Solden. Westport, Conn.: Greenwood Press, 1985.

Needell, Jeffrey D. "Making the Carioca Belle Époque Concrete: The Urban Reforms of Rio de Janeiro under Pereira Passos." *Journal of Urban History* 10.4 (August 1984): 384–422.

O'Donnell, Guillermo. "Corporatism and the Question of the State." In *Authoritarianism and Corporatism in Latin America*, ed. James M. Malloy. Pittsburgh: University of Pittsburgh Press, 1977.

Offe, Claus, and Helmut Wiesenthal. "Two Logics of Collective Action: Theoretical Notes on Social Class and Organizational Form." *Political Power and Social Theory* 1 (1980): 67–115.

Paoli, Maria Célia. "Os Trabalhadores Urbanos na Fala dos Outros. Tempo, Espaço e Classe na História Operária Brasileira." In *Cultura e Identidade Operária: Aspectos da Cultura da Classe Trabalhadora*, ed. José Sérgio Leite Lopes. São Paulo: Marco Zero/UFRJ, 1987.

———. "Working-Class São Paulo and Its Representations, 1900–1940." *LAP* 14.2 (Spring 1987): 204–25.

Pena, Maria Valéria Junho. *Mulheres e Trabalhadores: Presença Feminina na Construção do Sistema Fabril*. Rio de Janeiro: Paz e Terra, 1981.

Perrot, Michelle. *Les ouvriers en grève: France, 1871–1890*. 2 vols. Paris: Mouton, 1974.

Pinheiro, Paulo Sérgio. *Estratégias da Illusão: A Revolução Mundial e o Brasil, 1922–1935*. São Paulo: Companhia das Letras, 1991.

———. *Política e Trabalho no Brasil*. Rio de Janeiro: Paz e Terra, 1975.

Pinheiro, Paulo Sérgio, and Michael M. Hall. *A Classe Operária no Brasil, 1889–1930, Documentos*. Volume 1: *O Movimento Operário*. São Paulo: Alfa-Omega, 1979.

———. *A Classe Operária no Brasil*. Volume 2: *Condições de Vida e de Trabalho, Relações com os Empresários e o Estado, Documentos*. São Paulo: Brasiliense, 1981.

Pinto de Góes, Maria Conceição. *A Formação da Classe Trabalhadora: Movimento Anarquista no Rio de Janeiro, 1888–1911*. Rio de Janeiro: Jorge Zahar, 1988.

Piven, Francis Fox, and Richard A. Cloward. *Poor People's Movements: Why They Succeed, How They Fail*. New York: Pantheon, 1977.

Prado, Antonio Arnoni, ed. *Libertários no Brasil: Memória, Lutas, Cultura*. São Paulo: Brasiliense, 1986.

Rago, Magareth. *Do Cabaré ao Lar: A Utopia da Cidade Disciplinar, Brasil, 1890–1930*. Rio de Janeiro: Paz e Terra, 1985.

———. *Os Prazeres da Noite: Prostituição e Códigos da Sexualidade Feminina em São Paulo, 1890–1930*. Rio de Janeiro: Paz e Terra, 1991.

Ribeiro, Maria Alicia Rosa. *Condições do Trabalho na Indústria Têxtil Paulista, 1870–1930*. São Paulo: Hucitec, 1988.

Rodrigues, José Albertino. *Sindicato e Desenvolvimento no Brasil*. São Paulo: Difusão Européia do Livro, 1968.

Rodrigues, Leôncio Martins. "Sindicalismo e Classe Operária, 1930–1964." In *História Geral da Civilização Brasileira*. Vol. 10, ed. Boris Fausto. Rio de Janeiro: DIFEL, 1986.

Rubin, Jeffrey W. "Ambiguity and Contradiction in a Radical Popular Movement: The Peasant-Worker Alliance in Juchitán, Mexico, 1973–1992." Paper presented to the Ninth Annual Latin American Labor History Conference, Stony Brook, N.Y., April 1992.

———. "Rethinking Post-Revolutionary Mexico: Regional History, Cultural Identity, and Radical Politics in Juchitán, Oaxaca." Ph.D. diss., Harvard University, 1991.

Sabel, Charles F. *Work and Politics: The Division of Labor in Industry.* Cambridge: Cambridge University Press, 1982.

Saboia, João. *Salário Mínimo: A Experiência Brasileira.* Porto Alegre: L & PM, 1985.

Saffioti, Heleith I. B. *Women in Class Society.* Trans. Michael Vale. New York: Monthly Review Press, 1978.

Schmitter, Philippe. "Still the Century of Corporatism?" *Review of Politics* 36.1 (January 1974): 85–131.

Scott, James C. *Domination and the Arts of Resistance: Hidden Transcripts.* New Haven: Yale University Press, 1990.

Scott, Joan. "The Evidence of Experience." *Critical Inquiry* 17.4 (Summer 1991): 773–97.

———. *Gender and the Politics of History.* New York: Columbia University Press, 1988.

Sevcenko, Nicolau. *Literatura como Missão: Tenses Sociais e Criação Cultural na Primeira República.* São Paulo: Brasiliense, 1983.

Simão, Azis. *Sindicato e Estado: Suas Relações na Formação do Proletariado de São Paulo.* São Paulo: Ática, 1981.

———. "O Voto Operário em São Paulo." *Revista Brasileira de Estudos Políticos* 1 (December 1956): 130–41.

Simões Paes, Maria Helena. "O Sindicato dos Metalúrgicos de São Paulo, 1932–1951." Tese de mestrado, Universidade de São Paulo, 1979.

Skidmore, Thomas E. *Black into White: Race and Nationality in Brazilian Thought.* New York: Oxford University Press, 1974.

———. "Getúlio Vargas and the Estado Novo, 1935–1945; What Kind of Regime." In *Problems in Latin American History: The Modern Period,* ed. Joseph S. Tulchin. New York: Harper Row, 1973.

———. *Politics in Brazil, 1930–1964: An Experiment in Democracy.* New York: Oxford University Press, 1967.

———. *The Politics of Military Rule in Brazil, 1964–1985.* New York: Oxford University Press, 1988.

———. "Workers and Soldiers: Urban Labor Movements and Elite Responses in Twentieth-Century Latin America." In *Elites, Masses, and Modernization in*

Latin America, 1850–1930, ed. Virginia Bernhard. Austin: University of Texas Press, 1979.

Soares D'Araújo, Maria Celina. *O Segundo Governo Vargas, 1951–1954: Democracia, Partidos, e Crise Política.* Rio de Janeiro: Zahar, 1982.

Sodre, Nelson Werneck. *História de Burguesia Brasileira.* Rio de Janeiro: Civilização Brasileira, 1976.

Spalding, Hobart A., Jr. *Organized Labor in Latin America: Historical Case Studies of Workers in Dependent Societies.* New York: Harper Torchbooks, 1977.

Stein, Stanley J. *The Brazilian Cotton Manufacture: Textile Enterprise in an Underdeveloped Area, 1850–1950.* Cambridge, Mass.: Harvard University Press, 1957.

Suggs, Julia F. "Women Workers in Brazil." Master's thesis, Howard University, 1945.

Suzigan, Wilson. *Indústria Brasileira: Origem e Desenvolvimento.* São Paulo: Brasiliense, 1986.

―――――. "A Industrialização de São Paulo: 1930–1945." *Revista Brasileira de Economia* 25.2 (April–June 1971): 89–111.

Tavares de Almeida, Maria Hermínia. "Estado e Classes Trabalhadores no Brasil, 1930–1945." Tese de doutoramento, Universidade de São Paulo, 1978.

Teixeira, Palmira Petratti. *A Fábrica do Sohno: Trajetória do Industrial Jorge Street.* Rio de Janeiro: Paz e Terra, 1990.

Teixeira Mendes Torres, Maria Celestina. *O Bairro do Brás.* São Paulo: Secretaria de Educação e Cultura, 1969.

Telles, Jover. *O Movimento Sindical no Brasil.* Rio de Janeiro: Vitória, 1963.

Touraine, Alain. "Industrialisation et conscience ouvrière à São Paulo." *Sociologie du Travail* 3.4 (October–December 1961): 389–407.

Topik, Steven. *The Political Economy of the Brazilian State, 1889–1930.* Austin: University of Texas Press, 1987.

Versiani, Flávio Rabelo. *A Década de 20 na Industrialização Brasileira.* Rio de Janeiro: IPEA/INPES, 1987.

―――――. "Industrialização: A Década de 20 e a Depressão." *Pesquisa e Planajamento Econômico* (April 1984).

―――――. "Industrialização e Economia da Exportação: A Experiência Brasileira antes de 1914." *Revista Brasileira de Economia* 34.1 (January–March 1980): 3–40.

―――――. "Technical Change, Equipment Replacement, and Labor Absorption: The Case of the Brazilian Textile Industry." Ph.D. diss., Vanderbilt University, 1971.

Versiani, Flávio Rabelo, and Maria Teresa Versiani. "A Industrialização Brasileira antes de 1930; Uma Contribuição." *Estudos Economicos* 5.1 (January–April 1975): 37–63.

Vianna, Luiz Werneck. *Liberalismo e Sindicato no Brasil.* 2d ed. Rio de Janeiro: Paz e Terra, 1978.

Villela, Annibal V., and Wilson Suzigan. "Government Policy and the Economic Growth of Brazil, 1889–1945." *Brazilian Economic Studies* 3 (1977).

Weffort, Francisco C. "Democracia e Movimento Operário: Algumas Questões para a História do Período 1945–1964." *Revista de Cultura Contemporênea* 1.1 (July 1978).

——. "Origens do Sindicalismo Populista no Brasil: A Conjuntura Após-Guerra." *Estudos CEBRAP* 4 (April–June 1973).

——. *O Populismo na Política Brasileira.* Rio de Janeiro: Paz e Terra, 1980.

——. *Por que Democracia?* São Paulo: Brasiliense, 1984.

——. "Sindicatos e Política." Tese de livre-docência, Universidade de São Paulo, 1972.

Weinstein, Barbara. "The Industrialists, the State, and the Issue of Worker Training and Social Services in Brazil, 1930–1950." *HAHR* 70.3 (August 1990): 397–404.

——. "The New Latin American Labor History: What We Gain." *International Labor and Working-Class History* 36 (Fall 1989): 25–30.

Welch, Clifford Andrew. "Rural Labor and the Brazilian Revolution in São Paulo, 1930–1964." Ph.D. diss., Duke University, 1990.

——. "United States Labor Policy and the Politics of 'Ordem e Progresso' in Brazil, 1945–1950." Master's thesis, University of Maryland, 1987.

Wells, John. "Industrial Accumulation and Living-Standards in the Long Run: The São Paulo Industrial Working Class 1930–1975." Center of Latin American Studies, University of Cambridge. Working Papers, no. 37.

Wiarda, Howard. *The Brazilian Catholic Labor Movement.* Amherst: University of Massachusetts Labor and Industrial Relations Center, 1969.

Winn, Peter. *Weavers of Revolution: The Yarur Workers and Chile's Road to Socialism.* New York: Oxford University Press, 1986.

Wirth, John D. *The Politics of Brazilian Development, 1930–1954.* Stanford: Stanford University Press, 1970.

Wolfe, Joel. "Anarchist Ideology, Worker Practice: The 1917 General Strike and the Formation of São Paulo's Working Class." *HAHR* 71.4 (November 1991): 809–46.

——. "The Rise of Brazil's Industrial Working Class: Community, Work, and Politics in São Paulo, 1900–1955." Ph.D. diss., University of Wisconsin–Madison, 1990.

——. "Worker Mobilization, Repression, and the Rise of the Authoritarian State: São Paulo, 1914–1924." Paper presented to the 56th Annual Meeting of the Southern Historical Association, New Orleans, La., November 1990.

Index